POET AND CRITIC

The Letters of Ted Hughes and Keith Sagar

Cheer up Keith. Your kids are turning out little aces, your finches are breeding. You had a great time in Cornwall.

You didn't give an address so I couldn't contact you to call anyway. You could have had cream tea and I could have given you some Laureate sherry, and shown Owen my skulls, and given him a skin or two.

Love to all

Ted

You were watching the wrong play. Racine's play is 5 Universes away from the Euripides. I read it as a (subconscious) analysis + total dramatisation of his (Racine's) rejection of the theatre (Phèdre) and his reversion to the Jansenist brainwashing of his youth (against which his whole theatre adventure had been a defiant escape). Hence Alicia etc. Yes, I was asked to do it. Production has quite a way to go, but it should be OK in Sept + London.

[left margin, vertical text] Authentic supersession of the female by hustling as you intellectuals (Pascal as an intellectual (I know also Jansenist)

[circled note in margin] Cornwall moments of French Culture were recovered

The second page of Hughes' letter of 14 August 1998.

POET AND CRITIC

The Letters of Ted Hughes and Keith Sagar

Edited by Keith Sagar

The British Library

First published in 2012 by
The British Library
96 Euston Road
London NW1 2DB

Cataloguing in Publication Data
A catalogue record for this book is available from The British Library
ISBN 978 0 7123 5862 0

Designed by Andrew Shoolbred
Typeset by Norman Tilley Graphics Ltd, Northampton
Printed in Hong Kong by Great Wall Printing Co. Ltd

Contents

Acknowledgements and Credits

It became obvious to me very early that my letters from Ted Hughes needed to be treasured. I believe I kept them all. It soon became clear that our correspondence was a unique phenomenon. After Ted's death I felt that the privilege of receiving such wonderful letters carried with it the obligation to oversee their publication. However, Faber rejected my proposal in 2009. Rather than wait indefinitely, I thought I would write a little book about my relationship with Ted, and wrote to Carol Hughes in October 2010 asking if it might be possible for me to use a limited amount of quotation from Ted's letters to me. To my amazement and delight she replied 'Why not use the complete letters?' The British Library was keen to publish the book, so from there it was plain sailing.

Thus my first and greatest debt is to Carol Hughes, not only for permission to publish the letters, but for her constant supply of information, suggestions, and corrections. She also contributed five previously unpublished photographs.

I must also pay tribute to the dedicated work of my editor at the British Library, Lara Speicher, my copy-editor Trevor Horwood, and Helen Melody, Curator of Modern Literary Manuscripts.

It had not occurred to me to keep copies of any of my letters to Ted until the advent of word processing, but fortunately Ted had kept nearly all of them, and Kathy Shoemaker, the Research Services Associate Archivist in the Manuscript, Archives, and Rare Book Library at Emory University generously sent me copies of them all, including their enclosures.

I should also like to record my thanks to my wife Melissa for her typing; to Olwyn Hughes for her invaluable letters; to Daniel Huws for transcribing and translating Ted's Gaelic (p. 73) and for permission to reprint his poem 'O Mountain'; to Michael Kustow for permission to publish part of Ted's letter to him in the Appendices; to the Henry Moore Foundation for permission to print the letter from Moore to me; and to Worcester Polytechnic Institute, Massachusetts, for providing a transcript of Hughes' notes in their copy of The Hawk in the Rain.

Having heard such horror stories of the petty rivalries and back-biting of other single-author academic specialisms, it was a great pleasure, at the beginning of my career, to find in D. H. Lawrence studies a high degree of friendliness and cooperation. I was doubly blessed when my fellow workers in the field of Hughes studies turned out to be equally generous. I cannot list all who have made some contribution to this book, but must mention particularly Ann Skea, Neil Roberts, Terry Gifford, Matthew Howard and Mark Hinchliffe.

My thanks to the Arvon Foundation for their help in locating the photograph of Lumb Bank; to Mark Gerson and the National Portrait Gallery for the photograph of the five poets; to Anthony Thwaite, and Judy Burg, the University

Archivist at Hull History Centre, for help with the Philip Larkin photograph; to Frieda Hughes for permission to use Nicholas Hughes' photograph of Hughes with the Nile Perch; and to Michael Daley for permission to reproduce his wonderful drawing of Shakespeare, the Goddess and the Boar.

Introduction

18 March 1969

A foul night. We were on our way, myself and four of my female adult students, from Blackburn to Manchester, to the first televised reading by Ted Hughes, at Holly Royde, my department's residential college in Didsbury. None of us had ever heard Hughes live. It was raining and very cold. We climbed slowly behind a lorry out of Blackburn towards the Grane Road, which crosses an exposed plateau to Haslingden. There was no motorway in those days, and we were short of time. When the road levelled, I pulled out to overtake the lorry, but realized as I drew level with it that I had no steering. The lorry driver, seeing I was in trouble, slowed. My beetle skidded sideways, then backwards into a wall. The back window came in. We bounced across the road into another wall, and the windscreen came in. Then we slowly keeled over into a ditch. We crawled out, and found that, amazingly, we were unharmed. We could barely stand on the road, which gleamed with black ice. The following day the Emley Moor television mast collapsed from the weight of ice on its wires.

The lorry driver stopped, and offered to send a taxi from Haslingden to pick us up. I doubted whether a taxi would make it, but sure enough, in less than half-an-hour, one came, and took us all back to my house. I made some soup and opened a bottle of wine. When the hilarity, which I suppose is a common after-effect of shock, had subsided, I played my recordings of Hughes reading a dozen of his poems.

The Holly Royde reading was chaired by Brian Cox, who had promised to introduce me to Hughes.[1] I had taken with me the first essay I had written on him, covering his first three collections, which I intended to give him. The next day I wrote to him, explaining why there were five empty seats in his audience, and enclosing my paper, together with a piece I had just written on Lawrence's tortoise poems, which I thought might interest him.

After a fortnight I gave up hope of a reply. Why should he reply? He must be bombarded with such letters. I did not learn until years later that Hughes probably received my letter on the day before the death of his partner Assia and their daughter Shura.[2] Amazingly, he did reply, and with the extraordinary generosity

---

1 At that time I was a lecturer in English in the Extra-Mural Department at Manchester University, where Brian Cox was a professor in the English department. He had known Hughes at Pembroke College, Cambridge, where he was reading English two years ahead of Hughes, though Hughes never mentioned to him at that time that he wrote poetry. In 1959 he had founded, with A. E. Dyson, the *Critical Quarterly*, which published many poems by both Hughes and his wife Sylvia Plath, and Hughes had participated in some of the Critical Quarterly conferences. Cox and Hughes held very similar views about the teaching of English at all levels.

2 Assia Gutmann was born in Germany in 1927, the daughter of a Jewish doctor of Russian descent and a German mother. Her youth was spent in Tel Aviv. She moved to London with her first husband, John Steel, in 1946. They emigrated to Vancouver where she met her second husband, the Canadian

which was to characterize the whole of our subsequent relationship. I had no reason to expect ever to receive another letter from Hughes, let alone 145 more over a period of nearly thirty years.

★★★

That I had struck the right note in that first piece was no guarantee that we would remain in complete accord. Such an accord between a major creative writer and a critic would seem to be almost against nature. The dirtiest word Samuel Beckett knew was 'critic'. He spelled it crrrritic, with several 'r's. The South African dramatist Athol Fugard wrote: 'Critics are poisonous snakes.' We critics are all too aware of the contempt in which our breed is held by the great majority of creative writers. In his book *Modern Critics in Practice*, Philip Smallwood writes: 'Criticism is seen as hostile to creation, and the critic is regarded as the enemy of the poet; paradoxically jealous of genius and a parasite upon it . . . Creation is making, criticism destruction' (p. 192).

The *Oxford English Dictionary* gives as its primary definition of criticism: 'The action of criticizing, or passing (esp. unfavourable) judgement upon the qualities of anything; fault-finding', and as the secondary meaning: 'The art of estimating the qualities and character of literary and artistic work'. It seems to me that the judgemental word 'estimating' allows these meanings to merge, as they frequently do in practice, not least in academia.

I first met this problem in 1959, when I was in the middle of writing my PhD thesis on D. H. Lawrence at Leeds University. Derry Jeffares, the head of the English department, read what I had written so far, and expressed himself dissatisfied on the ground that it was 'not sufficiently critical', by which he clearly meant that it was insufficiently fault-finding. I had chosen Lawrence because I was excited by his work and seemed to be, as it were, on his wavelength.

Ted Hughes claimed that the job of the critic, or any serious reader of imaginative literature, was not to judge it, but to submit to being judged by it: 'I have suspended scholarly disbelief, and adopted the attitude of an interpretive musician. As he reads the score, the musician imagines he finds the living spirit of the music, the inmost vital being of a stranger, reproduced spontaneously, inside himself.'[3]

My unquestioned assumption had been similar: if I could get a bit closer than most readers to the 'living spirit' and 'inmost vital being' of Lawrence through an adequate reading of him, that would qualify me to teach him and write about him. I am by nature pragmatic, having no interest in theory, and did not pay any attention to Jeffares. I just carried on writing the thesis the way I

economist Richard Lipsey. In 1956 she met the poet David Wevill, and they married in 1960. Assia worked in advertising in London, also writing poetry and translating. In 1961 the Wevills rented a flat in Chalcot Square from Ted and his wife Sylvia Plath. Ted and Assia became lovers. Sylvia committed suicide in 1963. Ted and Assia's daughter Shura was born in 1965. The following year Assia moved into Ted's home in Devon. On 23 March 1969 Assia committed suicide, taking Shura with her. In 1990 Hughes published *Capriccio*, twenty poems about his relationship with Assia.

3 *Winter Pollen* (1994), p. 291.

wanted. Eventually it became my first book, *The Art of D. H. Lawrence* (published in 1966).

My writing was an extension of my teaching, and as a tutor in adult education I had only one foot in the academy (the other in the real world). Another advantage of adult education was that I could choose what to teach, could teach almost exclusively writers with whom I felt in accord. I had admired Hughes' first collection, *The Hawk in the Rain*, on its publication in 1957. After the war Eliot wrote no more poetry. I attended an electrifying reading at the Cambridge Student Union by Dylan Thomas, but he was dead within a year. R. S. Thomas and Philip Larkin had not yet emerged. There was a lacuna in English poetry into which *The Hawk in the Rain* burst. After *Lupercal* (1960), I began to teach Hughes; and after *Wodwo* (1967) to write on him. After *Crow* (1970) I sent a proposal to the British Council for a monograph on Hughes in their *Writers and their Work* series, and in 1972 that became the first monograph to be published on him. I felt that I had much more to say about Hughes' work so far than was possible in the forty-three pages of that booklet, and so I sent a proposal for a full-length book to Faber & Faber, Hughes' publishers. They rejected it on the grounds that it was 'premature'. They were right. Presumably they knew what was in the almost bursting pipeline. *The Art of Ted Hughes*, published by Cambridge University Press in 1975, was overtaken by events even before it went on sale: many of the poems from *Season Songs* had been published, Hughes had read from *Gaudete* at the Ilkley Festival, and the original version of *Cave Birds* had been broadcast. Fortunately, the Press allowed me to produce a new edition in 1978, with added chapters on these three crucial works.[4]

★★★

It was obviously an advantage to me in writing on Ted to have so much in common with him. We were born within ten miles and four years of each other, into families of much the same class. We were both educated at West Riding grammar schools and Cambridge. Since Ted did his National Service before university and I did mine after, we were actually at Cambridge together, though we never met there. We shared a passion for animals, and for many of the same writers. However, neither this shared background nor a similar approach to criticism was any guarantee that the accord of our opening correspondence would continue.

In my work on Lawrence I had become very interested in the genesis of works of literature, in the process by which the imaginative writer transforms the raw material of his living into art. I followed up *The Art of D. H. Lawrence* with *The Life of D. H. Lawrence* (1980), and both with *D. H. Lawrence: Life into Art* (1985). Lawrence, being a man without a mask, who believed, like Yeats, that the writer must go naked, lent himself to this approach. Hughes, on the other hand, wore

4 After Ted's death I submitted to Cambridge University Press a proposal for a third edition, adding chapters on *Moortown, Remains of Elmet, River* and *Birthday Letters*. This was rejected. However, the chapters were written, and the first three are incorporated in my *Ted Hughes and Nature: 'Terror and Exultation'* (2009). The chapter on *Birthday Letters* appears as 'From Prospero to Orpheus' in my *The Laughter of Foxes: A Study of Ted Hughes* (2000). In 2008 the Press digitally reprinted the 1978 edition.

many masks, almost always spoke through alter egos: Fallgrief, the man seeking experience, Dick Straightup, Crag Jack, Dully Gumption, Wodwo, Crow, Prometheus, Nicholas Lumb, Adam, and the nameless protagonist of Cave Birds. But these masks seemed to me so transparent that I felt that to tap the living spirit of the poems, to reach the 'inmost vital being', I needed to relate them to the living man. When I sent Hughes the first draft of the opening chapters of The Art of Ted Hughes he recoiled from any such biographical element, from anything which might bring any aspect of his private or inner life into the public domain.

Hughes himself did not hesitate to delve deeply into the inner lives of Shakespeare, Coleridge, Eliot and Plath in his interpretation of their works; even into my life in his explication of my story 'The Beast'; yet he was hypersensitive to any reference to his life in criticism of his own work. He was deeply committed to Eliot's insistence that 'the more perfect the artist, the more completely separate in him will be the man who suffers and the mind which creates'. He was hostile for decades to confessional poetry, but gradually came to realize the cost of the 'continual self-sacrifice', 'continual extinction of personality', to which he attributed his final illness.[5] One sense in which the letters which follow have a narrative progression is that they reveal the gradual healing of that split, which is a measure of the fearless opening of his innermost self in his later work. This process culminated in Birthday Letters, which he described to me before publication as 'totally vulnerable'.

There were aspects of Hughes, both as man and as poet, with which I was far from being in accord. Hughes himself stimulated my interest in mythology, Jungian psychology, shamanism. But I was never able to work up the slightest interest in alchemy, Rosicrucianism, Hermetic Neo-Platonic philosophy, Cabbala, astrology . . . In his letter of 30 August 1979, Hughes castigated Auden for dismissing all such things in Yeats. I have to admit that my sympathies were more with Auden than with Yeats and Hughes. Fortunately, I do not believe that Hughes (with some exceptions such as Cave Birds) allowed these interests to come between the reader and the poems.

Nor could I share Hughes' enthusiasm for royalty and fishing. The former produced some of his worst poems, the latter some of his finest.

***

Hughes' reservations about my opening chapters gradually faded after he had received my chapter on Crow in October 1973: 'This chapter seems somehow the best. You certainly get my drift better than anybody else I've read. The book (Crow) is mostly blueprints, route-maps, reconnaissances, etc – so it needs creative as well as sympathetic imagination, not just critical attention.'

From this point onwards, his letters became larger and fatter, as he habitually enclosed carbons or photocopies of his work in progress. At first I

---

5   T. S. Eliot, *Selected Essays* (Faber & Faber, 1932), pp. 18, 17. Eliot's insistence was later belied by his description of *The Waste Land* as 'a wholly personal grouse against life'.

interpreted this as his generous contribution to my Hughes collection, and as material which he thought I might find useful in any future writings on him. Then it gradually dawned on me that he might be tacitly inviting a response – not mere flattery, but imaginative input. It appears from Hughes' correspondence that he frequently, not only in my case, invited this kind of cooperation from selected friends while a work was in progress, listened carefully to it, and, in a few instances, even acted on it. He was never aiming for any kind of perfection, but always looking for ways to open himself and his work in new directions. There were always several directions to choose from, sometimes opposite ones, and he needed sounding-boards for them. The sounding-boards did not, of course, have to be professional literary critics (this was more likely to be a disqualification). They had to be good readers – readers who could be trusted to approach his work, or any work, in the right spirit.

Among the typescripts Hughes sent me were several early drafts of Cave Birds. That sequence went through many metamorphoses, involving not only the heavy revision of individual poems, but the inclusion in the earlier drafts of several poems which later disappeared altogether. Hughes sent me the first draft on 20 March 1975. It contained the same thirty poems he had already sent to the editor of the Ilkley Literature Festival programme, with some revision and a slight change in order. This was the version of Cave Birds read at the festival on 30 May and subsequently broadcast. In his accompanying letter Hughes wrote that parallel to the alchemical cave drama 'goes a more human progress of correspondences, which are free & loose, contrast to the studied formality of the bird-pieces'.

Two years later Hughes sent me a much-revised version of Cave Birds which he had prepared for publication. I was appalled to find that five of my favourite poems from this 'more human progress' – 'After the first fright', 'She seemed so considerate', 'Something was happening', 'Only a little sleep' and 'A Loyal Mother' – had gone, thus tipping the whole work towards even greater artificiality. I wrote to him in dismay. He replied (10 June 1977):

> Thank you for your remarks about Cave Birds, because they made me dig out those pieces I'd deleted, and so it comes about that I rediscover their rough virtues, so much better than what I tried to replace them with, as you so rightly complain, and I think probably better than the main sequence, certainly better than many of them. In fact now I look at them I realise they were the beginning of an attempt to open myself in a different direction; a very necessary direction for me, the only real direction, and I'm aghast at the time and density of folly that has passed since I lost sight of it.

All five of these poems were restored in the published version.

I like to think that this, my first presumptuous intervention, not only led to a better Cave Birds, but helped Hughes to move forward in a 'necessary direction'. Two years later Hughes wrote to Gifford and Roberts: 'After the First Fright is crude — at one point I replaced it — but I put it back. Keith Sagar urged me not to drop it, and he's right, it has a kind of intactness — it states its case in a way I haven't been able to improve.'[6]

The first public appearance of *Cave Birds* had been at the Ilkley Literature Festival in May 1975, where the poems were read by professional actors. After the interval Hughes himself read from *Lumb's Remains*, the poems which became the epilogue to *Gaudete* (1977). It seemed to me that the two halves of that evening represented two extremes of Hughes' work to date, *Cave Birds* being at the extreme of artifice, complexity and obscurity (which undoubtedly delivered its own riches); and *Lumb's Remains* being at the extreme of stripped-down nakedness, directness and artlessness. I felt very strongly that the second was the direction in which Hughes should be going.

Most of my input in the eighties did not relate to specific poems or collections, but took the form of persistent nagging at Hughes to avoid what seemed to me unnecessary complexity and obscurity in his verse. He seemed to write on the assumption that every reader had read and remembered everything he had read himself, even in his own specialist fields, such as mythology, folklore, alchemy, etc.

✷✷✷

In 1984 Hughes became Poet Laureate. The news came as a shock to many of his admirers, since it was hard to imagine a poet further removed from the Establishment. The first poem Hughes published in his capacity of Laureate was the superb 'Rain Charm for the Duchy', a poem already written, but subtly adapted to a royal christening through the theme of water. The main purpose of the poem is to keep alive or revivify in the imagination of the reader our innate but inert sense of the sacredness of water, not as something that comes out of a tap, but as a fundamental and indispensable source of life, as part of the miraculous system of delicate interrelationships on which life on earth depends. As such it serves as a metaphor for all relationships and creativity, and is perhaps the most common and potent image in all poetry. This poem demonstrated how Hughes could use his new position as national poet to subvert the Establishment by placing its institutions within a far larger context, to reopen the circuit of fertilizing interchange between the secular world and the world of spirit, which is also Nature. Thus the poet has the huge responsibility of taking over this essential task from priest and shaman. The shaman brought power from the spirit world to heal the sickness of his people. This, for Hughes, was the raison d'être of all poetry.

In his review of Mircea Eliade's *Shamanism*,[7] Hughes had written: 'The shamans seem to undergo, at will and at phenomenal intensity, and with practical results, one of the main regenerating dramas of the human psyche: the fundamental poetic event.' He described Shakespeare, Keats, Yeats and Eliot as shamanic poets, but doubted whether in our world it was any longer possible

---

6 Terry Gifford and Neil Roberts, *Ted Hughes: A Critical Study* (1981), p. 259.
7 Mircea Eliade, *Shamanism* (Routledge and Kegan Paul, 1964), reviewed in *Winter Pollen*, p. 58.

for poetry to function in this way: 'Everything among us is against it'.[8] 'Rain Charm for the Duchy' seemed to me to imply that Hughes felt that the laureateship might put him in a privileged position to answer that call. I wrote a paper on 'The Laureate as Shaman', which I gave in several places, including the National Poetry Centre in London.

I was not the only one with such high expectations. Seamus Heaney described 'Rain Charm' as 'deeply bardic and public', and hoped that Hughes would establish 'a sacerdotal function for the poet in the realm'.[9] Neil Roberts expressed the hope that Hughes 'might turn the Laureateship into an organ for creatively exploring the role of religion, ritual and mythology in our society'.[10] We were all disappointed. Hughes did not write another serious laureate poem. It was the publication of his poem 'The Dream of the Lion' which prompted me, in January 1986, to challenge him on this point. His reply demonstrated at length the symbolic/heraldic ingenuity of the poem, but revealed that he regarded the laureate poems as semi-private letters to members of the royal family, written 'in an amiable way'.

★★★

The next occasion on which I was able to make a significant contribution was in relation to *Shakespeare and the Goddess of Complete Being*. In 1971 Hughes had published a remarkable introduction to his *A Choice of Shakespeare's Verse* (1971),[11] where he had found in *Venus and Adonis* a template for the myth or 'Tragic Equation' which is the basis of *Shakespeare and the Goddess*. It inspired Donya Feuer, a director of the Royal Dramatic Theatre in Stockholm, to devise *Soundings* in 1978, in Hughes' words 'a full-length performance of interlinked verse extracts in which a solo actress relived her Shakespearean earlier incarnations, following the evolution of one of the myth's figures from play to play'.[12] In 1979 she was mounting a production of *Measure for Measure*, and asked Hughes for his view of it. His reply occupies fifteen pages in the *Letters*,[13] but does not take the opportunity to develop the Tragic Equation in relation to that play. In 1989 Donya Feuer contacted Hughes again,

> wanting to know if anything could be done with our old notion of the last fifteen plays, hugely shuffled and rearranged to make a *perpetuum mobile* maze of metamorphic episodes, play dissolving into play, characters going through their transformations, in and out of each other's worlds, like supernatural, dying and resurrected entities in a real myth.

8 Ekbert Faas, *Ted Hughes: The Unaccommodated Universe* (1980), p. 206. Despite his overt refusal of the call, Larkin did write a number of shamanic poems, using water as the primary image: 'Wedding-Wind', 'Water', 'Church Going' and 'The Whitsun Weddings' for example. See the essay on Larkin on my website: www.keithsagar.co.uk. Hughes acknowledged the shamanic quality in Larkin when he made use of the phrase 'devout drench' from 'Water' in his dedication of 'Rain Charm'.
9 *Belfast Review*, 10 (Spring 1985), p. 6.
10 *Critical Quarterly*, vol. 27, no. 2 (1985), p. 5.
11 The American edition was called *With Fairest Flowers while Summer Lasts*.
12 *Shakespeare and the Goddess of Complete Being* (1992), p. xii.
13 Christopher Reid, ed., *Letters of Ted Hughes* (2007), pp. 405–19.

I had no clear idea how such a thing might ever be practicable, but the thought of it would intrigue anybody. However, it did occur to me that if I anatomized what I had identified as Shakespeare's myth, as it revealed itself in each work, and followed through what are to me its fascinating evolutions, and set it all out in letters to Donya Feuer, bit by bit, as simply as possible, who knows, maybe something would emerge.[14]

Hughes sent me copies of the first fifteen of these letters on 29 April 1990, and of the rest as he typed them up. He seemed to expect a detailed response, and I was in a good position to make it, since I was in the throes of writing my own three chapters on Shakespeare for *Literature and the Crime Against Nature*, and was also preparing to teach a three-year course on the complete works of Shakespeare the following session. My comments, over the next year, ran to scores of closely typed A4 pages.

In the final text of *Shakespeare and the Goddess*, Ted made several attempts to sum up in a single paragraph what he meant by Shakespeare's myth, or 'Tragic Equation'. The clearest of these seems to me the following:

> Confronting the Goddess of Divine Love, the Goddess of Complete Being, the ego's extreme alternatives are either to reject her and attempt to live an independent, rational, secular life or to abnegate the ego and embrace her love with 'total, unconditional love', which means to become a saint, a holy idiot, possessed by the Divine Love. The inevitability of the tragic idea which Shakespeare projects with such 'divine' completeness is that there is no escape from one choice or the other. Man will always choose the former, simply because once he is free of a natural, creaturely awareness of the divine indulgence which permits him to exist at all, he wants to live his own life, and he has never invented a society of saints that was tolerable. In other words, always, one way or another, he rejects the Goddess. This is the first phase of the tragedy. Then follows his correction: his 'madness' against the Goddess, the Puritan crime which leads directly to his own tragic self-destruction, from which he can escape only after the destruction of his ego – being reborn through the Flower rebirth, becoming a holy idiot, renouncing his secular independence, and surrendering once again to the Goddess.
>
> From the human point of view, obviously the whole business is monstrous: tragic on a cosmic scale, where the only easements are in the possibilities of a temporary blessing from the Goddess (an erotic fracture in the carapace of the tragic hero) or of becoming a saint. There is a third possibility, in some degree of self-anaesthesia, some kind of living death. But man has no more choice in the basic arrangement than the blue-green algae. (pp. 392–3)

14 *Shakespeare and the Goddess of Complete Being*, pp. xii–xiii.

Once Ted had committed himself to demonstrating the presence of the Tragic Equation in full in every play from *All's Well that Ends Well* onwards, he was doomed to being, in places, over-elaborate, tortuous, and incomprehensible. I felt that if he had confined himself to a selection of those plays and parts of plays where the underlying equation can be clearly demonstrated, he would have written a better book in a fraction of the time.

I was perfectly happy with the idea that there was a shadowy but consistent mythic meaning behind the surface drama and characterization of many, perhaps even most of the plays, but I demanded a minimum level of congruence between the two, which Ted did not always provide. If the myth required white and the play delivered black, he simply proceeded on the assumption that the play could be ignored. This played into the hands of those reviewers who resented his invasion of their academic territory.

Hughes' reactions to my comments were very mixed. In the case of *Hamlet* he did not take into account any of the themes I outlined, presumably because they would have diverted the flow of his argument. But he did act on almost all my more local objections without demur, often in such brief sentences as 'OK, that's gone' or 'I'll change that'. But when I challenged the equation itself, or rather his application of it to a particular play, it was a very different matter.

The plays on which we disagreed most fundamentally were *Measure for Measure* and *The Tempest*. Ted's response to my attack on Isabella, in *Measure for Measure*, was fourteen A4 pages of impassioned eloquence. Our dialogue about her continued long after the publication of *Shakespeare and the Goddess of Complete Being*.

In the case of *The Tempest* I felt that Ted's equation fitted the play perfectly, but that he had arbitrarily, perversely, assumed that Prospero, 'obviously with Shakespeare's fullest and most fascinated collaboration' (p. 413), actually repudiated the equation. This involved Shakespeare repudiating most of his earlier plays. So I attacked Prospero, and Ted stoutly defended him, with no quarter on either side.[15]

When Ted thanked me in the acknowledgements for playing 'devil's advocate to some effect', I think he meant that I had been most useful to him in forcing him to extend and fortify his arguments, particularly in these instances. If he also believed that I was deliberately taking up opposing positions I did not actually hold, or expressing some academic consensus, then he was wrong.

When Hughes sent 'Shakespeare and Occult Neoplatonism' to William Scammell, the editor of *Winter Pollen*, he sent with it an introductory paragraph which Scammell did not use. In it he wrote: 'With a book about such a questionable and touchy subject (the psychological/religious/mystical root-system of Shakespeare's dramatic vision) naturally I want my readers to approach it with the cooperative, imaginative attitude of a co-author.' This was an approach I had adopted to almost all of Hughes' earlier work. But in this case I also felt impelled to play Shakespeare's advocate.

15 I subsequently developed my case against Ted's account of Prospero, in *Ted Hughes and Nature*, pp. 130–40.

In the proofs of *Shakespeare and the Goddess* Hughes had given an account, dropped from the published text, of how in the late sixties Peter Brook, when he began to think of making a film of his famous production of *King Lear*, had invited Ted to see what he could do 'in the way of converting Shakespeare's massively verbal text to dialogue more suitable for a film'.

A twenty-five year devotion to Shakespeare's concept, and to his every line and expression, made this task more difficult for me than it might have been for many others. Every move I made reconfirmed how each word – in that first act, for instance – is like a vital gland in the whole organism, and how exclusively verbal, as a delicate flying machine, that gigantic seraph-pterodactyl is. But imagining how ruthlessly Shakespeare himself would have stripped the play down for performance in country tavern yards, I plucked up my courage and for some weeks hacked away, trying this and that. Until one night I had an odd dream. A pounding at the back door of my house, in the middle of the night, awoke me. I opened the door to find Shakespeare himself there, magnificently arrayed in dazzling Elizabethan finery and utterly enraged with me and with what I was doing.

I imagined Shakespeare 'utterly enraged' at many points in *Shakespeare and the Goddess*. Enraged, for example, that the 'vital words' he gives to Isabella in *Measure for Measure* when she avows that pre-marital sex is 'a vice that most I do abhor, / And most desire should meet the blow of justice', should be transformed by Hughes into their opposite, Isabella pleading 'on behalf of fornication, for sexual licence . . . for the sanctity of her brother's impregnating his betrothed Juliet' (pp. 168–9).

My most significant contribution to *Shakespeare and the Goddess* was perhaps structural. Hughes' original intention had been to publish the material simply as *Letters to Donya*, but he felt the need to expand on those letters, and rewrote the material as *The Silence of Cordelia*. His account of *King Lear* was the culmination, the later plays being virtually relegated to an afterword. I persuaded him that the culmination had to be a full account of *The Tempest*. Once he had committed himself to that, it became a chapter of over a hundred pages, and generated another hundred pages to account for the plays between *King Lear* and *The Tempest*. If Hughes was right that his preoccupation with prose in those years contributed to his final illness, he had nothing to thank me for.

***

When Hughes published his two essays on Coleridge in *Winter Pollen* in 1994, he began the first of them, 'Myths, Metres, Rhythms', by confronting the issue of communication. For adequate communication to take place, he states, author and reader must share a mythos, that is, an inherited fund of 'the deeper shared understandings which keep us intact as a group': 'When the shared group understanding of all members is complete then a mere touching of the tokens of their mythology is enough for complete communication. Each verbal signal illuminates – with the voltage of the whole group's awareness and energy – those members of the group who exchange it' (p. 310).

Such a mythos is perfect for the poet, since 'nothing needs to be explained'. But in our modern, multicultural world no such mythos exists. The writer is obliged to try to find a lingua franca which will communicate across a global network: 'While that new global multiculture writhes like a sandstorm out of every television, the writer can only grope along, transmitting what are intended to be meaningful signals, the most meaningful possible – in the hope of . . . meeting antennae lifted and vibrating in joy' (p. 312).

Hughes gives as an example the total incomprehension of an American urban poet when confronted with 'The Unknown Wren'. For him the wren was literally unknown. He had never seen one, and was uncertain what it was. The poem demands, like every other Hughes animal poem, that the animal should be part of the reader's mythos. This shared mythos can no longer be taken for granted even within one's own culture. On one occasion I collected Ted after a reading at a school in Eccles, and asked why he seemed gloomy. Apparently he had read 'Swifts', with little or no response from his audience, and was afterwards told by a teacher that probably none of the children knew what a swift was.

But what Hughes regarded as his essential mythos included much more than a thorough knowledge of English flora and fauna. It included the whole of classical, Celtic and Nordic mythologies, 'the whole tradition of Hermetic Magic (which is a good part of Jewish Mystical philosophy, not to speak of the mystical philosophy of the Renaissance), the whole historical exploration into spirit life at every level of consciousness, the whole deposit of earlier and other religion, myth, vision, traditional wisdom and story in folk belief, on which Yeats based all his work'.[16] Philip Larkin had solved the problem by dismissing the 'common myth-kitty' as irrelevant to his own or any other poet's concerns, but at a great cost to his poetry and criticism. The point is that what for Auden and Larkin was merely a facile add-on for the purpose of gaining spurious resonances, was for Yeats and Hughes their essential discipline and poetic life-blood. Hughes could not write without that huge resource. Without it he would have been 'gagged'. Yet he could not continue to write on the assumption, already problematic for Yeats and Eliot, that there was a readership equipped by education and culture to tune in to all that.

When Ted sent me the first draft of 'The Snake in the Oak', the second of his two essays on Coleridge, on 27 May 1993, he asked me to provide a list of the places where I thought clarifying notes were needed: 'My sense of what is necessary, in that line, is defective.' He was shocked that I did not know what he meant by the 'Keeper of the Threshold'. He regarded all such stories from myth and folklore as 'standard features' which he could take for granted as common ground with his readers. He was surprised to find that his copy-editor did not know what Samadhi were. Neither did I. Neither, I was sure, did the vast majority of his potential readers.

16   See 30 August 1979.

Given the intractable problems of communication he had bewailed in the first Coleridge essay, it was incomprehensible to me that in the second he should have indulged in so many esoteric and exclusive references. 'The goblins of the sangsara on a Tibetan tanka', for example, have never been part of any Western mythos. In 1984 Hughes had read *Phoenix*, Lawrence's posthumous prose, and described it as 'straight oxygen'. The pity of it, it seemed to me, was that Hughes was perfectly capable of writing prose of similarly energizing directness and lucidity.

On 1 August 1993 he wrote: 'I managed to take account of almost all those suggestions you gave me, in the Coleridge piece. Thanks a lot for that.' His taking account took the form of adding footnotes in *Winter Pollen*, such as those on Hamadryads (p. 386) and 'Psyche's incognito visitant' (p. 393). He had written on one of Coleridge's notebook entries:

> But here, in the exhalations of the underworld from which 'Kubla Khan' rises, the Nightingale's 'fast thick warble', 'that crowds, and hurries, and precipitates', can be heard through the Alph's
>
> > ceaseless turmoil seething,
> > As if this earth in fast thick pants were breathing,
>
> and through the wailing of the woman in the dark chasm, uttering her 'love-chant' and striving 'to disburthen her full soul' for her demon lover, and no less clearly through the bellowing of the alligator whose convulsions, by now, are rising more insistently into the boil of the 'mighty fountain'.

I told him that many readers would find this interminable sentence unintelligible. He kept the sentence, but inserted a lengthy note on page 396.

But the problem, it seemed to me, could not be solved by mere notes. Hughes protested that in requesting such clarification I was 'imagining readers on the margins of illiterate' (27 June). But in most cases I needed the clarification myself. He seemed to me to be working to an altogether unrealistic definition of literacy.

Fortunately, there was a solution, which Hughes belatedly discovered. *Birthday Letters* (which he had already begun) was to be hailed by the reviewers as unpremeditated art, an outpouring of spontaneous, 'confessional' verse – a notion disingenuously encouraged by Hughes himself. It was nothing of the sort. Those poems are completely dependent on the inspiration and discipline which Hughes drew from Cabbala. The eighty-eight poems, as Ann Skea has incontrovertibly demonstrated, correspond exactly to the eighty-eight paths of the Cabbalistic journey.[17] What is new about *Birthday Letters* is that Hughes had found that he could draw the poetic discipline he needed from an esoteric source without requiring readers to understand or even be aware of it. It is the

17 See 'Poetry and Magic 1: *Birthday Letters*' on http://ann.skea.com.

scaffolding which can be removed entirely when the building is finished. But it is more than scaffolding, since Hughes no doubt assumed that something of the ancient power and spiritual truth of his source would invisibly inform the poems and subliminally infiltrate his readers.

★★★

As we moved towards the end of the century, post-modern critical theory and its offshoots gradually strangled literary criticism as I understood and practised it. The fashionable anti-literary critics gained such influence in the academies that they reduced the demand to the point where even appreciative publishers could not see a market for it.

The very success of my repeated efforts to get inside Hughes' works began to tell against me. In 1998 I sent Christopher Reid, as reader for Faber, what I had so far written (most of it) of The Laughter of Foxes. He found the book lacking in critical objectivity, and 'disconcertingly ventriloquial'. Ted had better things to do than spend his time putting words into my mouth. He never suggested that I should write anything on his work. I would draft an essay or chapter in full before sending it to him for his comments. Then I would incorporate most of his useful corrections and additional information. After the publication of Birthday Letters I had ventured for the first time onto the dangerous ground of Sylvia Plath,[18] with a chapter called 'From Prospero to Orpheus', tracing the gradual but complete reversal of Ted's sense of his role in relation to her work over a period of forty years. I was apprehensive about his reaction. He replied: 'Your account of the cooperation between S.P. & me is pretty much as I see it'. If this kind of validation constitutes ventriloquism, I am content to disconcert those readers who are hoping for sterile theory and judgemental confrontation.

★★★

The flow of criticism between Hughes and myself was by no means always one way. I had published a few poems in the Bradford Grammar School magazine, but Cambridge English quickly cured me of the presumption of writing poems. I did not write another for sixteen years. In 1968 I wrote a handful of poems,

---

18 Sylvia Plath was born in Boston, Massachusetts, in 1932. Her German father Otto was a professor of biology at Boston University, and a world authority on bees. He died when Sylvia was eight. Despite academic and literary successes, increasing depression led to Plath's first suicide attempt in 1953, which was followed by insulin therapy and electoconvulsive shock treatment. These horrific experiences were the basis of her novel The Bell Jar (published by Heinemann in 1963 under the pseudonym Victoria Lucas). In 1955 Plath won a Fulbright Scholarship, and began postgraduate study at Newnham College, Cambridge. In February 1956 she met Ted Hughes at the launch of the St. Botolph's Review, which contained several of his poems. They were married in June. Sylvia submitted Hughes' first book, The Hawk in the Rain, to a competition run by Harper & Row. Hughes won the competition, the prize being publication (by Harper/Faber & Faber in 1957). Her own first book, The Colossus, was published by Faber & Faber in 1960. Their daughter Frieda was born in April 1960, and their son Nicholas in January 1962. In September of that year Hughes and Plath separated. Plath committed suicide the following February. Hughes edited Plath's second collection, Ariel (Faber & Faber, 1965), her short stories Johnny Panic and the Bible of Dreams (Faber & Faber, 1977) and her Collected Poems (Faber & Faber, 1981). He also contributed a foreword to The Journals of Sylvia Plath (Dial Press, 1982). His Birthday Letters is a poetic account of their relationship.

most of them about Lawrence's paintings,[19] but I soon fizzled out. In the spring of 1977 Ted sent me an advance copy of *Gaudete* (inscribed 'The head is older than the book'). I wanted to share my excitement, so I organized free weekly meetings at my home for friends and adult students I knew to be interested in Hughes. All that summer several of us went through the book page by page. Not only was I bowled over by the book in its own terms, it also had the dramatic and immediate effect of fertilizing my own imagination (an effect Ted's poems had on many others). I wrote more and much better poems in 1977 than any other year.

I sent the best of my poems to Ted, and his response was so encouraging that I asked him if he would expand his comments a little to form an introduction to my poems in a series called 'Proem Pamphlets' being published by the Yorkshire Arts Association. The idea was that in each a new poet's work would be introduced by an established poet. To my delight Ted came up with an essay on the virtues of simplicity in poetry.[20]

The Lawrence trail also took me several times to Italy. In 1978 I visited the Etruscan tombs at Cerveteri, north of Rome, a magical place, and that night I had a very strange dream. Out of the reality and the dream I made my first short story, 'The Beast'. On my way home through London I bought the latest issue of *Bananas*. It contained a new story by Ted Hughes called 'The Head'. It was a long story, but the further I read, the more aware I became that it was the same story as 'The Beast', not only in essentials, but occasionally in detail and even phraseology. In each story a modern man from our despiritualized world, makes a journey into a nightmare world, which is also the animal world and the spirit world. In each case he must pass through the territory of a primitive race with an animistic religion. In each case the dreamworld is a dark, steep, heavily forested valley. In 'The Beast' the ancient trees are 'like standing fossils'; in 'The Head' the forest is 'like a cave full of stalagmites'. In each story the sacredness of the animal/spirit world is violated by senseless, barbaric cruelty. Each narrator is watched by an elk. Mine has 'massive antlers', Hughes' has 'antlers the breadth of a lounge'. My elk looks at me 'with its empty eye-sockets'; his looks at him 'with his dead brilliant eye'. In each story what should kill an animal, many stakes driven into its head, or many bullets fired into its body, fails to do so. It refuses to die. In each story the narrator is transformed, purified, by 'animal wounds and animal pain'. There is much more in Hughes' story, but it contains the whole of mine. Hughes' story must have been written first. How was it transmitted across Europe to me in my sleep in Tarquinia?

I sent the story to Hughes, expecting him to comment on the astonishing similarities. Instead he sent me a lengthy analysis of it in psychological terms. His interpretation had never occurred to me, but may well be right. It brings the story into a much closer relationship to my poems than I was aware of.

After the publication of my first book, *The Art of D. H. Lawrence*, in 1966, my

19 I had seen the original paintings in Taos, New Mexico, and Austin, Texas, and they demanded that I should record my response to them in little poems, like Lawrence's own *Pansies*.
20 See Appendix VI.

publishers, Cambridge University Press, asked me if I had another book in preparation. I did not; but I rapidly invented one. It was to be called *Worshippers of Nature*, and was simply an excuse to write about some of my favourite poets. But the project did not have enough shape or substance to draw me from my continuing work on Lawrence, or my budding work on Hughes. Three factors came together in the seventies to reanimate the project, all three involving Hughes.

Stimulated particularly by Hughes' passionate review of Max Nicholson's *The Environmental Revolution* in 1970,[21] I became increasingly interested in ecology, and the relationship between ecology and the creative imagination. I now had a much more interesting and challenging sense of 'Nature' to deal with. Rereading Eliot's essay 'Tradition and the Individual Talent', I was struck by the implications for my book of his statement that every new work added to the tradition changes the whole tradition. I realized that what I really wanted to write about was how the addition to the Western canon of Lawrence and Hughes had changed the way we must now read the whole canon. For this new way of reading I coined the term 'ecocriticism', and even added the subtitle: *A Primer in Ecocriticism*, though I later discovered that the term was already in use in the USA.

Thus from being too small a project to grab my attention, it became a dauntingly large, almost megalomaniac enterprise. I needed a clearer focus to enable me to work with a manageable number of texts. At the Cheltenham Festival in 1977 Ted gave an unpublished lecture on the east-European poets, in the course of which he made the striking claim that critics and readers are not judges of literature, they are criminals being judged by literature. This gave me not only a clearer focus, but also a new title: *Literature and the Crime Against Nature*. I decided that the climax would be a large final chapter on Ted: 'From World of Blood to World of Light'.

I did not write the chapters in chronological order, but used my teaching throughout the eighties to engage with works before writing about them. I sent Ted several of the chapters as I wrote them. His replies were invariably encouraging, as were the responses I got from other creative writers to whom I sent chapters – Peter Redgrove, Barry Unsworth, Lindsay Clarke. I was increasingly in need of such encouragement as the rejections from publishers mounted up in the early 1990s. When the number reached seventy-two, I gave up. Only six had wanted to see the book. Four of those praised it highly, but, understandably in that climate, could see no market for it. It remained unpublished until 2005.

★★★

I have concentrated on the relationship of Hughes and myself as a unique relationship between a poet and a critic. It will be obvious from the letters, however, that it soon became much more than that. We recommended books to each other, and exchanged accounts of our travels and the achievements of our children. We visited each other. At North Tawton I enjoyed walks with Ted along the Taw, and salmon caught that morning by Ted and deliciously cooked by

21 Reprinted in *Winter Pollen*.

Carol.[22] I held Ted's huge tiger skull. One evening when Ted was staying with me, he suggested that we each sit in front of one of my two large tanks of marine tropical fish, select a single specimen, and focus on it to the exclusion of all else for at least half and hour. This exercise did not produce a poem for Ted, but produced my 'Bicolour Blenny'.[23] On a later visit our son Arren, then aged eight, overheard Ted and me talking about Ted's tiger skull. He went to his room and came back with the shoebox in which he kept his collection of rabbit and sheep bones, and his dried squashed toad. These he proudly showed to Ted, who examined them intently. A few days later came a parcel for Arren containing the skull of the first badger Ted had ever skinned.[24] He subsequently sent Arren several other skulls.

★★★

29 October 1998

Returning to our campsite in the New Forest, I caught through the open door of a caravan a phrase from the six o'clock news: 'the late Poet Laureate'. It seemed a strange way to describe Betjeman. But moments later our own radio gave me the appalling news that Ted had died. I knew he had been treated for cancer, but, as far as I knew, successfully. The last sentence of my last, and first unanswered, letter seemed now strangely valedictory. I tried to express my sense of loss, not just for myself, but for the world, in a brief elegy:

> A ghost crab sidled into his body
> By moonlight
> Laid its thousand eggs.
> *
> When that oak fell a tremor passed
> Through all the rivers of the West.
> The spent salmon felt it.
> *
> A rare familiar voice
> Entered the October silence
> While red leaves fell.

22 Hughes had married Carol Orchard in August 1970. The following spring he wrote to Peter Redgrove: 'I'd like you to meet my wife. She's from Devon, daughter of a farmer, half Welsh, very young, not very interested in literature but with perfect taste & judgement for what really counts in what she does read. Exceedingly good for me' (Reid, Letters, p. 311).

23 See Appendix IV.

24 See plate 5.

A Note on the Text

The letters of Ted Hughes to me are at the British Library. The great majority are in longhand. To stay as close as possible to these, Hughes' spelling mistakes have been retained, indicated by [sic], as have his irregularities of punctuation, unnoted. The letters are reproduced in full, except for that of 9 July 1992, where two sentences which might be construed as libellous have been omitted. All Hughes' letters are from Court Green, North Tawton, Devon.

I did not keep copies of my letters to Ted until the dawn of word-processing. Fortunately, Ted kept nearly all of them, and included them in the archive he sold to Emory University in Atlanta in 1997. I have included here only such extracts as are necessary to maintain the continuity of the correspondence.

Square brackets around dates of letters indicate that they are conjectural; pm indicates that they derive from the postmark.

The Letters of Ted Hughes
and Keith Sagar

1969–1972

In March 1969 Hughes abandoned *The Life and Songs of the Crow*, the 'epic folk-tale' studded with hundreds of poems which had been the main focus of his work for two years, and published a selection of poems from it as *Crow*. His adaptation of Seneca's *Oedipus*, which had been performed by Peter Brook's company at the Old Vic the previous year, was published in December.

1970 saw the publication of *The Coming of the Kings*, four of Hughes' plays for children, and his review of Max Nicholson's *The Environmental Revolution*. In August Hughes married Carol Orchard. In October Hughes and his sister Olwyn founded the Rainbow Press. The first publication, *Poems: Ruth Fainlight, Ted Hughes, Alan Sillitoe*, appeared in April 1971.[1]

Hughes spent the whole summer of 1971 working with Peter Brook's company in Persia. He wrote *Orghast* for performance at the Shiraz Festival, and *Prometheus on his Crag*. In *A Choice of Shakespeare's Verse* Hughes first formulated the 'Tragic Equation' which was to be the basis of *Shakespeare and the Goddess of Complete Being*. Hughes took up again a film-scenario he had written in 1964 and began to transform it into *Gaudete*. In November he read at Manchester University.

In 1972 Hughes dramatised the twelfth-century Persian story *The Conference of the Birds* for Peter Brook, and wrote 'about 100 poems and scenarios for Peter Brook's company to improvise with' on their tour of Nigeria. Hughes began farming at Moortown farm, in north Devon, with his father-in-law Jack Orchard.

[19 March 1969]

My first letter to Ted Hughes (which has not survived) described the accident which had prevented me from attending his reading in Manchester the previous evening. I enclosed my first essay on his work, and a paper I had just written which I thought might interest him, '"Little Living Myths": A Note on Lawrence's Tortoises', subsequently published in the D. H. Lawrence Review, 3, Summer 1970.

[Early April 1969]

Dear Mr Sagar

Thank you for showing me these essays — which I'm now returning. Rather belatedly, I'm afraid.

---

1 Olwyn Hughes had been two years ahead of Ted at Mexborough Grammar School. She encouraged him to take Shakespeare seriously. In 1952 she went to live in Paris, working at the British Embassy, then at NATO, and finally with a Hungarian Film and Theatre Agency, Martonplay. After the death of Sylvia Plath, with whom she had found it difficult to form a relationship, Olwyn gave up her job in Paris to help Ted with the children, and gradually drifted into becoming his agent. She also represented, among other writers, Robert Nye, Jean Rhys, Yehuda Amichai and Elaine Feinstein.

Apart from the accidents, your compensation for missing my performance in Manchester seems to me to have been much better than what you missed. The three cameras not only fussed and distracted everybody, two of them eventually failed to work. So there'll be very little entertainment there.

It's difficult to say anything about an article about one's own work. What I have actually got down on paper seems such a small part, up to now, of what I concern myself with, that it is disturbing to have my intentions divined as generously as you divine them in your paper. But it is a great change to read an article that concerns itself with the imaginative and vital interior of poetry, rather than the verbal surface exclusively, and yours seems to me both bold and sensitive in that respect, keeping the surface qualities just in the right perspective.

I greatly enjoyed the piece on Lawrence, which surprised me in several places, and always into agreement.

I can't say at present whether I shall be doing any more readings for some time, so I'd like to decline your invitation for the time being.

Yours sincerely
Ted Hughes
P.S. In the quote from Skylarks you miss out the word 'crested'.

[September 1972]

I sent Hughes two books I had published in 1972, my British Council booklet on him in the Writers and their Work series, and my Penguin Selected Poems of D. H. Lawrence; also, having become aware of many parallels with Crow, a copy of David Lindsay's Voyage to Arcturus.

6th Oct 72

Dear Keith Sagar,

I'm very conscious of your understanding and good will. There are so many little things I haven't thanked you for, but I must say how much I like your Lawrence poetry selection. It's several years since I read his work closely so I had the intense pleasure of being overwhelmed afresh. Putting the best, in fair bulk, all together, has made something overwhelming.

Thank you also for Journey to Arcturus. I wrote a play of sorts, years ago, which I showed to Peter Redgrove[2] — he immediately recognised themes & events, & lent me his copy, which was a surprise to me at the time. His was a 1st Edition, so he took it back — I tried to keep it.

Best wishes to you

Sincerely

Ted Hughes

12 December 1972

I am a member of the Drama and Spoken Word Panel of the Mid-Pennine Arts Association. We had a meeting last week to discuss plans for the 1973–4 season. I put up a proposal for a Ted Hughes Festival or Fortnight which received unanimous support. It could be in the autumn of 1973 or spring of 1974.

This is the sort of thing we have in mind:

1. Readings by you at opposite ends of the area (say Todmorden and Blackburn). We could pay £60 for two.

2. Productions of some of your plays by Theatremobile, a professional company sponsored by the Association.

3. The publication of two poster poems – Pennines in April in an unlimited unsigned edition, and a new commissioned poem in a signed edition of 250. Payment could be in the form of a fee or a royalty or both.

4. An exhibition of Mss., first editions, poster poems, photographs, etc.

5. Talks and seminars on your work, perhaps in the form of a couple of Saturday day-schools run by my Department, in which Brian Cox and I would be the main contributors.

We shall no doubt get further ideas if the thing gets off the ground. We shall expect to get national coverage. It might give you some satisfaction to be recognized in your own country. However, we don't want to proceed unless the whole scheme meets with your approval, and unless you are prepared to participate by giving at least one reading.

2 Peter Redgrove (1932–2003), though primarily a poet, was also a novelist, playwright, and co-author (with his wife Penelope Shuttle) of The Wise Wound (Gollancz, 1978), which has a paragraph by Hughes on the dust-wrapper. Hughes and Redgrove had met in Cambridge, where Redgrove (who read Natural Sciences but left without a degree) founded the literary magazine Delta.

1973

Hughes wrote most of the poems in *Season Songs*, first published as *Spring, Summer, Autumn Winter* in 1974. He kept diary records in rough verse of his most memorable farming experiences, which were published as *Moortown Elegies* (1978), the 'Moortown' section of *Moortown* (1979) and *Moortown Diary* (1989).

[March 1973]

My letter to which the following letter from Hughes was an answer has not survived.

I had just signed a contract with Cambridge University Press for The Art of Ted Hughes, *and was beginning work on it. I asked Hughes the following questions: 1. Did the Billy Red described in the short story 'Sunday' actually exist? 2. Had 'The Court Tumbler and Satirist' appeared anywhere else before* Poetry from Cambridge 1952–4? *3. I can only guess that my question was: Which poems in* The Hawk in the Rain *were written before Hughes met Plath? However, in that case his answer would not tally with his dating of the poems in a copy of* Hawk *at Worcester Polytechnic Institute, Massachusetts (see Appendix I). 4. Where was the house in 'Wind'? 5. Where were the poems in* Lupercal *written? 6. Where is Yaddo?*

[pm 26 March 1973]

Dear Mr Sagar,

Sorry to have kept you waiting about September. A reading would be fine. Anything more complicated or prolonged I'd rather defer.[1]

I'll answer your questions:

1. — Yes there was. My father knew him quite well. And he killed rats at the pub I describe — called Stubbing Wharfe, at Mytholm, just outside Hebden Bridge. (Not Mytholmroyd.)

2. Can't remember where 'Court Tumbler' was first published. Chequer editor had it. (Not sure if it was published before the Anth.)

3. Dove-Breeder, Modest Proposal, Incompatibilities, after. Others before.

---

1 I have no record of the reasons, but the projected Hughes Festival never materialized. It was no doubt both premature and overambitious.

4. The Beacon, Heptonstall.[2]

5. Last piece (first in book) written at Yaddo. The whole book was written in the States.

6. Saratoga, N.Y. state.

I hope you have an interesting stay in America.

No — I did not go to Africa. I see they're just back. Probably missed something wonderful there — but things happen here too.

Best wishes

Ted Hughes

[Early October 1973]

Dear Keith Sagar,

Sorry to be so long answering your letter with the M.S. of your book. I find it very difficult to clear up my reactions to its contents.

Whatever person I've projected, in the body of my poems, will have to bear whatever ideas people have about him. I've freed myself fairly successfully from too great a concern about his fate. What does disturb me, I'm afraid, is to see him identified with me — in the details of my life. It is ridiculous, of course, but the sense of constriction and over-exposure I feel, reading the biographical parts of your book, is something I would rather be spared. I would be extremely grateful if you could delete anything of that sort.

A great concern of mine, over the past few years, has been to disperse in myself that sense of *the wrong audience* — which is so inhibiting, & falsifying, & wearisome. The more concentration one achieves, the more one is aware of its real enemies. By wrong audience I mean all those who, without being the people for whom you write, yet have a strong idea about you and enough scraps of your hair & nails. I'm trusting you'll understand. I'm always telling people about myself, then always regretting it when I see myself outlined in the 3rd person.

Your book made me regret the months & even years I've yielded to the serpent Ophuichon — who always appeared, to the day, when I had at last managed to take a real step. But he wasn't always ugly.

Best wishes Sincerely Ted Hughes

2 While Ted was at Cambridge, his parents had moved from Mexborough back to the Calder Valley, to The Beacon at Heptonstall Slack. See plate 1.

7 October 1973

Yes, I know what you mean by "the wrong audience". If any of them start to read my book, I don't think they'll get very far. But surely it is perfectly natural for members of your right audience, powerfully affected by the poems, to ask what sort of person writes such poems and out of what sort of background and experiences. I find myself in my teaching continually having to try to close the gap between art and life caused by formalism, aestheticism and preciosity, which prevents so many intelligent and sensitive people from taking poetry seriously. This tendency has been encouraged, I suppose, by my work on Lawrence, who created so directly out of his living. But I realize that your work is quite unlike his in this respect, that you have striven for and achieved a great impersonality in your work. Also, of course, one cannot approach a living author in the same way as one who died before one was born.

I offered to omit or rewrite any passages Hughes disliked, but he did not take up the offer. I enclosed a copy of The Art of D. H. Lawrence *and asked for Hughes' reaction to the idea of following the pattern of that book in having a chronology of works and a photograph at the head of each chapter. I also enclosed the first draft of my chapter on Crow, in which I pointed out the similarity between these lines from 'A Kill'*

> Flogged lame with legs
> Shot through the head with balled brains
> Shot blind with eyes
> Nailed down by his own ribs
> Strangled just short of his last gasp
> By his own windpipe
> Clubbed unconscious by his own heart

and the following lines from Marvell's 'A Dialogue between the Soul and Body':

> O Who shall, from this Dungeon, raise
> A Soul inslav'd so many wayes?
> With bolts of Bones, that fetter'd stands
> In Feet; and manacled in Hands.
> Here blinded with an Eye; and there
> Deaf with the drumming of an Ear.
> A Soul hung up, as 'twere, in Chains
> Of Nerves, and Arteries, and Veins.

[October 1973]

Dear Keith Sagar,

Thank you for the letter & the Crow chapter. This chapter seems somehow the best. You certainly get my drift better than anybody else I've read. The book (Crow) is mostly blueprints, route-maps, reconnaissances, etc — so it needs creative as well as sympathetic imagination, not just critical attention.

I'd forgotten Marvell's lines. I was paraphrasing — as he was — "the Gnostic commonplace". I came to it as an apocryphal explanation for Crow's colour — a sort of joke.

2 statements in your interpretations contradict what I intended —

In 'A horrible Religious Error' the serpent is — in a way — a form of Crow's own creator. He/she is a consistent figure throughout the overall story.

In 'Crow's last stand'. Crow's reactions, through the 3 first stanzas, correspond to separate phases of intensifying psychological pain — where the forms of hilarity & anguish are indistinguishable.

The lines "From one of his eyes . . ." to ". . . in a column", are transcript from the Tain — description of Cuchullin's battle-fury.[3]

If a poem doesn't work as an event in itself, no armorial embellishments from its distinguished lineage can help it — they rather embarrass it, I think. But if it works, then they help — they enrich it. To him who has etc. I wonder now if I wouldn't have defended my bird from the common reaction — that he's a disgusting creature, evil omen etc — if I'd been a little more forward with his lineage.

Crow as the totem of England (history of Bran — his ravens — the tower of London)[4]

Crow in early Celtic literature — the Morrigu, the death-Goddess, a Crow, & the underground form of the original life-goddess — as Hecate was of Aphrodite etc.

Apollo the Crow god. Crow in China. Crow among the Siberian peoples & the North American Indians. Crow in Alchemy.

Crow is a modern evil omen bird only insofar as he is a fallen god — he is Anathema because he was originally Anath.[5]

Except that my main concern was to produce something with the minimum cultural accretions of the museum sort — something autochthonous & complete in itself, as it might be invented after

3 See *The Táin*, trans. Thomas Kinsella (Oxford University Press, 1970), pp. 150–53.
4 Bran was a gigantic Celtic god and ruler of Britain. After he was mortally wounded in battle, his head was buried at the Tower of London, where it served as a protection against invaders. See p. 36.
5 Chief West Semitic goddess of love and war, the sister and helpmate of the god Baal (Bel).

the holocaust & demolition of all libraries, where essential things spring again — if at all — only from their seeds in nature — and are not lugged around or hoarded as preserved harvests from the past. So the comparative religion/mythology background was irrelevant to me, except as I could forget it. If I couldn't find it again original in Crow, I wasn't interested to make a trophy of it.

The poetic works that summarise cultures — as in Eliot, Joyce, David Jones — and those whose gyroscope is the vision of a new culture (vain as that dream must be) — as in Lawrence — are very distinct kinds, I think — both doomed to different kinds of failure. Doomed, probably, because both imply the two extremes of a culture at the point of collapse — so the one is loaded with obsolescent material, & the other is too naïve — implies an exclusive attitude, in opposition to too much, and a visionary projection which reality will always find wanting.

In the small scope of my operations I tried to get the best of both worlds. Crow's account of St George is the classic nightmare of modern English intelligence in particular — as Hercules Furens was of the Roman. I tried to dissolve in a raw psychic event, a history of religion & ideology rooted in early Babylonian Creation myth, descending through Middle Eastern religions, collision of Judaism & its neighbours, the mannichees [sic][6] & the early Christians & the Roman Empire, the reformation & its peculiar development & ramifications in Englishness, down to linguistic philosophy & the failure of English intelligence in the modem world — failure in comprehensiveness, depth, flexibility, & emotional charge. Which seems to me true & true again. The immediate source of the fable is a Japanese folk tale — where the exclusive, hubristic, ossified professionalism of a Samurai, & the madness behind it — unacknowledged because it contains everything rejected & ignored — is analogous to the sort of 'intelligence' my protagonist relies on. That's not a very good poem — but it's a real part of my story. But it's only part of my story because I could exclude from it the Japanese tale — Hercules Furens — the whole repetitive history of the militant ethos.

6 Manichaeism was one of the major Iranian Gnostic religions, founded by the prophet Mani (AD 216–76). Manichaeism taught an elaborate cosmology describing the struggle between a good, spiritual world of light, and an evil, material world of darkness. Through an ongoing process which takes place in human history, light is gradually removed from the world of matter and returned to the world of light from which it came. Manichaeism thrived between the third and seventh centuries, and at its height was one of the most widespread religions in the world.

As for the style — I simply tried to shed everything. It was quite an effort to get there — as much of an effort to stay there — every day I had to find it again. It was like hanging on to 9.5 second 100 yards. I tried to shed everything that the average Pavlovan [sic] critic knows how to respond to. It was a wonderful sensation when I finally got there. My idea was to reduce my style to the simplest clear cell — then regrow a wholeness & richness organically from that point. I didn't get that far. 'Horrible Religious Error' is a sort of fable of the idea of the confrontation in the style, I suppose, (mainly it's Crow mis-recognising the object of his quest) — but that was the last poem, March 20th 69, on the train leaving Manchester.[7]

Since then I've written virtually nothing. The Prometheus sequence is an expression of limbo — limbo in Persia, but limbo. A numb poem about numbness.[8]

But things have looked up a bit lately.

I'd be grateful if you could let me see your final draft. I'll assume this copy is only interim, until I hear from you.

Yours
Ted Hughes

7 I have been unable to ascertain whether Hughes' dating of his departure from Manchester is correct. According to Yehuda Koren and Eilat Negev in A Lover of Unreason (Robson Books, 2006), p. 201, it was 22 March. In his letter of 10 October 1998 he claims that the poem 'was written on the train to Manchester'.

8 Prometheus on His Crag (1973) was not yet published, but I had bought the entire archive from Ted's sister Olwyn the previous December.

1974

After receiving nine bird-drawings from Leonard Baskin, Hughes wrote the first draft of *Cave Birds*. Baskin then produced more drawings, and Hughes more poems. Having been introduced to the vacanas of the Siva-worshipping mystics of Southern India by A. K. Ramanujan's *Speaking of Siva*, Hughes began to adopt their naked, personal and colloquial style in the brief poems which became the epilogue poems in *Gaudete* and *Orts*. The Queen's Medal for Poetry was presented to Hughes on 21 November.

Hughes' comments on the first typescript of The Art of Ted Hughes, *relayed to me by Ted's sister Olwyn, who was also his agent. Since that draft no longer exists, I have omitted the opening page references.*

16 May 1974

Your photographs — one is enough.

If this biographical material is used, quote its source in POETRY IN THE MAKING.

Ted felt these first three pages read very oddly, and wonders whether they couldn't be written more coolly and tentatively. As far as the truth goes, nobody knows how much or what really happened, so it seems false to describe so few things so definitely. Up to the middle of page 4, it seems to him the facts should not be written up in any way.

Estate [Crookhill] with woods and "a lake". Only one.

Woodpecker song — delete this reference. It's a misleading reference, he thinks, and it's not the only germinal rhyme or phrase he picked up.[1]

Mention that it was a succession of English teachers, not just one. Culminating in John Fisher, who was able to do a great deal for him, as he did also for Harold Massingham.[2]

Ted wonders to how many of his contemporaries did he seem "massive and brooding"? This ought to be cut. Also Wendy

---

1 I dropped the woodpecker song, but did use it at the beginning of the final chapter of *The Laughter of Foxes*.
2 Harold Massingham was born in Mexborough in 1932. He taught at Manchester University, and published three volumes of poems, *Black Bull Guarding Apples* (Longmans, 1965), which Hughes described as 'very exciting stuff' (Reid, *Letters*, p. 243), *Frost-Gods* (Macmillan, 1972), and *Sonatas and Dreams* (Littlewood Arc, 1992).

Campbell's piece, which though good spirited and generous, is nevertheless overstated, and gives what seems to him a false impression.[3]

It is misleading to state that he read any particular thing at Cambridge, and he had learned the Yeats long before.

The sentence about "rivals" reads oddly. He's sure some readers disliked these poems very much.

He asks you please not to loose his beasts on the world. His beasts, if he's right, are all either dead, or in cages, or are harmless, or are in a distinctly other world.

Please don't quote THE WOMAN WITH SUCH HIGH HEELS etc. It was a bagatelle.

This party [the launch of the St. Botolph's Review] was on 25 February 1956.

Your definite statement about his influence on her [Sylvia Plath] seems to him simply wrong. The literary influence he did perhaps help to impose on her was that of John Crowe Ransome, whom he and his friends admired unreservedly at that time. She visibly adopted some of Crowe Ransome's mannerisms. After that, the only obvious influences on her are Wallace Stevens, and later Roethke. She was pretty resistant to influences. There is no sign in her work of any response to Ted's writings until he wrote VIEW OF A PIG, and later in 1961, when she seized on THE GREEN WOLF, the third part of OUT, and one or two other of the Wodwo poems. If you call special attention to the character of her poems from when Ted met her he feels you will seem to be unaware of what she was already writing. The real immediate influence he had on her, apart from increasing her concentration on poetry, was that he supplied a fully worked out belief in the poetic mythology expounded by Robert Graves in his book THE WHITE GODDESS.[4]

Their [Hughes and Plath's] flat was in Eltisley Avenue — neighbouring, but not overlooking Grantchester Meadows.

The quote from that Faas interview ought to be deleted.[5] The

3 Wendy Campbell was a friend of Sylvia and Ted at Cambridge. I had quoted her description of Ted at that time from her memoir 'Remembering Sylvia' in Charles Newman, ed., The Art of Sylvia Plath, Faber and Faber, 1970.

4 Since I regarded Hughes' statements about his early influence on Plath as matters of interpretation, I left unchanged the passage where I argued that 'his was the stronger, surer poetic voice, and the immediate effect was of ventriloquism' (The Art of Ted Hughes, pp. 10–11).

5 The passage about the New Lines poets (Faas, Ted Hughes: The Unaccommodated Universe, p. 201), was deleted. The 'relationship' between Hughes and those poets is discussed at length by Annie Schofield,

generalisations in this paragraph seem to Ted intolerable. His "relationship" with the poets born in the early 1920s simply does not exist. He wasn't even aware of their names until he was 26 or 27, let alone what they wrote. At 24, he couldn't have named five English poets born after 1913. He was totally wrapped up in books of another sort. The only contemporary poet he was aware of in those years was Thom Gunn — because at university he was already famous, and Ted greatly liked his poems. Ted's excessive devotion to the poetic world of THE WHITE GODDESS literature made him quite as intolerant as Graves on quite similar principles.

THE THOUGHT FOX is not really about writing a poem. It is about a recurrent dream, like CASUALTY.

Over-specific interpretation of A MODEST PROPOSAL. Marriage not mentioned. And surely marriage would be more fittingly symbolised by the greyhounds?[6]

He asks please find a way of not using the prose quote. There is an awful falsity about the whole piece — which crystallises in the phrase about "too much of the wrong sex". He's quite sure homosexuals are as brave and rash as anybody else.[7]

Don't you think this part culminates a little too high and purplish?

The last sentence on this page — Being aware of how much is evaded, etc. — couldn't this be phrased more tentatively? One lays a course by ideals, but "however far we go, we have to start here", etc.

First line of first quote, typing error.

Reading through this, he repeatedly flinched where you make the claims for his talent. Among many primitive peoples, open praise for somebody else's possession is regarded as a curse. If you do wish to make claims, he would be grateful if you would circumscribe them carefully, as your general opinion, rather than introduce them as a general assumption — which you tend to do, he thinks.

While Sylvia taught at Smith, he taught at the University of Massachusetts — for half the year.

'Hughes and the Movement', in Keith Sagar, ed., The Achievement of Ted Hughes (1983), pp. 22–36, and briefly by me in Ted Hughes and Nature, pp. 70–72 (where I do quote the passage in question).

6 I did not change my readings of 'The Thought-Fox' or 'A Modest Proposal' (where I had taken the greyhounds to symbolise marriage).

7 Hughes had used the phrase 'too much of the wrong sex' in 'The Crime of Fools Exposed', an essay on Wilfred Owen which appeared in The New York Times Book Review in 1964. He removed it when that essay was reprinted (as 'Unfinished Business') in Winter Pollen.

MAY DAY ['Mayday on Holderness'] was the introductory poem to what was to be a series, and which included the better pieces in LUPERCAL. The whole thing was to be a celebration of the serpentine spirit of the hungry erg. That serpentine course threads them all together.

The week after this poem was read over the radio, Dick Straight-Up (he listened to it) died.

Can anything be made of ACROBATS? This poem seems to Ted not worth notice.

Crag Jack was his father's father. An Irishman, a dyer, who acted as a local sage and scribe. His two close friends were the Protestant (Ted supposes Methodist) minister and the Catholic priest. On his death bed (he died young, of tuberculosis), the Protestant minister brought him flowers and the Catholic brought him whisky.

The distinction continually made between predators and others is a limitation. The predator quality of a predator is not completely incidental to it, but nearly so — almost like defining a human being as a communist, a liberal, etc. Jove's eagle was not a predator, Rome's wolf was not a predator, etc.

FIRE EATER — bad poem etc. This was Sylvia's favourite poem in LUPERCAL.

Correction of dates of the stories in WODWO: THE RAIN HORSE was written in 1958 — in the States. THE HARVESTING in 1958 — in the States. SNOW was first written in 1956, then rewritten in 1959 in the States. THE SUITOR was written in Devon in 1962. MEET MY FOLKS he wrote in the States — 1958. In 1960–61, apart from odd poems, he tried to write plays. Much of the time he spent on a grand oratorio of the BARDO THODOL for the Chinese composer Chou Wen Chung — never used.

He wrote HOWLING OF WOLVES in February 1963. SONG OF A RAT in March. Then nothing except a long play (from which GHOST CRABS and WAKING) until 1966, when he went to Ireland, and started with GNAT PSALM and SKYLARKS.[8]

Sorry you don't like end of LUDWIG'S DEATH MASK. He has a

---

8 'Waking' was an early title for 'Gog I'. When Hughes read 'The Knight' ('Gog III') and 'Nightfall' (an early title for 'Ghost Crabs') on the Third Programme 17 October 1965, he described these as 'detachable poems' from *Difficulties of a Bridegroom* (1995), which went into rehearsal 11 January 1963, and was broadcast on the Third Programme on 21 January, *before* the death of Sylvia Plath in February. The broadcast version did not contain any poems.

soft spot for it. The woman looking after Shakespeare's New Place House told Ted in 1951 that Shakespeare was buried 17 feet deep at his own request. If it's true, he really did want to get away — like Timon. Ted merely connected this with the tenable theory that Beethoven's own gift — recognising its own obstacles — caused him to go deaf.

THEOLOGY dates from 1961 — long before any Popa appeared in English.

The quote: There's one tiny grain of truth in this — but no mention of several other, bigger grains. So it is misleading.[9]

THE GREEN WOLF is in Frazer's GOLDEN BOUGH. The neighbour — same as in Sylvia's BERCK-PLAGE — died at midsummer. The beans, the tiger reference, the hawthorn, the fire, etc. all refer to a specific event.

In the Hopkins quote, typing error: "worn" for "worm".

Part 3 of GOG was from the same play as GHOST CRABS and WAKING.

Parts 2 & 3 of GOG were added as a control. Later, when it seemed all the potential damage of the first part was surely exhausted, he removed the second parts — which were probably not good enough to do the job anyway.[10]

WOMAN'S WEEPING uses the proverb, "Woman's weeping is secret laughter". Rather cynical proverb.

The earliest story, actually, is SNOW. Then SUNDAY. Probably there was some memory of Lawrence in THE RAIN HORSE. He read THE RAINBOW when he was about 18. Curiously enough, he read it in a field which held horses. During the night, a heavy rainstorm came on, and the horses spent the whole night charging from one corner of the field to the other around his tent. But the story derives partly from an experience of his mother's, partly from a story of his brother's about a mad cow, partly from a brief experience of his own, and partly from a recurrent dream when he was a boy. THE RAIN HORSE and THE HARVESTING take place on the same hill.

Sylvia pointed out, academically enough, that SUNDAY contains

---

9 I had described 'Theology' as 'inspired by Popa's "the heart of the quartz pebble"'. Ted had written an introduction for Anne Pennington's *Vasko Popa: Selected Poems* (Penguin, 1969; repr. in *Winter Pollen*).

10 'Gog' appeared with all three parts in the English edition of *Wodwo*. The American edition and the 1972 and 1995 *Selected Poems* all had part I only.

all the characters of the crucifixion — in which Ted appears as the helpless archangel Michael, while the rat is Christ.

He wrote THE SUITOR the day Nicholas was born, ie the day after the night. When he read the story to Sylvia, she said: "That is your best story. But the girl is me, and the flute player is death."

The hare is the moon. It is one of the elect totemic beasts of the British Isles. And elsewhere.

THE WOUND is what he managed to retain and put into shape of a dream. The dream was of a film, complete, very long, with many episodes. Along with the action, in which he was Ripley, he dreamed somehow a very full written text, which was both dramatic and descriptive at the same time. In his dream, the whole thing was by John Arden. (He probably had just read SERGEANT MUSGRAVE'S DANCE). He woke up, terribly disappointed that Arden had written something that Ted felt was so absolutely his own. Then of course he realised it was his — his dream. He drifted off to sleep and dreamed the whole thing again, in exact detail, perfectly repeated. He woke up and wrote down all he could remember. The text faded very rapidly, but he managed to get lots of the episodes and main thread. As he wrote it up for radio, he changed it a great deal, and much of the dream was too cinematic for him to convert — so it seemed at the time.

He dreamed this as he was working on the Bardo Thodol, and his first interpretation was that this was his parallel Gothic-Celtic version. That idea was somehow in the dream.

Lines describing the larks' stoop. It is a fine point, but there is a suggestion in your comment here that larks do not stoop, that the description here departs from the immediately literal, as in the "screams". Could that be made clearer? The most spectacular phase of the lark's flight is the least familiar. The Cuchullin section was written with the others, he kept it out because it did seem odd. He put it back because he felt an insistence that it belonged. The italics translation of part of a Gaelic charm.

These Wings are "made" poems — in the same sense as are the dispensable pieces in LUPERCAL. Except for KAFKA.

Shouldn't you give the Gawain first in the original?[11]

11 I had quoted the four lines from *Sir Gawain and the Green Knight*, which Hughes used as an epigraph to *Wodwo* only in a translation into modern English.

The quoted line should be two lines: the first line "Any minute", the next line "A bat will fly out, etc."[12]

Baskin <u>was</u> "obsessed" with dead bodies — and a variety of other things attended this obsession, of which the crow was one.[13]

The phrase, "sheer malice", etc. Please delete this. First, because it might be thought he meant any one of a number of women; secondly, because the malice of gossip is so innate it can't be singled out for specific blame; thirdly, because he would like you to ignore these stupid verses altogether.[14] EAT CROW was the first appearance of a crow.

Say "<u>One</u> Celtic name for him was Bran". And "Crow is <u>a</u> totem of England". You should also mention the persistence of the tradition of Bran's protective power, in the scare there was during the war when the Tower ravens died out — new ones were supplied, and their wings clipped to prevent them escaping.

Delete "except that" from the opening of this quote.

"Black, black, black" etc, ['Two Legends'] was (a) from the folk song; (b) from a Gaelic charm.

In support of his lines against Marvell's: "Flog lame with legs" — this refers to the oath used by drill sergeants to raw recruits: "I'll rip your arm off and beat you to death with the soggy end of it". "Shot through the head with balled brains" ['A Kill']

---

12 The version of 'Full Moon and Little Frieda' published in the *Atlantic Monthly* in December 1963 had these additional lines:

> The cows submerge.
> The moon has opened you wide and bright like a pond.
>
> The moon lifts you off the grass —
> A cat's cradle of spider's web, where the stars are trembling into place.
>
> The brimming moon looks through you and you cannot move.
>
> Any minute
> A bat will fly out of a cat's ear.

13 Hughes had met the American artist, sculptor and printer, Leonard Baskin (1922–2000) in 1958 at Smith College, Northampton, Massachusetts, where Baskin and Sylvia Plath both taught. They became firm friends, and from 1974 Baskin lived for nine years at Lurley Manor, near Tiverton, in order to be near Hughes. Baskin designed the covers of many of Hughes' books, provided illustrations for the 1973 limited edition of *Crow*, the American edition of *Selected Poems* (1973), the American edition of *Season Songs* (1975), the Scolar Press *Cave Birds* (1975), the American *Moon-Whales and other Moon Poems* (1976), *Under the North Star* (1981), and *Flowers and Insects* (1986), and published at his Gehenna Press *A Primer of Birds* (1981), *Capriccio* (1990) and *Howls and Whispers* (1998). See the CD *The Artist and the Poet: Leonard Baskin & Ted Hughes in Conversation* (Noel Chanan, 2009).

14 I had said that 'Bad News Good!' (Paul Keegan, ed., *Collected Poems of Ted Hughes*, 2003, pp. 106–7), published in 1963, was 'about a woman Hughes felt had helped to kill his wife out of sheer malice, "under crow-possession"'.

refers to Conchubar, who was sling-shot in the head by a missile made of the dried brains of an enemy (an ancient Celtic missile). To keep the wound closed, the missile was allowed to stay in. Eventually, hearing of the crucifixion, Conchubar went mad with rage against Christ's crucifiers, and attacked a forest — the brain ball then burst from his skull, his brains followed it, and he died. "Shot blind with eyes" — simple folk variant on the same story. "Nailed down by his own ribs" refers to the bloody eagle — the sacrificial method of execution used by the Norse. The ribs were cut either side of the spine, and twisted outwards, and the heart taken out through the hole. In all these, the disaster of each organic part involves a psychic positive. The other parallel was a Mannichean [sic] text in which strength and beauty of each organic part involved a psychic negative. He attempted a short circuit from one to the other — in the reduced terms of the body that actually suffers them (ie without metaphysical or hysterical association). As paradoxical deadlock statements to which there is no resolution.

Quote at bottom of page: you should, in all fairness, quote what he also said about the prose of the authorised version of the Bible — otherwise you seem here to dismiss "free verse" somewhat.

He composed DAWN'S ROSE deliberately as an imagistic poem in the style which — in all the rest of CROW — he was trying to get past. DAWN'S ROSE is in contemporary "poetic language" — our present version. He intended to write a few, because he thought if he didn't, he would lose touch with some readers altogether. It's dismaying to see it repeatedly chosen as the best piece in the book. Though he likes it too.

Not "the whole myth is to be told", but "was to be told".[15]

"He is the unkillable urge" etc. He is also simple energy. Infinitely corruptible, infinitely educable and transformable.

"This poem is about . . ." etc. It is also about Lear and Cordelia, Tolstoy and his muse, etc.[16]

Perhaps your immediate connection of this poem to the description of the Sphinx limits my meaning. The FRAGMENT OF AN ANCIENT TABLET is the clay of Eve, considered as the Smaragdine Table of Hermes Trismegistus. The poem is really a

15 In fact Hughes held on for many years to the hope that he might one day complete *The Life and Songs of the Crow*.
16 The poem in question is probably 'Revenge Fable'.

straightforward description of a very weird natural correspondence which seems to him endlessly revealing and interesting.

APPLE TRAGEDY is a joke, but he intended the meaning seriously. It is a rereading of the icon figuring God, the serpent, the tree, Adam and Eve, Judas hanging himself, Christ crucified, the crucified serpent, and several other details. One imagines the iconographer looking at these dumb images from which the official stories were constructed by priestly manipulators, deciding that the whole thing had been misinterpreted. (As obviously did happen). His reconstruction is more to his tastes — also more in line with what is now known about the real meaning of those early images.

"No love in CROW", etc. False. What Crow pronounces is the Logos. He doesn't pronounce the word love, he disgorges Eros itself, etc. "Terrible as an army with banners". As for the Tennyson, the love which moves the sun and the other stars presumably moves the claws and teeth too. In Dante's sense, when we say God is love we are saying he is the pressure of energy into being.

SONG FOR A PHALLUS was what he boiled out of an attempted satyr play to follow SENECA'S OEDIPUS — it recapitulates the main episodes of Seneca's play, with reinterpretations.

No, these conditions do not suit his purpose, but he has nowhere else to live than everywhere. (ie in heavens, earth, hells, etc., simultaneously).[17]

Re "short on conscience" etc. Crow is crucified on "conscience" (CROW AND THE SEA), he is potentially all conscience (CROW BLACKER THAN EVER). His aspiration (to find how to live according to the laws of creation) is what keeps him going at all, but he starts from the "nothing" — and Ted wanted to show him at all stages of the journey, and didn't get far.

CROW'S ACCOUNT OF ST GEORGE. This maligned piece perhaps needs some scholarly moral support. Maybe stories behind it could be enumerated. The Japanese tale, Seneca's Hercules Furens, the apocryphal notion about St George, the Middle Eastern legend, the Babylonian creation legend, etc. The St George legend being the summary parable of all these, so especially honoured in England.

A DISASTER. Your choice of the word "war" surprised Ted.

"Owl is not afraid enough" etc. Owl's discovery is that his fear

17 This probably refers to 'Oedipus Crow'.

is sophistical, ie. no part of himself, i.e. his singing, which is fearless, in that it sings, and is in harmony with the star and rock, which are fearless in that they maintain their order (like the doings of an infinite Owl). So all [that page] seems to Ted badly misleading.

THE CONTENDER is THE GREAT DEAD MAN OF ETERNITY. He is the undefeatable corpse.

The form of CRIMINAL BALLAD is that each snapshot of his life is a double exposure. That each situation or object of his attention, tunes him to its identical but opposite correspondence — not separated in his life by time and place, as it should be, but instantaneously co-present.

Crow's battle-fury is "<u>riastartha</u>"[18] — his "distortion" is the mutilations, psychic and physical, with which he advances towards the worst enemy — i.e. all that he can suffer. The mutilations becoming the "horrific majesty" of his advance — and half the means by which he subdues that enemy. Second quote. This process went only through the first phase.[19]

CROW WAKES: a speech from a play. The writing ended at "called" abruptly, and he's not been able to find a satisfactory following word since.

Whatever Crow means — he imagines that's it, since the subsequent dialogue was what he gradually fitted to it.

Ted is surprised that you make anything of THE NEW WORLD — he can't find any worth at all in these pieces except "I said goodbye". Why not exclude all mention of these.

This emphasis may be too specific.

Perhaps this page should end at "out of bounds".

This page seems to Ted out of place and somehow bad. He thinks it would be a good idea to delete it.

The quote from the FAAS review would need enormous amplification to make sense, Ted feels. "Shifting of foundations"

18 Gaelic for 'contorted'.
19 In my commentary on 'Crow's Battle Fury' I cited two quotations from R. D. Laing's *The Politics of Experience* (Penguin, 1967), in which Laing quotes one of his patients, Jessie Watkins:
    'The journey is there and every single one of us has got to go through it, and – um – everything – you can't dodge it . . . the purpose of everything and the whole of existence is – er – to equip you to take another step, and so on . . .'
        '. . . it's an experience that – um – we have at some stage to go through, but that was only one – and that – many more – a fantastic number of – um – things have got to impinge upon us until we gradually build ourselves up into an acceptance of reality, and a greater and greater acceptance of reality and what really exists.'

seems to him a vast topic, hardly to be dealt with in a page.

This St George chapter seems to Ted not good at all — a big let down. To talk about THE IRON MAN and the children's radio plays (written very casually and hastily) is <u>extremely</u> diluting in effect. Also, St George emerges as too ponderous a simplification, in this form. He would be grateful if you would cut this chapter up to page 266.[20]

The chaotic paragraphs from Myths and Education was taken from impromptu rambling talk — to make the real connection with this, much more space would be needed. And a clearer statement of the case. He thinks this should be deleted. Ted doesn't exactly offer education through myth as an alternative plan, he says.[21]

<u>No</u>, the story came first, and along with everything else. Quite true, only a few poems in CROW relate to it directly.[22]

You call the serpent "ugly". The whole point about serpents is that they are not ugly, surely.

This Orpheus and Merchant of Venice seem to Ted dragged in and too remotely relevant.

The last quote on the page: the line should be "And under it — the woman again" (not "<u>that</u>")

5th line of the quote: "wombs" — should be plural.

Correct end of quote to:

Image after image. Image after image. The vulture Etc etc

Penultimate line of the quote:

And balances. <u>And</u> treads. (Not "he")

A type of crocus sprang from the blood of Prometheus.

Re Prometheus in general: Your interpretation leaves Ted wondering. Though he has no alternative theories.

To end with Orpheus seems too weak — this was a commissioned piece for children, and is a very weak dilution of things — despatched hastily. A serious treatment would have to be infinitely different. Please delete it.[23] If you feel a positive close is needed, maybe you could find it, a hint of it, in a collection of

20 In response to this I wrote:
It is a big wrench, I put a lot of work into it, but I agree to drop St. George. Except that I can salvage a couple of pages on 'Gog' for the *Wodwo* chapter where they originally came from, and a few other cherished paragraphs can go into the notes.

21 This refers to the earlier of the two essays with this title, published in *Children's Literature in Education*, March 1970, and uncollected. I discuss it at length in *Ted Hughes and Nature*.

22 On the dust-wrapper of the first printing Hughes had described *Crow* as a selection of poems 'from about the first two-thirds of what was to have been an epic folk-tale'.

23 I compromised by including two pages on *Orpheus* in the notes.

poems he wrote for children — THE SEASON POEMS — in which he tried to set down in a simple old-fashioned way, but scrupulously, some country pleasures — there are a few poems extra to those in Olwyn's limited edition.[24]

OMISSION The ELEPHANT TOTEM SONG is basically a bagatelle of astrological particulars. The elephant is supposedly a certain combination of Taurus and Cancer, the hyenas are the demons of Mars squared by Mercury.

Note 3: Ted feels that if you quote this you should also quote some opposite opinion. If you can't find the opposite opinion you shouldn't quote this (those who point out failures fill up with failure, etc.)

In fact Ted did not read MEN IN PRISON.[25]

23 May 1974

Where matters of biography, fact and tact are concerned I shall try to comply with your wishes to the letter. On matters of interpretation I shall look very carefully at what you say and see if my account can be modified or extended accordingly, but this may not always be so. It is not to be expected that any critic's interpretations will coincide at every point with the author's; and you will agree that they are not necessarily invalidated when they do not.

27 May [1974]

Dear Keith Sagar,

I came through Clitheroe the other day — but you weren't at home.

I wanted to leave the typed M.S. with you, & ask you one or two things.

Olwyn will be sending you a number of comments I made about various points — mainly factual adjustments. Two things I would like to ask. First is — could you reduce the number of photographs to not more than one.

This concerns me directly. This mass exposure intensifies my sense of being 'watched' — (which maims all well-known writers,

24 *Spring, Summer, Autumn, Winter* (Rainbow Press, 1974), in effect the first edition of *Season Songs* (Viking, 1975, with Baskin's illustrations, and Faber, 1976).

25 As part of their research into the Manichaean themes of the myths and of Pedro Calderón's *La Vida Es Sueño*, Peter Brook's company studied a book by Victor Serge called *Men in Prison* (Doubleday, 1969).

& destroys many). It sharpens, in any readers, the visual image of me, making their telepathic interference correspondingly more difficult to counter. (This might be laughed at, but not for much longer).

Your book, in general, of course, is going to increase both these types of harrassment [sic] immeasurably, in my awareness. Which is why I asked you to cut the biographical element to the minimum. If I were the sort who could migrate from country to country, finding a succession of acquaintances who knew nothing about me, with whom I could have ordinary relationships, I would be happier. As it is, everything written or said about me goes into the heads of the people among whom I live — so with everyone I have to allow for this unreal element. After trying to ignore it for some years, as part of the danger of the trade, I am finally having to reckon the cost. The photographs I've allowed to be published, the remarks I've made in persona, the degree to which I've let it be known that the writing's [sic] under my name belong to this particular person living this particular life, & then what others have said about me — all this seems to have an awful effect on the people round me. Now my children are becoming aware of it at school. They are beginning to realise that to some degree they are creatures in a peculiar museum — which my anonymity could have saved them from. They are having to adjust their directions against the crosswinds from their mother & from me. My daughter has a quite unusual natural poetic gift — quite some stages beyond what her mother or I were capable of at that age — but she is beginning to detest the word 'poetry'. Which will be too bad if — as seems quite likely — it is going to be her only real way out.

It would be ideal if your book concerned the verse alone as if nothing at all were known about me personally — as if my name were a pseudonym.

Another favour I would like to ask, is that you make no mention of any comments I might have made. Do not thank me in the preface. Because at present, the preface gives the impression that I have approved all you say in the book — almost as if you had ghost-written it for me. No matter how you qualify & limit what details I have given you, the response to your book will be confused by these other suspicions. I've tried to give your text factual support, & to suggest my debts to certain sources & sites in the way of subject matter, but everything speculative or to do with interpretation & evaluation are anybody's own business, yours as much as mine, finally. I know how absolutely meaningless it would be to try to impose mine, or attach it somehow to the poems as if it were part of them. Finally, poems belong to readers — just as houses belong to those who live in them & not to the builders.

I'll post off the M.S. I hope you're well.

Yours   Ted Hughes

p.s. Have you heard of the Arvon Foundation? They have a biggish home in Devon, where students come to live together with 2 poets, for a week or so, & write. Extraordinary effects, as a rule. They are just about to open another at Heptonstall in Yorks. I'm renting them my house there. Would your students be interested? The manager is: David Pease

Kilnhurst Farm

Todmorden, Lancs.

He'll give you the details. Courses are being set up now for the first 6 months (starting September)[26]

Very glad to hear Leonard will do a drawing.[27]

More interesting than any of the pictures you have, and also cheaper, and also both more personal and more impersonal, & not reproduced anywhere else, would be a picture Philip Larkin took, with delayed exposure, of himself, Richard Murphy, Douglas Dunn & me, in a rural churchyard in East Yorks. It's at a slight distance, but amusing.[28]

---

26 The Arvon Foundation was founded by John Moat and John Fairfax in 1968. (See *The Founding of Arvon* by John Moat, Francis Lincoln, 2005.) Their first centre, Totleigh Barton, was near Sheepwash in Devon, not far from Hughes' home in North Tawton. Hughes had first planned to buy Lumb Bank, a deserted mill-owner's house overlooking Colden Clough, and only yards from his parents' house, in 1963, and eventually did so in 1969. Hughes and his wife Carol, whom he married in 1970, attempted to live at Lumb Bank, but it proved unsuitable. When Hughes learned that Arvon was looking for a northern base, he offered them the use of the property. Arvon could not raise the whole cost of the necessary renovation, and Hughes contributed a good deal of the money himself, partly from the sale of his manuscripts. Hughes himself never ran an Arvon course, but was the visiting reader at many. See plate 2. David Pease was Arvon's national director from 1974 to 2001. He was awarded an MBE in 2011.
27 Leonard Baskin's cover design was used for *The Art of Ted Hughes*. His original drawing was subsequently lost while in the possession of Cambridge University Press.
28 See plate 4. The photograph used as frontispiece was of Hughes in Persia in 1971.

1975

The first major Hughes exhibition was staged at the Ilkley Literature Festival in May. Seeing the thirty photographs of the Calder Valley by Fay Godwin there stimulated Hughes to begin the collaboration with her which culminated in *Remains of Elmet*.[1] The Festival also staged a reading (later broadcast) of *Cave Birds* and *Lumb's Remains* (the *Gaudete* epilogue). The Scolar Press published their collectors' edition of *Cave Birds*, with prints of ten drawings by Leonard Baskin. Hughes wrote *Adam and the Sacred Nine*. My *The Art of Ted Hughes*, the first book-length critical study of Hughes' work, was published in August.

4th January 75

Dear Keith,

Thank you for the lovely Lawrence poem. Also for the very good suggestion about the collection of Crow poems. It might be interesting to expand it into a miscellany of crow-lore of all kinds — it is mostly interesting and often surprising. I've written quite a bit more, lately. I shan't leave it till I've exhausted my notion of it. Also a few other things which I hope will amuse you.

Crows and oaks seem related. These are lines from an abortive series about The Oak — from before I did the crow poems.

At the pure well of leaf

Waist-deep, the black oak is dancing.
My eyes pause, aghast,
On the centuries of its instant
As gnats
Try to winter in its wrinkles.

Dancing
In an ecstasy of the Annunciation
Of clay, water and the sunlight —
They tremble under its roof.
Its agony is its temple.

---

1 Fay Godwin (1931–2005) was Britain's best-known landscape photographer. Her books included *The Oldest Road: An Exploration of the Ridgeway* (1975), and *Land* (1985). She also photographed many of the country's leading literary figures. Fay said that *Elmet* (1944), which contains sixty of her photographs, was the book she would most like to be remembered by. Her archive is at the British Library.

The seas are thirsting
Towards the oak.

The oak is flying
Astride the earth.

  With a crow in the top.

  I requisitioned most of it lately for something else. Minus
crow.[2]

I hope to be at the Ilkley Festival with something I've been doing to
some of Leonard Baskin's bird drawings — the characters of a bird
drama, some of which I quite like.[3] He'll be there too.
Olwyn has just assembled the whole final mss of Sylvia's collected
poems — after a near-disastrous involvement with so-called
editors.[4] Whoever becomes involved with that material seems to
succumb to the hysterical supercharged public atmosphere that
surrounds it.
  Happy New Year to you   yours   Ted

15th Jan 75

Dear Keith
  Thanks for the letter & the programme.[5] I'd prefer to keep as far
out of the Festival as possible — the single reading — which I've
arranged to do — will be more than enough, considering
everything else going on.[6]
  I talked with Baskin tonight, and he'll be delighted to lend the
exhibition 12 of his drawings for Crow — never used (not the ones

2 This oak poem became 'Your tree – your oak', the penultimate poem in Gaudete.
3 An early version of Cave Birds and Lumb's Remains (epilogue poems from Gaudete) were read at the Ilkley
   Literature Festival on 30 May by Harvey Hall, Frances Horovitz, Peter Marinker and Gary Watson. The
   Baskin drawings were projected on a screen.
4 Sylvia Plath's Collected Poems was published by Faber in 1981 with an introduction by Hughes.
5 The 'programme' was for a three-day course 'The Achievement of Ted Hughes', sponsored by Leeds
   University Extra-Mural Department at Ilkley Grammar School, 28–30 May, in which I had invited
   Hughes to do a reading.
6 The 'single reading' he gave was shared with James Kirkup and Vernon Scannell on 31 May.

in the Faber limited edition).[7] Michael Dawson[8] is also using 20 of his cave-bird drawings — which go with a series of poems (which will make ½ my commissioned piece). Very different from the Crow drawings. His address is

    LURLEY MANOR
     LURLEY
     NR TIVERTON
     DEVON.

I'm hoping to get him up there with me when I come.

Pleased to hear you saw the brighter side of Heptonstall. Can you do anything for Lumb Bank? What it needs is (a) beneficent millionaires (b) courses of students. I've poured a lot into it because I've seen what those courses can do for students. I never believed it possible until I saw for myself. The difficulty is, to get potential backers (rich men) to believe it — not easy.

      Yours
       Ted

27th Feb 75

Dear Keith,

I'm sorry you didn't come to the meal with us the other night — I assumed you would be there, then you had vanished.[9]

Thank you for the Prometheus poem. An anthology of Vulture pieces would also be interesting, though there aren't many modern ones.

I wrote a little four-part poem about the luminous predatory fish in the deep seas. I call it Photostomias — it started as a poem to go with some spectacular coloured photographs, for Realites. When I finally did my piece, after about two years, they rejected it as incomprehensible, It seems to me only slightly cryptic.[10]

I've given the photographs away, and now that Olwyn is wanting to do the piece as a tiny LTD Edition, with some drawings by LB, I'm wondering where I can find pictures as good as those I've

---

7 I staged a Hughes exhibition during the Festival for which both Hughes and Baskin lent exhibits.
8 Michael Dawson was the director of the Yorkshire Arts Association and of the Ilkley Festival.
9 I was seldom able to join Ted for a meal or drink after an event because I had a long journey ahead of me, and adult students I had brought with me to deliver to their homes.
10 This poem was first published as 'Chiasmadon' by Charles Seluzicki in 1977 as a limited-edition pamphlet. In Moortown the title reverted to 'Photostomias'.

parted with, to show Leonard what I want. He has an absolute block about fish (if somebody eats fish in a restaurant within three or four yards of him he has to go out). He's done some drawings, very weird fantasies of those protozoa monsters — which are intense, but not quite what I was writing about. I thought you might know where the right pictures could be found.[11]

Thank you for buying the Prometheus papers. The last bunch include one or two things I abandoned. I needed the cash acutely — it comes at just the right moment. Lumb Bank has cleaned me out for quite a while to come. But up there it might just work the one or two miracles, and it will be a great thing for a great many, if it can get through this next two years.

Yours
Ted

17th March 75

Dear Keith

I meant to write after your last letter to say we would love to come to the Bay Tree with you. Carol can't remember whether she mentioned that the Baskins will be with us — pretty inseparably — but I don't want to corner you into paying for a fleet of people when your first invitation was for only two. I know what that's like because it's a situation I always seem to be getting into. Also, almost certainly, Eric White and his wife will be there, and since he has more or less managed my own contribution to the Festival from beginning to end, and since he's quite a close friend, and since most likely we shall be in Ilkley only that one evening — well, you see how it is. So what I propose is that you book for six of us — plus yourself and whoever else you want to invite — and we will pay a slightly bigger proportion of the bill — which I've heard is on the high side always. I think we ought certainly to do that — otherwise those little embarrassments start. The trouble with these Festivals, they are always a mass of people moving around in a herd. Beyond Eric I dare say there will be John Commander,[12] Michael Dawson, all

---

11 Ted knew that I kept tropical fish, including marines, and was working on a book, The Love of Tropical Fish, which would be illustrated with my own photographs.

12 The owner of the Scolar Press in Ilkley, which produced the remarkable limited first edition of Cave Birds to coincide with the Festival.

wanting to be host. The answer might be to stay in Ilkley a day or two more. When there are more than five or six at a meal nobody talks to anybody and the whole thing becomes a strain.

We're coming up to Yorks by Tuesday of that week because I've agreed to give a reading at Lumb Bank. On the Friday I've arranged to give a reading at Hull.

If we can keep the party to the Baskins, the Whites and ourselves it will be manageable — though only on condition that we have part of the Bill.[13] I imagine we shall have great difficulty in stopping the Baskins and the Whites paying, actually. Do you know Eric White? He's been a real friend in need at times to me, and to many others too. He was Secretary of the Literature Panel at the Arts Council till three or four years ago, but now he's busier than ever. He's on the council of all these Festivals, and on the committees of all these Manuscript libraries.[14] He wrote the great book on Stravinsky — life work. He's very entertaining and the Baskins get on with him.

Thank you for the fish pictures. They really are beautiful. Leonard was not to be lured any further into that kingdom, though. I'll be sending the material back.

What I wanted to ask you — do you know of anybody with a big second hand fish tank. I want something fairly long. The idea is to put a flow of water through it and keep trout in it — just to keep an eye on. Our son Nicholas is an extremely keen underwater creaturist, and that's been his dream for some years.[15] If you hear of anything of that kind going for sale.

I shan't read the Holbrook piece — everything about that man is so sad and unnecessary.[16] At one time he was giving in Exeter a lecture on Sylvia Plath — (Olwyn had a long cold war over his

---

13 The Whites did not attend the dinner, but David Pease and his wife Tina did.
14 He was also secretary of the Poetry Book Society.
15 Nicholas was to read zoology at Oxford, and pursue a distinguished career as a freshwater fish biologist.
16 David Holbrook (1923–2011) dedicated himself to making the glories of English literature available to all classes. His early books, English for the Rejected (1964), English for Maturity (1967), and his anthology Iron, Honey, Gold (1965), all published by Cambridge University Press, were very popular with secondary school teachers. Holbrook had contributed an essay, 'Ted Hughes' Crow and the Longing for Non-being', to The Black Rainbow (ed. Peter Abbs, Heinemann, 1975), in which (misreading Crow like many other critics of the time) he described it as 'a sad event for English poetry'.

statements on that front).[17] I wrote a very brief note — saying I trusted he would be as discreet as possible since he was in the territory of many friends and acquaintances of her children. I received back a four or five page letter — more like an essay — analysing her language and imagery in a way you would have expected of some pornographer or exhibitionistic voyeur. The impression of the whole thing was of a gibbering, spluttering half-frenzy. I didn't answer, and in fact he never turned up for the lecture. All his audience did.

I once met him and that was enough. I know exactly what to expect of him. The truly alarming thing is the authority he seems to have among schoolteachers. I suppose it's based on those early books of his. But he speaks for his tribe. Everybody speaks for their tribe, don't you think? Culturally, England is breaking up again into tribes, it seems to me.

I'm enclosing the poem you asked about.[18] It is one of the answers to the Hag, as Crow carries her over the river. The idea was that each of the seven answers recapitulated Crow's progress from his earliest desolation to his ultimate marriage in the Happy Land — which lies on the other side of the river. This one is a late answer. The question was: Who gives most, him or her? It was just a note at the time of Crow — though it is still not much more than a note. I've put it provisionally in the Cave-bird sequence, which now contains about thirty pieces. Rather abstract pieces, though I quite like some of them, and one or two are good. When I get a final typed copy, I'll send you the whole thing. It depends quite a bit on the drawings.

Anyway, we'll be seeing you in Ilkley in what looks like not long after next week. All the best meanwhile.

Yours   Ted

---

17 In a letter of 7 June 1975 Holbrook complained to Craig Robinson (a student of mine who was doing a PhD on Ted at Lancaster University) that Olwyn Hughes had held up his book *Sylvia Plath: Poetry and Existence* (Athlone Press, 1976) for four years, and had caused the publisher of his *Lost Bearings in English Poetry* (Vision Press, 1977) to remove all references to Sylvia Plath.
18 'Bride and Groom Lie Hidden for Three Days'.

20th March 75

Dear Keith,

Here is a copy of Cave-Birds.[19] I don't have a copy of the pictures alas. The pieces that go with certain drawings have descriptive titles. Finale is a tiny drawing in the middle of a big page.

The idea is to judge & condemn the guilty party — as a cockerel. He emerges in the underworld as a Crow of sorts. Through various initiatory ordeals, of a quasi-alchemical nature, supervised by varieties of owls & eagles, he is resurrected as a falcon, finally.

Parallel & somewhat counterpoint goes a more human progress of correspondences, which are free & loose, contrast to the studied formality of the bird-pieces. For Ilkley — and maybe it's a good idea anyway — I distributed the text among 4 voices — one female, & two male "judges", and one male protagonist. He is the one things are happening to. Some pieces are divided line by line among the first 3 voices, but then others fall complete to one voice or another. So the whole thing becomes a static mystery play. I'm leaving it to some producer to try & bring it off.

All the best Ted

About the love-poem — the Crow poem — which I sent you — number 28 of this lot — use it all, if you want to.[20]

18th April 75

Dear Keith,

One thing I meant to mention on the phone: the other Baskin Crow drawings, the ones used in Faber's Ltd edition, are still being held by Mr Volpe, at Fabers. Leonard is quite agreeable that you collect them from him — maybe you could arrange to do that the same time as you collect these others from Olwyn's.[21]

All the best yours Ted

19 *Cave Birds* went through many metamorphoses, involving not only the heavy revision of individual poems, but the inclusion in the earlier drafts of several poems which later disappeared altogether. This draft was the version of *Cave Birds* read at the festival on 30 May and subsequently broadcast. For a list of the poems included in this typescript, together with Ted's introductory comments, see Appendix II.

20 There was just time for me to insert 'Bride and Groom' in the notes of *The Art of Ted Hughes*.

21 Since it was much easier for me to get to London than to Devon, we had arranged that Ted would leave with Olwyn on his next visit all the material he and Leonard Baskin had agreed to lend me for the Ilkley exhibition. When he arrived at Olwyn's he discovered that he had forgotten to put this material in the boot, so I was obliged to drive to Devon.

[May 1975]

Dear Keith,

Thank you for the poems.[22] If these are all you've written, it's surprising. You must know they're pretty good. A summary simple selecting of essentials — and great tact of phasing — which amounts to a very strong style. Each one works on its own terms. You also have a very rare gift — to be perfectly straightforward and yet surprising. Most writers get that essential surprise by going to right or left of the direct forthright. The greatest surprise of all though is when somebody goes directly to the point — even if it is an oblique point.

Your visit was a real pleasure.[23]

Just to keep you up-to-date on the Ilkley business, I'm enclosing a commentary for the Cave-Birds — written for the actors, but the more I think about it, for the readers too.[24] If the reader cannot follow my story-line on one level, it could be he'd be lost, & bored, among all the words.

Best wishes till we see you in Ilkley

Yours   Ted

22 I had written very few poems at that time, most of them descriptions of Lawrence paintings.
23 My first visit to Court Green, was to collect the material Ted and Leonard were lending me for the Ilkley exhibition. I had stayed overnight.
24 See Appendix II.

1976

Hughes wrote several elegies for Jack Orchard, who had died in February. The livestock at Moortown farm was gradually sold. In March he attended the Adelaide Festival, where he gave readings and interviews. He co-edited and wrote the introduction for *János Pilinszky: Selected Poems*, Carcanet Press, 1976, and read from the translations at the launch at Manchester University in September.

31st March 76

Dear Keith

Olwyn told me you were looking for this Antaeus. The other is makeweight. Somewhere I've hidden away 'Realités' — I think it's in the roof, which is like saying it's somewhere up the Amazon.[1]

Thank you for the book — a lovely generous gift.[2] The Australian book is spectacular, some of the best impressions of the place I've seen. My 5 days, or 6, in that country was one of the best jaunts I've ever had. I saw very little of the land. Just the primaeval scrub of Ti trees between the bijou bungalows on the promontory south of Melbourne. Then on my last day I visited a farm — an 18c Manor farm — 70 miles or so outside Adelaide. I got a taste of it there. The whole place hit me very hard & deep. The most peculiar thing is the light — a glare even when there's cloud. It casts a weird disastrous starkness over everything — like a primitive painting. A dream brilliance & strangeness. Everything stands or moves in some eerie significance — rather sinister & very beautiful. I couldn't get over it. And I couldn't quite locate exactly what created the impression — except the light. The second great wonderful surprise is the birds. Every bird behaves at least as queerly as our cuckoos. And they have a class of cries utterly different & unique — imagine the calls of lizards & prehistoric freaks. Cries completely unmodified by the revisions & bird-masterpieces of the last 50 million years. And behaviour to go with the cries.

1 I had begun to collect everything by or about Ted, with a view to compiling a bibliography, and both Ted and Olwyn helped me to keep track of things. *Antaeus* had published five poems from *Prometheus on his Crag* in their Winter 1973 issue; and *Realités* three others in March 1973.
2 This was my book *The Love of Tropical Fish* (Octopus Books, 1976).

I met some attractive people. Quite a few young poets hung around the Festival & I got to know them well, in that wine-saturated city. Three or four seemed to me good on an international level. One of them — a girl — really put the icy finger on me. Only about 23 years old. And looks like a genius as well as writes somewhat like one. Susan Burgess — lives with a poet called Alan Aftermann.[3] She's published nearly nothing.

The English 'Season Songs' comes out in May. Contains 5 more pieces than the U.S edition, minus one called The Defenders, & minus the paintings.

I'd written a great deal this last 6 months — all on the way to where I want to be. But my wife's father died very suddenly — cancer plus heart — in February, which has dropped the farm onto me complete, & stopped everything. It will be a long sad job unloading it this summer.

Thank your stars you didn't get to Exeter.

The Wodwos are nice. I'd always hoped female Wodwos would be Sheila-na-gigs. Do you know those lovely ladies?[4]

   all the best   Ted

I'll be returning the Australia book.

---

3 Allen Afterman, American-born poet and author of *Kabbalah and Consciousness* (Sheep Meadow Press, 1992).

4 'Wodwo' is a Middle English word of very imprecise meaning: wild man of the woods, troll, satyr, wood-demon . . . Hughes had exploited this ambiguity in the 1961 poem 'Wodwo', and had used the passage from *Sir Gawain and the Green Knight* where Gawain fights wodwos as the epigraph to *Wodwo*. The frequent images of wodwos across Europe in the fourteenth century, in engravings, tapestries, stained glass, and memorial brasses, consistently depict them as naked, very hairy men wielding clubs. I had sent Ted two brass-rubbings I had made of wodwos. One of them depicted a wodwo with a club defending himself and a female wodwo from a knight with a sword. John Starkey, in *Celtic Mysteries* (Thames and Hudson, 1975), wrote:

> The characteristic manifestation of the devouring-mother aspect of the goddess in Celtic symbolism — and analogous to the bloody Kali of the Hindus or the Coatlicue of the Aztecs — is graphically illustrated by the stone effigies known under the name of Sheela-na-gig, found in medieval churches and castles. The usual characteristics of Sheela-na-gig are 'an ugly mask-like skull-face with huge scowling mouth, skeletal ribs, huge genitalia held apart with both hands, and bent legs', offering a fantasy of unlimited sexual licence but at the same time a comic reminder of our origins (p. 8).

See *Gaudete*, p. 110.

1977

Hughes was awarded the Order of the British Empire. He finished his Elmet poems. *Gaudete* was published in May. In July he gave readings in the USA, some of which were interrupted or picketed by feminists who held him responsible for the death of Sylvia Plath. In October he gave a talk, never published, on Herbert, Holub, Amichai and Popa, in which he claimed that their poetry was the first ever written which did not lose significantly in translation. In December he paid tribute to Henry Williamson at his memorial service.

[21 April 1977]

Dear Keith,

Thanks for the interesting letter. Pity you didn't get to Mexico. I don't know what MS. will compensate. I'll give Olwyn a list.[1]

I'm enclosing 4 typescripts — rather a miscellaneous lot of marginal stuff. It seems marginal, except for one or two poems here & there. It will be something to enlarge on — with Gaudete — if you manage to get to add a chapter to your book.[2]

CAPRICHOS goes with 16 drawings of Leonard B's — some of his most interesting.[3] John Commander at Scolar has them at the moment — a book is being considered. The drawings are not linked in any way — the poems did develope[4] some links. Not quite sure what to make of them. I wanted to keep them simpler — i.e. closer to me — than Cave-Birds — which became so intricately elaborate in their internal narrative/dramatic machinery, & so cold in their baroque surface, I can hardly feel I wrote most of them. But Cave-Birds put me through a process, in a therapeutic way, and brought me out changed in a real sense. I'm not sure Caprichos have the same magical operation on my dream-works, though I think I like them better. Numbers 1, 13 & 14 are from continued Crow — not typical, just suitable for this sequence.

Cave-Birds is final, I think. Number 17 was from continued Crow — though I don't know that it's so vital to reclaim it from

---

1 I bought the entire *Adam and the Sacred Nine* archive.
2 In the 1978 second edition of *The Art of Ted Hughes* I added chapters on *Season Songs*, *Cave Birds* and *Gaudete*.
3 See Appendix III.
4 Ted misspells this word repeatedly throughout the correspondence.

its place here. 'Actaeon' ought also to be in continued Crow —
so ought the poems about loving couples — though I wrote them to
go here. I'm sorry poem 25 is missing (it's the one you quote in the
appendix of your book) but I'm in the usual belated mess of no
copies after seeming to type dozens.

"Moon-Bells" is odds & ends I put together for a children's
book in Chatto's series. 'Pets', 'Fox-hunt', 'Birth of Rainbow', 'He
gets up in dark dawn', 'Coming down through Somerset" are pieces
from a verse diary I've kept from time to time. It's a casual way of
getting down the details without bothering about making a poem
— quite often they come out as passages that I can't alter in any way
at all for the better — they're old-fashioned and all that, but I don't
know how else I could get what they get. (That poem 'Sheep' in
Season Songs is about the best of them). They can only be done
right on the spot, pretty well. If I leave it more than a week, the
thing becomes a more conventional sort of poem — with all sorts
of other intrusive requirements to be satisfied.[5]

'Nessie' & 'Horrible Song' I wrote long ago, for Winter's Tales
for Children. 'Tigress' and 'A mountain lion' are sketches —
written in front of the cages (like second glimpse of a Jaguar).
'Water' is from Recklings. 'Off-days' was a verse diary bit that I left
too late. 'Roe-deer' the same. 'Earth-Numb' — the best — I wanted
to put in Season Songs, to balance December River, but I didn't get
it finished. The day after I finished & typed it, I caught 2 salmon,
and the next day another — the first for 3 years. Hunting magic.

'Amulet', 'I see a bear' and 'Earth-Moon' were all off-cuts from
the first batch of Crow. Earth-Moon was the first where I hit the
style for the Bedtime Story type of narrative.

The 3rd M.S. 'Moortown Elegies', is made up of verse diary
pieces I wrote while I was farming — some came off better than
others. At the end are a few brief bits of elegy for Jack Orchard —
Carol's father. I wanted to do much more of that but perhaps his
death was too close at the time. They don't carry anything of what I
wanted them to carry, but they do carry something. The whole lot
will be a Rainbow Limited Edition — a memorial edition, for
Carol.[6] Though I think I'd put them in a collection too, in spite

---

5   See Hughes' Preface to Moortown Diary; Collected Poems, pp. 1204–5.
6   Ted and Olwyn had founded the Rainbow Press in 1970. In the next decade it published sixteen titles,
    ten of them by Hughes.

of their carelessness. I would have put more in Season Songs but somehow they are largely downbeat — and I deliberately made Season Songs up-beat, to buck me up. Diaries tend to record downs & disasters anyway. I just wish I'd written more.

Finally a final Cave-Birds. Quite a bit changed, as you'll see.

Gaudete comes out May 18th.[7] Charles Monteith[8] is giving a party — for which you'll receive an invite. That book will be everybody's opportunity to rip me to bits for 5 years. However, it's a big thing for me & shows me many directions. I think I know exactly what it's worth, so I'm quite willing to take my amount of protest & abuse & ridicule too, which I suppose I shall get. The M.S., by the way, weighs several pounds.

I've just about finished my Calder Valley text for Fay's photographs.[9] I began to feel my way there. Some of them I like quite a bit. I hope you will too.

All the best Ted

17 May 1977

I have started a weekly seminar at my house to discuss *Cave Birds*. I suppose the group represents the top end of your readership: two ex-students of mine now doing Ph.Ds on you; two Senior English Masters; one of our part-time tutors; and a couple of my brightest students.

[I reported the difficulties we were having with the first few poems, and complained about the changes Hughes had made in his 'final' text since the Ilkley version.] The poems have got much worse since then from the point of view of impenetrability. Many of the more accessible and direct poems and passages seem to have gone.

22 May 1977

I am very worried about *Cave Birds*. The main problem is not really the obscurity, it is the fact that you seem to have left out all the best poems and

---

7 Ted sent me a copy with this letter. It has the inscription: 'The head is older than the book'.
8 Charles Monteith (1921–95) was Ted's editor at Faber & Faber until his retirement in 1981.
9 Hughes had met Fay Godwin in 1970 when she was commissioned by Faber to take some publicity photographs of him, and he had suggested that they might do a book together on the Calder Valley. She later contributed a portfolio of Calder Valley photographs to *Worlds: Seven Modern Poets*, ed. Geoffrey Summerfield (Penguin, 1974). These prompted me to ask her to lend me some prints for the Hughes exhibition in Ilkley in 1975. She replied, 'I have lots more and still try to go to Yorkshire when I can'. She provided thirty prints for the exhibition. When Hughes saw these, they revived his interest in a joint book, *Remains of Elmet* (1979). For an account of their collaboration see Sagar, *Ted Hughes and Nature*, pp. 227–30.

passages, the ones that go home without having to find their way through a mental labyrinth. By the time you get through, if you ever do, the charge is dissipated. In the first draft you sent me your effort seemed to be to anchor the elaborate bird-drama as firmly as possible in contemporary human experience. Now you seem to be deliberately draining it of humanity and making it as remote and formal and complex and allusive as possible. Who wants to read about Socrates when he can read about himself? Of course you get back to the self eventually if you're lucky, but why go round about when going straight through is so much more compelling and makes so much better poetry.

'The speechless upside-down corpse/ Hanging at your back' just sends everybody off to Frazer and the Tarot pack and gives them an excuse for not confronting the reality which is inescapable in 'With a bonfire unconcern for the screaming/ In the cells'.

'After the first fright' – a tremendous poem – gone. 'She seemed so considerate' – the same. 'The Plaintiff' – now drained of everything – gutted. 'In these fading moments' – the same. 'First, the doubtful charts of skin' and 'The Knight' – a sigh of relief that they have been left alone. 'Something was happening' – another good poem gone. 'Only a little sleep' – beautiful – gone. 'A Loyal Mother' – the same. 'A Riddle' – the only one actually improved.

All this is, I know, impertinent; but better to say it now than in the book. Is there no chance that any of these will be restored?

30 May 1977

Dear Keith,

The sequence of the pieces you have is: Gaudete, 73–76; Cave Birds, mid 74 and early 75, then intermittently through to 76; Caprichos (yes, Baskin's reference to Goya) mid 76; Moortown Elegies, 73 to 76 — as a farm diary or at least an odd-day journal; Pets — various times over the last ten years; Adam and the Sacred Nine — late 75. So you see they overlap somewhat. Cave-Birds seems to me too cold and far off except for one or two of the poems about couples. Caprichos I quite like, though it is still not very close to me. Adam etc I like up to a point. Moortown I like — they are very close to me as records, but I wouldn't like to think I was confined to that kind of writing. Gaudete seems to me the best — both the narrative and the poems at the end. The narrative sketches a style of writing and a style of composition I would dearly like to be able to take further and make complete. At present Gaudete is a prototype — but not to be altered. The poems at the end seem to me about my furthest point so far, some of them. Even so, they leave me very unsatisfied.

So this whole batch of writing has an odd character for me — it looks provisional and interim. Probably because I did it when I was preoccupied with farming and crises, that disrupted every line of thought or work.

The original film scenario of Gaudete — 1964 — is still extant. I haven't read it since. The subject was novel in 1964 — charismatic priests, harem congregations, black magic or at least Old Religion magic in church precincts. But then of course it all became common-place. I wish I'd kept cuttings of the priests who here or there came near to living out Lumb's situation. By 1972 I began to see what looked to me very like reminiscences of my story in other people's books — Fowles, Redgrove etc. I decided to write down the outline in simple summary form, just to stake my claim. I'd hit on that rough narrative verse — each line, ideally, a compressed paragraph — while I was writing a scenario of Burke and Wills. Once I started writing, I started to redream it, in various forms — in that way I got the whole notion of the two men, the real and the changeling, which I now see is full of potential. Also various small episodes, the bull-killing consecration of the non-man etc. I've probably told you all this.

Why an Anglican priest? How could that adventure happen to a Catholic?

The 'healing' refers to the task for which living men were carried away by spirits in various scots and Irish tales: sometimes to cure a sick person, usually to work some recovery on a woman, or deliver a child.

What he actually did there is a whole separate possibility. Difficulty — if it is one — is to keep that distinct from continued Crow.

The consciousness of the original real Lumb and that of the changeling leak into each other, at times change places — a little of that in the Gaudete narrative. I didn't push it or develope it for its own sake because I wanted a story that (a) could somehow happen like that if the priest was eccentric enough (b) would rush from beginning to end with natural acceleration, like a runaway truck downhill — a small compact sequence, really a short story. Obviously, it could also have been a big sprawling fantasy of two worlds but I didn't want that.

Idea in the style was to crush an elemental dimension into the dead end of tea-cups, spectacles, bits of stone etc. I wanted the feeling of a collision — a disastrous one — between something unlimited and insatiable and something trapped and itself a trap, between a keen sense of something supernatural or at least unnatural going on while the actual world yields nothing but the commonplace visible surface of inert objects and the skins of people's faces. I don't confuse this at any point with dialogue — nobody says anything. If they do, it's indicated at a remove, as if it were the track of a fly on a window. That helped determine the style. Also part of it, a collision between a debased demonish spirit-power, in wood-goblinish form, and the sterile gentility of a Southern English village.

I wanted to suggest all that, and say nothing about it. No detail but what radiated the right feeling I've described. No explanation of cause and effect — just juxtapositions or symmetrical relationships.

Various bits and pieces that might seem 'difficult' seem to me right in the overall pattern. The goblin figure that gets into bed with Betty, for instance is a truant demon imitating Lumb and emanating from the tom-cat —he copulates with Betty's astral body, as it were. The changeling Lumb, plus his magical operations, is a doorway for the general influx of a debased demonish spirit-life — this is partly what has got control of the women. I don't say anything about this because that would be ridiculous and mechanical — and anyway it is only a way of speaking, a metaphor for feelings and energies that Lumb somehow evokes. The wolf-dream is part of what would have been a larger half of the scheme if the book had been leisurely and ample. That touches the circumstance that the consciousness of the women in this world — affected by Lumb — and that of the ailing one in the other world, the elemental one, also leak into each other. Usually it's just a whiff of the elemental one in this world, but in this case a reinterpreting dream image. But as I say, I didn't want anything of that that wouldn't work naturally into a 'realistic' sort of story — so I deliberately ignored the developments that kept trying to turn the main idea into a cosmology. I wanted to keep it to the dimension of the spirit-life of stones, rivers, starlings, rising and falling like little flames in a wet reluctant fire — sometimes there, sometimes just damp sticks. The way I think it really is.

The shift from Anglican to something like a tenth century anchorite in the West of Ireland surely has its meaning.

The fact that this — mistaken — summoning of spirit through sexual life of women is shot through the head also has a meaning I intended.

What interested me was to see if I could get all this into terms of cosy English village life, and the sort of people who live it.

It's also a story about English Maytime, about the doom and horror and otherworldliness of sexual life, a little bit.

Probably I abbreviated everything too much. But maybe not. It will take more than a few reviewers to unpick the codes. The main thing is, for it to stay alive and interesting.

Could you ask Olwyn about the poems for THE NEW YORK QUARTERLY — I'll ask her today.[10] Thank you for the cash. I wouldn't know how to direct the student's reading — thing is, to follow the nose. I suppose he's read Frazer — you don't mention that.[11]

All the best   Ted

10 June 1977

Many thanks for the most helpful letter about *Gaudete*.

Something very strange has happened. I must be turning into a poet belatedly at the age of 43. In the two years between sending you my poems and last month I had written only one poem, and that so wretched that I dare not show it to anyone. Then I started some little word sketches in front of my tanks, out of which I have so far made two poems, neither of which anyone seems to like, but I enclose them. On Wednesday morning I posted off to my friend in New York 'Ravens' (which Olwyn said we could have) and my review of *Gaudete*, and a couple of my own old poems Polly had asked to see again. That same afternoon I suddenly wrote a new poem, out of the blue – 'Risk', which I like. Next morning I woke up in the middle of a dream, which in half-an-hour I had down as another poem 'The Nightingale Man', the first time I have ever been able to make any use of dream-material. – I've never been able to retain it long enough. Also these are the first two poems I've written which I don't fully understand, which I have to approach as though they'd been

10 A friend of mine, Polly Whitney, had written to tell me that she and two colleagues were launching a new literary review, the *New York Quarterly*, and asked if I could persuade Ted Hughes to submit a poem. Presumably because they discovered that a *New York Quarterly* had existed since 1969, they quickly changed the name to the *Provincial Review*. At my suggestion, Ted offered them 'Ravens', which was scheduled for publication, along with my review of *Gaudete*, in the first issue. In March 1978 Polly reported that the launch had been slowed by funding problems. I heard no more from her, and can find no evidence that the review ever got off the ground.

11 One of the research students in my seminar was Craig Robinson, who was about to start a PhD on Hughes at Lancaster. He had done all the obvious background reading, and had asked for my suggestions for further reading. His thesis eventually became *Ted Hughes as Shepherd of Being* (1989).

written by someone else, with only partial, hesitant and provisional interpretations. I suppose that's all to the good. That makes thirteen poems I've written now, not counting my little nonsense jingles for children (sample included). At this rate I'll have a book by the time I retire.[12]

I really don't know why I'm burdening you with these trivia.

[pm 10 June 1977]

Dear Keith,

Forgive me for bombarding you with notes, but I'd like to thank you for your remarks about Cave-Birds, because they made me dig out those pieces I'd deleted, and so it comes about that I rediscover their rough virtues, so much better than what I tried to replace them with, as you so rightly complain, and I think probably better than the main sequence, certainly better than many of them. In fact now I look at them I realize they were the beginning of an attempt to open myself in a different direction, a very necessary direction for me, the only real direction, and I'm aghast at the time and density of folly that has passed since I lost sight of it. However.

When I first did that book with Leonard, I jibbed at the idea of a trade edition, thinking there weren't more than four or five of the poems I would want to keep — The Raven, The Knight, then in the complementary pieces His Legs Ran about and Bride and Groom. But his precious drawings gradually pushed themselves towards wide public display naturally etc. I'm now somewhat disillusioned by the whole thing. But does it really matter? I've restored After The First Fright and She Seemed So Considerate and Something was happening, and Only a Little Sleep and A Loyal Mother. I've deleted Two Dreams, and one or two others, maybe The Advocate as well. But for Leonard's drawings as I say I'd delete the whole damned lot. There's a funny atmosphere about them that I really dislike. Caprichos came off a bit better, I think, because I took little or no note of the drawings and no care for any sequential development. It's the last time I enter that sort of crabbing handcufflinked teamwork or three legged race or whatever it is. I did twenty pieces after his drawings. Then I added eight pieces (the ones I'm now restoring and the ones about the couple). That's the difference

---

12 Unfortunately the spate of creativity largely inspired by *Gaudete* did not last. It took me another twenty-six years to produce enough poems for a book, *Mola* (Arrowhead Press, 2004).

between pieces derived from a set piece artifact and pieces just pulled out of the bag. He then drew eight more drawings for my eight new pieces. And those last eight drawings, like my first twenty poems after his drawings, are crabbed, dead, abstract, in just the same way — glad I got my own back to prove the point. Actually, he'd lost the thread of his inspiration for those birds. He produced just one big-footed wingspread eagle — nearly my favourite, very small and intense, that was a new thing. The rest were afterbirths.

Who are Neil Roberts and Terry Gifford?[13] Faber are a peculiar lot. They've just fouled up Gaudete publication — printed 5 thousand, bound two and a half. All gone from the shops — many shops never even got their first order. By the time they get the next wave out the curiosity impulse plus the fresh electrification of those Sunday Paper reviews will have died. The attempt to buy a book exhausts the desire to read it. After that you wait for the paper back. It's like a debt you don't pay immediately — if it can go unpaid why should it ever be otherwise. (Don't take that personally, will you.) But Faber have no sense of their reading public.

I'd like to outflank Cave-Birds with a general collection of miscellaneous things — maybe the Prometheus poems, the Adam pieces, the Moortown journal, odds and ends. Something to outflank the narrow reaction to the verbal baroque of Cave-birds. But then I thought the epilogue poems would outflank the narrative in Gaudete. But those little poems seem to be invisible.

I knew when I made a narrative that eschews all the kisses and carressings [sic] that switch on the Englishman's cultural reflexes I was probably making my tale invisible. Still that won't matter so long as it can haunt. I knew the moment one of my characters opened his mouth I'd be stuck on the gramophone record with Iris M[urdoch] et al. Since my characters are all stuck on the record — that's the point. And what happens is off the record.

It's going to be published in the States in December. It will be even more invisible over there I imagine. Fran McCullough at Harpers and her readers were against it — too English. Then after three months she decided its limitations had a purpose. All her readers evidently came to the same idea. Now she wants to publish it, but to send review copies out six <u>months</u> before publication —

13 I had informed him that Gifford and Roberts were writing a book on him for Faber. It appeared in 1981 as *Ted Hughes: A Critical Study*.

so the reviewers can go through the same process before they shoot their mouths off. So she hopes.[14]

There's really only one thing wrong with it. That it wasn't the twentieth of its kind out of me. Instead of the first. So I had to invent the code as I unearthed the idea.

Didn't you like Arnold Feinstein? Isn't he a marvellous character?[15]

Keep well   Ted

[early July 1977]

Dear Keith,

Must thank you for the poems. I like the close-ups of your beasts — dead-pan & silent sinister. The dream is also effective — completely mysterious, unfaked, and disturbing. I would like to carp about something, but the children's pieces seem to me very funny. Especially the Anteater & the Wombat.[16]

Olwyn showed me your review of G.[17] It seems to me, so far as my own interpretations go, right. The variable is — how well or otherwise did I manage it.

I'm off to the States on Monday for a couple of weeks. All these readings have given me a good look at what I've done and cleared the air.

Keep well   Ted

[1 August 1977]

Dear Keith,

Thanks for the chapters. You read Gaudete as I hoped it might be read. If nothing of that is taken into account, the thing can only seem confused & arbitrary. Once that's taken into account, the lines can be seen in focus, & judged properly. It's like a mathematical

---

14 One of the problems for American reviewers was their inability to pronounce *Gaudete*. Some of them even changed the spelling to *Gaudette*.

15 Arnold Feinstein, the husband of Hughes' later biographer Elaine Feinstein, was head of the Department of Immunology at the Babraham Institute in Cambridge. He became a founding Fellow of Robinson College in 1977. I had spent most of an evening in a Soho restaurant with the Feinsteins, Ted, Carol and Olwyn, talking to Arnold about the immune system of sharks.

16 See Appendix IV. The nonsense poems for children eventually grew into a whole alphabet, *Animal Crackers*, which can be read on my website, www.keithsagar.co.uk.

17 My review of *Gaudete* was not published.

problem — to which the style is the correct answer. It's only when the whole problem's understood, that the style will be seen for what it is. To hear it called crude, clumsy etc (all of which it is) means that the reader hasn't understood why I took so much trouble to make it that way. But whatever people say about the book, I'm confident it's the genuine article — however mutilated, fragmentary, awkward etc.

I once knew the White Goddess pretty well. I deliberately avoided any conscious rigging of the themes, any archaeological showbiz with the material. So your Hercules' reference came as a surprise. The 'oak' business was just part of my infatuation with oak — I have hoards of oak, new & old, beams, boards, panelling etc. One of the first things I found — in a junk-shop in Moretonhampstead — was a snuff-box of oak. On the bottom, a stick-on old label reads 'Herne's oak' in early 19th C handwriting. I don't know when Herne's oak fell — but I imagine it was worked into curios & souvenirs.

The hand torn off episode was a tidied-up vivid dream. A quote in it from Beowulf, just for auld lang syne.

Cave Birds yes is harder to like. I'm sending you the final text. Nearly the original text. The genesis was: ten drawings — the first 8 birds, plus the falcon & the tiny goblin face. I wrote to those. Then Leonard became enthusiastic & produced another ten birds. From The Knight onwards. But since in the first 10, I'd executed & resurrected my hero, I had to create an underworld episode between execution & resurrection — between raven & falcon — to absorb the new drawings. I then added the others, for relief & contrast. The general idea is as you say — and an Osirian death & rebirth.

Caprichos are better poems — though less of a story. Adam & the birds is much better — though still a bagatelle.

There are 45 poems with Fay Godwin's photographs — quite like several of those.

However, the real thing must be something quite different from any of these.

Gaudete is published in the States in December.

All the best   Ted

[3 October 1977]

Dear Keith,

Not to worry about the cash. I'm sure somebody will do the book of pictures & biog.[18] Did George Nicholson of Viking ring you?

The installments [sic] will make nice surprises.

Yours   Ted

[pm 22 December 1977]

[The second page of this letter was written on a carbon of an unpublished poem called 'From PROBLEMS OF AN ANDROGYNE'.]

Dear Keith,

The poem you sent me is as you have it, verbally, but arranged as follows[19] — Should be in Orts.

Glad to hear you are onto Maddy Prior.[20] Thanks again for all the hospitality etc in Manchester. I quite enjoyed that trip.

A rich producer, partner of Polanski, was given a copy of Gaudete by his girl-friend, and is now all keen to persuade Polanski to do it as a film.

It came out in the States last week — deathly silence so far.

Xmas cheer greetings to Pat, & to yourself

all the best   Ted

18 I was in the process of writing a pictorial biography of D. H. Lawrence, and had been involved for months in negotiations with Rainbird for its publication, for which I was expecting to receive an advance of £4,000. I was depending on this to pay for the Adam and the Sacred Nine Mss. which I had bought in April. On the brink of signing the contract, Rainbird withdrew its offer. The biography was published by Eyre Methuen in 1980.

19 I wanted to give the whole of 'If searching can't find you' in the new edition of The Art of Ted Hughes, but had only my transcript from a tape of Ted's reading of it at Ilkley. Here he wrote it out for me as it was later to appear in Orts (1978).

20 Maddy Prior was the lead singer with Steeleye Span. Their version of 'Gaudete' from the Piae Cantiones of 1582 had reached number 14 in the UK charts at Christmas 1973. Hughes' study was close to his daughter Frieda's room, where she played her records. On one occasion Ted picked up a voice which fascinated him, and went to Frieda's room to listen. It was Maddy Prior singing 'Gaudete' (meaning 'Rejoice'), from which he took his title.

1978

Hughes became president of Farms for City Children. He read and discussed some of his poems for Norwich Tapes, where he claimed that poetry, like magic, is 'one way of making things happen the way you want them to happen'. In April he read at the Lancaster Literature Festival. 'The Head' was commissioned by Emma Tennant for *Bananas. Moon Bells, Orts, Cave Birds* (trade edition) and *Moortown Elegies* were all published. Hughes began collecting poems for *The Rattle Bag*, an anthology of poems for children, with Seamus Heaney.

[pm 19 July 1978]

Dear Keith,

Queer surprise to meet those Ur-Orghast syllables — a crude Hexameter, as I recall. Where on earth did you find them?[1]

The formula for preserving fish and a good deal of their colour is 1 teaspoon of formalin and 1 teaspoon of glycerine per pint of water — very simple. It would be marvellous if you could get me some of the small — 2" to 5" fish. I expect the fluorescences go, but the main colours should be O.K. Don't overdo the formalin, can overdo the glycerine.[2]

I shall be at Lumb Bank the 3rd August so I'll give you a ring.

Started writing a few stories — one in the current Bananas.[3]

Just put together a mass of odds & ends into a book which I'll call Moortown — 1st section is the farm diary pieces, 2nd section is Prometheus, 3rd section about 35 miscellaneous oddments — 4th section Adam & the Sacred Nine. Just clear a bit of the deck.

I shall be in Yorkshire with my brother and his wife.[4]

3 August 1978

During a recent holiday in Italy I had written my first short story, 'The Beast', based on a dream on the night after visiting the Etruscan necropolis at Cerveteri. I was amazed to find

1 This probably refers to Hughes' translation of Book V of *The Odyssey*, broadcast in 1960, of which I had obtained a copy from the BBC. *Collected Poems*, pp. 93–6.
2 I did obtain some corpses of marine tropical fish for Ted. I can't remember what he wanted them for.
3 'The Head', collected in *Difficulties of a Bridegroom*.
4 Gerald Hughes was ten years older than Ted. He was Ted's guide to 'the secret magical places'. He had emigrated to Australia after the war, where he still lives. Ted tried unsuccessfully for decades to persuade him to return, and take up farming, or some other enterprise, with him.

uncanny resemblances between my story and Ted's just published story 'The Head'.
I immediately sent mine to Ted, pointing out the parallels:

Both stories move from the normal world, the world of tourists, to a super-natural world, which is also the world of animals. Your tourists are after skins, mine photographs. Both stories feature primitive races with an animistic religion, who appear to be on good terms with the animal world, but are helpless in the crisis. Both stories move into an eerie land with steep forests, 'a vast mouldering of ancient trees' in yours, 'a steep valley with strange primitive trees and giant mosses and ferns' in mine. Your forest is 'like a caveful of stalagmites'; mine has 'ancient trees like standing fossils'. Both stories are about animal suffering and mutilation at the hands of men. In both stories are creatures which will not die in spite of several great holes in the head. In both are mute appeals for compassion. My beast and your final victim are both elks. Your elk looks at the man with dead eyes, mine with empty eye-sockets. The sentence 'I wondered if my touch were painful to it' could come from either story. I don't see how all these parallels could be mere coincidence. I wrote my story on 5th June at Gsteig. Yours must have been written well before this. Who beamed a preview of it across Europe?

In his next letter Ted gave a lengthy analysis of my story, but never mentioned the parallels. See Appendix V.

[pm 7 August 1978]

Dear Keith,

Sorry I couldn't get over to you. I was in a more than usual dash — my brother's here from Australia, which has foreshortened the day somewhat.

I meant to tell you in my last note. I thought your dream-story was very <u>impressive</u>. Quite convincing, interestingly & well written, and <u>unforgettable</u>.

How do you interpret it?[5]

The beast is, I imagine, among other things, your original being in all its undeveloped aspects — primitive & still out of this world aspects. The great stakes in its head were probably — among other things — all the theories & ideas, derived from your reading etc, about this original self, which are not natural to it — i.e. have not developed naturally out of it, but have been imposed on it by you,

---

5 I had not interpreted it at all, being a follower of Thurber's advice to 'leave your mind alone'. Had I done so, my interpretation would have borne no resemblance to Ted's, which is not to say that I rejected his.

in your thinking about yourself. These were a torture to it, a false head-load, a false crown.

The fact that you took these out — that you were able to find the beast & take those terrible stakes out means — among other things — that you have inwardly come to an understanding of the artificiality & wrongness of those notions, & have inwardly — by some inward change — removed them. Rejected & rubbished them. The beast weeps, because you have released him from these misunderstandings, which were like monstrous electrodes of imposed signals, having nothing to do with his real truth, & because you have, by implication, recognised his real nature, & are concerned for it.

The next dream in the series he will not be blind, & probably won't even be a beast.

Interpreted like this, it records a big change in your life — the transition from an intellectualised steerage (and mismanagement) of your real power, which actually immobilised it — 'froze up' your life in some way, to a phase in which, we hope, it will reveal its true direction & possibilities, under your understanding respect. Propitious dream. Though it depends how you follow it up in your behaviour.

No doubt there are other interpretations. But I think it's important to interpret dreams — if at all possible — positively. And this dream is so general, it seems quite clearly good.

All the best   Ted

29th Oct 78

Dear Keith,

Thanks for the note — and the copy of The Art of. I hope you sell plenty of those. I'm an A level author next year — evidently — so I hope that wind blows you some good.

Yes, the bottled fish were just what we wanted — they've kept extremely well. If it's not too much trouble, I hope the supply will keep up — let me remunerate the senders through you. Especially welcome any long small slender fish — up to 4″ or 5″, but all are welcome. Even the very small — 1″ & 2″.

I have a few manuscripts. Will see about getting some together.

Olwyn saved a copy of the very beautifully bound 'Moortown' for you, I hope you still want it.

It's been a scatty summer — too many people, too many dates & appointments. But I hope to clear some time now.

Keep well

Yours   Ted

1979

In February Ted read at the Commonwealth Institute, in March at Leeds University, and in May read from *Remains of Elmet* on ITV. Nicholas Hughes published the first of his Morrigu Press broadsides, for many of which Hughes did the illustrations. In July he spent three weeks fishing with Nicholas in Iceland. In August and September he was working with Richard Blackford on an opera for children, *The Pig Organ*, with the photographer Peter Keen on *River*, and with Leonard Baskin on *Under the North Star* and *A Primer of Birds*. In the autumn the Victoria and Albert Museum staged an exhibition of 'Illustrations to Ted Hughes Poems'. *Remains of Elmet, Moortown* and *Adam and the Sacred Nine* were published.

[pm 29.1.79]

Dear Keith,

Happy New Year.

I see your Art of TH is out. I expect it will sell quite well since this year my verses are general all over Os & As, it seems.[1]

I've recently finalised the M.S. of a collection which I shall call Moortown, simply, but which will contain, along with the farming journal pieces, & the Adam and the birds pieces, and some miscellaneous pieces, (4 x 35 page sections in all) the Prometheus pieces.

Three of these I replaced with new ones.[2] Certain things were missing, & certain pieces were pointlessly weak. But it occurred to me, since you have the Prometheus M.S., that you might like these new ones. I think there are about 30 pages — 2 of them took a lot of searching out — all three did, in fact. Among these pages there's another — rather crude one — that I didn't follow up much. There's also one page — just a draft of a Prometheus poem I never followed through, from the earliest batch, which I found recently. Let me know if you're interested.[3]

Leonard had a curious illness last week — all the signs of a big coronary. Hospital. His blood pressure dropped nearly to twenty

---

1 Ted's poems were set books in both the Ordinary level of the General Certificate of Education (which was usually sat at fifteen), and the Advanced level, sat at eighteen.
2 The three poems replaced from the Rainbow Press edition were 5. 'Prometheus ... Knew what was coming', 12. 'Prometheus ... Can see Io', and 17. 'Prometheus ... Was himself the fire'.
3 I believe I was unable to afford these Mss. My Prometheus archive is now at Emory University in Atlanta.

(at 50 the kidneys pack up) for a short time. But they got it back up, and within 2 or 3 days he was O.K., with no signs of any malfunction of any sort. But they kept him in, & finally decided he'd had Pericarditis with some odd complication. After a week of tests, they've decided he has a thyroid deficiency. They're taking him to London next week, to scan him in depth & detail. For a night there we sat in the ward waiting for the news that he'd gone — they gave him very small chances.

In the first two weeks of March I'm doing a reading tour in the Manchester & Birmingham areas — or I hope to. Carol's brother's trying to organise it, but we've left it a bit late. My idea is to hire various large halls, & fill each with 3 or 400 students from ten or fifteen schools — each school contributing a bit. This way I get to lots of schools which I would normally never visit, because they can't individually offer more than £25. Alltogether [sic], they make a reading worthwhile. But I shan't do it unless plenty of schools respond. Any ideas?[4]

I hope your tanks are thriving.

All the best Ted

26th Feb. 79

Dear Keith,

Sorry we didn't see more of you the other night — I expected you to be at the reception after.[5] We went for a meal at the Armenian Restaurant in Church St — and there was Evtushenko[6] with his girl friend — he'd darted off after some idiot came up and said 'And is this your wife?' at the 'Reception'. So that turned into an Evtushenko floor show and an international incident — outbuying each other in Lebanese wine & Dom Perignon at £15 a bottle. Everybody was glad to get away alive.

I've just been glancing through Terry Gifford's et al Book About

---

4 I was able to arrange a reading for Ted at the Leeds University Adult Education Centre on 10 March.
5 On 24 February I had attended a reading by Ted at the Commonwealth Institute in London. The occasion was the Award of Prizes for the Poetry Society's National Poetry Competition, for which he had been one of the judges.
6 Yevgeny Yevtushenko (born 1933) is a Russian poet, novelist, essayist, dramatist, screenwriter, actor, editor, and film director. Always controversial, Yevtushenko attacked several aspects of the Soviet State, but some other dissenters, including Joseph Brodsky, accused him of duplicity. His most famous poem 'Babi Yar' and four others were set to music by Shostakovich in his 13th symphony. In 1978 Yevtushenko had married Jan Butler, his third wife.

Me. Very odd — everything just slightly — often not so slightly — mis-taken. A general underswell of carping, quibble & pettifogging critical remonstration — apart from their declared liking & admiration etc. They tend to count & analyse misses, instead of hits — which is exasperating.[7] Opinion stated as critical judgement etc. I expect they wrote alternative chapters — one seems to have a better grasp than the other. They seem very genial — and yet at bottom their sympathy doesn't seem to be with the poems.

Leonard B. is under treatment at the moment — pituitary trouble. Result is — new life. I don't know if it's connected, but he's just done some watercolours which seem to me <u>the most</u> beautiful of anything he's done for some time.[8] And he had a peak of new productions last summer.

All the best. Looking forward to my tour up there.[9] Keep well.
Ted

9th July 79

Dear Keith,

I'd certainly like to go to Taos, but I've had my fill of literary ambience, for a year or two, & I'm trying to find the control panel knobs to turn down that wavelength, so if I go to New Mexico it will be on my own steam, or on Carol's, & well clear of Lawrence jamborees.[10] I should have gone in the last 2 years, when I was indulging my craving.

I'm quite pleased with the Elmet book — in spite of knowing too well what it lacks. The impulse is to supply what it lacks, elsewhere.

There are 12 lines missing from Grouse Butts — it goes on: as in The Listener.

The translation — of what the grouse say — is from Gaelic:

---

7 'The good man counts the hits; the bad man counts the misses' was a favourite saying of Ted's.
8 Baskin produced beautiful watercolour illustrations for Ted's Under the North Star.
9 Ted stayed with me 8–10 March. I took him to give school readings at Penwortham (Preston), Bury and Eccles (Manchester), and on the final evening at Leeds.
10 In April I had attended a Lawrence conference in Southern Illinois, and met there Tony Branch, President of the Taos Arts Association, and Director of the projected festival in Santa Fe and Taos in 1980, to mark the fiftieth anniversary of Lawrence's death. He wanted to bring together as many as possible of the leading contemporary writers who seemed to owe anything to Lawrence, and get them to talk informally about what Lawrence had meant to them. I did not have to persuade him that Ted's presence would be highly desirable.

Faic thusa'n enoc ud's an enoc ud eile

and Faic thusa'n la ud's an la ud eile[11] — onomatopoeic. In English, all they can say is Go back go back go back. Grouse are loyal to the Gaels.

In Crown Point Pensioners, 5th line from the end, should read Furthered in <u>their</u> throats.

No plans to come North. Any plans to be in London? On 19th July I go to Iceland for 3 weeks with Nicholas.

I've just marked the proofs for Moortown — which clears the decks of all occasional pieces — except for freakish pieces — written up to 1977 or thereabouts. Published Autumn.

The £1000 would be exceedingly useful at the moment. I'm trying to prepare for the final Tax assessment on Sylvia's earnings 71–75 — and it could well sink me for good, in the way of these things. However, I remember my Seneca & carry on calmly. Also — great Arab proverb: Take what you want — and pay for it. (They mean: Take life in full measure — because the payment is life)

Leonard is pretty well recovered — supercharged with pituitary secretions in pill-form supply. So I expect great things from him. Peril is — to be drawn too much into harnass [sic] with other egos — it promotes one kind of production, but displaces several others. And he's a demon for making books of drawings plus poems. Seems easy for him — he does the drawings in a week: he's a whole factory.

All the best   Ted

11 July 1979

Michael Dawson edits a series of booklets called Proem Pamphlets, published by the Yorkshire Arts Assoc. (I enclose a sample), and has offered to devote the next but one to a selection of my poems, <u>if</u> you would write a brief introduction. Of course I would not have suggested this to him as a possibility if you had not already expressed some enthusiasm for the poems in two letters which could easily be expanded into a little essay. It needn't be as long as Douglas Dunn's – I'm sure two pages would be ample . . . I do hope you'll be able to do this, but if you have any reservations, forget it. One problem with

---

11   There's this hill and that hill
      There's this day and that day.
    In the poem the grouse say 'I see a hill beyond a hill beyond a hill' and 'I see a day beyond a day beyond a day' (*Collected Poems*, pp. 472–3).

my poems is that they are really little scripts meant to be read aloud by me. You seem to be able to hear what they sound like in my voice; but many readers can't. I always get a much better response when I'm able to read them to people, but I seldom have an opportunity to do that . . .

My Bicolour Blenny has disappeared. Normal one minute, gone the next. Everything else is flourishing.

I enclosed a copy of the piece I had written for Poetry Wales, *'The Last Inheritance: Ted Hughes and his Landscape', published in their Winter 1979/80 issue, and reprinted in* The Achievement of Ted Hughes.

July 16 [1979]

Dear Keith,

Thank you for the letter, & the article.

When you mention the high proportion of 'Celtic' poets among contemporary writers in these islands, you could go back 200 years & find the tendency the same. You have to count Larkin (Irish name) & Gunn (Cornish) as Celtic too. The English sounding ones probably had Celtic grandmothers if not mothers. (Redgrove's mother is Italian)

Crag Jack was the local name for my father's father — an Irishman, a Catholic. His two closest friends were the Catholic priest & the (I expect) Wesleyan (whatever that church at Mytholm, bottom of Colden Valley, was) priest. On his death-bed, (died of T.B. — he was a dyer) the Catholic priest brought him a bottle of whisky, the other flowers. He lived originally in Cragg Vale — hence his name.

In the Fairy Godmother piece (which I deeply dislike) 'the ladder' is the RNA molecule — basis of the genetic code.[12]

The fox-dream story really goes as follows: in 1953, my second year at University, I was going through some kind of crise. The problems attached themselves to the writing of the weekly essay. It became impossible for me to write a sentence, except in lucky moments. (It varied with the author in question. — I remember writing fluently about Blake). The difficulties became chronic towards the end of my second year. One night I sat up late writing & rewriting 3 or 4 lines I had managed to compose — the opening of an essay about Samuel Johnson (a personality I greatly liked). I left

12 'My Fairy Godmother' was added to Meet My Folks! (1961) in the paperback edition.

the page on my table & went to bed. Then I dreamed I was still sitting at my essay, in my usual agonising frame of mind, trying to get one word to follow another. The door opened & a creature came in, with a fox's head, & a long skinny fox's body — but erect, & with human hands. He had escaped from a fire — the smell of burning hair was strong, & his skin was charred & in places cracking, bleeding freshly through the splits. He came across, & set his hand on the page & said "Stop this. You are destroying us." He lifted his hand away, & the blood-print stayed on the page. The hands in particular were terribly burned.

The dream had total reality. I woke soon after, & went to look at the page.

The following night, I dreamed that I woke, with the knowledge that somebody had come through my door. 2 or 3 steps led down from the door, into my room, — I could make out a tall figure standing on those steps. I got out of bed (in my dream) & went across to see who it might be. As I crossed the room, the creature opened two eyes & I saw that it was a leopard — but standing erect. My exclamation "It's a leopard", is the most vivid thing about the dream. As I spoke, it stepped towards me & began to push me back, — I resisted & wrestled for a moment, before it pushed me backwards over my armchair.

This was a less striking dream than the fox dream, but the very peculiar thing was I woke soon after lying over the chair — as if I had sat into it, over one arm, in backing from the door. I woke up because I was so uncomfortable. The leopard said nothing I remembered.

So that's the account as I remember it. I made a note of it at the time. The room was on K staircase, 1st floor, & looks out over the small courtyard halfway up Pembroke St.

These are dreams I should never have told, I expect.

I connected the fox's command to my own ideas about Eng. Lit., & the effect of the Cambridge blend of pseudo-critical terminology & social rancour on creative spirit, & from that moment abandoned my efforts to adapt myself.

I might say, that I had as much talent for Leavis-style dismantling of texts as anybody else.[13] I even had a special bent for

13   F. R. Leavis of Downing College was the most influential English don in Cambridge at that time, through his teaching, his books, and Scrutiny, a periodical he had founded, and edited from 1933 to

it — nearly a sadistic streak there, — but it seemed to me not only a foolish game, but deeply destructive of myself. I think it was something peculiar to Cambridge at that time, that nurtured it, & in particular separated the spirit of surgery & objective analysis from the spirit of husbandry & sympathetic coaching. I don't think it happened at Oxford, for instance.

I would be delighted to write the introduction to your book.[14] Let me have a full copy. I'm off to Iceland for 3 weeks, so it will be mid-August before I'm active again.

Sorry to hear about the Blenny. Sad to think of all that busy alert anxiety coming to an end. You should get two.

The cash would be very useful — give it Olwyn, in a reasonably tough envelope. Thanks again.

Just marking the proofs of Moortown — 10 broken letters per page.

I told you, didn't I? that I found a few more Prometheus sheets — I knew they hadn't been destroyed.

Yours   Ted

[pm 20 August 1979]

Dear Keith,

Thank you for the cash.

Olwyn showed me the letter — very kind to note the errors — 2 of which (commas) I hadn't bothered about, but then did.

I kept finding new errors right up to the last minute — so it's not possible the text will be perfect. I made one or two textual changes.[15] The cover is vile peppermint green.

The Lancaster Festival Programme makes me tremble.[16]

1953. He brought an Arnoldian high moral seriousness to the close reading of texts. However, he believed that great writers were a race apart, and he had no interest in the creativity of students.

14 The Reef and Other Poems (Proem Pamphlets, 1980). He produced a three-page piece which, in addition to introducing my poems, constituted an important essay on simplicity in poetry. See Appendix VI.

15 Olwyn had lent me a proof of Moortown in which I had made many corrections. All previous printings of 'Tiger-psalm' (as 'Crow's Table Talk') had repeated 'Does not kill' in lines 40 and 41, but in the proofs Ted had removed the repetition. For reasons I could not formulate, I felt the repetition had added a great deal, and asked Olwyn to plead with Ted to restore it, which he did.

16 In my letter to Olwyn I also told her that the Lancaster Literature Festival Committee had accepted my proposal to include a Ted Hughes Festival in May 1980. I had suggested five possible elements: 1) A five-day international conference, with two lectures a day open to the public, and a coach-trip to the Hughes country. 2) An exhibition similar to the 1975 Ilkley exhibition, 3) The commissioning of a new work from Ted. 4) Productions of two of Ted's plays for children. 5) A reading by Ted.

Somehow I feel all this will have to be paid for. Once you're dead it's OK, you've paid. Otherwise, the Japanese saw holds: Applause is the beginning of abuse.

I would like to see items 4 & 5 deleted for sure. And I'm not sure about 3. Any personal connection with that event conducts the current directly back to me. Do you know Rilke's story about poetic fame? A very little of it can feel like a great deal. Insofar as it becomes a point of the patient's attention, it's poison in the water. It's not what it is in itself, so much as what it prevents. And to be free of its effect, you need more than seclusion — you need geographical distance. I'm over-conscious of it at the moment — I suppose because I've indulged in all those readings, T.V. etc. So I hope you'll understand if I say I don't want anything to do with any Festival of the sort you've outlined. Purely survival common-sense.

Nicholas has an aquarium full of varieties of caddis larvae at present — writing notes, & making lists.

We had a memorable 3 weeks in Iceland — very tough country. Caught some very big fish, & in plenty. Wore ourselves out.

Hope you're keeping well.

Yours   Ted

[pm 30 August 1979]

Dear Keith,

Sorry if my letter seemed sudden. My only reservations were about the children's plays, the commissioned work and the personal appearance. Usual reasons.

The children's plays seem to me awfully weak and inadequate even to do their own job — so I can't see them stretching themselves to represent what I suppose I should call my more serious intentions, as inevitably they would be called upon to do, under the eyes of a studiously serious adult audience.

And the idea of taking on any more 'commissioned work' at the moment is a painful one. It seems to me I've spent years now embroiled in writing on request, to some specification or other — and vital time has shot past in total neglect of the work I ought really to have been doing, where I could have given a much fuller account of what there is to be given an account of. Even now, Keith, just for the record, I am looking at an urgent request from the composer Richard Blackford, a very sweet fellow and a talented musician, for the last lines and verse and oddments of our operetta — and he's quite right to ask for exactly what he's asked for, he knows what he's doing and I'm keen to give him just what he needs.[17] But beside him are twelve rather fine dream-landscape drawings by my close friend Reg Lloyd, the painter in Bideford, whose work I would dearly like to see represented in the V & A exhibition, and so before 11th sept [sic] I must somehow support their entry with passages of suitable verse.[18] Beside his drawings, are my friend Peter Keen's photographs of rivers and their environs and populations, which I would also like to see brightening up that exhibition, and for that I have somehow to pull together some verses which I'm anxious to make good, because they are pieces I've wanted to write for a long time.[19] Then beyond that lies a contract with Leonard to write three books of verse with his illustrations, for which he desperately needs the cash.[20] One of them I've done except for the all-important last revisions, for which I need a special degree of concentration, and another lies there in draft, and the other — at the moment — I feel reluctant to start at all. None of this is really my own line of work, but there it is. And for each one I'm making all the adjustments and adaptations, necessary it seems to me if the piece is to work at all, but for which no doubt I shall only have the doubtful reward of reprimands and correction from some of our guardian geniusses [sic].

So you see, Keith, — the idea of a commissioned work at the moment — it's rather like the idea of yet another personal appearance. My personal appearance batteries are just about exhausted, for the time being. The readings etc I'm still committed to I live with by ignoring. Otherwise my sense of audience has for some reason become so overwhelming that any concentration is just about impossible, and I expect it will be quite a while before I get back to an easy sense of privacy. This Exhibition at the V & A —

17 *The Pig Organ*, with music by Richard Blackford and libretto by Ted Hughes, had its world premiere at the Round House, London, on 3 January 1980.
18 Mark Haworth-Booth staged an exhibition of *Illustrations to Ted Hughes Poems* at the Victoria and Albert Museum, London, in September and October 1979. The only exhibit by Reg Lloyd was his 1970 poster-poem 'Crow's Last Stand'.
19 The exhibition included two photographs by Peter Keen which appeared in *River* in 1983.
20 The next collaborations with Baskin to be published were *Under the North Star* (by Faber) in April 1981, and *A Primer of Birds*, published by Baskin's own Gehenna Press, in July 1981. There was nothing else until *Mokomaki* in 1985.

the idea and work of Mark Hayward [sic] Booth, who seems to be a very sweet man and an enthusiastic reader of my verse, has become an obligation, on me, not to let him down — not imposed by him, but just by the circumstances — so that when I say I shan't go near the place people cry You can't do this to Mark when he's doing all this for you.

But is he doing it for me or for my writings or for the general opportunity to make an interesting cultural display of some quite interesting assorted visual art loosely assembled around the incidental thread of my publications? Well, I suppose I reap the fruits of whatever fair weather promotes my writings — but in that role I'm only a predatory goblin who happens to be still around from the age when such things were created. On the other hand — well, it's the old story. Whatever agitates and strengthens and consolidates my sense of my public ego strengths [sic] the very thing that all my writing has to dissolve and break down before it can begin to live.

I'm not against the Conference — any sympathy and help of that sort cheers me greatly. And the argument needs to be kept up. Do you remember that article about Yeats in the Kenyon Review, where Auden dismissed the whole of Eastern mystical and religious philosophy, the whole tradition of Hermetic Magic (which is a good part of Jewish Mystical philosophy, not to speak of the mystical philosophy of the Renaissance), the whole historical exploration into spirit life at every level of consciousness, the whole deposit of earlier and other religion, myth, vision, traditional wisdom and story in folk belief, on which Yeats based all his work, everything he did or attempted to bring about, as "embarrassing nonsense". The article concerned Yeats as an Example.[21] Auden's example, following the example of most cultured English sensibilities that awaken to the morally responsible life, was the solemnly-intoned, shuffling, high-minded, pedantic, frivolous, tea-and-biscuits Oxford High Anglicanism, dignified with whiffs of the old incense and murmurous latin — which seems to me closer to the pride, pomp and circumstance of the High Table than to any altar of uncut stones.

Well, we mustn't be thrown I suppose by the sharp reaction to

21 Auden's essay was reprinted in James Hall and Martin Steinmann, eds., *The Permanence of Yeats* (Macmillan, 1950).

the follies of the Sixties. The Sixties also produced that mass of newly published or republished texts of the essential literatures, which were swallowed whole by a generation that is still only in its thirties. And it produced the whole idea of our ecological responsibility, fully developed — maybe the crucial awakening. And the idea of ecological interconnectedness, which is the fundamental assumption now of children under 18, is only the material aspect of the interconnectedness of everything in spirit. But traditions — like Auden's — aren't changed by argument, only by death of skulls and brains. Argument changes the children, I suppose, who eavesdrop.

I'm beginning to babble, I think.

If Carol and I are in London around the 11th we must fix a meeting. Keep in touch through Olwyn.

The poems by the way are just awfully good. I'm looking forward to writing my piece.

All the best and to Pat

Yours Ted

2 September 1979

I can well understand your feelings about personal appearances, especially after your marathon of readings last year. We shall drop any idea of trying to involve you in person in whatever happens at Lancaster. The idea with the children's plays was that they would be performed by children for children in local schools; but we'll drop that too. I have obviously raised unnecessary fears by using the word 'commissioned'. Neither I nor the Lancaster Festival Committee had the slightest idea of asking you to write something to order, or of making any kind of specification. All we meant was that we would pay you a considerable sum for the right to 'unveil' some new work; that is, to give it its first public reading or first publication, or both — something you would have written anyway . . .

I don't know if I told you that I am doing an anthology of contemporary British poetry. It was originally intended to be translated into Danish by Steen Thorborg (the chap who translated Crow and Season Songs and Gaudete) – he has his own press, the Prometheus; but now the Manchester University Press has become interested in doing an English edition of it. I want fifty poets altogether to be represented in it, and so far I've selected 45. I enclose the list. Can you, at a glance, see anyone really good who is missing? I don't see any obligation to include people just because they are well known, if I don't myself like their work. All I'm looking for is poems with some life in them – I've read hundreds without this summer.

There's no hurry for that introduction, by the way. When you list all those commitments stopping you from getting on with what you really want to do, you make me ashamed that I should have added yet another.

[9 September 1979]

Dear Keith,

If the Lancaster series of lectures happens, & I've finished something unpublished and interesting, I expect there'll be some way it can be included. If that can be left vague.

Your list of poets isn't quite my own list — If I marked poets A, B & C. I'd introduce one or two A, & relegate one or two C. Abse would be a good B — an A insofar as I'd certainly have him in a list of 50. Early poem about 2 faces, poem about brain operation, etc.[22]

I'd find something from Walcott — recent book.[23]

W.S. Graham — I'd look hard there.

Tomlinson — must have the edge on several on the list. The Mexico anecdote.[24] Odd poems here & there? Surely he's very good when he's good.

Peter Porter — some things in his last book.[25]

Keith Douglas — (isn't he contemporary?) Should be in, I think. He'd only be sixty.[26]

Leslie Norris — Ballad of Billie Rose. Etc.

Michael Baldwin — Hoval. (several of his unpublished poems, about Goats etc)[27]

Geoffrey Hill — I don't see how he could be left out. Quite a few permanent poems — first quality. A plus plus, surely.

Two or three of your list I'd think hard about.

Glad to see you've got Massingham.

Seamus Heaney showed me a marvellous volume — last one — by Ian Crichton Smith (is that right? The Scot) Very good. You'd like it. Different from the earlier books.[28]

22 Probably 'The Trial' and 'In the Theatre'.
23 Derek Walcott's most recent book of poems had been *Sea Grapes* (Cape, 1976).
24 Possibly 'In the Emperor's Garden'; but Charles Tomlinson wrote many poems about Mexico.
25 Peter Porter's most recent book was *The Cost of Seriousness* (Oxford University Press, 1978).
26 See Hughes' essay on Douglas in *Winter Pollen*.
27 For Hughes' assessment of Baldwin's poetry see Reid, *Letters*, p. 363. Baldwin has never published a collection called *Hoval*, or anything like it. *King Horn: Poems Written at Montolieu in Old Laguedoc, 1969–1981* (Routledge, 1983) contains several poems about goats.
28 Iain Crichton Smith's most recent volume had been *River, River* (Macdonald, 1978).

Late Spender? — some diary-ish blank verse pieces, one about Auden. No? Roy Fisher?

My undiscovered poet is Daniel Weissbort. Read "Soundings" — Carcanet. And "In an Emergency" My opinion — his verse will be a fascinating & completely alive record, in 100 years. Unique pure writing. No blockbusters — just steady. Very true. Nothing quite like it.

Do you think 50 names — or a lot more with just odd poems. Craig Raine? Patricia Beer? Gavin Ewart? Thomas Kinsella? (Brilliant recent book)[29]

Keep well   Ted

Tony Harrison? Livingstone — some of his African poems.

Thwaite? I like Tom Loewenstein.[30] Anthologies that advance like a vast anonymous herd are more alive than those which sit like a roomful of statues. Cut down on the main names, spread over the barely known — many writers have one really marvellous poem, don't you think?

10 September 1979

Many thanks for the invaluable list of poets. I find I have been falling between two stools as a result of trying to kill two birds with one stone (visualize that if you can!).

What Steen wants for the Danish anthology is something to introduce the six or ten best living British poets to an audience which knows nothing of British poetry since Eliot and Dylan Thomas. Thus he will want at least ten poems by each. But there is really no need for such an anthology here. There are plenty of them, and the six best poets hardly need introducing any more. For the Manchester University Press anthology your idea might be much more attractive – one poem each by 100 poets. I agree that a great many poets whose general output is unimpressive have produced one splendid poem; the problem is finding them. I would have to plough through all the little magazines and small press publications. I think the best thing might be to get something short and simple prepared for Steen this autumn, and then take a year of further reading (most of which would be needed to follow up your list)

---

29 Kinsella had published three poetry collections in 1979: *Fifteen Dead*, *One and Other Poems* (both Oxford University Press) and *Peppercanister Poems 1972–1978* (Wake Forest University Press).

30 Tom Lowenstein had published translations of Eskimo poetry in 1973. Hughes wrote that his translations 'are at once works of detailed scholarship and of high poetic achievement'. In 1977 Lowenstein had published his first full-length book of poems, *The Death of Mrs Owl*. Hughes wrote: 'Your writing is unlike anything else – very new and alive, very strange and memorable'.

to find my 100 poems. I can't devote a lot of time to this or put it very high among my priorities – it has to be strictly a matter of bedtime reading. But it can be very exciting when you discover a fine poem by someone you'd never heard of – for example John Smith's 'On Motril Beach' – absolutely harrowing.[31]

The Lancaster project has been transformed since I last wrote to you. I have spent a good deal of the last two days in consultation with Martin Spencer and John Banks (the manager and literary editor of the MUP) and Brian Cox and Cecil Davies (who is director of studies in literature in my department), and a number of disadvantages of having this conference as part of the Lancaster Festival have been brought home to me, the most serious and ultimately decisive one being the time of year. Most of the people coming to such a conference would be in educational establishments, and mid-May is the very worst time of the academic year. Many would find it quite impossible to get away for a week at that time. Added to this is the fact that the elements which, at your request, we dropped, were the very ones the Lancaster people were keenest on, that accommodation in Lancaster is impossible to find during term time, that my own programme would have been almost impossibly cluttered for May . . . and you see why we have decided to take the conference away from Lancaster and hold it at Holly Royde, our own very pleasant residential college in Didsbury (you gave a reading there in 1969), 13–17 August 1980. It will have the backing of the university press, the Manchester Poetry Centre, the Critical Quarterly, and, we hope, the North West Arts Association. There will be eight lectures, six seminars, a small exhibition, and an optional coach trip to Haworth and Lumb Bank – nothing else (unless you could let me have something unpublished to read to them on the last evening). The capacity of Holly Royde is 54, which would be a nice size for such a conference. We'd hope to get most of the people who are working on you all over the world.

[pm 4 October 1979]

Dear Keith,

I don't suppose there's anything here you're not very familiar with. But just in case there's anything you can use.

Terry Gifford sent me the text of their book — and I had to get one or two notes in response off my chest. This is a copy.[32]

All the best   Ted

31 I abandoned this project when, in October, I was invited by Murray Mindlin, editorial director of Mansell Publishing, to compile (with Steve Tabor) the bibliography of Ted Hughes which Mansell published in 1983, a hugely time-consuming undertaking.
32 The bulk of this letter is in Reid, *Letters*, pp. 427–9.

1980

Hughes published the first of his poems about Sylvia Plath: 'The Earthenware Head' and 'You Hated Spain'. *The Pig Organ* opened at the Roundhouse in London in January. On 26 April Ted read from *Remains of Elmet* in Hebden Bridge. In July he went fishing in Alaska with Nicholas. He finished *River*, and edited Sylvia Plath's *Collected Poems. The Unaccommodated Universe*, by Ekbert Faas, contained extracts from many of Hughes' prose works, and two of the most important interviews he ever gave. The first international conference on Hughes took place in August at Holly Royde College, Manchester, in conjunction with a major exhibition in the City Art Gallery. In November Hughes was one of the judges (with Heaney, Larkin and Causley) of the *Observer*/Arvon Foundation Poetry Competition, which he had founded to raise funds for Arvon.

7th Jan. 1980

Dear Keith,

Here is what I wrote as foreword — I sent it on to Michael Dawson.[1] I've gone on a bit, but I had to get some of my own back, and I did want to give some context to my liking for your poems. If it's too long, what cuts do you suggest?

I expected to see you after The PIG ORGAN, but you vanished. What did you make of it? Richard (Blackford)'s difficulty was that having set out to write a children's opera, and got me interested in writing something that would be performed in every school in the world, with little simple school orchestras and irresistible timeless tunes, he was then pounced on by the Royal Opera Company and invited to Grand Opportunity in Tails — and how could he then go ahead with the Big Bad Wolf sort of music I was trying to imagine? Well, of course he couldn't. So the pig was split down the middle.

Maybe he will pull it together, and make the readjustments (write something for the actual pig-organ for one thing) to make it a successful work on his level. I can't tell. But it seemed to me rather difficult music. My ideal, unfortunately, was the Steeleye Span, so it was a mental collision for me.

He gave me a cassette of an earlier piece he wrote for a version — for children — of Gawain and the Grene Knight and after a hearing or two that was rather lovely.

1 See Appendix VI.

I've been trying to wring [sic] you about the MS etc. Let me hear from you.

Happy New Year meanwhile.

Yours   Ted

13 January 1980

Dear Ted

Very many thanks for the introduction to my poems. I expected nothing so grand. If by getting your own back you mean embarrassing me with praise, you have certainly done that — My only reservation is that after such a build-up the poems are bound to seem an anticlimax. When the Proem-Pamphlet comes out I shall send a copy to Faber to see if they would be interested in a book — I have just about enough poems for a book now. One more thing I should like to ask of you in connection with this: could you please send me a list of your ten favourite poems of mine in order of preference. I will then do a line-count on them to determine exactly how many there will be room for, and arrange them in some sort of order. Having been so excited by my Red Sea experiences, I was surprised that I had felt no inclination to write a poem. Then suddenly, on Friday evening, I felt impelled to pick up a paper and pencil, with nothing more in my head than a title — 'The Reef' — and the intention to write a eulogy of the fishes I had seen. But that isn't the poem which wanted to be written — in half an hour I had written the enclosed, which you can now take into consideration when making your selection. What do you think for a title? *City Boy? The Nightingale Man and Other Poems? The Reef?* If we had *The Reef* perhaps they would use one of my underwater photographs for the cover.[2]

We didn't disappear after The Pig Organ — simply went into the bar, where Olwyn and David and Tina already were. Then, after a few minutes, they disappeared. We stayed about quarter of an hour, but didn't see anybody; so we got an early train. I didn't much like The Pig Organ, but then I don't like opera — I've never been at home with its conventions. As is always the case with opera, I could hear only about a quarter of the words, which made the story difficult to follow. Why did the music-master die? Why was the king ill? Why did his illness take the form it did? The programme said he was suffering from a lack of music. Yet he was ill before the music-master died, and the music went on all the time anyway — from the eight players. The programme said the piglet was possessed by a dancing devil, yet it did not dance, and gave no sign of possession — just seemed mischievous. A lot of importance seemed to be attached to the pig organ, yet it didn't play, and didn't cure the king. I could work out subtle answers to some of these questions after the event, knowing how your mind works, but I imagine they would leave children

2   I had just spent a week at Nuweiba on the Red Sea, snorkelling every day.

bewildered, as would the music. There were so many opportunities to involve them — as in a traditional pantomime — none of which were taken. In fact I thought the production amazingly amateurish all round. The music was pleasant enough, but a far cry, as you say, from Steeleye. If it had to be written in a sub-Ravel idiom, then it should have been the Ravel of The Mother Goose Suite, where there are ravishing tunes throughout. Here there was only one a child could possibly register. But I'd like to read the whole text. Is it to be published in any form?

The Mss were fascinating, and of course I'd like to have them. How much do you want for them? But I still don't have the full set of Prometheus Mss. What about the three new poems you added for Moortown? I really need those too. Every new batch makes the history of the poems more complicated. Some day I'll ask you to go through them and arrange them in something like chronological order.

I hope your New Year resolution was to finish Crow this year!

All the best   Keith

20 Jan 1980

Dear Keith,

The whole point of assembling those Prometheus odds & ends was to include the M.S. of the 3 new ones (plus 2 or 3 abortive extras). The question is, where are they. I see they aren't on the list I gave you — as I would have sworn they were, before I looked. I assembled them very carefully not long ago. Where the hell are they! I'm so well organised these days, anything lost is really lost — there's no general catch-all mess any more.

They'll come out, as Olwyn says. I've a feeling I may have left them for you at her place — which means an Archaological [sic] find in 3 centuries, maybe.

I was hoping to use the cash to buy a boat.

I tore a notebook to pieces — one section had the Prometheus bits — written on the way to the States & in the States — at Leonard's — in 78 October — & adjusted since. Another section had a book of children's poems about birds & beasts in the Northern Woods which I also wrote at Leonard's (It's a wonderful thing, having nothing to do but write). I have this section carefully lodged with all subsequent drafts etc.

What I dread is the 3 or 4 hour search, of increasing mortification.

None of my ideas really emerged in the Pig Organ. The piglets were to be older, & abler. i.e. The first piglet was to be at least as demonic as a good Puck, & preferably more voodooistic by a good stretch. The musical debacle, to accompany that, was to rend heaven & earth, & leave us all trembling.

The Fantastic instrument was to be assembled laboriously & fantastically — in itself always a very theatrical thing — & then to produce notably fantastical artificial music.

The Pig-Song was to rise from among bellowings, screechings, ramblings, & abdominal explosions of a generally bestial underworld, & to extricate itself with musical art, & form itself in a realm of pure & simple beauty — such as the piglet could sing.

The King was to have been noticeably a King (not a 13th Century Maltese money-lender) & was to have descended into piggery by clearly marked jolts of intensifying horror. — trotters, ears, whole face & body, dragging the music down into the deafening operatic underworld from which the dancing pig erupted. The Princess was to have searched for her swineherd to the very end. The Swineherd was to have remained concealed till revealed at the culminating chorus of the pigs. Etc Etc. All good operatic & musical stuff — but probably too crude for Richard.

all the best   Ted

Don't repeat this — I wouldn't want to dishearten Richard. And it had to [be] my opera or his — i.e. it had to be his.

At Olwyn's suggestion I had invited Henry Moore to collaborate with Ted in designing a poster poem for the Manchester Exhibition.

4 April 1980

I enclose a photocopy of a letter from Henry Moore. I read it as not quite closing the door on doing something in the longer term in connection with you, so I have replied (after consulting Olwyn) with a number of further suggestions. As for the poster, we are now looking for a local artist to do a poster of one of the Elmet poems.

John Newton, fellow of Clare College, Cambridge, and one of the founders of the Cambridge Quarterly, in which he had published several enthusiastic reviews of Ted's poetry, had sent me a poem, 'Cassandra' by Sue Lenier, with the claim that he had discovered a new genius, and a request to forward it to Ted.

I had no intention of doing that, since I thought the poem was abominable and told him so in no uncertain terms. I told him it was the sort of thing most of us get out of our system at about eighteen and can only laugh at at twenty-two; that he would be doing her no good at all by encouraging her to go on in that second-hand posturing manner; that the best thing for her would be to get out of Cambridge, preferably out of the academic world altogether, perhaps stop writing for a while, and get on with living until something happened important enough to her to release her own simple voice from underneath all that clutter of superfluous metaphor and pseudo-Shakespeare. I enclose the poem, his letter, and his second letter, after which I could hardly refuse to forward the stuff to you without really offending him. Also I must allow for the possibility that I am completely wrong. You will probably need to read only the first page or two of the poem to see the sort of thing it is. Sorry to burden you with this — but you will see from his letters what an impossible position he put me in . . .

It only recently struck me how much better the Prometheus poems are in the Rainbow Press edition than in *Moortown*. The book itself conditions the reader to approach the poems with more respect and concentration than when they are badly printed on cheap paper and squashed in among lots of unrelated poems in a disposable paperback.

[pm 22 April 1980]

Dear Keith,

Thanks for the envelopefull [sic]. That is a very sweet letter from Henry Moore.[3]

Yes, I read the letters from John Newton — with horrible fascination. Sue Lenier's poem too — it fell in the thick of 3874 entries to the 1980 PEN Anthology, which I've been editing, so I saw it in context.[4]

If I read John Newton's letter aright, whatever I said would be superfluous, so I shall say nothing.

Last thing I want to do at the moment is pass comment on young geniusies [sic] — or old ones either. What a perilous thing, though, to be an English Prof. The poetic anima is bad enough, but the poetic animus is a pterodactyl. And no doubt beautiful too [sic] boot. Poetic animus is even more overwhelming when she's plain, I dare say.

3 See Appendix VII.
4 Sue Lenier subsequently published two books of poems, *Swansongs* (Oleander Press, 1982), and *Rain Following* (Oleander Press, 1984). Extravagant praise, comparing her to Shakespeare, Tennyson and Baudelaire, attracted some attention in the popular press. Christopher Reid, writing in the *Sunday Times*, shared exactly my opinion, describing her as 'a striving, clumsy, humorless imitator of antiquated modes, with nothing original to say, but an earnest desire to make impressive gestures'. She later concentrated on playwriting.

If you do visit Olwyn, I don't know what you'd find in the way of miscellanea. I accompanied her move, — I was supposed to help, but the chaos overwhelmed me. If anything survived that — it will belong to a whole extra category in rarity. One removal equals two fires. Anyway, not a lot survives Olwyn's day to day existence — or mine either. Since 1962 I've been making efforts to shed what wilfully adheres with fair success.

I'm sorry about the reading in Hebden Bridge.[5] I'd been led to think it was a small favour to the local literary & historical society, of which my cousin is one of the activists — favour to him really. Somehow he's spun it out into the usual giant web — a latest collapse, on my part, towards what seem inevitable nationalization of my vocal & verbal parts. I'm not sure I can redeem it, either, by exacting a percentage of the gate. These readings now have become peculiar psychological trials — for instance, this time my audience will be exclusively, pretty well, people who want to see if I'm making an ass of my mother & father. I no longer get audiences of people interested to hear verse — only audiences pursuing some perverse publicity-curiosity. That's the feeling. It's an odd thing to watch.

Curious what you say about the Prometheus poems. Are you sure you're not being influenced by what people say about them? It's true for me too, the printing counts for a lot — the distinctness of the visual impact is inseperable [sic] from my sense of the actuality and organic fullness of the poem. The same part of the brain enjoys both. Still, I'm not absolutely self-indulgent. Those pieces are O.K., within their terms, they serve their purpose. The other poems aren't unrelated. Earth-numb pieces all relate to events along that fringe where vivid & awakened sensation, sensitive alertness & sympathy, finds its limits — confronts what it cannot feel or share or for some reason openly contemplate — because of sheer physical limitations. It's where spirit awareness is humbled to physical body-cell confinement — and the prevailing sensation is like that in the dream where you try to see through blindfoldedness or nearly sealed eyes something very brilliant or strange which you

5   The Hebden Bridge Literary and Scientific Society, as part of its seventy-fifth anniversary programme, staged a Literary Evening at the Birchcliffe Centre on 26 April, the climax of which was Ted 'reading his own poetry including selections from his new book The Remains of Elmet'.

know is in front of you, it's a sense too of mutilation, & related to the amputated feeling after somebody's death. That's the magnet bundle of feelings holding that section in its pattern. The God, last piece, is the child in the womb, as you'll have divined.

So the first part is a life embedded in mud, body of death etc, & seeds. Prometheus is what tries to waken up inside this. Earth-numb is his failing effort to come to terms with it. Adam is his succeeding means of coming to terms with it. That's the general plan. The whole drift is an alchemising of a phoenix out of a serpent. An awakened life out of an unawakened.[6]

Anything that was not satisfyingly inter-related, I kept out, or rather, it kept out.

Prometheus is related to the main protagonist of Earth Numb — in his various phases. The Vulture not unrelated to the 9 birds.

The death in the natural labouring external world of Moortown, which is mainly dung & death acting as a crucible for repeated efforts at birth, is a counterpoint to the 'birth', in a supernatural, spirit, inner world, of Prometheus. That's it's [sic] symbolic role.

etc etc.

It was a case of me finding the dominant or a dominant pattern in all the stuff I had from 3 or 4 years, & making positive sense out of it, rather than negative. And as it turned out, I didn't have to wrench & remake anything, it was all there simply.

What it lacks, as a simple pattern, is a sense of purposive or dramatic motive. Maybe it's better that way. But it means its growing into other people will be a slow business — as it was with Wodwo. Assuming that it isn't encapsulated by white corpuscles & rejected, like a transplanted organ.

Still, it's time to do something different.

Yes, by all means pay me for those papers, if you want to buy them. I promise you the others — when they emerge. So long as they don't emerge in some sale catalogue.

Latest curious incident — the almost completed rolls of film (20 odd in each) disappeared from inside both Nick's & Carol's camera — the camera wound back to show the right number. Nick's had some irreplaceable evidence of our last pike expedition

---

6 In *Ted Hughes and Nature* I quarrel with Hughes' own account of the 'whole drift' of *Moortown*.

on Loch Allen. Fortunately he lost the really giant fish — looked about 30 lbs or more — very dramatic, in a boat in a rainy gale — or the now missing evidence would have been priceless to him.

Yes, your selection seems to me the right one but — (1) I'm sorry to see no The Beast. (2) Achilles Tang, Mantis Shrimp, Bicolour Blenny, ought definitely to be in. I would put these in, in place of 'The Reef'. These are really sound & surprising. But best keep The Reef as well.

Also, unless the book is lavish with empty spaces, I would like to see Boccaccio Story & Red Willow Trees fitted in. Also, Gluttony and Lechery.[7]

Do you think I should cut my foreword? I wrote it without interval, and no doubt after an interval, I would have changed it, as no doubt I would now, if I re-read it (I've no copy somehow). I could maybe give you an extra page, too.[8]

We just sent off a book to Viking titled Under the North Star. It began as a birthday book for Lucretia — Leonard's little daughter. Then blossomed in a frosty sort of way. Poems about creatures North of the 49th parallel — with 13 of Leonard's most intense & beautiful watercolours, different completely from Season Songs illustrations. Several of them are small masterpieces.

He's in good shape — changed, but for the better. His work is a new start, in some way. His world has been very effectively renewed. Monkey-gland effect.

Finished more or less a text for a book of Peter Keen's photographs of rivers & their associates. What I'd like to do, while I'm still in the material, is write a whole other book of pieces not intended for readers. Writing for accompaniment sets subtle limits — it's a different kind of contract with a different kind of audience. But maybe one poem is all that's needed.

Probably see you next week.[9] Keep well. Ted

---

7 The format of the Proem Pamphlets allowed for only sixteen pages of poems. Of the poems Ted suggested I was able to find room for only 'Mantis Shrimp', 'The Reef', 'Boccaccio Story' and 'Lechery'. All the others were included in my collected poems, *Mola*.

8 The foreword was printed as Ted had first submitted it.

9 Ted spent the last weekend in April with David and Tina Pease in Todmorden, and visited me on the Saturday.

1 June 1980

We have commissioned Norman Adams to do the poster poem for the Manchester exhibition. Do you know his work? He has several things at the Tate, and they have just bought another last week from the Royal Academy Summer Exhibition. Very nice chap. Lives in Horton-in-Ribblesdale. Did a book with Glyn Hughes several years ago. Glyn thinks very highly of him.[10] He was already very keen on *Crow*. In fact he says he wrote to you about it at the time and had a nice letter back. His wife, Anna Adams, is a pretty good poet. I lent him a copy of *Remains*, and as soon as he got to the poem 'Open to Huge Light' he knew that had to be the one; it coincided incredibly with experiments he was already engaged in; the poem brought his somewhat vague ideas suddenly into clear focus . . . Norman goes straight for the apocalyptic. So it should be a useful opening up. What he intends to do, if he sticks to his initial plan, is to have a dark, obscure frieze, as it were, made of shadowy people, sheep, cattle. The poem itself will be in the centre, as though in an opening torn through to this other world of bright emptiness and silent music. The letters will be in many bright colours — every letter broken up, prismatically, into several colours, scattering bright, too bright to be looked at by the stooping benighted figures. A touch of Blake. I hope you like it.

The conference is all very exciting, but dreadfully time-consuming. I go to the States for the New Mexico Lawrence Festival on 11 July. Before then I have to write a paper on 'Lawrence and the Etruscans'; one on 'Fourfold Vision in Ted Hughes'; edit *Sons and Lovers* for the Penguin English Library; make arrangements for three summer schools I am directing as soon as I get back (I'm only going for twelve days); write the exhibition catalogue, and get all the pictures mounted and framed for it.. Also I'm supposed to be getting on with the Hughes bibliography, the Lawrence letters,[11] and all the reading for my classes next session! It's a great life if you don't weaken.

July 16th 80

Dear Keith,

Just a note — so it will be waiting for you — to say I'm sending the bits & pieces up with David Pease. Would it be possible for you to collect them off him? He lives at Kilnhurst, Kilnhurst Road, Todmorden — in Billy Holt's old House. They're having a Billy Holt Exhibition opening August 2nd, in Tod. That should be interesting.

10 Glyn Hughes (1935–2011) was a poet, novelist and artist. He lived in and wrote about the Calder Valley for the last forty years of his life. In his introduction to a reprint of Glyn Hughes' first novel, *Where I Used to Play on the Green* (Gollancz, 1982), Ted, who was no relation, wrote that 'the total effect is convincing, alarming and memorable'. Norman produced several wonderful paintings, but none was suitable for use as a poster. 'Open to Huge Light' and 'Dead Farms, Dead Leaves' are now at Pembroke College, Cambridge.
11 I was co-editing vol. VII of *The Letters of D. H. Lawrence* for the Cambridge University Press.

He painted giant holy canvases — spiritual revelations of the Mills, the dark Satanic Mills as a Jerusalem — very grand & bad.[12]

His horse, Trigger, died the other day. The Vet estimated its age at 35 (human equivalent of about 120) Billy rode it to Rome & back when it was 15 or 20. A white Arab — he bought it from between the shafts of a coalman's cart. I've just been rereading his autobiographies "I haven't unpacked" etc. I'd forgotten what a marvellous record they are of that world of my parents, full of the real details. He joined up same time as my father — they were 3 apart in the queue — but was so clever they gave him a more or less special Army career to himself. He invented a shuttle & lost the patent somehow — it became the standard shuttle. Fascinating chap. Glyn Hughes is writing his biography.[13]

Alaska was everything I'd hoped. Everything happened I wanted to happen, & a whole lot more. We caught salmon until we were actually sick of catching them. We got ourselves off great lakes (living time, 5 minutes of immersion — so cold) by the skin of our teeth two or 3 times. We fished alongside bears. Lay awake listening to wolves. And generally sleepwalked through that dreamland. Unearthly valley, of flowers between snow mountains. Miles of purple lupins. 300 thousand people in a country the size of all Europe. Mostly new residents — fleeing from the States for one of several usual reasons — a picked lot of dreamers, escapists, self-elected red Indians, hoodlums & generally infatuated freedom addicts — it is extraordinarily free. But the Americans are there like migrants resting in transit — a very shallow hold. And the Indians & Eskimos are gradually getting all their claims back — interesting.

Keep well   Ted

25 July 1980

When we first discussed the symposium you offered to put on tape for me to play there a few of your latest as yet unpublished poems. I enclose a blank tape. Could you do a few North Star poems on it? We are having a little concert

---

12 William ('Billy') Holt (1897–1977) was a self-educated weaver, author, artist and inventor, born in Todmorden.
13 Glyn Hughes subsequently abandoned the project. But see the long description of Billy Holt and Trigger in his Millstone Grit (Gollancz, 1975).

as part of the opening on 11 August – I thought I might play the tape then. Shusha's concert is at Holly Royde on 14th August.[14]

[pm 9 August 1980]

Dear Keith,

I hope this is O.K.

I'm having to dash to get the last post.

Ted

28 August 1980

I'm working on a book of essays arising from the conference. I enclose a list of the contents. I wonder if you would be prepared to allow us to print an appendix of some of your uncollected poems – poems which you have no plans to collect, but which are of sufficient interest (perhaps in relation to earlier phases in your development) to be made accessible? Anyway, I enclose a list of all your uncollected poems, marking in red the ones I'd particularly like to reprint, though we should be delighted with any, and the more the better . . . It should be a pretty substantial book. The essays converge remarkably without overlapping. The contributors are seven British, seven American, and one German – a good balance . . . I hope you can get the corrected proofs of the Proem Pamphlet back to Michael quickly. There should then be time to sell some at the exhibition bookstall, where, you'll be glad to hear, they have been selling large quantities of your books. He wants each of us to sign 50 copies in exchange for 50 free copies. I have agreed, but I have not committed you to doing so.

[pm 12 September 1980]

Dear Keith,

I sent off the Ilkley proof.

Not quite sure about the poems you ask for — it's almost a collection. We'd have to have some sort of agreement.

Whiteness — will be in the River book

---

14 Shusha Guppy (1935–2008) was an Iranian singer and composer whose work Ted much admired. In a sleeve-note to her *Song of Long-time Lovers* (1972), he wrote that her voice 'opens an impossible door'. 'Somehow she puts us in touch with the ancient experience of a whole people . . . the real river of souls and physical ritual history which is the genius of Persia'. On that disc she sang a setting of 'Water Song' by Stanley Myers. On *Durable Fire* (1980) Shusha sang 'Thomas the Rhymer's Song' (*Collected Poems*, p. 628) set by Myers, which Ted had written specially for her. On *Strange Affair* (1986) she sang her own setting of 'Adam and Eve' (in *Collected Poems for Children* as 'Lobworms').

Eclipse — No, it's going in a book I'm doing with Leonard, & I'd like to keep some novelty for it.[15]

Wycoller Hall — No — I'd like to rewrite it & develope its potential.

Squirrel — I think this is really too weak, just curious, don't you think so?

Her Magic — I don't know this piece.[16]

Magpie — ditto[17]

Caprichos — no I'm using these in a limited edition, & want to keep them fresh.

Birdsong — don't know this.[18]

Foal — no — I made an agreement with Mike Morpurgo, and I should really not publish that for a while.

Barley — the same here.[19]

Irish Elk — No, I'm using this

A Dove — Same.

The rest seem to be O.K., though they amount to 19 or more pieces.

If Faber is going to do the book, maybe a simple deal could be arranged.

One or two of the Crow Pieces (Crow's Courtship) are in Faber's Ltd £40 edition.

Surely Scapegoats & Rabies is in Wodwo — Later editions.[20] It's in the Faber Selected.

The Poem 'Children' (from the New Yorker) is in Moortown.

The Viking Colour prints were so poor, they're being redone.

Signing the proem pamphlet is O.K.

Our River book is about finished. The Observer are interested in doing a splurge edition (as with Jane Bown's photographs). Not a

15 *Flowers and Insects.*
16 An unpublished poem which Ted had written on the endpaper of my copy of *Recklings* (1963).
17 This was not the 'Magpie' which was to be included in *A Primer of Birds* in 1981, but an unpublished poem beginning 'Grabbery as usual'.
18 'Birdsong' had appeared in the *London Magazine* in September 1966.
19 On one of my first visits to Court Green, Ted took me to the home of Michael Morpurgo and his wife Clare. In 1976 they founded Farms for City Children to provide children from inner-city areas with experience of working for a week on a farm. 'Foal' and 'Barley' were both published in Morpurgo's *All Around the Year* (John Murray, 1979). In 1999 the Morpurgos were awarded MBEs in recognition of their work for youth. Michael Morpurgo has published many stories and anthologies for children, and was Children's Laureate from 2003 to 2005.
20 'Scapegoats and Rabies' had been added to the American edition of *Wodwo*.

coffee-table book, but an ambassador's gift, or at least a Fishery officer's gift. Hugely expensive. But they have the means to find the buyers — which are no doubt widely-scattered, thinly.

The verse text is simply text — nobody, who's going to buy the book, is going to read my verses. They could as well be middle-kingdom curses, in the original. They're just decorative — with a respectable aura.

Faber talk of doing a trade edition, ordinary poetry book format, with just a few pictures, but I'm not so sure. There might be 8 or 9 pieces I would put in a book, if I were being conscientious. One collection of the whole lot, & nothing else — ! Like a feast of cheeses & nothing but cheeses.

I'm in danger — with my natural history — of moving into a confinement — as with poems about architectural styles or horticultural rarities.

Do you know Agrion Splendens? Do you distinguish male from female?[21] I have a poem about a female rôle in an archaic insect drama — the point being that it's performed by the male, as in Noh etc. I like it a lot — but who'll know what I'm talking about? Is that too fine a point?

Isn't Scigaj a charming fellow?[22]

Excuse me Keith, if I seem loth to take part in such things as the Conference. Apart from the ego-nightmare-of-fairground-distorting-mirrors aspect, & apart from the curious experience of having your ossified past clamped round your neck like a chinese cangue,[23] there's the evil eye aspect also — not to be under-estimated.

One of Nicky's Axolotls is looking a bit off-colour — wobbling about, hanging night & day from the surface, won't eat — though they rarely will eat.

His last print — Mosquito — is a superb piece of printing, He's really getting very good.[24]

---

21 The Banded Demoiselle damselfly. The male is smaller than the female, and much more brightly coloured – an iridescent blue-green. The poem in question is 'Last Act' in River.

22 Leonard Scigaj was to publish two books on Hughes, The Poetry of Ted Hughes (1986), and Ted Hughes (1991), and edit Critical Essays on Ted Hughes (1992). He became the leading American Hughes scholar, but sadly died young in 2005.

23 An instrument of punishment formerly used in China for petty criminals; consisting of a heavy wooden collar enclosing the neck and arms.

24 Nicholas had founded the Morrigu Press in 1979 to print broadsides of Ted's poems on an Albion hand press. Mosquito was the ninth.

I'm going to keep some pieces for his press alone — so they're never published anywhere else. I've one coming up about an eel.

Any publicity ideas for our Poetry Competition — it's going pretty well, but we'd like it to break the sound barriers.

This Yorkshire visit has also to contain London & Wales — so once again it's a scramble. I'll give you a ring though.

keep well   Ted

5 October 1980

I have delayed writing to you waiting for the arrival of *The Reef*. The printers have made a complete mess of it. The cover photograph has been printed much too faint, and should have been blue not green. The printer has left off most of the information which should have been on the cover – Proem Pamphlet 6, Introduced by Ted Hughes (the main selling point!) and the price. Can you imagine Michael letting them print hundreds of copies without ever looking at a proof of the cover! Why does he bother with these things if he has so little interest? They certainly don't make any money.

I'm delighted you will let us use some uncollected poems in *The Achievement*.

7th Oct 80

Dear Keith,

The Reef is nice — it is a pity the cover wasn't better done, but the poems have now flown. Only an unusual holocaust can annihilate them.

Let me know which poems you want to use. Talk to Olwyn. Some of them (some of those you enclose) I wouldn't want to publish. No point in parading misses ("The base man calls out your misses" — why give him opportunity?) Such things have a kind of interest as notes in tiny print buried in the appendix of a variorum — otherwise they are simply taken as new poems. Some of them seem actually weak.

You know that big U.S. college Anthology of Modern Lit where I'm represented by a comic/malicious pastiche once published as a winner in a New Statesman competition? The 'critical' text rolls on confidently — then demonstrates its point by this inanity. So much for literary judgement appreciation etc. For most readers, you could slip in the odd Shakespeare sonnet just as well. My point is — you can't rely on anybody, even the most amiable reader, setting a poem in its proper category. You have to stamp across it — in purple — "2nd team", 3rd or 4th or 5th or whatever.

Because in a real way — I see it more and more clearly — everything one writes modifies the life of everything else one has written.

Caprimulg & magpie are drafts of what finished otherwise.[25] Her Magic is simply poor, I think. Adam Lay is a draft. The flower bulb Prometheus seems to me to have no more than the odd phrase. 'voices quarrelled' is weak, & a bit mechanical.

The other Prometheus pieces only have life really as notes & jottings, I think — but I'm sure very few would distinguish them in any way from what I kept in the book — advanced to the book.

That leaves Crow Compromises (loaves of blood) Two Dreams, A Crow Joke (weak), He Shouted, She is the rock (penultimate line 'Rest' not 'Sleep'). Water: what do you think? They all seem a bit faint.

And there's always the problem of Rainbow Press — but do talk to Olwyn.

My piece about Agrion Splendens is in Quarto.[26]

Nicky's Axolotls died — we think they caught something from a minnow he put in with them. The River Taw has U.D.N. badly.[27]

We'd like to see you but leave it a month — it's just one thing after another at the moment.

Keep well   Ted

25 'Caprimulg' became 'Nightjar'.
26 'Last Act' in Quarto, October 1980.
27 Ulcerative Dermal Necrosis, a disease affecting river fish.

1981

Under the North Star was published in March, and *A Primer of Birds* in July. Hughes co-edited Sylvia Plath's *Journals* and prepared his *New Selected Poems*. He chose thirty uncollected or unpublished poems to be printed as an appendix to my *The Achievement of Ted Hughes*, the first critical anthology on his work. In June Ted and Carol were guests when Melissa and I were married in Bath. Hughes began *What is the Truth?* at the suggestion of his friend and neighbour Michael Morpurgo.

[pm 5 January 1981]

Dear Keith,

Happy New Year.

Very good news about your domestic plans — I hope all goes well. though I expect it will curb your collecting, alas.[1]

Nicholas is just packing off the most recent of his press productions — Mosquito — the best so far. (Writing this with his horrible rapidograph)

We've had a fallow year, at Morrigu. He's been too busy with his exams — to good purpose, as it turned out.

Now we've planned about 6 productions for this year — slightly more elaborate. I'm going to reserve the poems we use henceforth — so they're published nowhere else. I publish too much in books anyway.

Pity you didn't order yours direct from us — but since Ben Kane's doing the dealing he'd best be looked after.[2] We're only selling 40 — so the distribution is tight.

Are you interested in the enclosed picture — it's nicely framed & mounted?[3] Poem published nowhere else. Do you know anybody who'd like one? The painter is a friend of mine — owns the local

---

1 I had informed Ted of my intention of marrying Melissa Partridge in the spring or early summer.
2 Ben was a London bookseller who in 1970 had taken me to Olwyn's house to look at some of Ted's manuscripts she was selling. The door was opened by Ted, who happened to be staying there. It was the first time I had seen him.
3 The order form stated:
   Caricia Fine Arts are pleased to offer the first collaboration by painter Roger Vick and poet Ted Hughes in an edition limited to 150 prints of Sky Furnace each signed and numbered by artist and author. Ted Hughes' holograph is the first publication of this poem and the picture which has been finely printed by the Scolar Press is the sole reproduction of the original oil painting by Roger Vick.

cattle market, auctioneer etc. Something of a character. (Carol's sent it to you)

Trying to get going again and shake off distractions. Time for a putsch.

I hope you're well.

Yours   Ted

[pm 20 February 1981]

Dear Keith,

Thank you for the supper, & the pleasant evening. This is rather a belated note, because on the Sunday my father died. We took a friend of ours to top [sic] Withens — a desecrated site if ever there was one — (they must have sent a Haworth lunatic up there with a cartload of cement and asked him to 'tidy it up').[4] It rained & snowed & displayed a few grouse, & soaked us in style — & we got back to this news.

So in fact we were up again this last weekend, nicer weather but a harder occasion.

I hope we shall see Melissa & yourself down here, maybe before June 14.[5]

Trying to rid my life finally of the carnival ribbons I've got myself tied up in these last few years.

What did you make of the winning poems?[6] There were some quite good things among the lesser prizes. Nothing to come near the baboon. That is the last judging I shall ever do, Ever. Ever. Ever. Ever. Ever.[7]

We're not going to Leonard's Exhibition for a while — maybe

<hr />

4 Top Withens, on the moors above Haworth, is the ruin of a house Emily Brontë may have envisaged as the site of Wuthering Heights. For decades it had been a very atmospheric place, with crumbling walls and exposed rafters; but it had already been 'desecrated' by the time Fay Godwin photographed it (back cover of Remains of Elmet, p. 18 of Elmet (1994)). The photograph on p. 17 of Remains (p. 21 of Elmet) shows the view from it. See 'Two Photographs of Top Withens' (Collected Poems, p. 840) and 'Wuthering Heights' (Collected Poems, p. 1080).

5 Our wedding, in the event, was on 13 June.

6 Hughes had set up and judged (along with Seamus Heaney, Philip Larkin and Charles Causley) the Observer/Arvon Foundation Poetry Competition. There was much disagreement between the judges. The final winner was Andrew Motion's 'The Letter', but Hughes and Heaney had preferred 'The Baboon in the Nightclub' by Kenneth Bernard. Hughes makes his case for this ribald poem in a letter to Larkin in Reid, Letters, pp. 440–41. An extended version of the poem was published by Asylum Arts in 1994.

7 Hughes here echoes Lear's line: 'Never, never, never, never, never'.

2 weeks time.[8] Interested to see which way the dogs bark. English taste doesn't take readily to what he does, or didn't — maybe it's matured a little.

I like our last book — The North Star — seems wholesome & alive. Though I should have included some more gentle creatures — mice beavers & snow birds maybe balance it better. There'll be copies at that show.

Did you see James Joyce's recording of Anna Livia made only £300 — there were evidently all kinds of notes & oddments with it. I wonder who bought it.

Good luck with your house-hunting. Keep well.

Ted

[pm 13 March 1981]

Dear Keith,

Please don't feel any qualms about selling the MSS. If they enable you to get a house, they've worked quite profitably for both of us. And as you say the house will be just as good an investment & much more useful.[9]

I hope the photos of the house work on Melissa.

I've ticked on the list the pieces that seem O.K. I'm not sure what poems hide under A Lucky Folly and Crow Compromises or An Alchemy. If you just tell me the first lines etc it should be enough.

I've not decided about Burning of the Brothel — I have a stack of copies, & haven't decided how much, if at all, they'd be devalued by a trade publication (more people are going to read the selection in this collection — students — than read my books).

Maybe you should allow me to write a little introductory paragraph to these Nisseldrafts.

I want to keep the Tiger for a book I'm doing with Leonard. Or maybe I ought to try writing another. Let me think about that.

I quite like Lines to a Newborn baby — there were three parts — one the longish piece published in the Texas Quarterly, two a

8 Baskin's exhibition Graphics, Drawings, Sculptures was at the Cottage Gallery in London from 20 February to 21 March.

9 To buy our new house I was obliged to sell either my Hughes collection or my Lawrence collection. Fortunately, I was able to sell the latter.

shorter piece in 3 line paragraphs (it was the template for Sylvia's much superior "Love set you going like a fat gold watch")[10] and three a short 2 verse poem about trawlers — last line "To fill England with stale herring" Do you have it?[11]

I quite like Small Events

Fighting for Jerusalem is unpleasant but finished on a higher plane than most of these.

The Lovepet is in Moortown.

Sorry for this cryptography — I'm writing in the car.

All the best   Ted

What I'll do when I get back to Devon, end of the week, I'll send you 4 or 5 odd Crow pieces never published anywhere and you can fill up the complement from there, perhaps, (if you like any of them.)[12]

I've just been talking to Roy Davids — head of the M.S.S. dept at Sotheby's, who's become quite a close friend. I don't know what you're asking from Manchester, but he says a collection of the size you describe might be more valuable than you think — and it is possible to get a high price without paying Capital Gains, still keeping the details quiet.[13] He specialises in poetry MSS. (last night he was selling a Raleigh (Sir Walter) commonplace book (Elizabeth's Raleigh) for £40.000 — private deal. He is one of the most interesting & congenial characters I've met for a long time — absolutely honest — and the most knowledgeable about poetic M.S.S. (and others) in England (i.e. or in the U.S.). Singlehanded more or less he's created the M.S.S. trade boom — by raising them to the status of rare paintings or drawings, (It's a boom of the last 6 or 7 years)

---

10 'Morning Song'.

11 *Collected Poems* prints parts 3 and 2 as 'To F.R. At Six Months'.

12 These were 'Crow Compromises', 'Crow Fails', 'Crow Outlawed', 'A Crow Joke', 'Carrion Tiresias Examines the Sacrifice', 'A Near Thing' and 'Opportunity'. Of these I chose to include the first two in *The Achievement of Ted Hughes*.

13 Roy Davids writes: 'Personal letters are chattels and therefore subject to Capital Gains Tax and not Income Tax. Each letter is a discrete object not part of a set. Therefore each has a separate value, even if sold with others for a single total figure. Unless the value of any one of them is individually of greater value than the allowance per chattel obtaining at the time of sale (which is rarely so) none will attract CGT.'

He's very much worth while speaking to: you might not want to change the deal with Manchester.[14]

He's a collection of literary portraits — some very fine (one of the best of Eliot — big painting), and I meant to ask you if you had a good special Lawrence portrait to sell him.

But do ring him. If he can double Manchester's offer — what do you owe Manchester?

Worth thinking about. (He might think Manchester's is a pretty good offer.)

Leonard B. thinks Nicky's printing is becoming 'quite incredibly good'. His old Gehenna printer is coming over — Leonard's setting up a new Gehenna at Tiverton — but he says he can't teach Nicholas a thing. The only flaw seems to be my drawings. From now on — beginning with the latest "Catadrome" — his printings are going to be the sole printing of what he uses.

[c. 19 March 1981]

Dear Keith — hasty note. I'm leaving for Ireland tomorrow — 6 am. — for Ireland. For one month. I shall be away till April 15th or so.

Yes, but anecdote is in the Limited Faber Edition Crow. Still — OK, use it.

Yes, Lucky Folly.

Yes, Crow Compromises.

OK, an alchemy.

I enclose some aged Crow crones, for your interest.[15] Let me have copies sometime. You probably know some of them.

The price you mention seems to me pretty good. I hope you get the house.

All the best Ted

14 At the opening of the 1980 Hughes exhibition in Manchester, Fred Radcliffe, the Manchester University librarian, told me that he would like to buy my entire Hughes collection for the university. However, since he would be leaving Manchester shortly in order to take up the post of Cambridge University librarian, he felt that he should not push the sale through without the approval of his successor, Dr Pegg, who decided against the purchase.

15 The final outcome of protracted negotiations was that the appendix to *The Achievement of Ted Hughes* contained thirty uncollected poems, including seven unpublished poems, 'Crow Fails', 'Crow Compromises', four poems dropped from *Cave Birds* – 'The Advocate', 'Two Dreams in the Cell', 'Your Mother's Bones Wanted to Speak' and 'She is the Rock' – and 'Skin' from an early draft of *Adam and the Sacred Nine* (published 1979).

8 April 1981

We bought the house, subject, of course, to selling this house and the Mss. I have now met the new librarian at Manchester, Dr. Pegg, who is sceptical. Roy Davids' letter saying that he thought I had rather undervalued the collection had some impact on him. He has now asked for a fortnight in which to consult Brian Cox, Philip Larkin and various other people, before giving me a decision. But Fred Radcliffe, the librarian at Cambridge, has said that if Manchester does not take them he will, so I don't anticipate any problems there.

[11 April 1981]

Dear Keith,

Glad to hear you bought the house. Interested to note development of the sale of the MS.

Slightly re-ordered the sequence — by dates. Quest was written within a couple of days of 'Thrushes' in 1957 or very late 56 — the lawns in Thrushes being the lawn inside the Univ. Library at Cambridge. It was a technique of composition that began with Quest — followed by Thrushes — by Groom's Dream 6 months later, on Cape Cod, and then, with major adjustments to the production line tooling, with Pig & Pike & then, after a pause, (interval with other pieces) with Pibroch, & then, after collapses etc, with Howling of Wolves, Gnat-psalm, Skylarks, & then — by then a fairly successfully internalized series of reflexes — by the Crow Pieces — culminated in Water Playing,[16] & Life is trying to be Life.

I've never used the technique since, because it is a curious physical strain — and I felt it was also in danger of becoming exclusive. I wanted to develope the plant a bit more widely & flexibly, for a while, then see. But it is odd, in retrospect, that so many of the pieces that seem most special came out of it.

Also, never since, until just lately, have I concentrated solely on writing.

All this is strictly between you & me only, Keith.

I think I'll not write an introductory note to the pieces. Little Boys & The Seasons seems woefully poor. I don't share your liking for New World — except 4, 5 & 6. I thought Ante-penultimate line of 5 was "Aeons, aeons, later" — which I prefer. But leave it.

---

16 'How Water Began to Play', the penultimate poem in *Crow*.

The ex-Cave-Birds seem better than I remembered — in a bare way. The Lotus Elite belongs to Al Alvarez.

Odd feeling re-reading such things as Brother's Dream etc — I see what it is about much of my writing that repels people — again & again I seem to be starting some sort of fight for life that admits only rough & ready counters of language — a sort of makeshift language, as if I might have time later to verbalise the thing more adequately, which of course turns out to be quite impossible because — evidently — the important thing is the fight. And as soon as I come to the second wind and fresh shirt of revision, I'm drawn back into the fight, & I'm soon gasping for air again. Brother's Dream has that — and Quest, I suppose. Both of which I seem to have rewritten — in other poems — several times over.

The ugliness in all that, for me & I suppose for others, is that it is a fight — and not a talk, or a marriage, or an agape, or a sweet friendship, or a debate.

Reading my prose — or rather the odd bits of self-defence (just looking at Roberts & Giffords book) I've set down here & there — I feel the fight coming on. That prose somehow expresses very little of what I want to say, as if it were said only in the tension of a fight.

Strangest of all, I've realised, it is the same feeling I used to get reading my father's letters — there was something about them so vehement, so much in over-drive, that I often couldn't read them. (He was mostly a very silent man.) Is it possible to inherit a brain-rhythm? Very curious — in a biological way, to see it in myself so clearly, really as plain as a colour in a calf. The rest of me observes it with some dismay.

When I see it in such things as my exegesis of Orghast — in Anthony Smith's book[17] — I feel slightly horrified — I see what barren wastes of intellectualism — in the worst sense — lie in wait if I let that monster fly off with me. What a fury of ingenuities! The real relieving thing comes from elsewhere if it comes at all.

Apologies for this self-centred digression — I must feel you're interested, but this business of my father's temperament & my mother's lying side by side in me in some antagonistic arrangement has only occurred to me lately, as a way of explaining things. And as a novelty.

17 A. C. H. Smith's *Orghast at Persepolis* (Eyre Methuen, 1972), pp. 91–7, 132–3.

Leonard's first Gehenna book is a collection of birds — real birds — about 25. He'll do some drawings.[18]

We had an interesting time in Ireland — Nicholas caught two very big pike 22½ & 23½ lbs. I caught one 22 lbs — biggest I ever caught. No salmon — the rivers are near enough cleaned out. Just got the beginning of the trout — and probably the last of the best — the last, because Ireland has gone mad with EEC grants to drain the land, which they do by taking the river beds down 14 or more feet, in a straight clean ditch, so the water sluices out all the insect life, & the fish vanish. They now have so many great diggers, & so many drainage experts, & experienced drain-cutters, & so much unemployment, that there's no way the army will be stopped till every waterway in Ireland has been reduced to a straight clean shute [sic]. Once they built great useless walls, for employment. Now they dig deep mostly useless drains. 200 years for a drain to remake itself as a river, properly, I read.

Keep well   Ted

26 April 1981

Melissa and I start a six-week course on Sylvia in Manchester on Thursday, so I've been rereading all her accessible poems – for the first time, systematically, in about ten years. I really think she must be the best woman poet ever. But I'm not so keen now on those famous *Ariel* poems: 'Lady Lazarus', 'Daddy', etc. Plenty of "crackling energy" indeed, but what is the good of that if you can't handle it, if it blows your mind?

I had read Hugh Kenner's essay 'Sincerity Kills' (in Lane, ed. Sylvia Plath: New Views on the Poetry, Johns Hopkins University Press, 1979), where Kenner wrote:

> We can say that when furies lurk just beyond the rim of consciousness there is paramount danger in improvising. All the formal defences are down. For that had been a final use of the intricate formalisms: they detained her mind upon the plane of craft, and so long as it was detained there, it did not slip toward what beckoned it.

In the Ariel poems, he claimed,

> She was somewhere on the far side of sanity, teasing herself with the thrill of courting extinction, as though on a high window ledge. Such

---

18   A Primer of Birds.

spectacles gather crowds and win plaudits for "honesty" from critics who should know better.

Have you read Hugh Kenner's essay on her 'Sincerity Kills'? I enclose a photocopy of the last three pages. Weren't you saying something similar yourself when you said that the poet's response to the horror is to 'retreat from it and sing to it'? Isn't there some truth in Kenner's claim that the earlier poems are strategies for survival, whereas in those last poems she was simply letting herself drop into it, be possessed by it?

Also I've been struck, at this reading for the first time, how remarkably few poems there are about sex or sexual love – how relatively few sexual images even – for someone so preoccupied with her body and feelings, with the other primal experiences such as birth and death, with the body/mind split, and for someone so keen on Lawrence. One would have expected the Elizabethan/Lawrencean idea of coition as a 'little death' to have interested her, and the larger idea of good sex as healing and respiritualizing – as atonement. Or is sex always for her – poetically – the snake in the grass, the loss of innocence and purity. Or a see-saw of submission and dominance . . . Did you do any more of those poems about Sylvia?[19] Is there to be a whole sequence or book?

[23 May 1981]

Dear Keith,

I think I dated all the poems I could.

Kenner is consistent — higher-minded than any of us — loyal to a poetics that would bring about an Ice-age if he were Lord of the Universe — which his tone sometimes suggests he might be. His principles set in the fifties, O.K. for some.

He's probably perceptive about some writers who suit his temperament.

But don't follow him too closely on the 'frigidity of S.P.' trail. After all, what if he's wrong? (Maybe that never occurs to him — many silent classes have polished his confidence) Lots of people didn't like her — for no reason at all. I never knew anybody else who got poison pen letters from complete strangers. And it seems to go on after her death.

Where does the 'lack of sexual imagery' trail lead?

If only I can get her notebooks etc published, you'd probably

---

19 In 1980 Ted had published 'The Earthenware Head' and 'You Hated Spain', the earliest poems destined for *Birthday Letters*.

get a better idea of her. The letters merely mislead. And the poems have been overlaid with other people's fantasy visions of her.

Kenner seems to me simply wrong about The Colossus. The metrics of those poems expresses limbo — immobility of fear — inability to come to grips with the real self. If a stasis of that sort, which she experienced as psychic paralysis, is a control of 'dangerous forces' — well, he can be said to be right. But he doesn't mean that.

Ariel — March–Nov. 62 — is the diary of her coming to grips with & inheriting this 'real self'. It isn't the record of a 'breakdown'. Growing up brought her to it — having children etc, + confronting the events of 1962 (and mastering them completely). (After all, in 1960, she was only 18 months out of College — nearly all the Colossus poems were written while she was still a student or teacher & the rest within the first year after.)

You know Goethe's remark about the labour & difficulty of actually laying claim to what we have inherited — and you know how few people attempt it, how few even know they need to make the effort, how some go through Primal Screams to find it etc. Well, Ariel is her record of her experience of it — of coming into possession of the self she'd been afraid of (for good reasons).

The developed strategies of the verse were invented at need, to deal with the unique self-revelations — revelations of herself to herself (only incidentally to us). You suggest you find much of it a language of disintegration. I see it as footwork & dexterity — the honesty (nakedness) to meet the matter on its own terms, & the brave will to master it — which she did.

It's a process of 'integration' start to finish. By Dec. 62 she was quite a changed person — greatly matured and a 'big' personality. In Dec/Jan she stopped writing (no poems really from early December to late January) & set up a new home, a new circle of friends, & a new life — and had almost completely repaired her relationship to me. She had set the Ariel poems behind her as 'a-Hell-of-a-necessary phase'.

Those poems enact a weird fusion & identity with the material & simultaneously take control of it, & possession of it. That's a hypnotic technique (which Crowley used to like to demonstrate)[20]

20 Aleister Crowley (1875 –1947), also known as both Frater Perdurabo and The Great Beast, was an

— imitating somebody, exactly, until, at some imperceptible point, the initiative passes to you, & they begin to imitate you, & can then be controlled — it's the fundamental dynamics of the artistic process, but in literature nowhere so naked as those Ariel poems, which are all little dramas. More like some painting, or music, than any other poetry.

So you see I read those Ariel poems as a climb — not a fall. A climb to a precarious foothold, as it turned out.[21]

But she was knocked off again by pure unlucky combination of accidents. No doubt that year exhausted her emotionally. The housemaking etc, the 62/63 snow & cold, the 2 kids exhausted her physically. Flu knocked her lower. Stirrers & troublemakers complicated our getting together again, in no small way. Then on Jan 23rd — I think — The Bell Jar came out — which you can guess was traumatic for her — to have all that suddenly at large. But the key factor, maybe, was that her doctor prescribed, for pep up, a drug that her U.S. doctors knew — but her English doctor didn't — induced cyclic suicidal depression in her. She was allergic to it. Probably she didn't recognise the trade name. She was aware of its effects, which lasted about 3 hours between the old pill wearing off, & the new one taking effect. Just time enough.

The group of poems she wrote in those last days record the exhaustion & resignation — and the precariously-held-off solution — always very close when she touched bottom physically.

I've been trying to find the quote in Jung where he describes the most dangerous moment of all, in any episode of psychic disturbance — it is the moment of emerging from it, after having conquered it — when the sufferer has turned her back on it — steps out of it & away — at that moment it gathers all its energy and makes a last all-out attack (which, as he says, very often proves to be fatal, because the victim has lowered her defences). If that can be weathered, he says, the episode is usually over. Relevant.

I tell you all this to qualify your attitude to the notion of her as a

influential English occultist, mystic and ceremonial magician who founded the religious philosophy of Thelema.

21 At this stage Hughes was still vociferously defending his interpretation of his own role in relation to Plath as that of Prospero releasing Ariel (Plath's 'real self') from the cloven pine of her formalism. In the chapter 'From Prospero to Orpheus' in *The Laughter of Foxes* I demonstrate how, in everything he subsequently wrote on Plath, including *Birthday Letters*, Hughes gradually moved towards Kenner's views.

young woman hurtling to disintegration shedding rags of poetry —
leaping into Aetna & bursting into flames as she fell.

Ariel poems are about successful 'integration' — violent
inheriting of a violent temperament.

The first sign of disintegration — in a writer — is that the
writing loses the unique stamp of his/her character, & loses its
inner light.

Mustn't underestimate her humour either.

The real question is — what would be the interpretation of
those poems if she hadn't died, if she'd gone on to write something
marvellous in a different way. As those very last poems suggest she
was about to do. They could only have been read as the scenes of a
victorious battle for so-called 'self-integration'. The whole accent
of subsequent commentary would have been different. The
interpretation generally given is a pure fantasy — induced by her
death, which was an accident (it could have happened at any
moment between 51 & 63, if she'd got physically low enough — just
as it could happen to thousands who never show a symptom,) and
not at all essential to the poems — except as one latent factor in her
mythology.

There were other factors, just as dominant in their phase. The
suicide factor, however, only needed a phase of 3 hours to remove
all other factors from the succession & seize the crown for itself.

It is more interesting to read Ariel as a series of dramas of
integration — though sometimes of diabolical material — but no
more diabolical than most women would become aware of in her
situation.

Nobody seems to have tried this approach, that I know of.
Perhaps it's less interesting.

I haven't seen the Irish book about me.[22] The Gifford Roberts
book prints 75 poems complete (4/5 of Cave Birds inc) — so there's
been difficulties there.

Just seen Egbert's chapter — (I'm now feeling I have to check
everything, after the G/R book nearly got away with the bulk of my

---

22 Stuart Hirschberg, *Myth in the Poetry of Ted Hughes* (Wolfhound Press, 1981).

Selected Poems)[23] I must say I don't much like this writer Ted Hughes, that Egbert goes on about. Is it really like that?[24]

Keep well   Ted

6th Oct 81

Dear Keith.

Roy's valuation was probably high, but since he's quadrupled the average price of manuscripts in the last three years, while Rota during all their time had never managed to up the market one bit, it may be that Rota's valuation is low. If you watch sales, you'll see that Sotheby's estimates are always on the low side. Which doesn't alter the fact that your manuscripts are only worth at the moment what you can get for them. But when I see one page of The Revolt Of Islam going for twelve thousand pounds etc, —! it makes you think.[25]

I can't remember about Gavin Robbins' prints and book — I doubt if he can either. He made it as a project on his Art course, so there was never actually a publication date. It's just that at some point we began to sell them. Even the sale was a total fiasco — I've no idea where most of them went, or how they went. Olwyn might have a record of when she sold the first — which would be the closest publication date. There was no other publication date, or date that could be called that. Maybe she could help you with price too. I daresay your copy — March 69, was a little after some of them

23 'Hughes took our royalties in permission fees, and when Ted Hughes: A Critical Study went out of print we each received from Faber a royalty statement of minus £11. Thus are academics often financially rewarded. Fortunately the real rewards lie elsewhere' (Terry Gifford, Ted Hughes, Routledge, 2009, p. xii). When Gifford and Roberts explained the situation to Hughes (who had seen the book before publication), he replied (30 May 1981):

I really think Fabers are a little to blame for our dilemma... Since it was their fault — and I think it was — that your book became my selected poems more or less, I had expected them to compensate you in some way for your work.

24 Ekbert Faas had contributed 'Chapters of a shared mythology: Sylvia Plath and Ted Hughes' to The Achievement of Ted Hughes.

25 Melissa and I had now been married for some months, and were still living in my tiny cottage. I was increasingly anxious to sell my manuscripts. Both Manchester and Cambridge having backed out, Roy Davids had tried to find a buyer through Sotheby's without success. Ted had suggested that we approach his old college, Pembroke, Cambridge, but this also drew a blank. In the event I avoided selling my Hughes material by selling my D. H. Lawrence first editions to Birmingham University library instead.

had been sold, though I'm not sure. I sold very few of the books. I don't know what Gavin Robbins did with his.[26]

Eric White (3 Hopping Lane, London N.1. 2NU) used to arrange the literary events at the Little Missenden Festival. He may still have all his files concerning that (it still goes on, and I think he's still involved, though he had a slight stroke last year and has been out of action a while). If he doesn't have a programme (if he does, he might sell it), he probably knows who would be likely to have one. I believe the woman who was the driving force of the whole thing recently died. Little Missenden is in Herts or Bucks, I'm not sure.[27]

Morrigu Tapir exists in about fifteen copies now, perhaps two or three more. But Nicky was dissatisfied with the typeface (he set it in an old face, I think), so the official project was abandoned — he said postponed till it could be done properly, but now he thinks better leave it, and do no more. So the fifteen are both the proofs and the only ones there are. He set it up with his girlfriend — more to amuse themselves than as an object for sale. The epigraph is his Letter From Iceland.[28]

---

26 Ted and Olwyn were both now helping me to gather information for my bibliography. The Gavin Robbins prints are *Gravestones* (1967), a set of six splendid linocut broadsides: 'Theology', 'Fern', 'Still Life', 'Thistles', 'As Woman's Weeping' and 'Bowled Over'. The following year the same set was published in book form by Bartholomew Books/Exeter College of Art as *Poems: Ted Hughes Linocuts: Gavin Robbins*, in an edition of 300. In 1969 Robbins added a seventh broadside, 'I Said Goodbye to Earth'. All the prints and books were signed by Ted.

27 Hughes had written five poems at the request of Pat Harrison, a teacher in Little Missenden. She assigned children to read them at the Festival. Richard Drakeford provided some interlude music. The texts were to have been published in the Festival Programme, but arrived too late, and were first published as *Five Autumn Songs for Children's Voices* (Richard Gilbertson, 1968).

28 *Tapir's Saga*. Ted and Carol had given us a copy of this as a wedding present. On the back Ted had written:

What can dog-eared doggerel add
To plus & plus, that they may live
Among the common good & bad
Summa cum superlative?

For Melissa's nuptial wishes
A fecundity
Of fluorescent fishes.

For Keith the key
To the honey crop
Of the honey bee.

And what subtract
To make the yes
Of the wedded fact
Greater not less?   (continued on p. 113)

You should see his latest thing. Not a Morrigu publication, because he printed it on commission for the Farms For City Children, and handed the whole lot to the couple who run that: Mike and Clare Morpurgo, Langlands, Nethercott, Iddesleigh, Devon. It's a poem about Cows (deadly drawing of South Devons by me). There are 26 lettered copies, in a folder, and fifty numbered not in a folder. Fabriano paper (Jap handmade mulberry & rag tissue overlays the copy in the folder). They will be sold to raise funds, at a Fundraising party in London in December. He hadn't fixed a price, when we handed them over. It's a nice broadside.[29] That and Visitation are Nick's favourites Now he's sick of broadsides. He's going to do small booklets etc, varied experiments. But he's keener than ever on the printing. Leonard thinks he's good — says all his problems would be solved if only Nicky would do the printing for the new Gehenna he's set up at Lurley.

Leonard's first new Gehenna book is printed. Exceedingly handsome — thirty birds. A few woodcuts. Called A Primer of Birds — just odd pieces, nothing special. Staggeringly expensive, I expect. (His early books — even reprints of well-known things, have increased in value — in catalogues — many hundred percent, and this is what justifies to his mind putting a good price on them to start with.[30]

The river poems ooze along. James McGibbon is keen to sell them in a package deal — which will be better than nothing if we can't get the Observer to do them magnificently, which they are again interested in doing. Meanwhile, I try to add a bit of variety.

All the best to you both. Good luck with the houses.

Yours   Ted

Overleaf – loaded with 'no'
By geyser steam & glacial snow
Into the bleak & boreal glow
Two scapegoats go.

Melissa means 'honey bee'.
29 'Cows', Collected Poems, p. 619.
30 A Primer of Birds sold at £450 for the 25 special copies, and £175 for the remaining 225. In 2010 used copies fetched £600–800 for the ordinary copies, and £1,000–2,000 for the special copies.

21 October 1981

I am now at last getting back to work on the bibliography . . . Would you be willing to have a section, an appendix, of Juvenilia at the end of the bibliography? The things I should like to include would be:

1. The three poems (enclosed) from a school exercise book which belongs to Mrs Fisher.

2. All the poems published in the *Don and Dearne* (6 poems) and one prose piece, 'Harvesting'.

3. Your first Cambridge poem 'The Little Boys and the Seasons'.

4. 'The Court Tumbler and Satirist'. This appeared in some Cambridge publication between 1952 and 1954 but I have been unable to trace it.[31] Any ideas?

5. 'The Woman with such High Heels She Looked Dangerous'.

6. 'Scene Without an Act'

7. 'The Drowned Woman'

8. 'Bartholomew Pygge Esq.'

9. 'O'Kelly's Angel'

That's all. I can send you photocopies of any of these.[32]

Oct 24, 81

Dear Keith,

I probably do have a Grecourt Review somewhere. Is there any particular reason you want it, or are you wanting to purchase a copy. I doubt if I've more than one, and it might take some finding.

I'd prefer to let that Juvenilia lie where it lies. My mistakes are turning to noisy hounds on all sides. It really is quite worrying. Why can't they just forget and be forgotten, like most people's. I wish it were in your power to destroy all trace of them, because I'd ask you to do it. So I'd be grateful if you could let all that sink deeper than did ever plummet sound etc

You ask me about writing a note for the bibliography: I would prefer not to, Keith. I'm just resigning from the curatorship of Sylvia's mausoleum, after eighteen years loyal service, and I'd hate to take up the uniform for my own.

I had no dealings with the BBC till some time in 1956, when I did some readings of Hopkins for Carne-Ross, and one or two pieces of my own, but I don't think any of it was ever used. I was

31 *Poetry from Cambridge 1952–4*, ed. Karl Miller (Fantasy Press, 1955).

32 3–7 are in *Collected Poems*; 9 is in *Difficulties of a Bridegroom*; 8, Hughes' first published story, was in *Granta*, 4 May 1957; 1 and 2 remain unpublished.

just doing a test run — hoping to get some employment as a reader. Then I went off to the States (and soon after so did he.) When I came back at the end of 59, I started doing odd things for Schools Programmes etc — but I can't remember the dates, and I kept no trace of them.[33]

Leonard's Bird Book is a very pretty book physically — a very pretty price too, I can tell you. They come in two costings — Regal, and Princely. They will be sold in England through Holga Brautsch (Is that how it's spelled?) The German who runs the Gallery in Hereford Street (no. 9). Holger Braasch, Leinster Fine Arts. I think it's W.11. They're not signed yet. Official date is end of next week I think.

It's the first hand-printed book Gehenna have done with damped paper — and I think the first hand-printed book. It's the first book of Gehenna in Albion. So if it goes the way of the other Gehenna books, it's spontaneous alchemy. Buy 3.

I'm just going to meet the Japanese No actor who worked with Peter Brook — still does I think.[34] He wants to conflate three No plays — all concerning Ono no Komache the 9th Century Jap poetess in her old age or ghost-hood — into a performance for Irene Worth, and he thinks I might have a clue.

　　Love to Melissa,
　　　keep well　Ted

28 October 1981

Sure, we'll forget about Juvenilia, and those pieces will remain safely tucked away in my file.

I'd certainly like to buy copies of the *Grecourt Review* for my collection, but that was not the main reason for asking about it. I desperately need the information for section C of the Bibliography – it's the only gap in that section that I'm aware of. My information is that the GR published at least two of your poems: 'Groom's Dream' sometime in the last three months of 1957 and 'Roosting Hawk' (sic) in May 1959. But I haven't yet been able to trace either. I need accurate information about what they published in exactly what issues

---

33 The earliest broadcasts I traced were a reading of 'The Martyrdom of Bishop Farrar' in *The Poet's Voice*, broadcast 14 April 1957, and a reading of six poems to be collected in *Lupercal* on 27 August 1958, both on the BBC Third Programme.
34 Katsuhiro Oida.

on what pages, but I also need photocopies of the poems to see if they differ textually from later printings in each case.[35]

28th Dec 81

Dear Keith,

Happy New Year to Melissa and yourself.

Are you surviving the weather at all? Imagine the worse places. Nick and I spent eight days in Ireland earlier on. The first four were the coldest over there recorded this century. The last four were the windiest. We saw fish actually blown out of the lake. Lifted in the wave and the wave ripped off and blown ashore. I would never have believed it.

Spent the best (worst) part of this year involved in the coils of the Plath journals — what a bad business. Trying to cut the text across the Atlantic. It verged on Legal Force, finally. But I could not have won my last point or two, and I didn't want to pay for Dial's advertising. So there it is, a mangled mess. The Editorial comments are not too good, in my opinion. Since there will have to be an English Edition now, we're having to re-edit it as we should have edited it in the first place. I wrote a poor introductory note for the U.S. edition. I'm trying to go one or two better for the English — difficulty is maintaining the right temperature for the operation. And the right spacing for the words. But the whole book provides what has been lacking: a real image of her, the globe of all angles.

My own compositions have been in hibernation now for pretty well a year.

Just to bring everything home together, (with all the other things that have either culminated, or come to an end this year) I made a reselected poems, and I shall send the corrected proof off to Faber tomorrow. I made it quite full — a book for a reader, perhaps. Rather than my nine-times distilled drop. It's a mistake, I think, to write for this audience (Season Songs) or that audience (Elmet) or that other (Cave Birds). It's one of the temptations of writing for a living. I'm in the middle of another. In the end it's like a charity match.

Are you still looking for a new house?

Keep well   Ted

35 The *Grecourt Review* was an undergraduate publication at Smith College, Northampton, Massachusetts, where Sylvia had taught 1957–8.

1982

Hughes wrote *The Great Irish Pike* and several poems for the Morrigu Press. He reviewed Glyn Hughes' *Where I Used to Play on the Green*. In October he gave a reading at the Cheltenham Literature Festival. In letters written to Bishop Ross Hook in November Hughes claimed that his own poetry was 'secular' and that poetry should offer an alternative to organized religion. In April Dr Jane V. Anderson, a psychiatrist, brought an action for defamation against Avco Embassy Pictures Corp. and Edward James Hughes, claiming that the 1979 film of Plath's novel *The Bell Jar* had depicted her as a lesbian. Hughes feared bankruptcy, since he and the other nine defendants were being sued for six million dollars.

19 January 1982

Dear Ted

We were in Cambridge for the weekend and called on Olwyn. She seemed in good spirits. She showed us the *Primer of Birds* and the *New Selected Poems* proofs and your introduction to Sylvia's Journals.

I ordered a *Primer* from Leonard when you first told me it was printed, but heard nothing. The when you said it was being distributed by the Leinster Gallery I ordered from there. Now Olwyn says they are not handling it after all – they said they knew nothing about it. Do you have any spare copies? I really need one of each binding.

Your selection looks pretty good, except that I should have liked to see a few more *Season Songs*, perhaps in place of some of the early poems.

Several years ago you offered to sell me your copy of *Pike*.[1] Can't remember why I didn't take it. Is it still for sale? It's the only A item I don't have. I expect to hand the bibliography over to Mansell in about a fortnight. Pity Murray is no longer there.

No progress yet with either house or mss.

25th Jan. 82

Dear Keith,

Olwyn tells me you're both looking well.

Leonard's Primer of Birds is to be distributed by Phaedon [sic] — evidently that is now settled (just), but I don't know whom you should contact. Ring them up & run him down.

Yes, I'm regretting not having taken out quite a few of those earlier pieces. I could have made it waterproof.

---

1 Woodcut by Robert Bermelin. 150 copies were printed by the Gehenna Press in 1959.

My copies of Pike are distributed 1 to N., 1 to F. & 1 to Carol. But odd copies are about — I met somebody who'd slept at a friend's where there was one over the bed. I gave away about a dozen — maybe more. Heedless days!

Sorry to hear about the house hold-up, & the wretched M.SS.

Love to Melissa

Keep well   Ted

7ᵗʰ June [1982]

Dear Keith,

Thank you for sending the Antipodean letter.²

Here's a note from Leonard. I thought the Exhibition was in Cork St. I don't have a copy or I'd Xerox it myself — Leonard might have difficulties getting it to a machine. Pester him.³

He says — by all means use something of his for the cover. Just let him know which piece you want.⁴

'Stare-boned' touches on starling yes — wretched mass-bird — as well as 'sticking out' etc.⁵

Great moment for gardens, just on the brink of drought, here. No rain since 1ˢᵗ week in April.

Give us a ring when you come down this way.

Love to Melissa   Ted

28ᵗʰ July 82

Dear Keith,

I've looked everywhere for that poem you sent me, about the salmon, which I'd put with my copy — corrected. It's vanished. Under the mountain of paper. Could you send me another copy quite soon — the moment I see it, I'll recall the changes.⁶

Keep well. Love to Melissa. Ted

2 This was a letter from an Australian reader in appreciation of *The Art of Ted Hughes*, which I thought Ted would like to see.
3 I was probably seeking a copy of the catalogue of the Baskin exhibition at the Royal Watercolour Society Galleries in London in 1962, for which Ted had written an introduction.
4 I used a photograph of Leonard's relief of Ted with a crow and a pike for the cover of *The Achievement of Ted Hughes*.
5 I had asked whether 'stare' in 'stare-boned' ('The Interrogator') meant 'starling'.
6 Ted had given me permission to print an unpublished poem addressed to a salmon, 'While the high-breasted, the halved world', from an early draft of *Gaudete*, but had asked me to send it to him for revision first. See *The Achievement of Ted Hughes*, pp. 309–10.

20th Oct 82

Dear Keith & Melissa,

It was nice to see you the other night.[7] Pity you couldn't come along with us. We went back to Alan Hancock's house & had a pleasant easy sit around for a couple of hours — tasty food, & were left alone (the Cheltenham team were too fagged to harry us). You would have appreciated Hancock's Lawrence collection — every published thing, an entire section of bookcase in the living room (walled with books) which is evidently continued below in the basement by as much again. But I expect you've seen it.

You were both looking well on marriage, I might say.

For some reason, the event was a great strain. I think it's Festivals. The last I remember the same was Ilkley, which unbalanced my nervous system (heart-beat etc) for nearly two years. I must be the wrong sort of budgerigar for those grand chorales. I've told myself I shall never read in public again.

I wanted to read some other River pieces. I mis-timed, as always.[8] I wanted to read one or two Moortown pieces as well. I intended to read the enclosed — no piece ever dragged me closer in, or wasted more paper. It was like screw jammed in my skull — & the top twisted off.[9]

Nicholas had a dream-time in Africa — he's come back love-sick for the place. He walked all over Kenya, fished everywhere, in rivers, the sea, & the big lakes, fished with the blacks. He's trying to fix up an Oxford Research Project (i.e. University Cash Backing) to analyse the feeding pattern of Nile Perch in Lake Victoria. He got hooked on Nile perch. After being extinct in the Lake for aeons, they were reintroduced accidentally ten years ago. All the species that have evolved in their absence are now having to take account. At the moment there's a boom of Nile Perch, & a crash of everything else. Interesting moment for a zoologist. And for an angler. The lake is jammed with fish up to 300 lbs. Nicky's found the papers of all the work that's been done on them so far. So if his project comes off, I shall go with him as consultant Anthropologist/cook & complainer. That would be next summer.

---

7 We had attended Ted's reading at the Cheltenham Literature Festival on the 16th. Alan Hancox was the director of the Festival.
8 Since Ted was sharing the platform with Seamus Heaney, he had only half his accustomed reading time.
9 'The Gulkana River', published as 'The Gulkana'.

I've gone over the river pieces, knocked out all I'm not sure about, rewritten some, added some new ones (like the enclosed). 45 in all. The photographs are done too. The book has to come out (say the Gas Board, who are subsidising it) by next summer.

Under the North Star won an International Prize — awarded in Italy.

All this sharing of title pages is going to be very bad for my PLR future. In future I'm going to keep my books to myself. So that's two pages of talk about me, and I haven't thanked you for the Lawrence books — which at last have got Carol reading Lawrence.[10]

Love to you both. Ted

I'll call on you in November. I'll ring first.

Your letter's just come.

The weekend we shall be up there is November 27th. I hope to be fairly free because I'm withdrawing a little from Arvon.

Monday 29th Nov. [1982]

Dear Keith & Melissa,

It was nice to see you on Friday. Now I can imagine you there in perfect focus.[11]

Here's an item for the list. It's the piece Barry [Barrie] Cooke used in his set of Lithographs.[12] Also Barry's flyer.

There are two poems in Alan Brownjohn's latest Poetry Book Supplement — New Year. Two of the river pieces — one cancelled,[13] the other a slightly earlier than final version (The Cormorant).

Keep well. Stock in some food. 5 ft of snow fell on the Upper Loire over the weekend.

Love Ted

10 One of these would have been The Complete Short Novels, which Melissa and I had just edited for the Penguin English Library. The other may have been my edition of Sons and Lovers in the same series.
11 We had moved into our new house at Wiswell, near Clitheroe, in March.
12 The Great Irish Pike (1982) contains a reproduction of a section of Hughes' holograph of the poem.
13 'Madly Singing in the Mountains', in Alan Brownjohn, ed., New Year Poetry Supplement (Poetry Book Society, 1982).

1. Ted's aunt Hilda Farrar with his parents, Bill and Edith Hughes, at their home, The Beacon at Heptonstall Slack. © Estate of Ted Hughes. 'This house has been far out at sea all night' (from the poem 'Wind', 1955).

2. Lumb Bank, Heptonstall. Now the northern centre of the Arvon Foundation.© Eddie Jacob.

3. On 24 June 1960 Sylvia Plath wrote: 'Last night Ted and I went to a cocktail party at Faber & Faber, given for W. H. Auden. . . . There Ted stood, flanked by T. S. Eliot, W. H. Auden, Louis MacNeice and Stephen Spender, having his photograph taken. "Three generations of Faber poets there", Charles [Monteith] observed. "Wonderful!" Of course, I was immensely proud. Ted looked very at home among the great.' [*Letters Home*, 386]. © Mark Gerson/National Portrait Gallery. When Mark Gerson asked Eliot to assemble the poets, Eliot called out 'Ducdame, ducdame, ducdame', which, according to Jaques in *As You Like It*, is 'a Greek invocation to call fools into a circle'.

4. 1969. 'A picture Philip Larkin took, with delayed exposure, of himself, Richard Murphy, Douglas Dunn & me, in a rural churchyard in East Yorks. It's at a slight distance, but amusing.' © Estate of Philip Larkin.

5. 'I'm sending Arren the skull of the first badger I ever skinned – about 1967 (I've got a photo somewhere of me skinning it).' © Estate of Ted Hughes.

6. Keith Sagar reading 'Climbing into Heptonstall' to the conference members in 1980. © Joanny Moulin. 'The Tourist Guide, with his Group, in the ring of horizons, Looked down on to Hebden'.

7. Ted Hughes with Keith and Melissa Sagar at their wedding in June 1981. © Carol Hughes.

8. Birthday greetings sent to Ted Hughes from the first International Hughes Conference. Among the signatories are Keith Sagar, Fred Rue Jacobs, Neil Roberts, Len Scigaj, Mike Sweeting, Craig Robinson, Terry Gifford, Shusha, Graham Bradshaw, Annie Schofield, Derek Hyatt, Steve Tabor, Ekbert Faas and Keith Cushman.

9. Ted proudly displaying a local salmon catch in the late seventies. © Carol Hughes.

10. With his letter of 14 November 1983 Hughes enclosed this photograph. He had written on the back: 'Hughes with his Nile Perch – 104 lbs. Ulugi Beach, Rusinga Island, Lake Victoria, August 1983. That's our coloured canoe.' © Estate of Nicholas Hughes.

11. A page from Hughes' letter of 18 September 1990.

12. Drawing by Michael Daley of Shakespeare, the Goddess and the Boar, which accompanied a review of *Shakespeare and the Goddess of Complete Being* in *The Independent*, 11 April 1992. © Michael Daley.

13. Hughes at Court Green with Leonard Baskin, April 1998.
© Estate of Ted Hughes.

1983

Hughes spent the first three months writing 'The Hanged Man and the Dragonfly', his tribute to Leonard Baskin. In the spring he worked on *Flowers and Insects*. In August he visited Nicholas on an island on Lake Victoria, followed by a fishing trip to Scotland, and attended the International Festival of Authors in Toronto. He resumed work on 'Complete Lives and Songs of The Crow'. Hughes was instrumental in forming the Torridge Action Group to combat the discharge of raw sewage into the Torridge Estuary at Bideford.

[pm 4 January 1983]

Dear Keith & Melissa,
    Happy New Year
      love from   Ted & Carol

On the verso is a fair copy of 'Honey Bees', later published in What is the Truth? *(1984).*

13th Jan 83

Dear Keith,

I meant to ask you two things — when it's convenient could you let me have a copy of the Dante Sestina — Dan Huws' version in that Botolph Review. I want to see if it's as outstanding as I remember it.[1]

Also, what is the first line (so I can look it up) of that Lawrence Poem about apples being roses — with the line 'and the lily, the considerable lily'.[2]

No hurry.

Yes, it's a very early year for all the sproutlings down here. I'm afraid they'll be surprised. What's happened to the mini Ice-Age, promised by the Chinese (and U.S.) astronomers, the 320 year cycle freeze-up, corresponding to the planetary magnetic concentrations

---

1 'Dante Canzone' was not in the St. *Botolph's Review*, but in *Chequer*, 7 (November 1954). Daniel Huws writes in a letter to me: 'He was very loyal to that translation. It was at his insistence that I included it as a sort of tail-piece in *The Quarry*, Faber, 1999.'
2 Hughes is here conflating two poems. The poem 'about apples being roses' is 'Grapes'. But the 'considerable lily' occurs in 'Leaves of Grass, Flowers of Grass'.

this last month? Is it on its way? They promised 'Abnormally severe winters for the rest of our lifetimes'.

How lightly people use that Pantechnicon word 'lifetime'!
love to Melissa   Ted

25 March 83

Dear Keith and Melissa,

Thanks for the two books. I'm amazed at your industry. Very handsome books physically.[3] The collection of poems seems strange to me — strange, I suppose, in that I would never have put together just these. In fact, they make a definite, consistent effect — a real book in their own little way. But perhaps it was a mistake to include 'Little Boys & The Seasons'. I wrote 'Song' in 1949 — then nothing till that piece in 1954. Five years in which I tried constantly to write. What happened to me? Then all I could come up with was Little Boys & the Seasons!

I'm not sure about 'Quest' either. I wrote that sitting on the bed in Eltisley Avenue one afternoon — and the following afternoon, writing in the same way, wrote Thrushes, which seems to me like a piece from a different brain.

I don't know how indulgent one ought to be to one's gaffes & wrong starts. There's a Jewish proverb Leonard is always quoting to me, "Never show a fool half-work" — i.e. half-finished work.

But I can't believe it's good to be so anxious about things, either.

Printing Errors:

Anecdote: 5th line from end 'where' should be 'were'. 3rd line from end — delete the 'a'.

Crow Compromises: 'leaves' should be 'loaves' — as you spotted.

Songs against the white owl Should be 'Song etc'

Snow Song: 'a new life' should be 'a new knife' — unless I made a change I've forgotten. 5th line from end — 'Herding' should be 'Flocking' — I avoided that word, can you imagine, because it was too richly apt — what Puritan idiocy! And, not tentative enough!

---

3 The books were The Achievement of Ted Hughes, and Keith Sagar and Stephen Tabor, eds., Ted Hughes: A Bibliography 1946–1980 (Mansell, 1983).

Crow's Song about God: lamp-post (o missing) 10th line from end, 'As he mutters' should be 'As He mutters'. Distinction between Cap and Lower Case carries all the argument there.
The Advocate — 2nd line, 'blood-edged'.

I must re-write The Bear, & Song About God is worth salvaging.

The River is all set up — though we still haven't settled a contract. Peter is wanting more cash, naturally. But unfortunately — and naturally — the publishers are presenting my own share as the only adjustable figure. So that's become delicate.

I've finished with these huge tomes that won't go on a shelf, & that booksellers hate & refuse to give room to — after that first little honeymoon. Remains of Elmet & Cave Birds have become like the Okapi in the 19th Century — to be found only in native legends & Hunter's memoirs.

Just one more — which is a Children's Book (the little Morrigu poems are from it) & so will go on the Children's shelf, which is big. I expect I told you about it 'What Is The Truth?" — good Tolstoyan title. Most wonderful (to my eyes) illustrations by Reg Lloyd — painter & general wheeler & dealer in Bideford. Absolutely perfect for the book. Reg is designing the book too — a jigsaw of illustrations & text.

The three months I should have spent on that text, though, I've spent writing the Introduction to Leonard's complete collection of prints — over 800 of them.[4]

I've sweated blood — as never. Imagine trying to make Leonard happy — and yet say what one means! I got to grappling with God knows what — yet I do think it's true. True about the real & best thing in his work. But I wrote it dead against the conviction that nothing can be said about visual art — (or about music) — that isn't simply aesthetic opinion. How do you get a reader to swallow twenty odd pages of opinion — which also has to be a monumental eulogy of the subject, almost a funeral speech? I think my opinion is true — but I know it's only opinion — the whole thing is a hypothesis. So the first problem was discovering what I really thought about Leonard's productive machinery — and the second was finding a <u>tone</u> that didn't revolt me. Anyway, there it is. A wreath. Leonard & Lisa are going back to the States — selling

---

4 'The Hanged Man and the Dragonfly', in *Winter Pollen*.

their home here. It's in Country Life this month — £175,000. I shall miss Leonard.

Are you both well — watching your garden reveal itself? Nicholas' research expedition into the Nile Perch on Lake Victoria is now a (one-man) University Project — so he's looking for sponsors. He needs about £2,000.

Carol sends her love — me too.   Ted

11 April 1983

Dear Ted

I've just had an aggrieved letter from Leonard about the book jackets. I wrote to him at least twice in the early part of last year asking for permission to use them both. He never replied. Had he done so, I could have tried to negotiate a fee with the publishers . . . The publishers were getting upset because they couldn't get started on jacket design without Leonard's permission. So in desperation I wrote to you asking you if you could get Leonard to give us the go-ahead. Your next letter (7 June 1982) enclosed a note from him in which he apologized for not answering my letters, but never mentioned the jackets. However, your covering letter said 'He says – by all means use something of his for the cover'. I took this to mean for each cover, and rang the publishers at once . . .

I suppose what he felt must have added insult to injury was that he disliked the jacket design on The Achievement so much. A pity. Everyone else seems to like it.

12th April [1983]

Dear Keith,

Please don't let Leonard's letter un-horse you even for a moment. I'm absolutely certain it was exactly as you said — I assumed it was, but you've confirmed it was even more so & in more thorough detail than I'd assumed. The odd thing was — the book with the plaque replica doesn't make any acknowledge-ment, the Phoenix does.[5] I'm sure if you'd managed to get a copy to him very early, he'd have been happy enough, because such things only bother him <u>on principle</u>. And he simply couldn't remember anything about it — he forgets everything of that sort instantly. And I'm no better. He likes writing outraged letters — who doesn't! Olwyn thought the plaque cover was very brilliantly done —

5 Both covers in fact carried acknowledgements.

a very good brilliant copy. She liked the colour. So there's 2 opinions.[6]

I will read the essay, but at the moment I'm deferring such things — I'm just trying to get airborne again.[7] Leonard suddenly pulled 2 books out of a black bag — evidently 2 partners to North Star which we've been paid advance for. 'Flowers & Insects' and Monsters — or something of that sort. I'm keeping the monsterish attributes of the monsters to invisible aspects, the visible aspects being innocent. Better for Leonard, & more interesting for me.

Love to Melissa   Ted

21st May 83

Dear Keith & Melissa,

It was my fault I didn't get in touch with you before you came on your garden tour (assuming you did come). Still, I thought you'd probably call — so I had scones, cream etc, and stayed in Wednesday. I thought there was just a chance. Our number is 713, (Please don't let anybody have it) for next time.

Overleaf is a piece from the latest combined operation with Leonard.[8] 6 flowers, 5 insects, and a spider. 12 watercolours, & 12 poems. He sold the book to Viking at the same time as Under the North Star — and suddenly he needs the rest of the advance. NOT for children — more or less straight. (He's sold his house)

Sotheby's are holding a Modern Literary Sale — proceeds partly for Arvon, so I put in the one remaining copy of PIKE. It's a proof — so far as I know the only surviving one. Maybe I'll see you up there.

Keep well   Ted

6th July 83

Dear Keith & Melissa,

Isn't this weather strange? Nice for holidaymakers, disastrous for everything else.

---

6 Leonard had intensely disliked the turquoise colour in which the Manchester University Press designers had reproduced his plaque.
7 I had asked for Ted's opinion of my essay 'Fourfold Vision in Hughes' in The Achievement of Ted Hughes, which I had described to him as 'about the furthest I have gone in my criticism in the direction I want to go'.
8 'Sunstruck Foxglove'.

Here's an odd publication you might not find — it doesn't say so (some student subtlety) but it's the Blundell's School Mag — just published.[9] The son (Rupert) of the Simon & Hilary (to whom I dedicate the poem) goes to that School — and the editor obviously asked him to ask me for a piece. I was going fishing with Simon (the father), when the incident happened. He wasn't there, but he told me that the Sligachan Hotel (from which I got the ticket for the fishing, and where they told me about the pools upstream,) was the noble & historical site of his conception — on his parents' honeymoon! Hence the dedication etc.

The River book — ("River") — is printed by July, but not published now till Sept. Summer's a dead time among books, as you know. So they're probably wise.

"What is the Truth" is looking good — Reg Lloyd in Bideford is designing it — a jigsaw of text & drawings. I'm really pleased with it.

Trying to push along something a bit different.

Faber will publish just the poems of 'River' and of Elmet (I'm going to rewrite the whole thing, quite different poems except for a dozen or so) in paperback without photographs in a year or two. Everything that isn't first intensity, or that doesn't contribute directly & organically to what is, dilutes, confuses, obscures etc. I've made some bad mistakes, grafting myself onto others.

Keep well   love   Ted

[30 July 1983]

Dear Keith & Melissa —

Please do go ahead and sell the typescripts and have a good holiday. I'll find out what happened to Pike.

This heat's dreadful. River was 78° the other day.

Yes, do call when you come down.

Best   Ted

9 'Milesian Encounter on the Sligachan', Enter Rumour, Spring 1983. On the enclosed photocopy Hughes wrote, 'Dashes instead of Dots passim'. In line 13 he corrected 'scapulars' to 'scapulae' and in line 38 'Searing' to 'Searching'. Twelve lines from the end he gave 'glaistic' an initial capital. These changes were all incorporated in River. At the end he wrote:
Dear Keith,
The Simon of the dedication is Simon Day – Hilary his wife. I was on my way to meet him on Harris. Then he told me he'd been conceived in the Sligachan Hotel (about 48 years ago) on his parents' honeymoon.
Ted

25 August 1983

River is a cornucopia. As you know, I like the salmon poems best (and the Canadian ones). But you have left out some fine poems, especially 'Everything is on its way to the river', 'Madly singing in the mountains' and 'This valley is a prehistoric temple'. Any chance that these will be restored in the next (pictureless) edition?[10]

14th Nov. 83

Dear Keith & Melissa,

Our trip to the North was converted to an Arvon trip to the South, so we shan't be up there before the New Year, & I'm not sure when then.

Africa was everything I'd hoped. Nicholas had done his job, quite thoroughly, by the time I got there — examined about 1,000 Nile Perch in intimate detail. He'd established himself as the white boss, 19th Century German style, among a group of about 20 black fishermen, on an Island in Lake Victoria. About 9–10 mud huts, a bay & beach, on the North point of Rusinga Island, where all the fish population going in and out of the Kavirondo Gulf seem to pass on a highway, about 70 feet down, & 400 or so yards offshore. The natives simply drag a beach seine across this highway — take it out in canoes 500 yards, & drag it in to the beach. They make 8 or 10 pulls a day — slow job. Each pull of the net, the net's full — average of 30 or 40 fish, average weight 15–20 kilos, all Nile Perch. What scenes! In the evening, all the fish (up to 2 tons) piled in canoes, a rough rag of a sail run up, & they go 7 or so miles across to the mainland, a market town where nothing happens but marketing, cutting up, frying & smoking of fish. Quite a place. We went over in a colossal thunderstorm, one night.

The group all worked for the chief — a young bloke exactly like James Baldwin — and the fish sold for 1 shilling a kilo. We lived with the chief, on sweet tea, chapatis & ugali meal — rarely fish, though the Nile Perch was pretty good eating. (But the women, if they cooked it, ate it.)

In the mornings we fished. Nick had a canoe — painted strange thing, but very good to handle. We used baby Nile perch & fished as

10 In the event it was ten years before *Three Books: Remains of Elmet, Cave Birds, River* was published. The first two of the poems I had mentioned were restored there.

for pike, jigging the baits across the bottom. We caught very big fish. Up to the last day, Nick had the biggest — 82 lbs. Then on the last day we only had one bait — a morning of strange flukes. (Usually we had more baits than we could use.) So I fished. I caught 3 fish, & lost two others — without losing the bait off the hooks. No bait had ever before survived the catching or hooking & losing of a fish. Then in the last half hour, our last drift across the hot spot, I hooked a fish that took me about ½ an hour to bring up. It took us ten minutes to get it into the boat. It weighed 104 lbs.[11] I only saw one bigger fish (at the fish market), and Nicky had only seen about 4 — among 3 or 4,000.

Strange other fish (though Nile Perch seem to have all but cleaned out the lake, and are now starting on their own juveniles). Strange incident with a crocodile (we thought it was a big fish & tried to catch it). Big lizards galloping down the slopes, & crashing into the lake. Eagles everywhere you look. Extraordinary small birds. Curious incidents with the blacks.

A great self-contained, blissful dream, but at the time every minute was physically quite rough — that part of Africa being mainly petrified fangs, tusks, talons, & every plant like a display of Halberds, a torture instrument, or a needle machine. But I like the blacks, the atmosphere, the infantile freedom from greed & the scramble for gain, the luxurious sort of collapse into the dirt, the laughter & high spirits everywhere, the cultureless prehistoric idleness, the amiable familiarity, with all the weird creatures.

I came back & went to Scotland, where 4 of us in 5 days caught 59 salmon. Then I went to Toronto, Poetry Festival, lived for a week in the Hilton, & in general recovered, or made the attempt. Since then, retyped Leonard's introd (enclosed)[12] — a transatlantic swimmer finally triumphantly ashore, (unconscious on the rocks).

Keep well   Ted

16 November 1983

I'm still shaking after reading that tremendous piece on Leonard. That must have taken it out of you. What you say about *mana* in relation to Baskin is very similar to what I try to say about fourfold vision in the last chapter of *The Achievement*. The hanged man is a victim of the release of the dragonish

11 See plate 10.
12 In *Winter Pollen* as 'The Hanged Man and the Dragonfly'.

energies. The dragonfly is a vision of the resolution, harmonizing, consecration, as you say, of those energies. [. . .]

I've been puzzling about your title 'Milesian Encounter on the Sligachan'. Presumably you are referring to the Milesian School of Early Greek philosophers. I found this passage in Burnet's *Early Greek Philosophy*:

Lastly, they thought, earth turns once more to water – an idea derived from the observation of dew, night-mists, and subterranean springs. For these last were not in early times supposed to have anything to do with the rain. The 'waters under the earth' were regarded as an independent source of moisture.

Am I on the right track here? Or were you rather thinking in more general terms of such sayings as 'All things are full of gods' on which Burnet comments: 'Thales held there was a divine mind which formed all things out of water'.

You recommended to me a book on ancient philosophy by a woman whose name I forgot.

Two questions for the next edition of the bibliography. Did you write the jacket note for Sylvia's *Journals*? Did you contribute anything to the *writing* of the manifesto of the Association for Verbal Arts in the T.H.E.S. of which you were a signatory?

Love to Carol.

Come and see us in the New Year.

Keith

14th Dec 83

Dear Keith,

Thank you for the two (three) emendations in my Leonard piece. I've rewritten the first 6 pages considerably — clarified & lubricated it, I hope.

The 'Milesian' — in 'Milesian encounter' refers not Greekwards but West — Irishwards. 'Greek on the Irish Sea' maybe. But more specifically as follows: 'Milesian' is the name given, in the legendary account of the Invasions of Ireland, to the Goidels — who came evidently from Spain around the 2nd Century BC, and were the last big invasion to impose a language & distinctive culture over most of the country. They set up Tara.

During I suppose the 18th Century, the remains of Irish Tales — Ossian etc — as English style culture became aware of them — were at some point called 'Milesian'. Meaning, I suppose, pre-Christian, monstrously exaggerated, incredible, Irish-fantastic,

Celtic-inordinate ridiculously barbaric. The Milesians, presumably, gave the final stamp to most of the early Irish stories that survived — and even the more serious pieces from earlier, the Tain etc, must have been bundled under the one disparaging epithet. 'Milesian' came to mean, as I've said, 'ridiculously exaggerated barbaric Irish tale, perfectly incredible, typical of the idiotic hyperbolical Irish," etc.

So I used it because Skye is part of that old Irish kingdom, because the Salmon came from the Irish Sea, because the Salmon considered as a primitive Irish daughter of the nobility — of the archaic nobility — is an Irish enough idea, because all fishing tales are 'Milesian', because the kernel of fact in Milesian tales can only be disappointingly small, and anyway lost beyond investigation, as my salmon, after all my effort and excitement, was only about 4 lbs, and also I lost it, & because the setting of my encounter, which should have been consummated in the legendary conquest & ingestion of a great Irish queen in the form of a hiding salmon, was the actual setting of the real Milesian stories — the bogs, mountains etc of that sea-fringe. Because in Milesian tale style I worked up the losing of a small fish into an encounter on the frontiers of this that & the other. Because I wanted to set my poem — which I'm fond of — in the court of sympathetic indulgence and understanding, as a mini mock-Saga episode. And so on.

"River" is doing quite well. They printed 15000 paperback, 2500 hard. A month ago they'd distributed 8,000 and 1400.

I rang up Peter Keen to offer support & moral solidarity — after The Sunday Times review where they even got his name wrong, and he'd just learned, that very hour, that his daughter is an advanced case of some very rare cancer — in the marrow, the blood, & in the bones.[13] Danny Weissbort, — did you ever meet him? — has cancer of the jaw, same as Freud's, and has been carved up in the U.S., & is now battling to recover.

I'm trying to get going on new things.

Nicholas has written up his thesis, or rather his project. He's wondering what to do next year (finishes at Oxford this next summer). Half thinks of Alaska, but seems to be veering back to

13   At the end of his very enthusiastic review of River in the Sunday Times, 23 October 1983, Christopher Reid had written: 'Peter Lane's photographs, which accompany the text – some brilliantly accurate, others merely gaudy – serve a decorative rather than vital function'.

Africa. Strangely enough, or not so strangely, he was talking the other day of the very moment that his English teacher stopped him writing poetry. He'd written a (I thought) marvellous poem about a dead salmon he found under the river bridge. He pulled it out, and noticed, as he waded there, salmon eggs coming up out of the gravel. He scooped up the gravel, & salmon eggs poured out & downstream. The fish was lying actually on top of a redd — right under the town bridge. He was about thirteen. His English teacher said, evidently "Don't try to write about things outside your experience". Nicholas said it was just like a guillotine — he cut off, from that second, from any interest in English lessons. No doubt he needed another way forward. But now he's evidently regretting it. He says he has a constant craving to be doing his potting — he makes very good primaeval animals & fish (didn't I show them to you?) — and his printing. He's an interesting mix. Some sort of artist.

Frieda has finished 18 paintings for her children's book — you did see the first ones, didn't you? The great hen on the nest etc. Surprising stuff. But then she wrote a story connecting them all together, which is really good — skillful [sic] & full of life, compulsive reading, comic. Very publishable. I wonder what sort of writer she will become. Her children's story is the story of a huge chicken egg hatching into a fat piggy green creature that doesn't know what it is, which mutates — splitting its skin — into a fantastically-beautiful whirling skyfilling blazing dragon.

Was the woman I recommended Marie Lou von Franz? Her books are Apuleius & the Golden Ass, Individuation in Fairytales, Shadow & evil in Fairytales, Alchemy, Fairytales, The Feminine In Fairytales, Redemption Motifs in Fairytales, Lectures on Jung's Typology, Creation Myths. She's a dogmatic Jungian — but so wild & immediate, & first-hand, that it seems less of a system than the passionate outpourings of a half-batty, half-inspired woman. The books are the texts of her lectures — more or less, & transcripts of her talking. I find everything she writes very suggestive & congenial. It's Jung, basically — and she surely would like it to be thoroughgoing & systematically so — but she's turned it into something else much freer & she draws it continually from her own little well, which is quite deep & dark, & full of her own twinkly stars.

You can get them from Robinson & Watkins, Cecil Court, off Charing Cross.

I wrote nothing to do with any part of Sylvia's journals.[14] And contributed nothing to the Manifesto of the Ass. For Verbal Arts.

In fact, I shall withdraw my name from that. There's no sense putting your name to something you can't control. I don't know quite how my name got on there. I expect I agreed in a daze.

We — two or three at Arvon — met Brian Cox the other day, & just generally discussed what might be done. Brian is simply trying to invent an exit from the English teaching deadlock.

What was proposed, finally, was to start with about 15 Arvon style courses, held at rentable big houses up & down the country, or at one of the Arvon Centres, and encourage students of English & Other Departments (especially Science depts, that is) to attend them. And to see how that goes. It may be, demand will help the idea grow — till all students attend that sort of course (5 day courses) 2 or 3 times a year. That's just one immediate possibility, that could be feeling its way. But I intend to keep out of it.

Did you see my piece in West Country Fly Fishing, edited by Anne Voss Bark, published by Batsford. An account of the Taw & the Torridge — intended to encourage visiting anglers. Anne Voss Bark is a close friend, so I was committed to her general brief. Also, the hoteliers on the two rivers are friends of one sort or another. So the essay is an attempt to glorify the rivers while suppressing the knowledge that they are going down the drain. Even twenty years ago they produced $\frac{1}{3}$ of all the salmon in the West Country. Last year only 43 salmon were caught on the Torridge. (It used to be a thousand to 1500). It's become a farm sewer.

Peter's (Redgrove's) article was a tight-rope feat. He should never have taken it on, perhaps.[15]

The poem of Charles Tomlinson's, in that issue of the TLS, about the river — he wrote after I'd been showing him where we fish on the Torridge.[16]

'What Is The Truth?" is coming out in March.

14 In 1982 the Dial Press had published the Journals of Sylvia Plath, edited by Frances McCullough. Ted had in fact contributed the foreword, and is described on the title page as 'Consulting Editor'. He had also published an essay on the journals in the Spring 1982 edition of Grand Street.
15 Hughes could hardly have been disappointed by Redgrove's thorough and perceptive review of River (Times Literary Supplement, 11 November 1983). Perhaps Ted was thinking rather of the second half of the article, a somewhat carping review of The Achievement of Ted Hughes.
16 'Coombe'.

Do you remember a letter I wrote, in response to some letter which was in response to some article about me in an issue of one of those magazines which suddenly appeared while the TLS was on strike?

I forget the name of the Magazine, & I've no copy of the letter (can't find it). Do you by any chance have a copy? Is there any chance of you making me a Xerox of it? I'd be grateful. I can't find it in the (invaluable) bibliography — must be later.[17]

Now Xmas — "A sudden blast of dusty wind, and after
Thunder of feet, tumult of images".[18]

Are you both keeping warm & busy? Enclosed, a remarkable photograph. The holograph was something we thought of doing in Morrigu — but then the poem seemed so bad, & the imposition of my script so offensive, we dropped it.[19]

Have a good Xmas   love Ted

---

17 The piece was 'A Reply to My Critics', Books and Issues, 3–4 (1981). See Appendix VIII.
18 From 'Nineteen Hundred and Nineteen' by W. B. Yeats.
19 Cormorants. A few copies were sent as Christmas cards.

1984

Hughes visited Ireland in May, and the St Magnus International Festival in Orkney in June. In August he added poems to *River* and *Remains of Elmet*. In November he gave twenty readings, to 'about 6000' children at schools in various towns and cities including Hull, West Kirby, Birmingham, Manchester and Oxford. Late November and early December were spent in Egypt. On 18 December Hughes became Poet Laureate.

9th March 84

Dear Keith & Melissa,

Congratulations. I expect you're very pleased. The only good thing about little Leos is that they never ail anything. But the genetic contribution can add lots of extras.[1]

Your two bibliographical enquiries, Keith, deadened me a bit. That 'love' feature was just inane — can't it simply be considered non-existent? And the playlet wasn't any better. Completely ridiculous. Why can't there be, in the bibliography, a crematorial chamber — to extinguish undesirable attempts to flame wetly.[2]

I think one of the dreary aspects of my life is the permanent company of the daft things I've done. My easygoing general readiness to let anything pass has cluttered me up with embarrassments. "Never show fools half-work" — one of Leonard's Jewish dicta. A lesson I'm learning too late.

I was talking to Craig Raine about his manuscripts — suggesting he sell some through Sotheby's in an Auction they held partly for Arvon. He was horrified at the idea of exposing his unfinished fumblings. He was quite decided about it. "Look at Eliot — he said — when they published that facsimile of The Waste Land MSS his reputation just crashed." I was slightly amazed. For me, if anything, that MSS made Eliot even more interesting. But Craig lives among the literary skyscrapers, where demolitions & collapses are headlines on the day they occur. Did Eliot's reputation tremble?

---

1 I had informed Ted and Carol that Melissa was expecting our first baby in August.
2 In February 1963 a magazine called *Town* had published a sequence of photographs by Art Kane with a prose text by Ted called 'Love'. The 'playlet' was a short verse play called *Epithalamium* which was performed at the 1963 Poetry Festival at the Royal Court Theatre, London.

Anyway, the point is, in some way, for most readers, Craig is right. You & I read an author by his best — or even by what we feel of his own inner idea of what he's after. But most readers are much more pragmatic. We read with idealistic good-will. Most readers read with actual ill-will. As Pascal says, at bottom most people hate everybody else. You & I, simple honest Northerners, (as distinct from bilious, rancourous [sic], envious, crooked ones) still think we should love one another, & operate on an instinctive expectation of good-will & affection, an assumption that in our foibles we'll always be given the benefit of the doubt — as we give others. Well, it's not so, is it.

It's too late to change, & re-jig the works on a more realistic appraisal of the Universal Condition of multi-lateral hatred & active malice. But I'm trying to be more careful. So the notion of resurrecting more of my inanities, to perch on my head, as I say deadens me a bit.

On the other hand — what the hell. Who cares.

The Pike was traded, after the failed sale, for a vast sum.

What I have left is a curiosity — a 'proof'. On proof paper — with only one pike in the illustration. (The final copy has a double pike — one in green superimposed over one in black). It's the only one in this condition — so far as I know — that ever existed. I had it repaired (it had been torn slightly).

Carol's busy gardening. Lovely spring weather just now, here.

I've been involved in a local battle, of sorts, over Bideford Sewage System. The Water Authority, mightily urged on by local building interests, are putting in a type of sewage system that merely screens the sewage (takes out 20% 'solids' — which aren't what you think they might be, hyena coprolites, but are mostly cardboard, plastic etc). The moment the decision for this is formally taken, the building embargo on Bideford will be lifted, & 1600 new houses go in immediately followed by whatever developments developers can develope. First result, instant increase, of about 30% raw sewage going dump smack flop in the estuary in the middle of the town. The shellfish are already poisonous. 75% surfers & canoists [sic] pick up infections & assorted dysenteries etc. The local hoteliers, & tourist association, see all hear all & say nowt — fearful of what a public uproar might do to their tourists (population doubles in summer).

My concern was — the river (Torridge) has all but lost its run of salmon & sea-trout. Maybe the fish won't face the plug of crap in the estuary, & maybe the baby fish get poisoned as they drop down to the sea. Anyway, the sewage doesn't help them, & more sewage will help less. Also, the estuary in general & on the whole & regarded from a safe distance & sub specie aeternitas is one 5 mile sewage sludge pit — with a halitosis that on occasions kills gulls & swans.

All our efforts at protest being shoved aside, one of the local lads produced the enclosed. Keep it to yourself, because it might be libellous.[3]

love to you both Ted

14.3.84

There is no need to mention the playlet in the Bibliography, since no part of it was ever published. I just wondered if it had developed into anything else or any part of it had been salvaged. The other item will have to be listed in the next edition. I can't really, with my bibliographer hat on, drop things in the memory hole on critical grounds. But that's a far cry from reprinting it. Only a handful of the most fervent scholars will bother to look it up. It might rate a footnote in a Ph.D. thesis some day. I don't have the power to call up the dead by merely listing their tombstone inscriptions!

11th June 84

Dear Keith and Melissa,

Just got back from Ireland and found your note. I'm terribly sorry about the miscarriage. What a blow! Would be worse, though, not to have conceived at all.

We're sitting rather dazed, wondering how to weather the inevitable migration of friends across our map. The Schaeffers are coming over — to stay in that cottage next to Lawrence's, in Zennor.[4] They've been infinitely good to Frieda, who's just been

---

3 'Ballad of the Bideford Browns'. Unpublished. The 'local lad' was Ted himself.
4 In Ted Hughes: The Life of a Poet (2001), Elaine Feinstein writes:

The novelist Susan Fromberg Schaeffer and her husband Neil Schaeffer, both Professors in the English Department at Brooklyn College, had become friends with Hughes while on vacation in England. They tried on several occasions to persuade him to take up an academic post in New York, which was his for the asking and would not involve him in a heavy teaching load. Ted always refused politely.

In 1916–17 D. H. and Frieda Lawrence had lived at Higher Tregerthen, Zennor, Cornwall.

to New York, and we'd like to open our arms to them — but my last six months has gone down the drain and now every fresh engagement with distractions seems like extra punishment. Yehuda Amichai & his family will come for a week — dear old Yehuda, I've got to free my spirits for him.[5] And now I'm trudging to Orkney, to a Festival, a place I greatly like — but it feels like a forced march deeper into Siberia — all because I couldn't shame to go on turning down their courteous annual invitation. I've surely got things the wrong way round somehow. Lawrence would laugh.

End of repining.

Our garden's been very beautiful. Now it's the June gap — and we have masses of green leaf mainly. Roses just beginning.

Olwyn's Richard died in Crete. He went back there — after falling in love with it earlier this year — to try and write. He got mixed up in a Shepherd's Festival, & no doubt drank for Ireland — haemorraged, [sic] & bled to death. Christmas factor. Big blow for Olwyn, in spite of his evil genius. She's gone out there to help with his funeral. A real cursed nature, Richard's. He had really unusual talents, very rich human qualities, grand spirit — all fouled up with Catholic guilt torments & the anaesthesia-fixation of booze. Genuine tragic flaw, there — the whole slow self-destruction very harrowing.

Frieda's weird children's story has been taken by Heinemann.[6]

Love from us Ted

---

5 Yehuda Amichai (1924–2000), Israeli poet. Hughes had met Amichai's work in 1964 when translations of some of his poems were accepted by Hughes and Daniel Weissbort for the first number of *Modern Poetry in Translation*. He met Amichai himself when he participated in the first Poetry International, which Hughes directed in London in 1967. In the following year Hughes and Assia Wevill (under her maiden name Gutmann) translated Amichai's *Selected Poems* (Cape Goliard Press, 1968), and Hughes collaborated with Amichai himself in translating *Amen and Time* (Oxford University Press, 1978 and 1979). Hughes described Amichai as his favourite poet. For an account of their relationship with extracts from Hughes' letters to Amichai see Daniel Weissbort, ed., *Ted Hughes: Selected Translations* (2006), pp. 49–58 and 210–12.

6 *Getting Rid of Edna* (Heinemann, 1986).

[pm 28 August 1984]

Dear Keith,

I thought Melissa and yourself might be curious to see the effect of removing all the photographs from river.[7]

There are some changes in Gulkana.[8]

I heard from Tina you were going to be at Glyn's, and I felt I'd like to be there, seeing Roya cope.[9]

Everything here proceeds as before — a general dearth of everything but heat.

I'm trying to add one or two things to River — and to Remains of Elmet — which Faber want to publish together, without pictures. I'd like to elevate Cave Birds to the level of the better pieces, but that means about 25 new poems — the purpose of that would be, to cancel the 25 old ones. There's no other way of cancelling them. You can't just disown them.   Once goblins get out
                                        They will run about.

Frieda wrote a children's book — Heinemann will publish it here — Harper in the U.S. A very bizarre & inventive piece.

Nicholas is going to Alaska to do his PHD — so he'll be there 3 years at least. Which means, I hope, I'll be seeing more of it. His Nile Perch Report is making all sorts of larger circles, so he's very pleased.

I've just been reading the big Phoenix Collection of Lawrence's pieces — straight oxygen. What is the great plastic megaphone mask of English, that gets jammed over the head of all English writers, & that he avoided? He is the only one quite free of it. Maybe what helped him — apart from the talent, the nerve etc — was marrying a German, & staying out of England.

But all (modern) English writers disappear into this Gallery Tussaud's of a non-language — which acts automatically as censor & suppressant of any real material as if it manipulated the brain-rhythms, which I suppose it does. I opened John Fowles Mantissa the other day — a chronic extreme case, I'd say. It's very strange,

---

7 The Harper & Row edition of River, June 1984, omitted Peter Keen's photographs.

8 Hughes revised and extended this poem for the US edition, again for Three Books in 1993, and yet again for New Selected Poems in 1995. The version in Collected Poems is the last of these, though the revisions are described in the notes.

9 Part Five of Glyn Hughes' autobiographical poem Life Class (Shoestring Press, 2009) describes his tempestuous relationship with his Greek wife Roya.

It introduces into all writing a sort of struggle — Alan Sillitoe's is a full battlefield display of it. Most writers simply capitulate, & join its Civil Service, & proclaim its regulations. Others just get worn out. It's a study.

Love to Melissa   Ted

20th Nov. 84

Dear Keith,

We had a flying tour through schools in the Midlands last week, got as far as Hull, West Kirby, Oxford. I toyed with the idea of ringing you, the night we were near Blackburn, but everything was too jammed. I was doing two readings a day, & lying low in the evenings to conserve nervous energy, early bed, no booze. So the whole thing finally went quite well. Must have read to about 6,000 or so, in all.

I asked them what they wanted to hear, & read & talked about that — so the onus was on them, to keep the interest going.

A poem in the collection for Norman Nicholson's 70th, edited William Scammell. If you haven't a copy, I have 2.[10]

A poem in a Mag. From Norwich The Rialto — I've asked him to send you a copy. (February)[11]

2 Poems in London Review of Books which I expect you saw.[12]

We're just away to Egypt. Saw one or two Faber staff — they were telling of a book they commissioned William Golding to do, about Egypt. He insisted on doing it the real way — so hired a dhow. His guide was Ian Hamilton's brother-in-law (an Egyptian). Golding discovered, once he got afloat, that the Nile has quite high brown banks — monotonous empty brown quite high walls of earth. So he travelled for some days down this deep trench, or up it, seeing absolutely nothing but the river's walls. Then he climbed out, and spent the rest of his time in a hotel. What he wrote is so disparaging of Egypt, Faber's hardly know whether they dare publish it — and his guide has disassociated himself. This is gossip.[13]

10 'A Tern' in William Scammell, ed., Between Comets: For Norman Nicholson at 70 (Taxus, 1984).
11 'Remembering Jenny Rankin', Spring 1985.
12 'Walt' and 'A Macaw', 15 November 1984.
13 William Golding, An Egyptian Journal (Faber & Faber, 1985).

I hope Melissa & Co are doing well.[14] Give her my love.
I'll drop a line when we get back.
                     Ted

18 December 1984

<u>Laureate</u>[15]

   Are they courageous or foolhardy, those
   Who led the bull within the palace walls
   And garlanded with bays the lowered horns.

     Congratulations. Keith & Melissa.

---

14 I had informed Ted that Melissa was again pregnant.
15 News had just broken of Hughes' appointment as Poet Laureate.

1985

In January Hughes continued to revise *Remains of Elmet*. In April he gave a reading at the National Poetry Centre. In May he fished in Scotland, and in June in Alaska. Hughes wrote *The Cat and the Cuckoo*. In October he did a tour of readings arranged by Faber. He also read at the Kent Literature Festival.

4 January 1985

I'm not sure that this is a suitable gift,[1] since so much of it leaves a bad taste in the mouth, what Lawrence called "the unspeakable baseness of the press and the public voice" – I suspect that the Daily Express really is the 'Voice of Britain' – the nauseating headlines, the witless cartoons, the confident judgements based on ignorance, philistinism and malice, not only by journalists, but also 'critics', ignorance not only of your work but also of the very raison d'être of poetry – a "common cry of curs", the same as hounded Lawrence, with Amis as Triton among the minnows . . . There are, of course, a few oases, notably Seamus' piece.[2]

21st January 85

Dear Keith & Melissa,

So far so good.

I've paid no more attention to the cannonading, pro & con,

Than to the horrible same old effluvia going down the River Don.

But thank you for the scrapbook — Carol sat over it crowing & cackling. I've now achieved near perfect allegy [sic] to any word about myself. I can see my name coming through the paragraphs by the premonitory arrangement of the first words on the page. Now for a Pseudonym. And thank you for the CUP![3]

1 I had sent a scrapbook containing all the cuttings I could find relating to the Laureateship.
2 The *Daily Express* printed Hughes' first Laureate poem, 'Rain-Charm for the Duchy', on 24 December 1984, together with Kingsley Amis' description of it as 'a terrifically boring poem and very hard to follow'. Seamus Heaney, interviewed in the *Irish Times* on 18 December, described Hughes as 'gentle, humorous, enormously learned and intelligent'. He spoke of the 'pure regional energy' of his speech, and his 'refusal of gentility', even claiming that Hughes represented 'an alternative source of authority' to the government.
3 I had sent a mug, with the words: 'Here is a present, not to be opened until Christmas day. I saw it in a sale and immediately thought of you coming in frozen after fishing at dawn'.

You ask about Crow — the answer is I've done quite a lot. I roam around in there, clearing spaces. I occasionally have good omens about bits of it. But I shan't publish a word of it till it's all done — otherwise the response would be immunised, my thoughts about it interfered with. etc. Even as it is, the problem might be — déja vu, for defensive readers.[4]

Are you in training for Lawrence's year? Isn't it also Ezra Pound's year?[5]

I've been chipping away at bits & pieces about Calder Vally [sic] — I expect you've seen one or two. If that Elmet book's republished, I want to take out some of the more facile pieces, & include some ballast, simple accounts of relatives etc., a few dramatis personae. More of my own feeling (as distinct from my mother's)

The Rain Charm poem began as an attempt to get into the River Collection a few pieces of different voice & focus.

Surprising what effect the Poet Laureate label has. The line in that poem about the pollution (quite mild & domestic) of the Okement caused great agitation in Okehampton (responsible for the refuse) — might even affect the Council's laissez faire. These are the perks.

Pity I didn't leave in the lines about the Torridge — they were

"And the Torridge, that hospital sluice of all the doctored and
      scabby farms from Welcombe to Hatherleigh to Torrington
Poor, bleached leper in her pit, stirring her rags, praying that this
      at last is the kiss of the miracle,
That soon she'll be plunging under sprays, splitting her lazar crust,
      new-born,
A washed cherub etc"

But I thought it might seem in poor taste.
Send some news. Love   Ted
I hope all's going well. What are your birthdays?

4 Hughes told me that it took weeks with no distractions to get back into the Crow mode.
5 Pound was born just seven weeks later than Lawrence, on 30 October 1885.

27th Feb. 85

Dear Keith,

Here's a copy of the Norman Nicholson book.

Can I delay about Tony Stott's poems, they've somehow got separated into this blizzard of mail.[6]

Did I see some of your poems in Outposts, or was it elsewhere? They gave me a good shock — a genuine bite, real things in the general wash.[7]

The Atlantic Salmon Trust are having a sale of Fishing Beats & Shooting Days etc, to raise Funds, at Hopetoun House, South Queensferry, West Lothian, on Friday March 22nd. They asked me if I'd write them a poem to auction. (Little do they know!!!) But I felt I couldn't refuse — I'm a little bit involved there, indirectly. Besides, I'd love to raise some money for the cause. (They're doing great work). I thought of simply sending MS of a River poem. But who'll be there to bid? It might go for next to nothing, and then some dealer make the money. Besides, I don't like low figures. In the end, I wrote a kind of ballad —

> The best worker in Europe
> Is only six inch long.
> You thought he was a bigger chap?
> Just wait and hear my song, so,
> Just wait and hear my song
>   etc

The worker is a salmon smolt of course, who never costs a penny, never lifts his voice, and after converting the deep sea for a year or two returns counted in millions, weighed in metric tons, and dumps the whole lot in your river to be collected — 2 fish to feed the whole country, for nothing. Ideally of course. There's a carefully adjusted river in Vancouver, 10 miles long, and half a million salmon return to it — 100,000 more than to the Entire British Isles!!! (In Alaska last year they had over 200 million — caught)

---

6 Tony Stott was our postman, and a fine poet. Several poems from his Whin Sill sequence were subsequently published in the journal Northumbriana.
7 My 'Seven Lively Sins' had appeared in Outposts.

Anyway I shall sell him like a slave to the highest bidder.
Glad to hear you're well Melissa
   Love   Ted

7th June 1985

Dear Keith and Melissa,

Well, congratulations to you both. Or to all three rather.[8] I hope
you're all still of the same mind — that the event was good. And
that you're all surviving each other, with evolutionary gains all
round.

Nothing so radical here — or anything near it. I've spent too
much time fishing — Scotland, 2 weeks. And on Wednesday I'm
off to Alaska to observe Nicholas in his new habitat there.

Also, I made the mistake of becoming too involved in the battle
over the River Torridge — fairly pointless. The battle is between
the Water Authority, which has let the river die pretty well, & the
Riparian owners & fishermen. The Riparian Owners have lost,
collectively, the best part of 3 million pounds, & Albion will
probably lose its run of salmon in the Torridge. But the whole
business is perhaps mostly busyness — and self righteousness,
and lies. I'm quite sick of it, but I don't see quite how to extricate
myself.

I started rewriting the pieces in Elmet which I feel need it.
Replacing some altogether. About 15 or 20 of them. Others I think
I'll simply delete.

Now it's a case of persuading Faber to re-set the book with
the new pieces. Since the photographs make it something of a
regional gift-book, it seems likely it will go on selling at some
steady trickle — and the idea of perpetuating many/some of
those verses grieves me.

The rewriting has been head-in-a-sack drudgery. I'm glad to
stop. It's the sort of book I should have written in my twenties,
when my feelings about the place were still innocent, and
unspoiled, & fairly simple. And the direct approach —
autobiographical style — is always least productive.

I hope my rewriting won't dislocate too much of Leonard
Scigaj's interpretation. He sent me his opus — all but a final

8 Our daughter Ursula had been born on 6 May.

chapter.[9] I've dipped into it here & there where Carol directed.
I liked Leonard — the hour or two I spent with him. But it's
difficult to know how to respond — even to such positive readings.

Leonard Baskin visited — on his way to a small exhibition of his
work in Vienna. He's etched some "shrunken heads" — Maori type
heads — and when he asked for a text, I dug out some of the
Caprichos I wrote for an earlier set of drawings which he never
printed. So his new press — The Eremite Press — will probably do
that.[10] He showed me a book he did recently of Imps & Demons[11] —
it seems to me his work has intensified somewhat, since he went
back to the States.

With these Elmet repairs out of the way, I'm looking forward
to getting back into something juicier.

The only conscious business of this Laureateship is dealing
with other people's projections. Properly used it should provide
means of boosting new distances in the opposite direction. Main
thing is to stay free of the nets they cast, & the mail-burrs they
sprinkle, & the threads they try to attach — funny thing, to be
suddenly so visible to so many, & so useful to so many.

Have I written to you since Egypt? Surely I have.

Our garden has been amazing. A prodigal sort of spring, for the
blossoms. I can't remember one like it. I wish I'd watched it more
closely.

Drop a note with any news —

Love   Ted

5 October 1985

Dear Ted and Carol

I promised you a fuller account of India. First impressions were like
everyone's – dirt, dust and din, chaos, crowds, smells, and, of course, heat,
though that was not as bad as I expected, especially in Hyderabad, which is
on a plateau. Even in Madras and Trivandrum, the heat and humidity were no
worse than I have known in Texas.

The food, on the other hand, was hotter than I expected, and not very
good. 'Where should I go for the best Indian food?' I asked my host, who
replied 'Back to England'. I believe the dishes are more subtle and varied in

9   Scigaj, The Poetry of Ted Hughes.
10 Baskin's Mokomaki (Eremite Press, 1985), contained thirteen etchings and three poems: 'Aspiring
    Head', 'Halfway Head', and 'Landmark Head'.
11 Imps, Demons, Hobgoblins, Witches, Fairies & Elves (Pantheon Books, 1984).

the north. Waiters in filthy jackets. Floors assiduously swept. Nothing higher ever cleaned or repainted.

The traffic is terrifying. Roads no wider than ours and full of bumps and holes. No-one walks on the pavements which are public toilets, rubbish dumps and standing for cows and water-buffalo. So the first strip of road is taken up by pedestrians, often three or four abreast, walking round the outside of parked vehicles. Then come the cyclists weaving in and out of the bullock-wagons. Huge steel girders transported by bullock-wagon, one girder per wagon, at a snail's pace. Then come the scooters, thousands of them, weaving in and out of the auto-rickshaws and cycle-rickshaws; then the taxis and private cars (fortunately few); then the heavy lorries and buses with people hanging all over them. Everyone advertises his presence and intention to overtake by continuous sounding of the horn. There would not be room for all this traffic if the street were one-way, but it is not one-way. Anyone wanting to overtake does so irrespective of oncoming traffic, which is expected to stop or swerve . . . Half the traffic lights are not working. The other half are largely ignored, as are all road signs, bollards, etc. The chaos is further compounded by cripples, sacred cows, dogs, goats and pigs wandering nonchalantly among the traffic, and water-buffalo lying in the middle of the main street. One's immediate reaction is an unexpected wave of sympathy and understanding for the Raj – My God, someone has got to clear up this mess and create some order!

After three or four days in the thick of this on the back of my host's scooter I became quite blasé. But it really is dangerous, not just unfamiliar. In Kerala which is a small sparsely-populated state (largest town Trivandrum 200,000) there have been so far this year 1,600 road deaths!

What I did not become blasé about was the beggars and cripples. A big fat man, virtually naked, with no hands or feet, lay on his back in the mud in the middle of the bazaar howling. A little girl came past with a strange contraption of twisted black sticks on her back. When she turned round one saw that is was a man. Later I saw him crawling among the tourists on the beach with a tin in his mouth . . .

There is also the inertia. A girl described a crocodile as an image of total inertia. A professor replied: 'You don't have to look at crocodiles for that: you can just open any door in the university'.

27 Oct 85

Dear Keith,

I hope Melissa and Ursula are doing well. Real touch of winter here today.

Thank you for the long account of India. You gave me a real impression — confirmed my worst ideas. But I expect you had a wonderfully rich experience — to alchemise at leisure.[12] I can't decide whether to go. Problem is, I don't have time for journeys I'd prefer. Also, I have a notion that the Indian type of impresario, who'd be manipulating my schedule, would be fifty times as unscrupulous as the English. But they keep inviting me.

Just finished my mini-tour of readings. Faber set it up — one in each of their counties, so I met each of their reps. They saw it as part of a publicity campaign. I saw it as a concession to Laureate-watchers. One of my conditions was — no newspaper interviews, no cameras, knowing that Faber's publicity techniques now include every possible facility, and that if I gave them free rein my readings would be little more than overtures to the main thing — talking to the Press.

Result was, we had a few close encounters with enraged journalists/cameramen demanding my head on a platter, as a public property. Desmond Clarke almost came to blows, in Cambridge, defending me from a photographer.

Funny business.

Every day confirms my ideas about interviews — with me, as I see by this latest book about my poems, by somebody called West, they are on a fair way to replacing what I've written.[13] Inane remarks casually made by me, becomes clubs & blunt instruments to coerce my verses, rather than doing what I intended — laying a smoke-screen, behind which I escaped the question.

Any answer suits an interviewer, & no answer, too, is just as good, & can be stretched just as far.

I've been rewriting Elmet, or some of it. Not quite sure what to do with the pieces I have. What began as rewritings became quite different pieces alltogether [sic]. Still haven't unlocked it in the way I'd like.

Leonard was over — in very good form, just briefly.

I've met a Marine Biologist (retired) who is not only a high-flying glass-engraver (pupil of Whistler) but was a specialist in deep-sea luminous fish, which he photographed in colour. The photographs for which I originally wrote Photostomias — 1971 I saw them — were his. He's a mass of slides. When you visit

---

12 I attempted to distil the essence of my impressions in a poem 'Intersections – Hyderabad'.
13 Thomas West, *Ted Hughes* (Methuen, 1985).

here next, I'll see if I can arrange a slide-show. He's quite a find.[14]

We've been adopted by a peacock.

Love to all   Ted

16th Dec 85

Dear Keith & Melissa,

I hope everythings [sic] sledging up to Xmas in style, Ursula in her furs etc.

Thank you for the tapes — quite a big job. I shall have to listen to them in the car — no other Cassette-player, though I keep intending to get one.[15]

Thank you for The Magic Wheel review too. It's an odd book (editors sent me a copy). A clumpy ¾ lb paperback, not especially gorgeous, published now, and a hardback at the end of January. They must have got their computers crossed. I daresay Anglers would have bought hardbacks for presents, but once Xmas is past they'll make do with a paperback.[16]

Did you go to the Lawrence unveiling in the Abbey? Typical piece of period punk journalism I read reporting it.[17]

The week before, I'd seen Graves' name on the plaque unveiled for poets of the first War. So he was reported dead, in the Times on his 21st birthday, and had a slab in the Poet's corner before he was dead indeed. And now he, Grigson & Larkin can stare at each other in dismay, where the 3 roads fork.

I suppose — what with an inflationary daughter & the seventy seven months of marriage — you're no longer buying Limited Oddities. The poem I wrote for the Atlantic Salmon Trust, printed (very beautifully) by Sebastian Carter, is for sale at £25. Here's a proof. You can get the real thing from me (I have one or two left) or from The Atlantic Salmon Trust

14 Peter David, whom Hughes had met through the Torridge Action Group.
15 I had sent Ted my recording of forty Lawrence poems for Audio Learning.
16 David Profumo and Graham Swift, eds., *The Magic Wheel: An Anthology of Fishing in Literature* (Picador, 1985).
17 In November a memorial stone to Lawrence had been unveiled in Poets' Corner, bearing the quotation: 'Homo sum! the adventurer'.

> The Cottage
> Druimuan House
> Killiecrankie
> Pitlochry
> Perthshire

156 in all.

I've written the odd thing this year, but it has been a very distracted time — I've been away too much. I'm getting clear to it now.

A retired Marine Biologist near here specialises in colour photography of deep sea luminous fish. It turns out he took the pictures for which I originally wrote that little piece Photostomias. He has all his slides. Very interesting learned chap — now a champion glass-engraver.

This is just a greeting letter. Wishing you a Merry Xmas, and an interesting, productive, happy New Year.

With a kiss for Ursula.

Ted

1986

Hughes' essay on William Golding, 'Baboons and Neanderthals: A Rereading of *The Inheritors*' was published in *William Golding: The Man and his Books*, ed. John Carey (Faber & Faber). The spring and summer were largely taken up with legal business relating to the film of Sylvia's novel *The Bell Jar*. In October Ted and Carol went to Spain and selected two sherries (Oloroso Seco and Fino), of which 700 bottles came with the Laureateship.

10th Jan 86

Dear Keith,

The Author sent me this — probably clearing his decks. For some reason I said I'd show it to you. I thought the sentences I read were good. (I haven't read more than just odd sentences)[1]

Everything here is cruising quietly along. I'm trying to keep it that way. Nicholas is home at the moment, full of Alaskan tales.

Works [sic] going along too, but I'm not sure it's arrived yet. A sign of my good conscience is that I'm spending this evening trying to rediscover the surface of the table where Carol piles letters (in neat, impregnable tower blocks).

I hope you're all well.

I slipped on a low wall top the other day, & somersaulted. Caught the wall edge — squared & quite sharp — with my left eyebrow. So now I shall have a little scar encircling the top left quarter of my eyesocket, from mid-eyebrow to eye-corner. And I know how Shakespeare got his.

Hugs & kisses to Melissa & Ursula.

Ted

Ted's poem 'The Dream of the Lion', the first of the 'Two Poems for Her Majesty Queen Elizabeth the Queen Mother on her Eighty-fifth Birthday' in Rain-Charm for the Duchy (1992), appeared in the Observer on 29 December 1985.

---

1 Roger Goodman had sent Hughes a copy of a thesis on him that he had submitted as part of his degree course at Manchester University in 1971.

16 January 1986

Goodman's thesis was very good . . . I wrote and told him so. Strange he never published anything. He must have been one of the first to get on the right track with *Crow*. It would have been useful to have had access to his thesis when I was writing *The Art of T.H.* Strange also that he should wait thirteen years to send it to you!

Sorry to hear about your fall. Nasty. Apparently you would otherwise have been appearing on TV to read a Larkin poem called 'Aubade'. There is no such poem in any of his four volumes. Where did you find it?

As you must have been aware, many of your admirers had mixed feelings about your acceptance of the Laureateship, wondering if it might indicate some sort of sell-out to the Establishment. I took a different line, and have given in several places a lecture called 'Ted Hughes: The Laureate as Shaman'. 'Rain Charm for the Duchy' supported my case very well; but I'm having trouble with 'The Dream of the Lion'. I'm not at all sure what the dream of the lion is, but it sounds suspiciously like a dream of Empire, with such lines as "Guardian of the weak and tame", with overtones of the Divine Right of Kings. It seems to support a hierarchical class system, with mare, raven, hyena and wolf knowing their places in relation to the lion. Nor do I see why salmon should spawn in honour of the Queen Mother, rather than the Goddess only. I realize that everything depends on the attitude to the monarchy which you expressed at the time of your appointment when you said that it embodied or focussed the "spiritual unity of the tribe". But I don't understand that either. Do members of the royal family see their function in any such way? Would they know what it meant? Could they affect the spiritual state of the nation in any way, even if they wished to? Is the unity of the tribe a desirable objective any more, except perhaps in time of war? Should we not rather be striving to break down tribal consciousness and replace it with a consciousness of ourselves as owing allegiance only to the living world? Hasn't that been the burden of all your mature work? Nor would I know how to begin to defend the poem against the charge (already made) that its primary function is flattery. I hope I'm misreading it. How do you see the purpose of such a poem?

19th Jan 86

Dear Keith,

Glad to hear Ursula's back is more or less OK now. I know how worrying those things are. But they seem to grow out. When Nicholas was a baby his Granny wanted his leg in irons — it seemed too short and she wanted it stretching. Managed to fend off that. Then she wanted operations on his eye, which seemed to squint. She wanted muscles cut and reset. Luckily a doctor convinced her the only oddity was a pronounced epicanthic fold —

heirlooms from his Slavic/Hun forebears on the windy steppe —
which created the illusion of a squint. His only trace of that now
is his determined courtship of a Chinese girl.

Larkin's poem Aubade is his best poem — by some way. It was
in a New York Review of Books three years or so ago, and reprinted
in The Observer December 8th last year.

Your comment about the Lions interested me. Here's how it
came about. Just before the Queen Mother's birthday The Daily
Express asked if I had any tribute ready for her — presumably they
would have liked to print it. I didn't answer, but then about five days
before the day I read that one of her more celebrated ancestors was
a scots Lord known as The White Lion. It occurred to me that she's
the focal point of odd coincidences: her maiden name Lion,[2] her
birth-sign Lion and the fact that she's astrologically very typical,
a text book case, in that facially she somehow resembles a Lion
(especially the eyes — even more so when she was younger —
and the profile), and her role as bearer of the mythic crown in a
collective psychic unity where the totemic symbol of unity was the
Lion. I thought something might be made of this that would amuse
her to read.

This starting point went into complications, once I began to
reflect that the Lion is the only totem under which the British Isles
have ever approached a state of unity, as one Federation with a
reasonably shared family feeling, and that their history as a united
people of the lion culminated — and collapsed — in her reign, in
the 2nd World War, which she seemed to survive as the sole sacred
representative of the idea of unity under the Lion (which she upheld
apparently quite alone and in her own person after she had
absorbed all the Royal qualities of her reign, on the death of
King George. In the poem I keep the Queen out of it, on the
understanding that she represents something different and new,
and not relevant here.)

As I say, my idea was to write something she herself might
get some pleasure from. The thing had already become rather
arcane. Casting it into the form of a fable gave some hope of a
simplification, and of bringing narrative leverage to bear. But
it introduced a whole set of new problems that I hadn't clearly

2 Actually Bowes-Lyon.

foreseen, in that it shifted everything back into my own super-totemised childhood. This was partly deliberate, since my own real feelings about this Lion totem are there (as I imagine everybody else's are, if they have any), and I thought I might be able to tap them. But those feelings are too obscure I suppose for a poem that has to be simple. My early days are tangled in lion ideas. The idea of Being English, of my father having won the war (when I was about four) etc was all tied up with lion. I was disappointed (I remember where I sat thinking about it) that my name didn't begin with L. When the war came and we were painting posters endlessly all mine were simple scenes of the giant lion in action. But that was simple enough (and common property I expect) compared to the purely accidental fact that it always seemed to me my mother looked a bit like a lion, compounded by the maybe quite odd circumstance that I identified her, from when I was quite young, with the Queen Mother. The actual resemblance is probably fairly slight, but it was enough to do the trick at the occult level where those tricks are done. Maybe this is a common English delusion (Marrying one of the Royal Family is one of the common English dreams).

Anyway, these incidental dramatic twists meant that I found myself involved with that whole business of mother as representative of the Queen as representative of the Crown centre of psychic wholeness and unity and harmony — in an immediate but quite unmanageable and also irrelevant way. My footsteps through that sucking ooze are visible from verse to verse.

The most I could do with it was to project an Eden — not just a childhood land of the animals, but a land of communal collective care, where all natural internecine impulses are suspended, before the fall into division, difference and conflict. In this land every creature, of whatever kind, is also, psychically, a lion — as in a totem group. Enjoying the spiritualising harmony of a benign symbol — which is also the life-giver and the sun.

The Wolf and the Hyena are simply two predatory types of the residential fauna of this land (island), which are all types of dog. I don't actually say that because I didn't want to raise the complications it would entail. I didn't want any allegorising to hog the scene. But I take it the natural British totem is Dog. If you take away the lion you have a cacophonous Dog show. Before Lion appeared, this was a Dog-show, dog-fight, dog-hole etc. Hengest and Horsa commented on the fact, and what a pity it was to leave such a fine land to such creatures. This nation of domesticated cannine [sic] curiosities I take to be what the Romans left behind — having bred them for amusement and servile use (400 years — 12 generations — a long time among dog-breeders). The Anglo Saxons and the Vikings found them simple prey and they brought in the Wolvish. So in the national mix I take the Wolvish to be the purer strain of Norse and Anglo Saxon, and the hyena to be the native british [sic] strain of opportunistic collaborator, joining forces in the common business of preying on the dog-show.

Now the lion, in this English mystery, came into being as a unifying self-mastery, the emanation of the whole genetic blend, when it attained self-control, self-restraint, and a common purpose. Then all the separate varieties (as in Macbeth) sunk their differences in the general species, and even the wolf and the hyena suspended their inclinations, and all let themselves be raised into the single-mindedness of another order of animal, all became subordinate faculties of the body politic and leonine, all imbued with the general self-respect of Lion, a common Lion self-confidence. So the cannines had real existence, but they united in the shared fantasy of a lion existence, and over them all presided a visionary lion, which incarnated itself, as collective visions do, in a single real representative, in this case, I suggest, the Queen Mother. The Wolf and the Hyena, as the armed and violent and enterprising, concealing for awhile or transforming or sublimating their natural inclination to plunder and devour, become the 'guardians'. In other words, in this unified and harmonised system of potential havoc, the predators are the very ones who become the protectors.

And this Lion-likeness, being such a powerful form of self-esteem and self-confidence, which all share in the collective psychic unity, is regarded as 'sacred' — there's a religious attitude towards it. (Was!)

This is what I understand to be the real meaning of Monarchy, of which the Monarch is the actual and visible guarantee and assurance. Monarchs aren't created by the individuals of a group. They can only reign if they are created by the unity of a group, and all their trapping[s] are investiture projected from that dream-level of unity. You're saying this isn't desirable — but I'm saying rather that it's simply a fact. And loss of the sense of a sacred axis is loss of depth & coherence. And where do most people get that sense from?

Now these Roman dog-varieties, the native islanders, i.e. the medley in possession post 450 AD, were formerly something else. The Mare is (for the poem's purpose) the Totem of those Celts that came in from the East or rather the South East corner, and the Raven is the Totem of those Celts who came in from the West — from Ireland and the Mediterranean.

The First — later in time — left their Totem cut into the chalk.[3] The second left their Totem in the Tower — Bran's Raven, guardian of his buried head, surviving earliest god, etc.[4]

These are the widest possible shorthand generalities obviously.

The peoples of these two Totems had been genetically transformed in the Roman Hypocaust, from which they trickled out as a lot of dogs

What I further had to keep out of the piece was the general sense that the Lion passes away with the Queen Mother. What's left after her is the breakdown of the Federation, the tribes seceding into their old local allegiances. Resurgences of the alignments of the Civil War which was itself a resurgence of the oppositions of Norse and Anglo-Saxon, Anglo-Saxon and Celt, Celt and Roman, Celt and Celt. The Pull [sic] for home rule in Scotland Wales and Northern Ireland are [sic] signs of it. That's why the Lion for me can be nostalgic pageantry but the Crow quite real, in its way. Incomprehension of the Lion in that piece is also a sign. The country's falling to bits.

I saw that the Lion piece was, in spite of all my efforts to make it quite simple, too complicated. So the second piece was intended to be again simple — but without any internal complications. Even so, maybe the notion of 'a people's dream' is no longer part of common understanding.

From the start I'd wanted to bring in salmon. The Queen Mother is President of the Salmon And Trout Association, and it's known that salmon fishing has always been her sport. But I didn't want to drop the last chance of a unifying totem. The ultimate Totem is a fish as you know. And the ultimate totemic fish because

3 Many white horses were carved out of the chalk hillsides, particularly in Wiltshire. Most can still be seen.
4 See [October 1973].

of its peculiar life is salmon. So my idea was that, since political unity at the level of the Lion has gone, and since all the fragments are now recoiling into their differences, the totem of the only unity to which one can appeal is not Christ as a fish, because even that is not general enough, but the fish as the totem of the sexual creation, the weaver at the source. And that's how I tried to combine mentionning [sic] salmon as the nucleus of an obsession, and projecting an image of a universal totem, a global unity.

It may sound overelaborate but that's the general idea from which I tried to make something as simple and clear as a hymn — since I was still trying to write something she herself might quite like.

Anyway, there it is. I understand the dislike. Verse written semi-privately or as if semi-privately to someone else and yet published openly is always somehow offensive. False interpretations are like the air — always there at 15lbs per square inch. Worse things too.

You don't have to defend it, Keith. You only have to say you don't like that kind of verse. And who can write in an amiable way to any member of the royal family without it looking like flattery? Can't be done.

Love to Melissa & Ursula
Ted

26 May 1986

For several years I've been employing a cuttings agency to send me cuttings about you. When I calculated my expenses for last year for tax purposes and realized that this service had cost me £415 largely for rubbish (twenty cuttings all telling me that you are judging the same poetry competition) – it's ridiculous, so I've cancelled my subscription. But I'll be much more dependent on you and Olwyn for bibliographical information. I'm trying to keep full records which will make it much easier when we come to do a second edition of the Bibliography.

27th May 86

Dear Keith,

Give us a ring — 883 — if you get down here. I'm coming & going all over the place at the moment, but we should be able to fix something.

Amazed at the cost of your cuttings.

All I'm aware of lately is: Poems in Grand St (about now or soon).

2 Poems in Listener last week. Poem in London Review of Books couple of months ago. Poem in a book for Famine Africa due out by some Irish girl. Lynda (something).[5] Poems in a new Gehenna book by Leonard — only one or two poems (etchings of shrunken heads). Essay in collection of pieces for Golding (September next).[6] Piece for Queen in Times, her birthday.[7] Bodley Head reprinting with 3 additional poems a little book Moon Bells (soon). Piece about Crow in a book by Tony Dyson about Gunn, R.S. Thomas & myself — out soon.[8] Piece on Cover of Verbal Arts Association Magazine — recently.[9]

Problem now is to make any money with my pieces. Everybody wants them free for Charity. Me too — free for Charity. Time — free for charity. Pressure for this is so constant that whenever I have a faintly generous mood I'm sure to be nailed by somebody for something —

Strange spring, & the days nearly drawing in.

Hope you're all flourishing even so

I'll expect to hear from you

Ever   Ted

1st Aug. 86

Dear Keith,

Very sorry to hear of your father's death, and your mother's distress. I remember him very well. How about yourself — what's the effect on you?

It shouldn't be too difficult to get you a set of Barrie Cooke's Lithographs of The Great Irish Pike. To tell you the truth, I've forgotten how many I have. One or 5. I just couldn't say. And I don't know where they are. But I'll see if he will do a discount deal. I'm sure he will.

5   I have been unable to trace this book, if it ever appeared.
6   John Carey, ed., William Golding: The Man and His Books (Faber & Faber, 1986).
7   'The Crown of the Kingdom', The Times, 21 April 1986. A revised version appeared in Rain-Charm for the Duchy as 'A Birthday Masque'.
8   This was simply a reprinting of 'In Defence of Crow'.
9   The Verbal Arts Association quickly became the Northern Association of Writers in Education, which later became the National Association of Writers in Education, still going strong.

If you drop him a note, & say how much you regret missing one at the time, that will soften him.[10]

This has been a chaotic spring & summer. I've hardly met myself, let alone anybody else. U.S. legal business boiling & bubbling, among other slips of yew & toad's eyes.

In some ways, the press of extraverting demands, from this Laureateship, has clarified some important issues for me. Clarified the priorities.

Sorry to hear you're feeling you undersold the Lawrence. I'm not clear how much in all you sold.[11] Though I was surprised you didn't sell it through Sotheby's. Seems to me they usually get prices well beyond the expected, or the sane-seeming.

A friend of mine in Cheshire, no great collector (he runs a disco & lives by dealing in jewellery) but mad about Lawrence, paid £800 for a letter of a few lines, in a Sotheby sale. And he was mightily pleased.

Somebody else paid £1,200 for the m.s. of Ed. Thomas's Cockrow [sic] poem, and thought it "incredibly cheap, considering what you pay for a car".

A Wilde letter — 3 or 4 small pages — went for £20,000!!!

I hope everything's going well — Melissa & Ursula blooming.

Love to you all   Ted

20 Oct. 86

Dear Ted

Just got my copy of *Flowers and Insects*. Very attractive, though I'd have preferred wider margins and less glossy paper. The poems are lovely.
I particularly liked the ones which are new to me – 'Brambles', 'Cyclamen' and 'Saint's Island'. Some of the already published ones I had missed. You don't have spare copies of the *Grand Street* with 'Saint's Island' or the *London Mag.* with the grasshopper poem, or the *New Republic* with 'Big Poppy' do you?

What are you working on now? [. . . .]

I have applied today for a vacant chair at Warwick. The present head of

---

10 When *The Great Irish Pike* had been published in 1982 I had baulked at paying £300 for it.

11 The editorial centre of the Cambridge University Press edition of Lawrence's complete works had moved from Nottingham to Birmingham University, and in 1982 Birmingham University Library had expressed an interest in buying my almost complete collection of Lawrence first editions and other printed material. Partly because I was desperate for the money to pay off a bridging loan on our new house, and partly because I had myself proposed Anthony Rota as independent valuer, I felt obliged to accept his valuation at less than half of what I believed its true value to be at that time.

the dept. is Bergonzi. Do you know him? Or Paul Merchant? I've no idea what chance I stand. In terms of publications, I shall probably be in a league of my own. Anyone with a better record there will already have a chair. The question is, how much will they penalise me for having spent my career in an Extra-Mural rather than an English Dept. There would be nice places to live around there. [. . . .]

Melissa is expecting another baby next June. She is so sick she's sure it's going to be a boy.[12]

Love from us both.   Keith

24th Oct 86

Dear Keith,

Congratulations — to Melissa & yourself. Another Sagar must be welcome against the falling birthrate. You must be pleased.

Grand Street didn't publish 'St's Island' — book came out too quickly. That poem's not quite finished somehow. It began as a much shorter piece — in the vein of Grasshopper. Then I brought the rest up into it — not quite.

I never saw the Poppy publication. Maybe Olwyn did — she sold it. The London Mag with the Grasshopper — also has the original Mayfly piece. I did have a copy but it's vanished.[13]

The Warwick job must be desirable. I know Paul Merchant pretty well — I suppose I could call him a friend, and his father. Used to know them in Exeter. Paul is (was?) a good poet — made some very good Translations of Modern Greek poets for MPT.[14] That was his speciality — & the old Greek Plays. I think you'd like his poems — hard and spare, rather bleak. But good, I think. I never met Bergonzi.

I had an interesting few weeks. Stayed with Nicholas in Alaska. He's doing some fascinating research into Grayling — on a stream about 100 miles NE of Fairbanks. Living one of my dream lives. I caught an 89lb halibut.

Called in on Victoria & Vancouver — and realised that's where I ought to be living.

12 Our son Arren was born in May 1987.
13 'Big Poppy' had been published in New Republic on 26 March 1984. 'The Mayfly', a few lines of which were incorporated in 'Saint's Island', was in the London Magazine, October 1983; 'In the Likeness of a Grasshopper' was not.
14 Modern Poetry in Translation.

Called in on New York, & found myself a new lawyer. A sort of Samurai tiger — Jewish — Victor Kovner. I like his name. If he can't extricate me, nobody can. Harper have agreed to help, at last.

Then went to Spain — to lay claim to my butt of sack. Had a high old time there, with the Sherry grandees, in Jerez.[15]

So now I'm back fairly exhausted, & feeling I haven't put two words together for a year. Though actually I wrote a children's book in Alaska — the one I meant to write when I got sidetracked into What Is the Truth. Here's an expunged version of The Goat:

> Bones, belly, bag.!
> All ridge, all sag.
> Lump of torn hair
> Stuck here and there.
>
> What else am I
> With my wicked eye?
>
> My nibbling lip
> My only tool
> With which I strip
> Your farm, O fool.[16]
>
> Love to the family   Ted

15 Originally 'a butt of Sherry Sack' was given by James I as payment to the first Poet Laureate, Ben Jonson, and this continued until 1800. The tradition was revived in 1984 by the sherry producers to mark the long commercial links between the sherry business and Britain. A butt contains 720 bottles. Ted designed the label, Laureate's Choice, with a hoopoe inside a laurel wreath. He numbered and signed each label.

16 A different version of this poem was included in 1987's The Cat and the Cuckoo.

1987

In January the US lawsuit which had dragged on since 1982 was suddenly resolved, Hughes' name being withdrawn from the list of defendants. In March he spent two weeks writing an introduction to the Oxford University Press edition of the *Complete Poems of Keith Douglas*. Hughes finished *Tales of the Early World*. In the summer he went fishing on the Dean River in British Columbia, where he wrote 'The Bear'. In November Hughes was working on *Wolfwatching*.

11th March 1987

Dear Keith,

How is everything going?

What happened finally about the job at Worcester? [sic][1]

How's the family?

How are the marine tanks?

After the Lawsuit flurry, I'm trying to readjust my ballast, & set a course.

Five years, about $180,000, and 15,000 tons per square inch of the sort of experience which leaves you incapable of using it, or turning it to account in any way!![2]

Plus the satyr play performance of the English tabloids, where I've obviously joined the cast of Disney characters.

I just spent 2 arduous weeks writing a fresh Introduction to Oxford's Keith Douglas.[3] They were threatening to reprint the piece I did for the Faber Selected — which seems to me very poor. Once I got back into Douglas, I was pleased to find how much I still liked it. But it would have been time better spent on other things.

I finished a collection of stories which I'd intended to be a continuation of How The Whale Became. They're different inevitably. Tales of the Early World, I call them. There's one in the

---

1 I was not even short-listed for the Warwick chair; a relief, since I had really no desire to leave house, area, or job.

2 A settlement had been reached awarding Anderson $150,000 and an admission that the film had unintentionally defamed her. Hughes was excluded from the list of defendants on the grounds that the defamation was entirely in the film, and not in the novel.

3 *Complete Poems of Keith Douglas*, ed. Desmond Graham (Oxford University Press, 1987). Hughes' earlier introduction to *Selected Poems: Keith Douglas* (Faber, 1964), is in *Winter Pollen*, together with two letters about Douglas to William Scammell.

Guardian's collection 'Guardian angels' — just published (stories by the winners of their Guardian's Children's Fiction Prize).

Reg Lloyd has done the most fantastic series of paintings to some nursery mnemonic poems about creatures, & has designed a stunning little book — about 5" by 3" — called The Cat & The Cuckoo. We're printing it ourselves, & it's to be sold through Desmond Clarke's Poetry Catalogue — 250 Limited Edition (signed & I think boxed), at £20 & 1750 ordinary, at about £8. (He's sold most of the Ltd, & it's not printed yet)

Reg is also making a series of prints — 28 pieces, £20 each, £500 the set — which he's launching at some Exhibition of his, at London University in May.

I'm suggesting we do them as a long connected frieze, for nurseries. They really are dazzling pictures — much better than 'What Is The Truth'.

Here's the Hen:

Dowdy the Hen
Has nothing to do
But peer and peck, and peck and peer
At nothing.

Sometimes a couple of scratches to right
Sometimes a couple of scratches to left
And sometimes a head-up red-rimmed stare
At nothing.

O Hen in your pen, O Hen, O when
Will something happen?
Nothing to do but brood on her nest
And wish.

Wish? Wish? What shall she wish for?
Stealthy fingers
Under her bum.
An egg on your dish.

Here's the old Crow:

Thrice, thrice, thrice, the coal-bright Crow
Baaarks — aaarks — aaarks, like a match being struck
To look for trouble.

"Hear ye the Preacher:
Nature to Nature
Returns each creature."

The Crow lifts a claw —
A crucifix
Of burnt matchsticks.

"I am the Priest.
For my daily crust
I'll tend your dust."[4]
The monkish Crow
Ruffles his cloak
Like a burnt bible.

"At my humble feast
I'm happy to drink
Whatever you think."

Then the Crow
Laughs through his hacker
And grows blacker.

The others are mostly shorter & simpler.
Love to Melissa, blessings on the kids
be well   Ted

[Mid-March 1987]

Dear Ted,
Thanks for the letter and poems. The nursery frieze is a good idea, but
then I'm rather nursery-oriented at the moment.

---

4 In the published text Ted changed this stanza to:
I am the Priest.
For my daily bread
I nurse the dead.

I didn't make the short-list at Warwick . . . The chair went to someone who apparently once published an essay on Eliot. One never knows why one has been ruled out – age? Extra-Mural background? Over-qualified (whatever that means)?

We are all well apart from the succession of coughs and colds all winter. Melissa is enormous, as big with three months to go as she was at full-term with Ursula. So it looks as though it's going to be a boy, which would give us the same pattern as yours.

Ursula is particularly fascinating now with her rapid language acquisition. She loves poems and songs. I wonder if she is the first 22-month-old to be able to recite (with great feeling) the first two lines of Blake's 'Tyger'?

The fish are fine. But I have a bad conscience now about keeping them – depleting the reefs.

The failure at Warwick may turn out to be a blessing . . . We got a new director of our department in January. Within a week of taking up his appointment he rang me out of the blue to say he wanted to put my name forward for a personal chair. Since we have really no desire to leave this house or area or job, that would be splendid.

I suppose the law-suit could have gone much worse; and no-one who matters takes any notice of *The Mail on Sunday*. Perhaps a time of wound-licking would be a good time to finish *Crow*. Or do you have anything major in hand or head in the way of poems for adults?

11 September 1987

People who are doing work on you are writing to me all the time. Many of them have discovered and are very excited by your prose writings – essays, interviews, introductions, reviews, etc. Many of them are asking me to supply then with photocopies of things they can't get hold of. They all ask the same question, why do you make your prose so inaccessible? Why is there no volume of 'Selected Essays' or 'Selected Literary Criticism'? I believe Olwyn was planning to publish such a volume at one time, but then lost interest in the Rainbow Press. But surely Faber would jump at it. I believe that the great creative writers are always also the best critics. If your work in this field were generally known you would stand alongside Eliot and Lawrence. If you don't want the bother of editing such a book and seeing it through the press, I'd be delighted to take it on, but I'm not mentioning it because I'm looking for work; I have far too much on my plate as it is. But I would give such a book the highest priority.

Nov. 14. 87

Dear Keith,

I hope Melissa & yourself and the exponential family are all well.

When did I last write. This has been one of those headlong years, like falling down a mountain. The court-case, in spite of all the positive things about it, left me mightily enlightened — and extensively rearranged.

I wonder, quietly & not letting myself respond too much to my own thoughts, just how deeply it has paralysed me for the last 5 years. I certainly feel deeply different, now I'm rid of it.

I greatly liked the Lawrence poems (I liked the piece too). Really some of your best.[5]

Once again I'm trying to get the old airplane down the runway. It's one of those climacterics — when it suddenly seems as if only now do I know what I ought to be doing, & how! I ought to be doing it.

I have what I suppose is a book — excluding most things. My only hesitation about it is — it's moulted feathers, rather than new flight. So it seems Elegiac — obsequies over a state of mind that is to me now defunct. It is actually, I suppose, the funeral, & the mourning. So it's sad.[6]

This summer I went back to British Columbia — went fishing on the Deane [sic] River, about 500 very wild miles North of Vancouver. Magical place & time. We caught Steelhead — sea-run rainbows. They grow big — 25 lb — and are maybe 2 or 3 times as boisterous as Salmon.

There were bears. Strange observation: in Alaska, the presence of bears is a sort of constant apprehension, as if you were creeping about in heavily guarded enemy country. In Canada the bears are just as dangerous — and yet you have no anxieties about them, only great desire to see them. It's odd. Something to do maybe with a critical point of human claim over the territory — in Canada that point has been passed, & the bears are living by permission. In Alaska, the bears still own it, & the traveller is living by permission.

I received the letter from the Cambridge graduate — proposing

5 I had sent Ted a copy of the first issue of Words International, November 1987, which contained my piece
   on 'Six Paintings by D. H. Lawrence', and incorporated six poems on them.
6 Wolfwatching (1989).

a collection of my prose. Recently Oxford republished — any moment now — the Complete Keith Douglas, & wanted to reprint with it the essay Introduction of mine from the 1964 selection. I was so appalled, re-reading that piece, I set to writing another, more to my tastes — which Oxford used. But to face that rewriting — not rewriting but total cancellation & replacement — for all my lapses of prose! If only the whole lot could volatolise! [sic] And vanish. I've engaged myself to reissue (I shall enlarge it a bit) my Shakespeare selection — because I do want to redeem & repair the mistake of that Essay — the mistake being in my unrealistic idea of the audience (16 year olds!) that would be reading it.[7] Taken me too long to realise that everything I put on paper is judged as if it were my heart-blood, my last ultimate offering, to the highest.

Love to all.   Ted

15 November 1987

As for your miscellaneous prose. It is extant, and scholars (like me) will forever be ferreting it out and quoting it. Would not publishing it be almost a way of disowning it, if you had an introduction saying that you would say it all differently now – if at all. There are all those snippets in Egbert Faas' book – so annoying when the paragraph one wanted is omitted. However inadequate it all seems to you now, it is so much better than anyone else's, and so <u>needed</u> in the midst of our present decadence that it seems to me a real waste and deprivation that it should be withheld.[8]

---

7 A Choice of Shakespeare's Verse.
8 In 1991 Hughes finally agreed to collaborate with William Scammell in compiling a collection of his prose: Winter Pollen.

1988

Hughes began writing *The Iron Woman*. He began compiling *Winter Pollen* with William Scammell, and a second anthology of poems for children with Seamus Heaney. In June he went fishing in Alaska. In September he delivered the T. S. Eliot Centenary address, 'A Dancer to God'.

7 June 1988

Dear Ted

I've just read the first chapter and a half of a 500-page Ph.D. thesis: *Poetry and Grace: The Dynamics of the Self in Ted Hughes' Adult Poetry* by Nick Bishop, whom I gather you know. It's the most promising beginning to a thesis I've ever read. Splendid so far. I'm the external examiner. I don't expect to be in any doubt that he'll get his Ph.D., but I still have to go to Exeter to interview him a week on Monday (20th) . . . It would be a good opportunity to call and see you if you'll be around and can spare an hour . . .

Another Ph.D. thesis on you is winging its way from Australia, by Ann Skea from Armidale, N.S.W. I've met her and read bits of her work-in-progress, enough to know that that's going to be another fine piece of work.[1] How lucky you are in your critics! Craig Robinson's pleasant book T.H.: *Shepherd of Being* will be published later this year by Macmillan. He's a former student of mine.

My only reservation about Nick Bishop so far is that he goes much too far for my taste down that currently so fashionable road of denying that language has any purchase on objective reality. He quotes Gurdjieff with approval:

People do not clearly realize to what degree their language is subjective, that is, what different things each of them says while using the same words. They are not aware that each of them speaks a language of his own, understanding other people's language either vaguely or not at all, and having no idea that each one of them speaks in a language unknown to him.

This seems to me pure affectation, especially in writers like Beckett who wring their hands at the impossibility of communication while in the midst of communicating the most subtle and complex meanings. If it were true there could be no literature. Language seems to me almost the greatest human accomplishment. It is little short of miraculous that you can put a few marks on paper and be understood by thousands. I prefer Whitman:

1 Subsequently published as *Ted Hughes: The Poetic Quest* (1994).

Were you thinking that those were the words, those upright lines? Those
   curves, angles, dots?
No, those are not the words, the substantial words are in the ground and
   sea,
They are in the air, they are in you.

That's what great poetry is – 'substantial words'.

10th June 88

Dear Keith,

Sorry I shall be missing you — I leave for Alaska on the 14th
June. Pity, for other reasons too.

Give Nick Bishop my regards. I'm glad you like his thesis.
I thought he'd left Exeter. I thought for some reason he was in the
U.S. He's a pleasant fellow — interested in arcane reading.[2]

Like you, I try to keep some faith in words. Though the Babel of
the Plath industry makes it difficult. When the subject is somebody
else, the accounts & reports & interpretations sound plausible.
When it's yourself, you realise what the creative demon is. So far as
I can see — in other words, so far as it touches me — the world of
biography is a world of lies. Perverse lies, too, mostly.

I have a jumble of bits and pieces — can't feel it's a collection.
And it's a bit too gloomy. I've had an elegiac few years, it seems.

Is everything going pretty well? And happily? And healthily?
If healthily then wealthily.[3]

   all the best to all   Ted

23rd Nov. 88

Dear Keith,

China must have been a change. Did you keep a journal?[4]

I went nowhere new this year — though the old places were very
good.

---

2 A revised version of Bishop's thesis was published as *Re-Making Poetry: Ted Hughes and a New Critical
   Psychology* (1991).
3 Ted is here echoing Petruchio in *The Taming of the Shrew*:
      I come to wive it wealthily in Padua;
      If wealthily, then happily in Padua.
4 I had attended a Lawrence conference in Shanghai, followed by a tour to Xian and Beijing. There were
   many bright and keen young Chinese Lawrence scholars at the conference. But it was a false dawn,
   destined to be stained in less than a year by the Tiananmen Square massacre.

This is only a note to send you a copy of my Eliot Centenary address — needs to be half the length. But it was trying to shorten it that made it so long.[5]

I trust all the family's well.

love to all   Ted

---

5   Published as 'A Dancer to God' in *A Dancer to God: Tributes to T. S. Eliot* (1993).

1989

In April Hughes wrote long letters to the *Guardian* and the *Independent* about the desecration of Sylvia Plath's grave at Heptonstall. He wrote 'Sylvia Plath: The Evolution of "Sheep in Fog"'. In July he became 'heavily involved' in the early stages of what was to grow, over the next two years, into *Shakespeare and the Goddess of Complete Being*. In November Hughes visited Bangladesh for the Asia Poetry Festival.

2ⁿᵈ Feb 89

Dear Keith —

Here's the missing page of that Eliot address.

If I can avoid it, I shall never again get into the position of delivering this sort of thing.

To say what you think is one thing. To parade it in ceremonial dress, on a pious occasion, where the aesthetic requirement is confined to 'eulogy for the dead — good taste for the occasion', is another.

So I see this Eliot piece as — maybe — 3 pages. I'll have a go.

Audience — one's idea of audience — is the great problem. One always has the dreadful notion that unless you (one) start with ABC, & go on step by step from there, with notes, sources etc to every reference, half nay 9/10 of your (one's) audience won't have the faintest idea of what you're (one's) talking about.

And when your subject is some apparently shared piece of the mythos — like Eliot's work — that's a kind of agony, a sort of writhing.

Don't you find that? How do you do it? Maybe all I lack is classroom fluency.

My Beatrice piece was published Dec 17ᵗʰ — Daily Telegraph.[1]

I auctioned it to the 4 main dailies. Guardian offered about £750 — apologising for the small sum. Independent cried off (after agreeing to join the Auction) saying they were sure they didn't have the money to equal what the Times would offer. The Times delayed — probably until they got the drum whisper of what the Telegraph

---

1 'For the Christening of Her Royal Highness Princess Beatrice of York Born: 8.18 8–8-88'. Collected in *Rain-Charm for the Duchy* and *Collected Poems*, p. 820.

had offered — then changed the rules & said they really couldn't make an offer till they'd seen the verses. The Telegraph offered £5,000 — which was split between Greenpeace & Friends of the Earth. That's the story. Good for Max Hastings, say I.

I sent Faber a small collection — just to get it out of the way. I'll send you a copy.

Also they're republishing Moortown — I've cut out everything but the farming pieces and added a few introductory pieces of prose.[2]

Did I write — surely I did, I remember it — about your Lawrence essay, which I did like.

Love to Melissa & the children   Ted

7th July 89

Dear Keith,

How was Spain? Nice photographs. I expect that paternal role packs your days tight. Nice chance to see the world afresh.

Small after-shock of that Guardian business last week. The letter that prompted my reply was written by Ronald Hayman, and signed by 7 others — including Joseph Brodsky.[3] I couldn't understand how (a) he would be interested (b) could have been contacted in the 3 or 4 day period between Hayman's letter and that earlier letter — by the 2 feminists — which prompted that.

He was in England last week, with Derek Walcott. We gave Walcott a Queen's Gold Medal for Poetry, & at the little ceremony I asked him about Brodsky's involvement. He asked Brodsky. It turns out — Brodsky knew nothing about it. Hayman had simply hijacked his name. I don't know what Brodsky's done about it.[4]

---

2 *Moortown Elegies* was republished by Faber in 1989 as *Moortown Diary*.

3 Joseph Brodsky (1940–96), Russian poet, essayist and dissident, was expelled from the Soviet Union in 1972 and spent the rest of his life in the USA. He was awarded the Nobel Prize for Literature in 1987 and appointed American Poet Laureate in 1991.

4 On 7 April the *Guardian* had published a letter from two academics, Julia Parnaby and Rachel Wingfield, complaining that Sylvia Plath's grave at Heptonstall was both hard to find and neglected. They also claimed, erroneously, that Hughes and Plath had signed divorce papers. Four days later the *Guardian* published a letter from Ronald Hayman in support of the previous letter, and co-signed by A. Alvarez, Joseph Brodsky, Helga Graham, Jill Neville, Peter Orr, Peter Porter and John Carey. On 20 April the *Guardian* printed a response from Hughes, in which he explained that the pebbles and shells with which he had decorated Plath's grave had been removed, and that the gravestone, which bore the name Sylvia Plath Hughes, had been repeatedly vandalized by chiselling out the name Hughes. He also explained that he had resisted suggestions that the grave should be signposted because he did not want it to become a tourist attraction. See Reid, *Letters*, pp. 552–61.

Lumb Bank is being bought by Arvon. The Northern Arts Associations refused to go on funding Arvon if it moved anywhere else. We were thinking of renting somewhere else, so your suggestion would have been useful. As it is, there's laborious fundraising afoot. Do you want a 100 per annum 4 year Covenant?[5]

Wolfwatching comes out Sept 18th — same day as Hawk in the Rain.

Heavily involved at the moment rewriting my Shakespeare introduction — not as an introduction, but as a series of letters (mightily simplifies the tone & prose). I see the whole thing much more clearly, & slightly differently. Last time, supposing I was writing for 17 year olds (how could I be so naïve!) I left everything to be unravelled by the reader — assuming my main point was interesting enough to excite a Shakespearean's curiosity.

I know more now about the solidarity of the Academic walls. So I am laying the whole pattern out in some detail, as in a theorem — as for a Theatre Director who wants to stage all the tragedies and romances as a single concertina. In fact, a Swedish Director, Donya Feuers [sic], who made a single composite monologue for one woman — following suggestions in that first intro. version, wants to do just that.

Problem is, of course — the secret of being boring is to tell all.

Also, republishing just the farm diary section of Moortown, with a brief intro & notes — to set it in context and make it readable.

Love to Melissa & the family   Ted

[July 1989]

Dear Ted,

I'm writing to ask a big favour. My favourite poem in Elmet is 'Curlew's Lift'. I was delighted to see it so beautifully and aptly illustrated by Robert Greenhalf in Birds [Summer 1989], and still more delighted when I was able to buy the original painting from the RSPB. The original is much better than the reproduction – bigger of course, but also the reproduction has lost the 'bilberry blue' of the rocks and clouds. I now want to frame it, but I'm searching for a bilberry blue mount . . .

I want to frame the text under the painting, and could, of course, blow

5   I had suggested that we might accommodate some Arvon courses at Holly Royde, my department's residential college in Didsbury, Manchester.

up the printed text, but it would be infinitely better if you would be willing to write it out for me.

21ˢᵗ July 89

Dear Keith

Here's the inscription. No trouble. Keep it out of the light — or it will fade right away. Unless you get special glass (Roy Davids — Sotheby's — knows which).

I heard from Faber about the proposed Schrekschrift.[6] The Eliot piece I've trimmed greatly — to its essentials. I'd prefer to keep it for a separate volume.

Brodsky wrote to Guardian, dissociating himself from Hayman's letter. Guardian rang Hayman who swore that Brodsky had read it and signed it. What next, I wonder.

Love to all   Ted

RSPB mag had a misprint in the other part of Curlews — a zoological howler at that.[7]

29 July 1989

I got hold of an advance copy of *Wolfwatching* from Bernard Stone. [. . .] I noted a few misprints. [. . .]

I'm puzzled by the reference to Cary Grant:

Born at the bottom of the heap. As he grew upwards
The welts of his brow deepened, fold upon fold.
Like the Tragic Mask.
Cary Grant was his living double.   ('Sacrifice')

He doesn't seem to me to have a particularly furrowed brow, and has no connection with either tragedy (having specialized in romantic comedies) or Westerns. You weren't thinking of Gary Cooper, were you? I have in front of me a photograph of Gary Cooper in *High Noon*. The caption reads: Though he has been in pictures thirty years, the lines which have settled in Gary Cooper's face seem to be imposed by the physical and emotional climate of his native Montana rather than of Hollywood.

---

6 I had informed Faber of my plans for the 1990 Manchester conference on Hughes, and had asked if they would be interested in publishing the resulting collection, which, I suggested, might include Ted's essay on Eliot. *Schrekschrift* means 'horror-writing'.
7 Curlews were described as 'web-footed' (which they are not) instead of 'wet-footed'.

5th Aug. 89

Dear Keith —

Thank you for the textual corrections — 'the imprimatur of printer's error is holy as it is inevitable'. 'The god of proofing oversight is stronger than the human eye' etc.

I got them all, I think (many that you missed, Keith) (some) — except maybe 'Duumvirate'. Plus some textual changes — slight & not so slight.

I wrote a couple of paragraphs for the Poetry Book Society bulletin, trying to explain nothing.[8]

Simultaneously, they're reprinting the Moortown Poems — separate & solus, with a brief introduction & commentary on a few of the pieces.

I've been thinking of making a selection of my verses and setting them in a commentary — like the Vita Nuova.[9] The pieces I mostly read.

This is heresy. But there seems to me a possibility that many poems simply slip from the great memory because they lack context. We assume the context is understood — but that is only so in a fairly stable society. I know quite intelligent people who have simply lost the keys to what one imagined were natural responses. And now they have the arrogance of their minority rights ("what I don't know must be trying to oppress me") to harden them in what is actually simple deprivation. (Not so simple)

Mainly, my idea would be to give a context as I might at a reading. An anecdote or two etc. Supply the subjective link — without which most readers don't know how to feel, I find.

Tricky, though. Historical change, I see, is mainly forgetting.

Black Rhino was first published in The Daily Telegraph — or rather the Weekend Telegraph 28th October 1987. Then in Antaeus. With an extra piece at the end. I'm trying to sell a limited edition — 12 copies only, poem written out fresh, with 12 drawings by famous wildlife artists including Prince Bernhardt of Sweden — one original with each copy — £5000 each for Rhino Rescue.[10]

Cary Grant looked like the subject in question, strong facial

8   The Bulletin published a few of Ted's notes on Wolfwatching in its Autumn number.
9   Dante Alighieri, 1295.
10   This project seems never to have got off the ground.

resemblance, & expression too. Imagine Cary Grant with a wrinkled brow. There you have him.

If Faber would do the revised Elmet, I would reprint the Elmetish pieces in it — plus a few others I have. Fay has new photographs. In fact, I heard from her only yesterday — she had just asked Henry [actually Ernest] Hall (the Halifax millionaire local culture renovator) to raise the £10,000 Faber would require. She said he was 'very interested'. Do you know him.[11]

Schreck — from Kinderschrek (child-frightener).

My Shakespeare rewrite is now quite long. Too long (several long letters to a Swedish stage director) but a tar-baby.

Love to all   Ted

17 August 1989

Dear Ted

I've found a framer in Manchester who can frame 'Curlews Lift' with UV filter Perspex and acid-free board and exactly the right 'bilberry blue' colour. So it's all systems go.

Yes, I agree with you about contexts for poems. But what is surely most needed is the full context for the Crow poems – the prose framework of the 'folk-epic'. I supply as much of this as I can when teaching Crow, and it makes such a difference to the reception of the poems.

20 September 1989

Craig Raine turned down the proposed book eventually . . .

I felt there ought to be a piece on your Mss. demonstrating what a prolonged and complex process often lies behind even the shortest and simplest poems, how they are kernels which have shed several layers of elaboration. I am limited to those poems of which I have all the drafts, that is the Prometheus and Adam poems. My first choice was 'Adam lay defeated', but after a week's weary work trying to decipher the drafts and get them in the right order I lay defeated. I had cracked most of the deciphering problems, but the ordering was very difficult. The conclusion I came to was that you arrived quite quickly at the version you eventually published, but then went on to expand the three dreams through many more drafts, eventually abandoning them all. Is that correct? If so, it is all very interesting, but not really typical. But if the published poem really is the end-product, whittled down from the elaborated dreams, then I'll have another go at the ordering. Anyway, I then had a go at 'The Dove Came', thinking that would be much easier; but it

11 Elmet was eventually published by Faber in 1994.

wasn't. I've transcribed the Mss. and put them in an order, but again I'm not at all sure it's the right one . . . Is there another poem in either the Adam or Prometheus sequence you think would lend itself better to my purposes.
I really want to counteract the idea (perhaps suggested by 'The Thought Fox') that your poems come to you complete in one sitting in a matter of minutes. On the other hand I don't want to choose an untypically factitious, laboured poem such as Prometheus 21, of which I have, I think, sixteen drafts, the last having not 1 phrase in common with the first!

27 November 1989

I abandoned 'Adam lay defeated'. But I went ahead with 'The Dove Came'. I enclose the first draft. Would you like to have a look at it? If you don't think it would do any good, I'll have a go at one of the Prometheus poems instead.

The other chapter I'm thinking of doing is called 'Crow and his Context'. Of course I'll drop that if you are thinking of publishing something along the same lines yourself. It would be mainly a summary of information you have yourself given in articles, introductions, sleeve-notes, interviews and readings. But I think there is one piece of information I should need from you to make the exercise worthwhile. The ogress asked Crow seven questions while crossing the river. Three of these were 'Who paid most, him or her?', 'Who gave most, him or her?' and 'Was it an animal, a bird or a fish?' What were the other four questions, and in what order? And what poems are the answers to these questions? Do you still see it as a possibility that you will ever finish The Life and Songs of the Crow?

14 December 1989

I have done a first draft of the sort of thing I had in mind. Every word is yours, but it is a composite made up of material from several sources. You will no doubt want to knock out and change some things. I have therefore printed it double-spaced so that you can make interlinear revisions. If, however, you dislike the whole thing in this form, the alternative would be simply to print extracts in chronological order from the various pieces. The trouble with that would be to avoid repetition, and the fact that there would be no order or progression or coherence.

There are two points on which I think it would be highly desirable to have some additional information. The reference to 'God's hidden prisoner' comes out of the blue. Could you briefly explain how the nightmare hand/voice, which appears to be quite independent of God at the beginning gets to be his hidden female prisoner? Also I think it would be very helpful if you could give the other five questions asked by the hag, and identify the poems which are Crow's answers to them. Does he give only one answer (poem) to each question? Is 'The Lamentable History of the Human Calf' one of his most wrong answers? It seems even more wrong than 'Lovesong', where at least they share the guilt. 'Actaeon' could be yet another wrong answer to the first question . . .

Let me know when you have time whether you think that piece on 'The Dove Came' is worth publishing.

1990

Hughes continued to work with Seamus Heaney on the anthology eventually published as *The School Bag* in 1997. He proposed to Faber a competition of plays for children based on myths, folktales and environmental issues. His proposal was taken up and resulted in the creation of the Sacred Earth Drama Trust, and the publication by Faber of the winners in *Sacred Earth Dramas* (1993), for which Hughes wrote the foreword. Hughes' brother Gerald and his wife visited Court Green for a month. Otherwise, Hughes remained preoccupied with his book on Shakespeare. The second international conference on Hughes was held in Manchester in July. Papers from the conference were published under my editorship as *The Challenge of Ted Hughes* by Macmillan in 1994.

5th Jan 1990

Dear Keith,

Happy New Year.

Sorry to be so laggard responding. I went to Bangladesh, and back here came under pressure to finish my Shakespeare pieces for Donya Feuers — who is wanting to make an attempt at the ultimate thing, blend all the mature plays into one i.e. from ALL'S WELL to the end. I've worked out in fair detail the particular unity that makes this possible — old stuff, the myth, but worked out for each play. I see it much more clearly now, and find the plays fit much more precisely than I'd anticipated. The truth seems to be, the internal system, in Shakes Imag, existed with marvellous consistency of form, and evolved in a step by step manner.

Odd incidentals: the language change — which begins in All's Well, comes at exactly the point where the myth emerges into the drama. (The change from the process of increasing simplification to the process of increasing complication — of meaning and music: though the process of simplification, of basic elements, goes right on to the end, as the musical compounds of those elements becomes all the time more complicated.)

As You Like It — play before ALL'S WELL — recapitulates opening of Dante's inferno — in many corresponding details: i.e. as if Shakes knew he was at this point committing himself to the serious business. Then — in next play — he enters the myth.

Cordelia descends in unbroken line of mythical evolution from the Eye of Ra (for which Horus and Set fought each other. Also source of Lucrece figure (Cordelia) = Crown.) via the Irish versions where she became the Crane Skin Bag (in which the god of poetry kept the letters of the Alphabet). Creiddylad (In the Welsh original, which also has the two brothers which all Shakespeare's known sources had lost, but which Shakespeare replaced — from Arcadia) is derived from welsh Creyr = crane or heron.

I've been writing it all out as a series of letters to her. I'll let you see it as soon as I type it up.

Also, a point I didn't make before (I don't know whether it had actually dawned on me (I've refrained from re-reading my earlier piece) the two plots, Venus and Adonis and Lucrece, are, the first of them the myth behind Catholic Christianity (Great goddess and the sacrificed God) and the second, a secularisation of the Marduk-Tiamat myth[1] via Jehovah-Middle Eastern Goddesses via Reformation Puritan Jehovan Christ — Catholic Church as great harlot, the myth, behind puritan Protestantism, so by fusing the two, he fused, literally, the religious history and pre-history of Europe — in exactly the form in which the two traditions were fighting it out in England between Henry VIII and Cromwell's regicide. At least I didn't make it clearly. But it explains why the myth did become the template of the great plays. It wasn't just some old myth — it was IT. Perhaps I did say it before.

All kinds of other incidentals.

I've written an extremely simplified scan of the relevant bits for introduction to an enlarged reprint of the Shakespeare Anthology. I'll send you that.

Of the prose you sent me, the parts that I penned with care seem OK. The other parts, from interviews, embarrass me. They also, I must say, interfere somewhat with what I was still trying to do about all that. It was a great mistake for me ever to be drawn into saying anything about the context of the Crow pieces. I've a feeling the other parts — the carefully penned — are being used by Tony

---

1 Robert Graves writes: 'Marduk, the Babylonian city-god, eventually defeats the goddess in the person of Tiamat the Sea-serpent; and it is then brazenly announced that he, not anyone else, created herbs, lands, rivers, beasts, birds, and mankind' (The Greek Myths (2 vols), Penguin, 1955, vol. I, p. 35). Anne Baring and Jules Cashford speak of the Enuma Elish as 'the first story of the replacing of a mother goddess who generates creation as part of herself by a god who "makes" creation as something separate from himself' ('Tiamat of Babylon: The Defeat of the Goddess', in The Myth of the Goddess, Viking, 1991). See Hughes, Shakespeare and the Goddess of Complete Being, p. 6.

Dyson in some book he's written about R. S. Thomas, Thom G and myself.[2] But I'm not sure just how he's using it.

I hope Melissa & the children are prospering — I expect they are.

Love to them   Ted

p.s. I'll write again about The Dove — very interesting (largely right, I suppose)

4th April 90

Dear Keith,

Sorry, as ever, to be so delayed, answering your specific points — in reverse order:

(1) The problem of making — as you propose, a selection of unpublished poems, is: that presents a meal, for the reader, of what I'd thrown out of the kitchen.[3]

My dear friends & fellow writers will no more miss the opportunity to comment on my evolutionary failures this next time than they did last time. Even dear old Peter (Redgrove), whose own miscarriages I regularly put on my private life support system, couldn't resist a public outcry or two.

Lord what apes we mortals be![4]

I should say, I'd prefer you not to resuscitate anything from any interview or recorded talk. Chat at readings only works on the occasion, and is a studied way, you know, of saying nothing about the verse — a studied way of putting the listener off-guard, or at least at ease. Like the soupy music slurped out to air passengers just before take-off & landing. It's basically a bit loathsome, and one of the reasons I've stopped doing readings is my rising gorge against the requisite introductory chat. Though my verses are too short and too arcane (?) to be read straight, I'm wondering whether I don't owe them — my verses — a commentary. Something like the notes to Moortown, if I could keep it very simple. I get the feeling, wherever I've heard that annotated Moortown Diary mentioned, that readers get more out of the notes than out of the verses.

2 A. E. Dyson, ed., *Three Contemporary Poets: Thom Gunn, Ted Hughes and R. S. Thomas* (1990).
3 I was trying to find a publisher for the essays to be presented at the forthcoming Hughes conference in Manchester, and had asked Ted if he would be interested in following the pattern of *The Achievement of Ted Hughes* by including an appendix of some of his unpublished poems.
4 'Lord, what fools these mortals be!' Puck in *A Midsummer Night's Dream*.

The piece about Crow that Dyson is using is the only piece of mine, about C., that seems of any use. Everything else seems positively destructive.[5]

I see they're considering deleting the set-books course for A level English. I thought set books were meant to help teachers — to give them something to work with. If there are no set books, presumably teachers will still need to pick some particular books to concentrate their teaching. How is English taught without texts? Without A level King Lear & The Woodlanders & Adonais I might be just about retiring from commercial fishing out of Sydney.[6]

Instead, here I am writing about King Lear. I've been writing up my Shakespeare piece as a series of letters to Donya Feuers — a Swedish Director who made a performance from some ideas in that first introduction to the Selection of passages.

I found it impossible to set out briefly — without making it hopelessly obscure. So I'm going through each play from All's Well onwards in detail — a letter of 9 or 10 written pages on each main point. I'm on my third letter about Lear — letter 33. About Cordelia's silence. The key to the whole complex. If I publish these I shall call it The Silence of Cordelia. Maybe I told you that. When I type them up, (what's left shouldn't take long — since I've laid out most of the groundwork) I'll send you copies.

Yes, I know the Story of Salt. (I mentioned it in that piece about Myth in Education).[7] I once told the story of King Lear to Frieda. She then told me the variants that she knew — one of them was the story of Salt.[8]

Sorry about this pen on this paper. 46 years ago today, I was looking up into a Holly Tree beside Crookhill Pond (Conisborough) where there was sometimes a tawny owl, and I thought: today is 4/4/44 and I shall never forget this moment. Now I orient all holocaust experiences, all 2nd world war events, by that fixed moment.

Love to the family   Ted

---

5 See Appendix VIII.
6 King Lear, Thomas Hardy's The Woodlanders, and Shelley's 'Adonais' were set books for the A level examination Hughes would have sat in his last year at Mexborough Grammar School.
7 See Winter Pollen, p. 153.
8 I had heard an Eastern European folk-tale related on radio (without reference to King Lear) in which the three daughters tell the king that they love him like sugar, like honey, and like salt. The king is infuriated with the third daughter, who means, of course, that she could not live without him.

15 April 1990

I think you are overreacting to (or misremembering) Peter's single sentence about the appendix of your poems in his review of *The Achievement*. All he said was that they contradicted the impression given by some of the essays in that book that you could do no wrong, being 'naturally uneven in quality' – hardly a 'public outcry'. Moreover, Peter was unique among the few reviewers in not welcoming those poems. Elizabeth Maslen, reviewing the book in *English*, said: 'The final section, incorporating the thirty poems, is an inspiration on the part of the editor and includes, for example, further Crow poems; and two poems used in the Ilkley Festival production of *Cave Birds*, which are omitted from both the limited and commercial editions'. And Peter Vernon in *Études anglaises* wrote: 'It is wonderful to have available "Light", "Skin" and "Two Dreams in the Cell" which would otherwise be lost poems. And certainly anything from the outstanding poet of our era is worth reading.' Also I'm sure that by no means all your uncollected or even unpublished poems have been 'thrown out of the kitchen'. Some get forgotten or lost, other fall by the wayside because of accidents of publishing – i.e. they are withheld from one book in the expectation that they will be included in another which does not, in the event, materialize. For example, what about those *Caprichos* poems Leonard was going to publish ten years ago? I'm sure there are a score of uncollected poems as good and important as many of your collected ones, though in any case no-one would apply the same standard to such a gathering as to one of your major collections.

29th April 90

Dear Keith,

Here are the first 15 (or so) of 45.[9] I'm away for a week — I'll type the rest when I get back.

I'm trying to be clear & plain. Here & there my ideal would be "Instructions for assembling a Greenhouse".

My correspondent — I think I told you — is a Director at the royal Theatre in Stockholm.

Love to the family   Ted

(There's no May 5th. April 31st becomes May 1st)

9th May 90

Dear Keith,

Here are some more sections of the tube.

Love to the family   Ted

9 Hughes' letters on Shakespeare to Donya Feuer. See 5 January 1990.

18th June 90

Dear Keith,

Here are the rest. Plus the first three rewritten.

The first one, 23rd April, is now a sort of introductory survey —
a map of the whole route, to help through the mazes of the earlier
part.

I also inserted brief introductions to five main divisions —
again, hill-top views of the next dark valley, with new bearings,
hot coffee & chocolate.

I've tidied up several of the pieces I sent you, though not
radically — I won't confuse you with new copies of those. April 31st
I've abbreviated & simplified. I'm always surprised what objections
are raised to the Catholic/Puritan conflict, throughout that period.

Wriothesley was a perfect example.[10] His family such fervent
Catholics (and his Mother's family) that his father's career was
ruined by his loyalty. His own allegiances suspect — in spite of his
protestations. His later years — militant Puritan. He must have
lived out exactly the internal Civil War that I'm talking about.

Extract 27th April — probably relevant, but too speculative, for
a reader & unnecessary. No reason why I should introduce her.[11]

Maybe I should add one or two other letters. One about his
verse, as a form of action — a sort of hieroglyphic audial drama
emanating from the visible drama.

Have a good time in Montpellier.

Love to the family   Ted

The details are less important that the principle. Obviously,
every detail is open to other interpretations. The plot of All's Well is
like a transcription of parts of Wriothesley's life. If he'd made a will,
in 1605, (Shakespeare) he would have been leaving his kingdom to

---

10 Henry Wriothesley, 3rd Earl of Southampton (1573–1624), was Shakespeare's patron, and probably
    the model for the 'young man' of the sonnets. He was deeply involved in Essex's conspiracy against
    Elizabeth I, and in 1601 was sentenced to death. This was later commuted to life imprisonment.
    After the accession of James I in 1603, he was released, and resumed his connection with the theatre.
11 Hughes deleted the several pages he had written on Emilia Lanier. Emilia Lanier (1569–1645), was the
    daughter of a court musician, Baptiste Bassano. She was educated at court, and became the mistress
    of the Queen's cousin, Henry Carey, 1st Baron Hunsdon, forty-five years her senior. When she became
    pregnant by him, she was married off to another court musician, Alfonso Lanier. In 1611 she became
    the first Englishwoman to publish a book of poems. In *Shakespeare the Man* (Macmillan, 1973), A. L.
    Rowse identified her with the Dark Lady of the Sonnets, and this identification has been taken up
    by other biographers, most recently by Michael Wood, *In Search of Shakespeare* (BBC Books, 2003),
    pp. 209–20.

3 women, but his title (his armorial crest & Gent.) would pass to Edmund, the bastard son of his brother Edmund. Etc.

The main point is not that the equation displaces anything — it still leaves every interpretation and thematic analysis untouched — but that it provides the dynamics of the motivation, which are (in realistic terms) always irrational, often simply crazy, yet they always seem right & always decide the drama of the situation.

As the letters go on, I think that becomes easier to see.

I was extremely keen to study these letters and respond to them, but it was not until after the Lawrence conference in Montpellier, family holidays in Brittany and Anglesey, the Hughes conference in Manchester, and a theatre course in Edinburgh, that I was finally able to give them the concentrated attention they needed.

My eventual response consisted of ten closely typed pages. Since Hughes took up most of my points in his replies, I shall give it at length.

26 August 1990

The whole thing is extremely exciting, but, as with anything really new, revolutionary, the danger is that you will try to make your equation the key to too much, your account too consistent and all-inclusive, or that you will fail to persuade your readers that you are not pushing it too far. Your method does indeed, as you say, occasionally try my patience 'by excluding consideration of everything in the plays except the role of the equation', but not just for the reasons you suggest.

My response varies considerably from play to play. Broadly, there are three reactions:

1. Of course! How obvious once it's pointed to! Why has no-one seen it before?

2. Sceptical. I'll need some persuading. But gradually your argument commands assent.

3. No! Though your argument seems as watertight on its own terms as in any other case, too much of the play's meaning is not just left out of account, but actually contradicted. There is no problem when the equation is visible on the surface, as in the sonnets or *Venus and Adonis* or *Macbeth* or *Antony and Cleopatra*, or when you enable us to see it running underneath the received meanings, deepening them, as in *King Lear*. The problem arises when your interpretation appears to run counter to the meanings which the play, read from any other angle, yields. It is not always clear whether you are saying or implying that the other meanings are not in fact there, or that your meanings override them, or that the opposite meanings can, in some paradoxical way, co-exist. Sometimes you show no awareness of the possibility that these other meanings might exist, even when they are meanings you have yourself argued for in the earlier Shakespeare essay. Your new Prospero, for example, is a long way from the old

('but what a wooden wedding!' etc.). I shall develop these points in relation to *Measure for Measure* and *Hamlet* particularly.

Since I shall concentrate in these notes on caveats of this kind, my response will appear much more negative than it really is. There are many consecutive letters which elicit nothing but admiration. I believe that this is by far the most important book on Shakespeare since *The Wheel of Fire*, and should similarly inaugurate a new era of Shakespeare criticism. It also, of course, has vast implications for the criticism of *any* imaginative literature.

26 April p.1
'Throughout his drama we never actually see any of his characters'. You mean his drama in the sonnets, of course; but the sentence is open to misunderstanding.

p.2
I have seen two portraits of Wriothesley, in both of which his hair is dark brown. One is at Montacute (or was when we were there). The other is reproduced on p 122 of Anthony Burgess' *Shakespeare*; it is from an oil painting (c. 1601–1603) by John de Critz the elder. It is at Boughton House, Northamptonshire. I'll get copies made of them when I go into Manchester later in the week.

28 April p.3
How can Gertrude be said to have colluded in her husband's murder by marrying the murderer when she does not know that Claudius is a murderer, nor, indeed, that her husband has been murdered? Her lust is crime enough for Hamlet.

29 April p.1
   O strange excuse,
When reason is the bawd to lust's abuse.

Call it not love . . .[12]

It might be worth drawing attention, at this point, to the virtual repetition of these words in Hamlet's speech to his mother:

You cannot call it love . . .
When . . . reason panders will. [III iv 67, 87]

31 April p.3
'The form and pressure of the times' is not a quotation. Nor is 'form and pressure of the age' on the next page. The actual quotation is: 'the very age and body of the time his form and pressure'.

12 These lines are spoken by Adonis in *Venus and Adonis*. See *Shakespeare and the Goddess of Complete Being*, p. 65.

2 May

I find it difficult in the case of Lucrece and impossible in the case of Isabella to accept the unqualified value you claim that Shakespeare is attaching to chastity. Already in his Argument, Shakespeare creates a moral context for the story in which virtue is a competitive matter, and coupled (in typically Roman fashion) with fame: 'Whereupon the noblemen yielded Collatinus the victory, and his wife the fame'. The word 'fame' and its cognates occur far too often not to have a morally determining effect. Our first introduction to Lucrece is in these terms:

> When at Collatium this false lord arrived,
> Well was he welcomed by the Roman dame,
> Within whose face Beauty and Virtue strived
> Which of them both should underprop her fame.
> When Virtue bragged, Beauty would blush for shame;
> When Beauty boasted blushes, in despite
> Virtue would stain that o'er with silver white.

> He stories to her ears her husband's fame,
> Won in the fields of fruitful Italy;
> And decks with praises Collatine's high name,
> Made glorious by his manly chivalry,
> With bruised arms and wreaths of victory.

We seem to be in a world where *everything* is judged in terms of name and fame, and life itself is sacrificed to it.

After the rape, the sole reason for Lucrece's distress and decision to kill herself seems to be that in losing her own good name she has also destroyed her husband's – all this based on the unquestioned assumption that by being raped she has lost her chastity, broken her wedding vow, committed a crime and a sin, done something unspeakably shameful. She is as preoccupied by 'reputation' as Othello:

> Let my good name, that senseless reputation,
> For Collatine's dear love be kept unspotted.

> In vain I cavil with mine infamy.

> But if I live though liv'st in my defame.

> To clear this spot by death, at least I give
> A badge of fame to slander's livery,
> A dying life to living infamy.

> Her sacred temple spotted, spoiled, corrupted,
> Grossly engirt with daring infamy.

So of shame's ashes shall my fame be bred,
For in my death I murder shameful scorn.

Dear lord of that dear jewel I have lost,
What legacy shall I bequeath to thee?
My resolution, love, shall be thy boast . . .

What an insult to her husband to assume that what will be of most value to
him will be to be able to boast of her dead as he had boasted of her living!

Mine honour be the knife that makes my wound;
My shame be his that did my fame confound;
  And all my fame that lives disbursed be
To those that live and think no shame of me.

    . . . the better so to clear her
From that suspicion which the world might bear her.

    . . . this act will be
My fame and thy perpetual infamy.

There are many, many, more examples. And equally weighty is the
conspicuous absence of what might be expected in the circumstances to be
of importance to her which she never once mentions – how her rape will
appear in the eyes of her husband or in the eyes of God, and the effect of her
suicide on her husband and children.

    The poem ends with an unseemly and absurd competition between the
father and the husband, who almost come to blows over which of them has
the exclusive right to mourn her. But long before this, Shakespeare has
convinced most readers that Lucrece was indeed guilty, not, of course, of being
raped, but of using the rape to make a quite unnecessary martyr of herself.

    If it be objected that I am distorting the poem by bringing modern
attitudes to bear, I quote the Duke in Measure for Measure who tells Juliet that
sorrow which is merely for the shame sin brings 'is always toward ourselves,
not heaven', and Tyndale, speaking in the same vein as many Elizabethan
moralists, who wrote of Lucrece (and of any woman who places an absolute
value on chastity):

    She sought her own glory in her chastity and not god's. When she had lost
    her chastity, then she counted herself most abominable in the sight of all
    men; and for very pain and thought which she had, not that she had
    displeased god, but that she had lost her honour, slew herself. Look how
    great her glory and rejoicing therein, and much despised she them that
    were otherwise, and pitied them not, which pride god more abhorreth
    than the whoredom of any whore.

4 May p.1
I have never found *Measure for Measure* lacking in resonance (or relevance)
for a modern audience either in the theatre or on television. The number of
productions in the seventies, and the high proportion of them which worked
very well in modern dress, testified to this. It was seen, correctly, I think, as a
play about permissiveness (the word is actually used in the play). It was seen as
a way of exploring the dilemma that freedom will always tend towards licence,
while those who presume to judge, to enforce law and order and 'traditional
moral values', are suspect and probably more dangerously corrupt for their
seeming purity. Therefore any rigorous attempt to curb refractory and unruly
appetites will probably be a jump from the frying-pan into the fire. The play
works perfectly well in these secular terms, with the 'theological parable' as
an optional extra for those who perceive it and want it.

4 May p.2
If Lucio is no more than a 'cynical Mephistopheles', how do you account for
1. His faithfulness to Claudio and deeper commitment than Isabella's to
saving him.
2. His respect for Isabella;

> I hold you as a thing enskied and sainted
> By your renouncement, an immortal spirit,
> And to be talk'd with in sincerity,
> As with a saint.

(One can imagine Thersites or Iago doubling up at that.)

3. His remarkable speech;

> As those that feed grow full, as blossoming time
> That from the seedness the bare fallow brings
> To teeming foison, even so her plenteous womb
> Expresseth his full tilth and husbandry.

which resembles nothing so much as the Gentleman's description of
Cordelia.

4. The Duke's leniency towards him.
    Isabella emphatically does *not* plead for sexual licence (except in the
twisted sense in which it could be argued that Christ saying 'Let him who
is without sin cast the first stone' is pleading for sexual licence), and never
mentions procreation or her brother's forthcoming child. I cannot see an inch
of common ground between her and Venus. Her first words to Angelo are that
she abhors sexual licence more than any other vice, and would approve the
sentence did not the condemned man happen to be her brother. Her plea
is not for any relaxation of the law, but for mercy in this specific case. It is

because she actually agrees with Angelo that she is so cold for so long and needs so much prompting.

Angelo and Isabella are not entirely in opposition. In a sense they are counterparts. Each is 'cold', lacking the normal range of human emotions, implying, by their claim to be above the flesh, a denial that they have been 'made by man and woman, after this downright way of creation'.

In terms of plot she is set against Angelo and suffers much at his hands. But it seems to me that in terms of the deeper meaning of the play she is essentially his female counterpart. Both are puritans dedicated to unusually harsh disciplines. Her seeming, screened by her youth and innocence and habit of a nun, is much less obvious than Angelo's, and less melodramatically revealed; but revealed it certainly is, if we are alive to the implications of the lines she speaks. She knows herself as little as Anglo knows himself, and is as deficient in common humanity.

It is not Lucio but the Provost, a man distinguished by a mature and balanced humanity, who describes Claudio as 'more fit to do another such offence, than die for this'.

Claudio is a very ordinary young man, concerned not with abstract morality, but with living and loving. The only people in the play who take his offence seriously are Angelo and Isabella.

The first we hear of Isabella is Claudio's expression of his high hopes that she, if anyone, might win him a reprieve:

    For in her youth
    There is a prone and speechless dialect
    Such as move men; beside, she hath prosperous art
    When she will play with reason and discourse,
    And well she can persuade.

It is indeed to be that 'prone and speechless dialect' which moves Angelo, rather than her arguments. But her first appearance in the play is inauspicious. For we find that she is so far from accepting her own sexuality that she is about to enter a nunnery where she will never again speak to a man but with covered face and in the presence of the prioress. The first thing she says is that the rules of the strict order of St. Clare are not strict enough for her. Her desire for 'a more strict restraint' upon the sisters parallels Angelo's desire for stricter law and law-enforcement in Vienna – and the previous scene had ended with the Duke's expression of his doubts about the genuineness of that.

Angelo did not recognize himself to be a man. Isabella is immediately presented to us as aspiring to be something more than a woman, not merely a nun but "a thing enskied and sainted", an "immortal spirit". She succeeds only in being something less than a woman. In the dichotomy the play sets up between nunnery and brothel, it is Mistress Overdone, a bawd, who exemplifies womanly compassion and Christian charity by taking in Lucio's bastard. Can we imagine Isabella doing as much for her brother's child? (Mariana has to give her another lesson in compassion at the end.)

The sterility of the life to which she aspires is underlined by the imagery of richness and fertility in which Lucio describes to her her brother's 'sin'. When Isabella comes to plead for Claudio she never asks what harm he has done, or why his offence should be a capital one (as do not only Lucio, but also Escalus and the Provost).

On the contrary, she claims that it is

A vice that most I do abhor,
And most desire should meet the blow of justice.

This goes even further than Angelo, who never claims that fornication is a more abhorrent vice than murder! Why should she abhor the lovemaking of a young man and his fiancée so much if not in fear of her own sexuality – for the same reason, that is, that she wishes to enter a nunnery?

She is as legalistic as Angelo:

I had rather my brother die by the law, than my son
Should be unlawfully born.

This sort of legalism is thoroughly undermined by Pompey when he says that prostitution is legal if the law allows it. What the law does and does not allow varies with time, place and circumstance, and is, in any case, merely the official voice of whoever happens to be 'dressed in a little brief authority', in Isabella's own words.

To the puritan, all things are impure. Just as Angelo's Puritanism ensured that sex could only present itself to him in perverse forms, so Isabella's also diverts her sexuality from its normal course. There is a kind of perverted sexuality in the language she uses when Angelo makes his proposition – what Leavis calls 'a kind of sensuality of martyrdom':

Were I under the terms of death,
Th'impression of keen whips I'd wear as rubies,
And strip myself to death as to a bed
That longing have been sick for, ere I'd yield
My body up to shame.

She glibly offers to give her life (which is not in question) to save Claudio, but not her 'honour', a term she never questions. She is in no doubt that her chastity weighs more than her brother's life:

Then Isabel live chaste, and brother die:
More than our brother is out chastity.

How can that vicious line be justified or even excused? There is certainly no theological justification for it. And there is worse to come. When Claudio suggests that a sin done in charity, to save a life, is no sin but a virtue (and he is theologically impeccable), she becomes as ruthless and sadistic as Angelo in defence of her puritanical self-esteem.

    Might but my bending down
    Reprieve thee from thy fate, it should proceed.
    I'll pray a thousand prayers for thy death;
    No word to save thee.

Mariana has no compunction about making love to a man to whom she is not yet married, and the duke not only sanctions but sets up the act. And it is Mariana who has to redeem Isabella in the end.

    It is Mariana who corresponds to Venus, a woman of candid sexuality defined entirely by her unconditional love for a man who rejects her, but taking him to her bosom in the end after he has undergone a symbolic death and resurrection.

5 May p.7
There is nothing specifically Christian about Venus' doves. Aphrodite was commonly accompanied by doves for the Greeks.

5 May p.8
You use the phrase 'psychological dynamics'; but you have said little about the matter in psychological terms, having used almost entirely mythic terms. I think your account would be strengthened if it included a new expanded version of the powerful summary account of the crossover on p.192 of the original essay.

28 August 1990

6 May p.1
'Noble' seems hardly the word for Macbeth's slaughter of Duncan, Macbeth, creeping under cover of night, jittery, with his hangman's hands, handing the daggers to Lady Macbeth to finish the job . . . Does the mere fact that he has a bad conscience make the act noble?

Introduction to Section II
At the end you say that you are going to start with *Measure for Measure*, but, in my version, you say nothing more about that play. Do I infer that you are planning to move your earlier discussion of it (4 and 5) to this point? In any case it seems to me that you lose more than you gain by not dealing with *Measure for Measure* in its rightful place.

8 May p.1
The reader will not be able to follow the argument that Jaques or even Jakes is the first syllable of Shakespeare unless you mention earlier the possible derivation from Jacquespierre (of which I had never heard).

This letter and the next are hard going, airless, until you seem to surface again in the last paragraph.

9 May p.9
You have already quoted this sonnet in full in the introduction to Section II.

17 May p.4
I don't know what texts you are using. Most of the scholars that I know use the New Arden. There are several differences in your quotation from *Troilus and Cressida* from the 1982 New Arden text:
l.1 I can't imagine any edition giving 'lamps', since Q and F are agreed on 'lamp'. The line ends with a ;.
l.2 ends with a comma.
l.3 has a comma after 'outward'.
l.4 ends with an !.
l.5 has no mark at the end.
l.8 'Of such a winnow'd purity in love – '.
There are the same frequent differences in punctuation in all your subsequent quotations from this play. I haven't checked quotation from other plays.[13]
It might be worth referring specifically here to Sonnet 116.

[p.m. 30 August 1990]

Dear Keith — I look forward to your comments. I can see they are going to be useful — especially your response Number 3.

I felt I treat the last 4 plays too cursorily (I began to feel my readers might have had too much already). So I'm rewriting that section — much more fully. I want it to be the real culmination — Tempest especially.

Other parts I've cut & patched.

Specific to your comment: Ap.26 — p.1. In general, do you think any of the characters are projected visually — except for Falstaff, Bardolph, Richard III etc — where some physical peculiarity is the badge of some extreme humour — and a point of comment? Is Othello snub or aquiline?

P.2. Yes — foolish error. Deleted. I have a good biog about him by Akrigg.[14] Yet, I've always imagined him blonde.

O.K. about Donne. "Usually" instead of "always". But as you say the 'wit' is an attempt to ward off — to maintain ego-control,

---

13 Hughes made some but not all of these changes. These may, of course, have been mere errors rather than a matter of the edition he was using.
14 G. P. V. Akrigg, *Shakespeare and the Earl of Southampton* (Hamish Hamilton, 1968).

Shakespeare's peculiarity is to embrace what Donne tries to keep at arm's length. But I will soften the words about Donne — though not much.[15]

P.3. Yes. The scar is a joke. Speculation — a way of saying his abilities are abnormal (like those of Hurkos).[16] But those remarks now deleted. I also deleted the letter about Emilia Lanier. Is my analysis of Sonnet 127 perverse?

Love to Family   Ted

I haven't re-read my Shakes Intro. in fifteen years: now I will.

P.S. Did you see the T.V. Joseph Campbell on the Goddess? — like a note for my letters.[17]

P.S. Do you know of any rentable property within commuting range of Manchester — for a young married couple for 1 year? Very nice son & daughter-in-law of a friend of mine. Husband just left army, now working for some big company.

30 August 1990

Dear Ted

Here is the third and penultimate batch of notes.

18 May p.2
'catalytic', not 'catylitic' (twice)

18 May p.3
Shakespeare goes out of his way to make the point that Hamlet's loathing of and rejection of his mother has nothing to do with his father's murder by having him express it in his first soliloquy *before* he knows that his father has been murdered. The line 'To post with such dexterity to incestuous sheets' reveals in its queasy disgust that it is his mother's sexual appetite alone which alienates him. It seems that in Hamlet's idealizing imagination, his father's love for his mother did not descend to bodies.

So loving to my mother
That he might not beteem the winds of heaven
Visit her face too roughly.

---

15 I had objected to Hughes' opinion that Donne's wit was mere dalliance.
16 Peter Hurkos (1911–88) was a Dutchman who claimed that he had acquired extra-sensory perception following a head injury at the age of thirty. He became a popular stage and television entertainer. He was acclaimed by some as 'the greatest pychic in the world', but most of his claims were refuted or challenged.
17 Hughes had been much influenced by the works of the American mythographer Joseph Campbell (1904–87), especially *The Hero with a Thousand Faces* (Pantheon, 1949) and *The Masks of God* (4 vols, Secker and Warburg, 1962–8).

Whereas his mother's love for his father had tried to drag him down into her world of appetite:

> Why, she would hang on him
> As if increase of appetite had grown
> By what it fed on.

It seems that the image of his mother and father making love is scarcely more palatable to Hamlet than that of his mother and uncle.

19 May p.1
Insofar as Ophelia is the 'rose of May', she represents that essential spiritual health in Hamlet which made him 'the expectancy and rose of the fair state' before the state was corrupted by Claudius, and in Hamlet's tainted vision the world became an unweeded garden. If 'things rank and gross in nature possess it merely', then there can be no roses, only fat weeds, canker and mildew, and the sun breeds maggots in dead dogs.

24 May p.1 section 1
There is no way Hamlet 'at the beginning of the play' can be so imagined. The first soliloquy shows him, as I said above, not just 'touched by doubts' but sick with disgust at his mother – spiritually jaundiced. The Puritan spectacles are already firmly in place (he acquired them in Wittenberg). But the early part of the play gives us plenty of evidence for reconstructing what Hamlet was like before he went to Wittenberg. That was 'Adonis in the idyllic phase'.

24 May p.1 section 2
The double vision towards his mother is as evident in the first soliloquy – *before* Hamlet meets the ghost – as it is ever to be.

24 May p.1 section 3
There is nothing unreal about Hamlet's accusation against Ophelia. Claudius has corrupted Polonius, Polonius corrupts Ophelia by ordering her to lie to Hamlet and to offer herself as the live-bait in his trap. She is given a prayer-book to pretend to be reading:

> 'Tis too much proved that with devotion's visage
> And pious action we do sugar o'er
> The devil himself.

When Hamlet asks her if she is honest, she is indeed being thoroughly dishonest (though for what seem to her the best of motives). The name 'Ophelia' means 'serviceableness'.

24 May p.2 section 6
You can hardly call Hamlet's response to the ghost's command an 'irresistible compulsion' when, in your own words, 'he goes on resisting it for five acts'.

> Do you not come your tardy son to chide,
> That, laps'd in time and passion, lets go by
> Th'important acting of your dread command?

In fact he resists it for only four acts. The Hamlet who returns to Elsinore in act five has fully accepted his destiny as heaven's minister.

24 May p.2 section 7
You earlier defined the Crown as 'the soul of external Divine Order'. But Claudius' crown is far from that. Claudius is 'a vice of kings',

> A cutpurse of the empire and the rule,
> That from a shelf the precious diadem stole
> And put it in his pocket –

The murder of Claudius is not a 'rape' but a cleansing of the state, a deed which, ultimately, has divine sanction (not from the ghost, but direct from heaven). It is a restoration of 'external Divine Order'.

24 May p.5
Claudius is *not* the self Hamlet must become. He is the self Hamlet thinks he is required to become during his mistaken phase (from 'O what a rogue and peasant slave' to 'From this time forth / My thoughts be bloody or be nothing worth'). Hamlet does not, in the last act, become a Tarquin; he becomes a Richmond or a Macduff or an Edgar killing the tyrant under divine dispensation. I can demonstrate this at length and in detail if you wish.
It is not so much Hamlet's murder of Claudius, but his delay in murdering him which leads to the deaths of all the other characters who die before Claudius. If Hamlet had indeed swept to his revenge, who else would have suffered?
   Your whole account of *Hamlet* is very unconvincing because it fails to take into account of so much of the play, not just parts of the play which are doing something else or operating on a different level, but what seems to me to be the essential dynamic and shape and meaning of the play. You leave out of account
1. the significance of the fact that Hamlet has come from and wishes to return to Wittenberg (mentioned six times in two pages) – the university of Faust and Luther and Giordano Bruno;
2. the first soliloquy, before the ghost's revelations;
3. the ghost not as Protestant demon but as authentic Catholic spirit;
4. the evil spreading from Claudius, and Hamlet's obligation to stop it;
5. the transformation of Hamlet on shipboard, and the different, mature,

spiritually calm Hamlet (no more soliloquies) who returns to Elsinore in Act V;
6. the function of 'minister', and the role of 'destiny', 'providence', 'heaven' in
the last act.

26 May p.3
Hamlet also, at one point, 'begins to exult in his murderous decision':

 For 'tis the sport to have the enginer
 Hoist with his own petard . . . O, 'tis most sweet
 When in one line two crafts directly meet.

And is he in the saddle, in full awareness, behaving rationally, when he
plays hide-and-seek with the body of Polonius? This is Hamlet at his most
benighted, immediately before his sea-change and spiritual rebirth. The new
Hamlet returns ready to declare his love for Ophelia, but it is too late. In his
madness he had killed her father, driven her brother into alliance with evil,
driven her to madness and suicide.

Ophelia is totally passive, 'an infinitely gentle, infinitely suffering thing'.[18]
She lacks the strength to move towards Hamlet and be waiting for him as he
emerges from his madness, like Cordelia and Lear.

6 June p.3
First line: how about 'papyrus' for 'alloy'?

Introduction to Section V p.1
The quotation from King Lear is 'That ever I have felt'.

The book is terrific in its general conception and execution and in relation to
all the specific texts I don't mention in my notes, working up triumphantly to
the climax of King Lear. But the big danger, as I said at the beginning, is that its
critics will be able to say (with some justice as the book now stands) that you
use your equation as a Procrustean bed. Most of the texts you deal with fit it
amazingly well; some awkwardly, requiring some distortion (including,
unfortunately, two of your templates, Lucrece and Measure for Measure); and
some not without near-fatal mutilation (Hamlet).

What is the significance of the fact that the sequence of letters begins on
Shakespeare's birthday and ends on mine?!
    Yours   Keith

---

18   T. S. Eliot, 'Preludes' IV.

[1 Sept 90]

Dear Keith —

Your industry!

28th April p3. Yes, but from Hamlet's point of view? And from the mythic pattern's point of view?

On the other hand, the murder is an extra. The equation only requires 'lust'. Then out of the lust (out of the Queen of Hell) unfolds murder, (her infernal consort — the 'hot tyrant' whose 'murder' is also a 'rape'.)

I tried to clarify my idea of 'lust' (the 'lust' which Adonis rejects) as a complex which contains (either as an intensifying metaphor, or as a male component that actually kills), the component 'murder'. That is the link, after all, between the Boar (Venus' 'lust') & the death of Adonis as a Puritan ego — (he is 'murdered'). And between Tarquin's rape & Lucrece's suicide — her soul is 'murdered' in that his act destroys it. And between the assault of the Boar on the Puritan ego generally, and the usurping brother's 'murder' of the Crown.

If I haven't made it clear that Gertrude's 'lust' is the intolerable factor — exactly as Venus' 'lust' is for Adonis — then I shall have to rewrite.

31 April p3: Yes — all that part is rewritten.

2 May: Yes, I agree with all you say about Fame. But in spite of Tyndale, I don't see that it disables what I say about chastity. My own impression is that Shakespeare is being fairly direct, and means what he says when he calls her 'This earthly saint adored by this devil". His description of her, throughout, it seems to me, is consistent with his portrait of her as 'saintly' — and consistent with his portraits of later Lucrece figures & their holy fidelity in married love, or even just in love. Again in spite of Tyndale, plenty of women have done as Lucrece did — simply because they couldn't face life or themselves, with the shame.

You make Shakespeare more interested in her sin of pride (which I have difficulty finding in the text) than in her role as the apotheosis of an extreme (almost an abstraction) of a kind of female virtue, which he continues to apotheosise right through to the Tempest. And even if he did pluck that string, I think he was being more human than Tyndale, who uses Lucrece as Sylvia's biographers tend to use me. I can't see that oversensitivity to 'fame'

& fear of public humiliation is incompatible with a woman's fanatically high valuation of a sexual union consecrated by religion — where her infidelity, or the fact that she has been raped, will destroy her husband's self respect and expose him to the derisive pity of other men (which may be daft, but which always to some degree happens) as well as destroy the respect she has for herself (which for some women, in some cultures, or in some situations, is reason enough for suicide).

Even if you were right, my whole point is that the dramatic motives, which Shakespeare develops in his realisation of the character, are incidental — as far as the equation goes. What I am saying is that the primary impulse, in this poem, is the myth — in which the martial God, as an obsessed tyrant, destroys the Goddess, as an image of sacred love. The created work is something else, but whatever it is it has to make that hidden requirement of the basic impulse (the myth) plausible. Tarquin has to be possessed, in his attack on Lucrece, & Lucrece has to be somehow destroyed. How her death is brought about is secondary to the mythic requirement (the requirement of the energy source, on which Shakespeare is drawing) that she must die as a result of his attack.

The same in each play: even though the physical details of the play may seem to contradict the design of the mythic equation, the overall pattern of the finished drama must obey it.

When Shakes. fitted the two poems together, he put his finger on the roles of sexuality and defensive ego in the succession of religions — suppression of the Goddess by the ego, Goddess as a madness takes possession of the ego, possessed ego tries simultaneously to express the Goddess-madness (lust without love) & to destroy the Goddess (attempted murder). Tarquin is the image of this double motive of the possessed ego: his lust proves fatal.

In All's Well (Bertram's assault on Diana) and Measure for Measure (Angelo's on Isabella) Shakespeare concentrates (as he did in Lucrece) on the 'lust'. The myth that is, is defanged — temporarily. But after Troilus, where as I point out the 'lust' cannot be expressed as such, the act of murder takes its place naturally (according with the requirement of the myth, where the Goddess must be destroyed).

After that, the perfect statement is Othello: as I explained,

Tarquin's lust has become Othello's need to murder (the Goddess) in punishment for her lust. So that is a direct transcription of the myth.

But just the same, in Hamlet the rejected female must die — even though the details of the finished play remove the act of murder from the hands of the hero who rejects her. — Hamlet rejects Ophelia but — unlike Othello — does not murder her, and yet, like Desdemona, Ophelia is asphyxiated. He rejects his mother, does not murder her, & yet she dies, gulping poison (as Ophelia gulped water). As a tabloid journalist would see quite clearly — Hamlet murdered both of them. His Tarquinian madness was the direct cause of their deaths.

In the same way, the tragic equation's requirement imposes the pattern on Goneril, Regan & Cordelia. On the mythic plane, which that tabloid journalist would recognise, Lear in his madness against them killed all three. Somehow. Exactly how does not matter — to the equation. However it happens, the hidden pattern will ensure that it will be interesting, dramatic, and will seem 'right'. All that matters is that the hero's Tarquinian madness brings about their death.

Again, the 'chastity' of Lucrece is as decisive as the 'chastity' of Adonis. That is part of the tight correspondence between LUCRECE & VENUS & ADONIS. V & A is the myth (I don't see how else it can be argued) of the head-on collision between the goddess of Love (life) and the Puritan absolute of chastity (faithful to Diana).

When this event in heaven is translated, & inverted into an event on earth, the Boar's fatal attack on Adonis becomes Tarquin's attack on Lucrece, & Adonis puritan ego (his idealism, his devotion to a sacred idea of chastity) becomes Lucrece's virtue — i.e. her devotion to a sacred idea of chastity (which may well be entangled with obsessions about 'reputation'). All this is anticipated in that image of Adonis' — about the 'hot tyrant' — where he imagines himself as the 'fresh beauty' which the 'hot tyrant' 'stains'. The 'chastity' in the second poem, it seems to me, is simply the embodiment in Lucrece of Adonis' ideal — which is certainly nothing but chastity, the worship of a sacred ideal of love, in practice.

Tyndale sounds to be stoking the fire at a witch-burning.

4 May p.1. Good. Then I will delete any mention of 'lacking in

resonance'. That's an example (I don't do it often, or rather I try to avoid doing it constantly) of batting at windmills operated by others.

Yes, too, about the theological parable, although I do think it is a little more than an option. — Shakespeare does embed the story squarely in Christian terms, fortified with Convent & Friar. Isabella finally, instead of marrying Christ, as a nun, marries the Duke — a consecrated ruler & quasi-priest, i.e. God's viscount.

And yes, I agree it works in a secular sense, if one reads the religious terms simply as metaphors.

But its closeness to the mythic equation — and to the original religious terms of the mythic equation (Catholic Nun and Calvinist Judge) — keep it wide open to the religious interpretation.

4 May p.2.: (1) I think you're assuming a more literal matching to the 'algebra' of the equation than seems to me necessary. Literal matching would preclude individuality. All it needs is enough congruity to pick up the magnetic field & electrical charge of the mythic pattern. I'm sure Lucio is a very complicated figure, but as an emanation of the Goddess, or as a reflection of her ability, his closeness to Claudio (a pre-puritan Adonis, an authentic lover) is consistent with his closeness to Isabella during her siege of Angelo, and with his rôle as mouthpiece of the brothel-world of Vienna. I think his closeness to Parolles is evident. (He is never tested, like Parolles).

Thersites & Iago, as I see it, are simply more evolved — complicatedly more evolved. But all are a sort of ox-pecker on the rhino of love.[19] One can imagine their relationship to the lovers as a series of fables: Parolles wants Bertram to be not what his true nature is (a rhino), but an ox-pecker, frolicking among the buffaloes (rejected forms of the Goddess, casual affairs). Lucio is an irrepressibly amiable loyal ox-pecker, happy among the buffaloes, but always faithful, too, to his rhino Claudio, & ready to go, on his behalf, with the goddess herself, the goddess of rhinos, Isabella. Thersites is embittered — for some reason soured, presumably because he cannot be a rhino himself, but can only flit from rhino to rhino, telling them they are all lousy buffaloes. Finally, Iago — embittered beyond all understanding by his metaphysical exclusion

19 Oxpeckers are birds which ride on the backs of Africa's large mammals, pecking off ticks.

from the rhino bliss, decides to do something about it. But all are ox-peckers — all live on the warmth of love, on the juicy tidbits that live in the crevices of the rhino of love.

At least, ox-peckerishness in a rhino world is a prominent characteristic that they all share. Each obviously has qualities that none of the others share.

2. Surely this is Lucio's horse for the course. "You have a daily beauty in your life / That makes me ugly — " Only it doesn't make him bitter. He is enthusiastic to give her superlatives that come easily, & anyway fit the case & the occasion. He is free to say this sort of thing because he isn't — like Thersites & Iago, preoccupied with critical revenge. He's frivolous, and he's trying to persuade her.

3. Again surely a courtly horse being given a trot. For a nun. Other occasions he brings out 'rebellion of a cod-piece'. etc.

4. Forgiveness is the word to all.

Your page 4. If you can't see 'an inch of common ground' between Venus & Isabella — well, I don't know where to start. I can only repeat what I said in the letter.

You have to let these figures ride very loose in the saddle. In court, if Isabella appeared as the defendant of one who had committed adultery against the law, surely she would be, in a sense, pleading the case for adultery. If she were to win, even if only on a battery of extenuating circumstances, and as a result the law were to be changed — from capital punishment to some kind of fine — then she would have won a case resoundingly for freedom of love. It seems to me, she is pleading for mercy towards their act in this way. And it seems to me, Venus is doing the same thing with Adonis: pleading, with his puritan prohibition, to permit his body & hers the act of love. I don't see your problem.

I agree that she is not specifically asking for a change in the law, for a licence to all lovers etc.

All I am saying is that her appeal, however specific & restricted, is a powerful image of Venus' appeal to Adonis — and, as I argue, has the same effect on him as is worked out in the mythic business of Boar into Tarquin.

And what about Isabella as Nun. Venus as bride of Adonis.

As for Isabella being cold: yes, the Lucrece/Diana figure is there, the nun, floating at the surface, & it takes control at moment

Angelo becomes a Tarquin. But surely the whole point of her suit is that it gives her physical beauty its proper role — making the appeal on behalf of love. Shakespeare's point, as I see it, is that her physical beauty speaks with "a prone and speechless dialect", with a heat that melts Angelo. — He is also making the point, which he also made in Lucrece, that modest or chaste speech in the mouth of a physically beautiful woman is sexually provocative. It is like a form of sexually teasing dress — articulating the opposite of what the body itself is actually saying. Or like love-talk expressed in opposites — 'you cannot do this' 'you cannot do that' — while arguing for a total permissiveness. No, that's not quite right.

But you know what I mean. Her virtue — her militant virtue, engages his conscious principles in a code through which her beauty speaks to his suppressed eros. Neither he nor she consciously understand the code. But the audience understands it, & his suppressed Eros understands it.

She is like those saints who, on learning that their eyes or their breasts have infatuated some wretch tear them out or cut them off — not quite like them but as surprised at herself, as dismayed.

All your page 4 seems to be arguing you round to agree with me — only stops short at making the metaphorical translation of the phase of her appeal into Venus' appeal.

She is a Lucrece, who by circumstances is made to act the part of Venus — whereupon it turns out that she actually is a form of Venus. But Lucrece always contains, latent, the full form of Venus, i.e. Desdemona contains, latent (for Othello) the Queen of Hell.

Throughout your page 5 I can only say stand back & see the pattern behind the details. The tragic equation is only a template — a foundation circuit of dramatic energy, not the fully realised, individualised complexity of a play.

5 May P7: My point about the 'doves' — in Ovid they are 'swans', which diverts Venus from her Christian lineage. But it's an unnecessary point.

5 May P.8. I translate it — maybe too fully — into psychological terms later on. 28th May. But I'll look again at the original essay, and see what I can cannibalise.

Thank you for going into such detail with Lucrece & M for M.

It makes me feel I should somehow say more about the actual

scanning method — the infra-red sort of detector — that I'm using, that one needs to use.

If the textual details, the weave of words & individualities, weren't so dense & so self-sufficient, & so fascinating, I expect the whole business of the tragic equation, the recurrent presence of this consistent but developing nuclear mythic pattern, would have been obvious to any reader long ago.

I ought also to make it clearer, perhaps, just what degree of importance it has (in my view) in any particular work. I don't think it goes further, usually, than providing the energy for the main dramatic situation. It does not matter whether Isabella is a heartless intellectual, an egocentric bitch, a sentimental idealist, a passionate heroine, a modest secretary, or what. All that matters is that she embodies Venus, for a while, in the eye of the hero & that he then sees the double vision, goes crazy, and tries either to ravish or destroy either her or some representative of her. What either of them say in the process will mightily affect the play — but not the outcome of the tragic equation.

How do I get that across? Perhaps I ought not to make any attempt to forestall the slings & arrows — but leave the idea to make its own way, with all its imperfections on its head.[20]

Have I said anything in this letter, that you feel I haven't said in the letters to D[onya].?

All the best & love to the family Ted

Dear Keith —

I'm having problems with this pen — so I've photocopied my letter, to improve the legibility. Otherwise you could hardly have faced it.

Ted

31 August 1990

Dear Ted

Here are the last of my comment on *The Silence of Cordelia*.

---

20 Hughes is here quoting Hamlet: 'The slings and arrows of outrageous fortune', and the Ghost: 'No reck'ning made, but sent to my account / With all my imperfections on my head'.

10 May p.1
Joyce spells it Dedalus

Further thoughts on chastity. Lucrece and Isabella are falsely chaste as Claudius and Macbeth are false kings. The latter think, or act as though, divine kingship were not a spiritual reality but the golden round itself, which can be physically snatched. So Lucrece and Isabella confuse chastity with its physical symbol, the vagina. To commit suicide because you have been raped is morally and spiritually the same as to commit suicide because someone has stolen your wedding ring. This false chastity is also the female equivalent of the false puritanism of Adonis – a form of egotism.

14 June p.8
It amazes me that you should say that the Sacred Bride/Divine Mother lacks an identifiable poetry, since the language Cordelia speaks after her return

>. . . all the idle weeds that grow
>In our sustaining corn.
>. . . All the bless'd secrets,
>All you unpublish'd virtues of the earth,
>Spring with my tears!

>Was this a face
>To be oppose'd against the warring winds?
>To stand against the deep dread-bolted thunder?
>In the most terrible and nimble stroke
>Of quick, cross lightning? To watch – poor *perdu!* –
>With this thin helm? Mine enemy's dog,
>Though he had bit me, should have stood that might
>Against my fire. And wast thou fain, poor father,
>To hovel thee with swine and rogues forlorn,
>In short and musty straw? Alack, alack!
>'Tis wonder that thy life and wits at once
>Had not concluded all.

>O! look upon me, Sir,
>And hold your hand in benediction o'er me.
>No, Sir, you must not kneel.

simplifying further into 'And so I am, I am'. 'No cause, no cause' – a language which seems to pass from Cordelia, like medicine, to those she comes in contact with – the Gentleman who describes her to Kent (IV iii) and Lear himself in the restoration scene – is not only a new and distinctive language, purged of style, but is, it seems to me, in its strong tenderness and simplicity, no less than the finest expression English has ever yielded. This is what her 'nothing' at last opens into: a speech which is capable of expressing the truth of the heart. The Restoration which flows from her lips is words, words completely of a piece with her gestures, her kiss, her kneeling, her tears. Shakespeare was unable to hold on to this language, but there are echoes of it in the speech of most of the late heroines.

The book seems to end very abruptly. Nor do I come away from your reading of The Tempest with any very clear idea of how your application of the equation affects your overall interpretation of the play. Unlike any of your other readings, you seem to be applying the equation to each character separately, without ever pulling the whole thing together. The nearest thing to a conclusion seems to come too early (p.5), and the words 'This suggests . . .' leave open the possibility that it is a suggestion you want to modify or even contradict in the remaining pages. I think you need – either at the very end or between your itemising of the plot and your coda on the language – another page or two to sum up the meaning of the play as a whole and what it tells us of Shakespeare's final position in relation to the Goddess. How does the play constitute 'the completion of Shakespeare's spiritual task'? Is Prospero no more than Adonis who, having narrowly escaped the boar, goes into hiding or retreat for decades to perfect his defences against Venus until he is powerful enough to exclude her from his magic circle? Does he succeed in this? Does Shakespeare approve of the attempt? Or are you saying that the attempt is doomed because, though Sycorax may be dead and Venus distant, the boar survives in Antonio and Caliban even on the island, and presumably marauds everywhere in the world beyond, where Prospero will be without his book and staff?

I enclose a copy of a talk I gave last year on The Tempest to a group of A-level students. It had to be both simplified and comprehensive, so much of it is irrelevant to your purposes, but you might pick up one or two interesting points in it.

I hope my comments have not seemed too presumptuous, and will be of some use. I have assumed that you sent me the papers not only for my own interest but also in the hope of some such feedback. It has been a great privilege to read them in this new-minted, almost molten state.

2 Sept 90

Dear Keith,

Thank you again.

10th May p.1. 'Further thoughts on Chastity'. I shall have to think about it, but I'm not sure I grasp what you mean — about Lucrece's & Isabella's 'false' chastity. As I said in my letter yesterday I can't help feeling that most women associate 'chastity' with the 'vagina' — I mean identify. And that 'chaste' women are absolutely violated, psychologically, by 'rape' — almost as men by castration. They can live with it, but the sanctity of their sexuality has gone. I imagine. Very chaste, naturally chaste, women — women whose 'chastity' is identified (also) with the sanctity of their ownership of their own bodies, & the sanctity of the love which they have to give. I do think there are such women. They belong to the heroic race — as do those men who "mourned more bitterly for their dogs than men do nowadays for their brothers, and who mourned for their brothers by mutilating their own limbs, hacking off fingers etc." To some women, heroic natures, these sacred principles simply mean more. I think I've known one or two women like that.

Also, according to my argument, chastity in Shakespeare is a symbol of the importance of the pure, 'total & unconditional' bond between a man and his soul. A man must be loyal to his soul. The idea of it. Possibility of his soul's being disloyal to him is an intolerable horror — a madness. The idea that a man's own soul could deceive him, or prefer others, or be defiled by others — is a madness. That idea is a key to the violence of the tragic equation.

This meaning of chastity in Shakespeare seems to me consistent with his fundamentalist valuation of the divinity of the soul — his fanatic insistence on a man being true to this divinity of the soul. Consistent, that is, with his quasi-insane loathing of all forms of treachery, dishonesty (à la Timon) and with the fact that this loathing focuses on the treachery of the female (i.e. of the soul).

Given this 'mythic' value, then Lucrece & Isabella are less real women, with the God only knows what dark horse under their tails, than they are my mouthpieces of Shakespeare's ethical system, his.

Yes, at the same time, chastity as a Puritan mode of 'control' — as a consensus-ruled coercion — I do agree (passim in my letter) is the 'error' of ego — from which the tragic equation, the revenge of the Goddess, duly follows.

14 June P.8. As a matter of fact, I agree with you absolutely. My wording is bad, as usual. I wanted to do a full-length analysis of the 'new' poetry of the last period, in which I trace it from the rebirth poetry of Lear, — exactly those pieces you quote, plus 'Come, let's away to prison'. And have done.

As I think I've mentioned, I'm rewriting Section 5. Everything you say about it I also feel. The introduction to that section (between June 7 & 8) is already the longest in the book (25 written pages) & begins to say what I mean.

Your Tempest lecture is full of points. Basically I feel I'm on your wavelength throughout — & I think it gives me the dog to round up my own scattered flock.

I'm sending you this in its original — so you can see how awful this pen is, & its ink.

Love to all,   Ted.

4–6 September 1990

Dear Ted

Thank you for the long letter. I think the last page gets to the heart of the matter. It isn't just the slings and arrows from conservative critics and jealous guardians of the field of academic Shakespeare studies that I'm thinking of. Any reader keen enough on Shakespeare to read The Silence of Cordelia is going to be so familiar with certain plays, so committed to certain readings and understandings, that an approach which requires, or seems to require, some of these cherished and perhaps hard-won insights to be jettisoned, since they cannot be reconciled with the demands of the equation, will provoke wholesale resistance. Of course you are not saying that the equation fits every play like a glove and yields an all-inclusive interpretation. I do think you need to say more about the scanning method. But even if you repeated these disclaimers every other letter, that would not be enough. I think you must also be very careful to say when you are talking not about a character per se but as seen by another character (i.e. what you say here about Isabella as seen by Angelo – which may have little or nothing to do with Isabella as seen by the reader in the rest of the play). Also I think your determination not to be sidetracked from following the equation makes it possible for the reader to wonder whether you are even aware of what else is going on in a play beyond the equation, or whether you are deliberately leaving out of account anything which might run counter to the equation. I don't think it would deflect you very much just to preface a paragraph occasionally with some such clause as 'In spite of her preoccupation with name and fame, Lucrece . . .' or 'In spite of her similarity to Angelo in her coldness, her legalistic harshness, her contempt for sexuality, Isabella . . .'

Even in terms of the equation, I think it needs to be said that the Venus role is divided between Isabella (unconsciously provoking murderous lust in the Puritan) and Mariana (redemptive unconditional love) . . .

I find what you say about chastity pretty convincing, at least in relation to Lucrece. But I still can't forgive Isabella, and when I come to Measure for Measure in my own book I'll give her a hard time.

18th Sept 90

Dear Keith —

Extremely grateful for this pen. With every new nib I change a nature.

I've rewritten the 5th Section. The interval refreshed me.

Is there anything extant concerning the conflation of Argosy story (Jason, Medea, Golden Fleece), Odyssey, Bks I to VI of Aeneid, and Tempest?

The key is: Tempest as hero's quest to win magical treasure (and daughter) from Ogre King, (prototype shaman's flight story) =

Jason as Ferdinand, Prospero as Aeëtes (Medea's father), and Medea as Miranda. Something must have been written about that.

But Medea, Circe's niece, was, like Circe, a Hecate — Goddess of the willow shrine in Colchis, worshipped by the Coraxi.[21]

Circe was a death-Goddess — Queen of Hell, with her sacred swine, converting men to swine.

As Persephone, she was the same who became a Boar to reclaim Adonis.

Ulysses ('thigh-scar' — his nurse recognises him by the old boar-tusk wound on his thigh) confronting Circe was a type of Adonis confronting the Queen of Hell & the Boar.

But Circe, or Sycorax (the Goddess of the black pig) overpowered by Ulysses (with the magic help of a flower), was a type of Sycorax overpowered by Prospero, who held the charge of her boar (Caliban) spellbound. (Ariel is a flower spirit — 'Where the bee sucks etc') (Marduk made himself immune to Tiamat's battle-magic — by smelling at a flower).

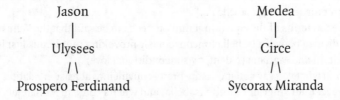

```
        Jason                          Medea
          |                              |
       Ulysses                         Circe
         / \                            / \
Prospero  Ferdinand           Sycorax  Miranda
```

The missing link is Dido. Dido's story supplies all kinds of detailed dovetails, mortises & tenons, & big nails — to fit and fasten her

---

21 *Corax* is Crow in ancient Greek. Scholars have pointed out that Sycorax resembles Circe from Greek mythology, and also a version of Circe found in the mythology of the Coraxi tribe in modern-day Georgia.

into the Tragic equation etc. He must have planned a play about Dido. Couldn't not have thought about it.

Jason
|
Ulysses
|
Aeneas
/ \
Ferdinand/Aeneas Prospero/Aeneas
(Meeting Venus whom he (rejecting Dido/Sycorax
takes to be Diana i.e. Miranda) but rescuing Miranda/Diana)

No, I've tangled that by jumping a few moves. Dido's Carthage — an island inside a bullskin — becomes the island where Ferdinand Aeneas, coming ashore, meets (his mother) Venus & tells her to be (Miranda) Diana (BK I. Aeneid). But it is also the island on which Dido, rejected by Aeneas, (becoming all those heroines rejected as Queen of Hell) died.

So, the island of Setebos is the place where the rejected Queen of Hell died (as Sycorax) but where the mistakenly rejected Lucrece can be rescued (reborn) as Miranda.

No, it's much, much clearer where I've done it at length, in detail, and in full. But the point is: Dido is the common factor of Sycorax & Miranda (and of all the loved-loathed double women).

Thank you for this book by Cobb.[22] Exceedingly interesting, as they say! I'm sure he's right — that Shakes had an Alchemical analogue running in all these later plays. But kept it in solution — as he did the Prot/Cathol. analogue.

22 Noel Cobb, *Prospero's Island: The Secret Alchemy at the Heart of The Tempest* (Coventure, 1984).

1991

For the first three months Hughes suffered from shingles. He visited Scotland in April, July and August. Apart from further work on *The School Bag*, Hughes was exclusively concerned with completing *Shakespeare and the Goddess of Complete Being*.

18 January 1991

I don't suppose you have ever heard of a poet called Enid Hudson (1907–1982)? Her daughter is one of my students, and has just given me a booklet of her mother's poems.[1] They. seem to me remarkable. Some of the early ones, from the twenties, are very like Yeats (and as good as some of the less ambitious Yeats). Later she developed a sparer style.

19 Jan 91

Dear Keith,

Thank you for the note. Yes, Enid Hudson is good isn't she. Never was aware of her. Could you show me more?

After your response to my Shakes letters, & a response I got from one or two others, I made a second run at it, cut a lot of the groping twaddle, made the essential mythology clear from the start, then went properly into Macbeth, Ant & Cleo, & Cymbeline onwards. I wanted to really make clear to myself what is so special about Macb. & Ant & Cleo — and The Tempest. So I probably doubled the length of the book. But I got what I wanted, I think. Anyway, I'm doing no more to it — though I'm still rewriting it every night in my sleep.

It's being typed (I put it all on tapes). So I'll let you see a copy when I have one. Clutter you up. Everything became more & more lucid as I went on — bad sign? or good?

It's a relief to get back to other things, even so. I always knew I would have to do it, and I always knew it would take a year or more. Still, I'm glad I've done it.

If it is still not clear why Lucrece & Angelo/Isabella are self-evident, could I use some of your letter in a <u>Note</u> — the letter in

---

1 I subsequently sent Hughes a copy of the book: *Kaleidoscope* (Outposts Publications, 1984).

which you argue your doubts? Then with my answer to your letter (some of it) added to that, a reader would have an example of the natural objections, & my accomodating [sic] explanation. Help in giving bearings. But obviously the whole thing must seem controversial to most readers. If not idiotic.

I still think I've hit on something.

The main difficulty, as you pointed out, I think, is that I set aside virtually everything that most commentators comment about — the individuality of the plays — and talk about something of which the existence has been, more or less, explicitly or implicitly, denied, certainly ignored. But in doing that, I'm not challenging or modifying anything said about the individuality of the plays — I'm simply adding an extra dimension, but one that they all share. And proving the coherence & consistency of it.

It looks as though Faber are bracing themselves to do "Remains of Elmet" afresh — Fay has a whole lot of new pictures, and I want to introduce some different verses here & there.

Are you all well? Happy 1991

Love to the family   Ted

15th March 91

Dear Keith —

The last section of my Shakespeare pieces became as long as the rest of it. As I made a second run through it, I couldn't believe how little I'd got into some of them. But the better I got a grip on the whole pattern, the more I saw the machinery of each one.

Macbeth & Ant & Cleo I'd hardly touched. Better now. Macbeth is the key — the apparition scene — to everything that follows. Ant & Cleo is the most perfect image of them all — for what he was doing. Incredibly ingenious cantilever use of the Rival Brothers & Equation — after mid point the whole structure turns inside out. As I got the theoretical part into the working of the plays, I cut out the waffly discourses.

Interested to know what you'll make of my genealogy of Ariel & Caliban — and of the Storm & the Flower.

It's being typed on a wordprocessor & I hope to get some copies end of next week.

I'm calling it "Shakespeare & the Goddess of Complete Being".

I went back through the Comedies. The bare bones of the equation & the Rival Brothers makes up Two Gents of Verona, Comedy of Errors, Taming of the Shrew, Midsummer Night's Dream. It provides Shylock, Falstaff. Simply as a plot-schema. Then in All's Well they pick up the same equation pattern, but in its mythic form, from the 2 poems. After that, plot-schema & myth are fused, & develope together.

Love to family.   Ted
Very much liked the Enid Hudson.

27th May 91

Dear Keith,

I like your writing paper. Who designed the designs?[2]

The Shakespeare book is still going to and fro with last bits and pieces between me and a wordprocessor. 684 pages. I call it SHAKESPEARE AND THE GODDESS OF COMPLETE BEING. Some bits as you saw it but mostly rewritten or new. I only began to see the meaning of my own ideas as I rewrote it. In the end I had to forcibly stop myself writing fresh chapters — the thing became a little factory of its own ideas. Also, where do you stop.

I look forward to seeing what you describe.[3] We've probably written some identical pages. I've gone on a good deal about Caliban. Also I got into the evolutionary process of the poetry — unearthed why the third phase poetry begins where Lear and Cordelia reunite, why it disappears again till Ant and Cleo, why it pervades which parts of Ant and Cleo, then why it fastens to which parts of Pericles Cymbeline Winters Tale, and why it fills the Tempest. Also proved why the much-maligned Masque in the Tempest is the culmination of the Complete Works etc etc. Learned a lot, as they say.

I'm trying to get into and pull together something else — using the work habit I developed with the Shakespeare if I can.

I scrapped the title THE SILENCE OF CORDELIA — a bit too fancy, but mainly because I read a first class book by Craig Raine's wife, Shakespeare as Director, in which she had almost the identical sentence as the axis of her whole argument, describing Cordelia's

<hr />

2 I was using Friends of the Earth paper, with pictures of an angelfish and a starfish.
3 I had described the section of the Shakespeare chapter I was writing for *Literature and the Crime Against Nature*, material which subsequently became a separate chapter, 'The Crime Against Caliban'.

silence as the axis of Shakespeare's universe, as I had in my pages about Cordelia. So I found a better title and shall use her sentence as an epigraph.[4] If you want to read her book, her publishing name is Anne Pasternak Slater. A really good book — it hardly got a review. That and a book by Milward called Shakespeare's Religion[5] are the most interesting works I've come across in my search for somebody who might just have touched on ideas similar to mine. After raking through dozens of books I've come to the conclusion that almost all, possibly nearly all, all but this one and that perhaps, would regard my argument as <u>irrelevant</u> — and that's why nobody's ever bothered to describe something so self-evident. Maybe the novelty of my approach is nothing else but to see that level of the content — for the first time — as important. But that means I still have to persuade my yawning reader — not that this stuff is in there, they knew that, but that it's <u>important</u>.

Thanks for the Wilson Knight Red Indian.[6] I've kept clear of Red Indians — I wanted to focus Caliban into a slightly different context. But of course I'm sure he's right, basically. On the other hand, Shakespeare grafts the Red Indian identity onto an older stock, to my mind. In a piece I wrote a few years ago for Donya Feuer I made a lot out of the Red Indian Joker in the Elizabethan pack — but in his aspect of genius of the spirochaete,[7] the Mephistopheles of siphilis [sic].[8] Which was Lawrence's idea, I think, wasn't it.[9] Though I can't link Caliban with that.

I've yet to read Wilson Knight however — maybe now I shall.

I hope you're all well, and enjoying this perfect spring

love to the family   Ted

4 'But Cordelia is the quiet absolute . . . her very silence is the still centre of this turning world.' Anne Pasternak Slater is the niece of Boris Pasternak, and has written on his translations of Shakespeare into Russian. In Areté 34, Spring/Summer 2011, which contains all Hughes' letters to Craig Raine and his wife, Raine writes that although he was the nominal editor of Shakespeare and the Goddess of Complete Being, his wife 'was the real editor'. For her analysis of the manuscript see pp. 43–53.
5 Peter Milward, Shakespeare's Religious Background (Sidgwick and Jackson, 1973).
6 I had sent Ted the chapter 'Caliban as a Red Man' from Wilson Knight's Shakespearean Dimensions (Prentice-Hall/Harvester Wheatsheaf, 1984).
7 The bacterium which causes syphilis.
8 If Hughes is here referring to the long piece on Measure for Measure he had written for Donya Feuer in 1979 (Reid, Letters, pp. 405–19), he has misremembered. There is no mention of Red Indians, and only a passing reference to syphilis:
    [Measure for Measure] can be read as an analysis of the deep psychological terror of venereal disease – as the culmination of the deep psychological/religious fear of sex in general, and its specific effect on religious feeling in Europe at the turn of the 16/17 centuries (p. 410).
9 Lawrence discusses the impact of syphilis on Elizabethan consciousness, and specifically on Shakespeare, in his essay 'Introduction to these Paintings'.

12 September 1991

When I had a native marine tank twenty years ago, I used to go collecting specimens at St. Bees Head in Cumbria (just south of Whitehaven). So we went there a fortnight ago. We found the rock pools empty and ourselves ankle-deep in raw sewage, so we fled. Today I read of Greenpeace blocking the sewage outlet at Whitehaven, which they say is the worst in the country.

Sept 21 91

Dear Keith —

Thank you for the note and photocopied pages.[10] Interesting. I was startled to see my name & that casual reference to Angelo's transformation into a Tarquin — the first reference to my old Intro that I've come across, in Shakespeare commentary, since I published it. I read it ten minutes after sending off my last readjustments of the Goddess to my copy-editor, (a brilliant girl, Gillian Bate, who's helped a lot getting the mass of it — 800 plus typed pages — into clear sequence, paced & shaped.) — who will give it to the production dept on Monday.

From what you read, the sections on the Sonnets, the 2 long poems, As You Like It, All's Well, M for M, Othello, T & C. Hamlet & Lear are the same — with a good bit of polishing up & additional material (a whole lot more on Jacques/Iago). Clarification & amplification of Lear.

Also clarified Ritual Drama chat. A chapter about Hippolytos [sic] (Euripides) & V & A. A chapter about 'A Lover's Complaint' (key poem). Ampler & clearer mythological background — to Lear. All the generalised discussions deleted.

Macbeth totally new — saw at last just how everything turns on Macbeth in the scene of the apparitions. Much more about Macbeth the pivotal work.

Timon & Coriol the same — but corrected, clarified, amplified here & there.

Ant & Cleo completely new — at considerable length. Now I know why I love that play.

Cymb. & Peric the same but amplified, classified etc — with the Gnostic mythic material laid out fairly fully, & related to the text.

10 I had photocopied several pages on Isabella from Graham Bradshaw's book *Shakespeare's Scepticism* (Palgrave Macmillan, 1987).

T.W.T. incorporates what I had, but mostly new & larger, at considerable length.

Tempest entirely new & at great length (about 1/5 of the book)

I divide it into 3 parts, & each part into 2 chapters. I enclose contents list to give you some idea. I wanted it to read like a Detective story.

In The Tempest final section, I gather up all the threads, talk a good deal about Shakespeare's poetry, psyche, development, thematic symbolism as it supplies the main factors of the Equation etc — the nature of the Boar & the Flower (of Caliban, Ariel & the Storm).

Good deal about Shakespeare's language. I thought I'd be able to find more about that — in the literature — but found very little, & none of it really helpful. I must have missed a good deal (in the literature) about that, I suppose.

In fact, reading through all I could of the Shakespearean shelves (scanning through), which I began to do in earnest after I'd finished the second rewrite — I found nothing that either (a) contradicted or (b) pre-empted anything in my thesis. Here & there I found incidental support (Milward's — Shakespeare's religious background Anne Pasternak Slater's 'Shakespeare as Director').

Apart from the obvious things that have to be said simply in mapping out the general features of the works.

But much as I read I suppose I read only a tiny proportion of what exists.

I added Notes here & there — my favourite bits, threepenny bits in the Xmas pud. Some of them turned into whole sections.

I added a fairly long Intro (50 or 60 typed sheets) in which I set out as fully as seems necessary the mythic/religious geneology [sic] of the Venus/Adonis myth (and of the Boar, therefore) and of the Jehovah myth, and of Brunoesque Occult Neoplatonism and the psychic disciplines (Cabbala, Memory Maps, visionary meditation, ritual drama etc) which passed from O.N, via Bruno & John Dee & the Secret Societies, into Rosicrucianism etc (and so through to Goethe, Blake, Yeats — as anathema to orthodoxy)[11]

11 Hughes gives a fuller account in his introduction to the new edition of *A Choice of Shakespeare's Verse* (1991):
      Archaic mythic systems, various traditions of spiritual discipline, drawn from Pagan, Asiatic,

Also, in the same Intro, I tried to make clear what I am trying to do (the strict limits of my suggestions) and what I am not trying to do. I had thought — at that point — of including something of our correspondence, but then merely acknowledged the value of it (in my little page of acknowledgements).

When your letter arrived, the other day, I saw that my solution was — to quote the section of the Arden M for M Intro in which Lever quotes the Tyndale — which enables me to make my point about the two different worlds within the drama — the fixed world of the mythic plane and the 'free' world of secular personality & action. My argument concerns the first, exclusively. Commentary, performance, & even Shakespeare's plot complications, concern the second. And it connects Isabella & Lucrece.

So I made my very last readjustment, & sent it off 'haste post haste' after the typescript.[12]

I'd thought of sending you a typescript — but it is such a mountain of mess (with the added notes, rearrangements etc, that it is probably a fair course in aversion therapy. Once you'd floundered in it, you'd never want to make the acquaintance of the fresh-faced, clean-limbed book, or even proof — which I'll send you.

For the front cover, I'm trying to get them to reproduce a Romano-British bronze boar (sold at Sotheby's a month ago for £11,000 — the best one I know. I thought of trying to buy it, but didn't — remembering how my beautiful bronze Roman wolf, and my Heracles candlestick, were stolen.)[13] For the back I found

Islamic, Gnostic and Hebraic sources, were incorporated in a giant, religious synthesis centred on a Christ figure, and based on love of the Divine Source (p. 167).

Giordano Bruno (whom Shakespeare may have known through their mutual friend Sir Philip Sydney) 'expounded this as a practical method of organizing the psyche and the knowable universe within an exalted vision of Love' (p. 168). 'Shakespeare and Occult Neoplatonism' in *Winter Pollen* is a revised version of this introduction.

Bruno (1548–1600) was an Italian Dominican friar, philosopher, humanist, mathematician and astronomer. He was burned at the stake for heresy in 1600. See Frances A. Yates, *Giordana Bruno and the Hermetic Tradition* (Routledge and Kegan Paul, 1964).

John Dee (1527–1608 or 1609) was a noted English mathematician, astronomer, astrologer, occultist, navigator, and consultant to Queen Elizabeth I. He devoted much of his life to the study of alchemy, divination and Hermetic philosophy.

Rosicrucianism is the theology of a secret society of mystics, allegedly formed in late medieval Germany, based on ancient esoteric knowledge, which gives insight into both nature and the world of spirit. This knowledge is symbolized by the rose and the cross.

12 I cannot find this final 'readjustment' in the published text.

13 The front cover was a drawing of a boar's head by Andrew Davidson. The painting on the back cover was 'Lotus World' from the Bharat Kala Bhavan collection *Banaras*. The cover of the paperback has a painting by Christine de Pisan of Robert de Vere, favourite of Richard II, being savaged by a boar.

a marvellous Indian painting of Krishna & Parvati (as the Goddess of Complete Being) in a world made of lotus flowers, each dressed in lotus petals, with lotus caps, he giving her a lotus. Exactly where my story ends up (Krishna was blue-faced — i.e. black — like Caliban & Aaron & the wild Boar.)

But Faber's design is in the hands of those collagists, who design, mainly, logos for accountancy firms, & who regard Faber's book-list as their permanent travelling public exhibition. If an idea is suggested, they complain that their creativity is being stifled.[14]

I thought I'd written about your Whitman piece.[15] It struck me as one of your best flights. And it brought Whitman's poetry to life — your approach seemed both new, yet spot on. By bringing his poetry to life, what I mean is — you isolated the most vital element, which is so startling, so naked & stirring.

You should have called when you came to Cornwall. That shoreline wipe-out is becoming more and more general. A face I know too well, these days. I hope you have some blennies — butterfish as the Irish call them.[16]

Love to the family   Ted

Did I show you my text for The Mermaid's Purse? — a follow up to the Cat & the Cuckoo, (though Reg Lloyd's illustrations, — very different from the C & the C — are a bit too adult for publishers, so we've run into a patch of quicksand. Here are two, for your aquarium)[17]

---

14   The Indian painting was in fact used on the back cover.
15   The first draft of 'Whitman and the Voice of Nature', in Sagar, *Literature and the Crime Against Nature*.
16   Blennies and butterfish are both found in British rock-pools, but are quite distinct species.
17   The first edition was published by the Sunstone Press, Ted's and Reg Lloyd's own press.

1992

Shakespeare and the Goddess of Complete Being was published in April to a largely hostile reception. Hughes published articles in its defence in *The Times* (16 April) and the *Sunday Times* (19 April). *Rain Charm for the Duchy*, his collected Laureate poems, was published in June. In October Hughes read at the Cheltenham Literature Festival, then went to Ireland. He finished *The Iron Woman*.

18 Feb. 92

Dear Keith —

Worms crawling around like Journalists in an earthquake, or am I seeing back to front. That Sunday Times news of the film about Sylvia set it all off. Fortunately, I've translocated — I hear journalists now more or less as I hear rooks.

I got you a set of proof sheets of the Goddess but didn't send them because I set about changing everything so much. Several words on most pages. Sentences in, or out, or both, on very many pages. 9 or 10 pages replaced, rewritten, radically changed. For instance, the anecdote of the dream out of the acknowledgements[1] (one page out) and an account of how I first located the idea, in the foreword (one page in). So on.

Thank you for the noted errors — I haven't checked, but I'm pretty sure they'll have been picked up. It was very thoroughly gone over, not only by me, several times.

But don't read any further. I didn't send you the sheets, because

---

1 In the proofs Hughes had given an account of how Peter Brook, when, in the late sixties, he began to think of making a film of his famous production of *King Lear*, had invited Hughes to see what he could do 'in the way of converting Shakespeare's massively verbal text to dialogue more suitable for a film'. Hughes worked on this for some weeks:

Until one night I had an odd dream. A pounding at the back door of my house, in the middle of the night, awoke me. I opened the door to find Shakespeare himself there, magnificently arrayed in dazzling Elizabethan finery and utterly enraged with me and with what I was doing. He then put on, as a demonstration of what he had meant, a performance of the full text of *King Lear*. The stage was the roof-space of my house, actually quite a large area, but the roof had vanished. The action took over the entire cosmos (seeming to absorb many pantheons) in unearthly colour, light and violence, and at tremendous speed. One of the most astonishing dreams that I ever had. Next morning I noted down what I could recall. I took the dream as a sign to withdraw from the film project, which I did. But my understanding of Shakespeare was totally changed, and I realize now that this book accommodates something of what I was shown that night.

I didn't want you to exhaust your first impressions on such a roughish draft. A different ending (very important) and some of the pivotal points much improved.

I'm enclosing two passages that couldn't be got into the British Edition (too late & long), but will be in the U.S.[2] Also a further refinement of the argument for the literal truth of Shakespeare's references to his lameness. (Not very important, but curious).

Cover's very good, for once.

Out on March 9th. I picked the day Astrologically (as I used to do when my books had good earthly fortunes). It could well be on that day the hemispheres might just twist apart. Lie low, over that weekend, says my Sybil.

I collected the Laureate poems, improved them here and there, and wrote some notes — which have somehow become a disquisition on the metaphysics of Monarchy — or rather, of the British Monarchy (different in kind from all others).

Strange migration of your books. Evil days in the bookshops. And out of them too.[3]

I got embroiled, as I knew I would, in one or two of those prose pieces. Still, I'm beginning to realise that poems need prose precincts. A mistake of mine, from the worldly point of view, to think they did not.[4]

I wish the Goddess could be a bit more readable (less detailed maybe) — to make its meaning plain a little more quickly (i.e. not in 50 years time).

Mermaid's Purse moves apace (I think) — with a new illustrator (a girl whose name I forget).[5] No publisher would touch Reg's paintings — 'too adult' they all said.

I thought I'd put Cave Birds, Elmet & River in one Vol.[6] (Elmet could still be a picture book — with the right cash). And maybe

---

2 In the first of these Hughes suggests that Shakespeare was, psychologically, 'as fully female as he was male', so that the Equation can be seen as 'the magical battle of the two shamans within his single body'. The second is a longer passage in which Hughes seeks to demonstrate that in the mythic sense The Merchant of Venice is 'a powerfully pro-Semitic work, a powerfully anti-anti-semitic work, in which (not surprisingly, in a Christian imagination) Israel = the Goddess'.

3 I was having difficulty finding publishers for both The Challenge of Ted Hughes and Literature and the Crime Against Nature.

4 Hughes was now working with William Scammell on the collection of his occasional prose to be published in 1994 as Winter Pollen.

5 Flora McDonnell.

6 Published in 1993 as Three Books: Remains of Elmet, Cave Birds, River.

Hawk Lupercal & Wodwo (without stories) in another. So get all published handily, but avoid the dreadfulness of a Complete.

Yes, drop a line before you come in August.

Love to all the family   Ted

9th July 92

Dear Keith —

My number is [enclosed].

I shall be around when you're down, first week in August. Get in touch!

Finally managed to stop writing addenda to the Shakespeare. Ideally, I should have sat on it another year, then rewritten it — half the length.

But the excitement of discovering my way through it would have gone.

Problem for almost everybody who reads it — they simply don't know the plays.

Reviews were interesting. The Academics identified themselves, to a man, (with a kind of naivety) with the Adonis character in his Angelo phase — confronting my argument as the brothels of Vienna, Juliet's pregnancy, Isabella's appeal. How right Shakespeare was!

Women were wiser — but still tended to identify themselves with the plaintiff Goddess, disturbed by what they saw as my puritan assault on them.

No single reviewer transcended the quarrel, & observed the transformations of both. Marina Warner nearest, by far.[7]

---

7 Marina Warner, reviewing the book in the Times Literary Supplement, 17 April 1992, described the Tragic Equation fully and accurately, with its 'densely woven insights – historical, biographical and psychological':

The readings Hughes offers again and again are dazzling; perhaps other people know Shakespeare's poetry as he does, but I've not come across them. His high-wire performance – as he cross-refers, sounds echoes and image and device, takes off with magnificent cadenzas on certain motifs – is never less than enthralling.

But she also expressed the same reservations my letters had reiterated:

In the same way as interpreting the plays as sacred rituals attenuates the moral subtleties of the tragedies, Hughes's psycho-sacralization of the anima, embodied by Cleopatra, or Hermione, or Imogen, empties the plays of some of their complex, spiritual, inner life, which flows in the sensitivity of individual predicaments and responses. Perceiving overall patterns can finally blind one to the interest of the stitches; questers for Woman tend to mistake or overlook mortal women: Goddesses screen persons from view.

I see now more clearly what the Introduction should be — a more forthright & simple "Instructions for the use of this book".

Also, those Academics didn't read it — not more than a few pages.

Pity I let myself be angry with Carey — missed the opportunity to state the case (which he missed because he hadn't read crucial sections).[8]

But he is a catspaw for the Sylvia Plath Society, and is a particular friend, evidently, of Elizabeth Sigmund.[9] [. . .] Carey signed Hayman's letter about S.P.'s grave, you may remember.

When Nicky sold one of S.P.'s books recently, & the dealer put it in Sotheby's with a reserve of £8,500, Elizabeth rang up The Times to inform the world that I was selling S.P. properties that ought to belong to her children. What a gel! And Carey her foghorn.

Look forward to seeing you   Ted

21st Oct 92

Dear Keith —

Thanks for the print.[10]

Just been in Ireland, with Nicholas. Read at a Memorial Concert for George Macbeth in Dublin — Brownjohn Thwaite, & myself. And about 100 cold pairs of ears in a Dublin church. A dimmish event — brightened by the M.C. and a busker brought in off the street to play a noble lament on the Irish pipes — as wild a fellow as you could ask for.

Nicholas caught some very big pike — and I caught nothing, according to the law: sons are built on the ruins of fathers.

Then read for Field Day, in Derry. Too late, to my horror, I saw great patches of school kids — 9 & 10 year olds — in the audience. Threw me rather. Between Royalty watchers & children my serious audience (if there is such a thing) has been squashed to a fossil.

My Shakes. comes out in the U.S. in a week or two. Had a

---

8   John Carey's review, 'Shaman Scandal', had appeared in the *Sunday Times* on 5 April 1992. 'Battling Over the Bard', 19 April, contained a lengthy reply from Hughes, and a further riposte from Carey. See Appendix IX.
9   Close friend and confidante of Plath.
10   I had been so impressed by Michael Daley's drawing of Shakespeare, the Goddess and the Boar which had accompanied a review of Ted's book in the *Independent*, 11 April 1992, that I had bought the original from him, together with a bromide print to send to Ted. See plate 12.

strange letter from a woman in Sussex — a nun I daresay: she sent me an essay she wrote in 1990, using exactly my method on David Copperfield — rather brilliant in a quiet, lucid way. She once wrote a book on the Christian Myth: Lois Lang-Sims.[11] — but, she tells me, it was instantly remaindered.

Love to all   Ted

22 Oct 92

Dear Keith —

Since I let my mail bank up, I don't see what comes when I'm away — till long after. Dangerous policy, maybe.

I've just unearthed a letter from you — sent in April. With the chapter about the Sphynx.[12]

This chapter makes it very clear — an ideal drama for our day would be those Greek dramas up-dated. Not translated, but totally re-imagined. Your chapter is a meaty synthesis — grandly moulded & inclusive, to my mind. But so timeless.

How was dancing at Lughnasa? I met Friel recently — very engaging fellow.[13]

Publishers are all in a funk.

Finished The Iron Woman. Carol likes it. (And she's a very tough critic)

Love to all   Ted

11 Lois Lang-Sims, The Christian Mystery: An Exposition of Esoteric Christianity (Allen & Unwin, 1980).
12 'The Curse of the Sphinx', subsequently published in my Literature and the Crime Against Nature.
13 Every Easter I run a residential course for theatregoers in London. In 1992 one of the six plays we saw was Brian Friel's Dancing at Lughnasa, a memorable production.

1993

At the beginning of the year Hughes began writing the two essays on Coleridge which were to be included in *Winter Pollen* the following year. In March he contributed to the Wilfred Owen Centenary at Oswestry. His revised versions of *Remains of Elmet*, *Cave Birds* and *River* were published in one volume: *Three Books* (June). In August Hughes gave several readings in Canada. On 31 October he read with Tony Harrison in York. He produced translations of four of Ovid's *Metamorphoses* in response to an invitation from Michael Hoffman and James Lasdun to contribute to their collection of translations by living poets.

17th Feb 93

Dear Keith —

I blundered into the pit of sorting out what exactly is going on in Coleridge's 3 poems — Kubla, Mariner, Christabel.

Now I'm wondering if all I've done is regurgitate somebody else's banquet. <u>What books ought I to read?</u> (I know the Notebooks) I mean — to look at, just to check.[1]

I expect I've rewritten your chapter 11. !!![2]

The paperback Shakes looks O.K. — nice cover too. Don't buy one, let me send you one. (Obviously, it's not to be read again.)

Love to Melissa and all   Ted

27 May 93

Dear Keith —

Thought Melissa and yourself might like to see the enclosed.[3]

Thank you for the Albatross pages. As you see, my conclusions are similar. But I became intrigued by the curiously ingenious <u>mechanics</u> of the whole thing. Real sign language.

Hope all goes well. love to all   Ted

Let me know if you find some bits unclear. (Must rewrite last page and ½)

---

1 I recommended Norman Fruman's 1971 biography *Coleridge, the Damaged Archangel* (G. Braziller). I offered to give him Richard Holmes' recent biography, *Coleridge, Early Visions* (Hodder & Stoughton, 1989), and to lend him the Macmillan casebook on *The Ancient Mariner and Other Poems* (ed. Alun R. Jones and William Tydeman, 1973).

2 Chapter 11 in *Literature and the Crime Against Nature* is 'The Curse of the Albatross'.

3 The final draft of 'The Snake in the Oak', first published in *Winter Pollen*.

10 June 1993

Dear Ted

Many thanks for letting me see the Coleridge draft. It is very exciting. Also dispiriting, since one's own work suddenly looks very dull and superficial. Perhaps the hysterical antagonism of so many reviewers (especially from the Oxford establishment) to your Shakespeare book was a defensive reflex — their only alternative to admitting that in the light of the real thing they ought really to pack up shop. In my own case I suppose I can console myself that I am dealing also with the real thing, though paddling in the shallows of it, and can therefore justify publishing it as a sort of elementary swimming lesson in preparation for the deep-sea diving of your work. Having seen this essay, I see that it would have been more helpful to have sent you not my Coleridge paper but the part of my Lawrence paper which deals with 'Snake'. So here it is.[4]

I don't have many comments on your paper, but here they are for what they are worth . . . The main problem as I see it is that you are speaking a language which will be foreign to the bulk of your readers, including many academics. More so than it would have been twenty years ago, since then it was still common for students to be taught in higher education and even in good schools the rudiments of reading imaginative literature. Now we have a generation of critics and teachers who have no idea how to read poetry, and don't regard such an ability as an essential part of their equipment or concern. You can't take anything for granted. Simultaneously with expounding your interpretation you have to teach your readers your language. As it stands it is, in places, so concentrated and allusive as to become gnomic. Many of your allusions which are intended to make helpful connections and to clarify, in fact obscure your meaning because they lead the reader into unknown vertiginous territory without a guide. You use at times a shorthand which is decipherable only by those who have read and thoroughly digested their Eliade,[5] Campbell, etc. Such people would give you a tiny readership. The vast majority will know nothing of shamanism, or have any idea what a 'Guardian of the Threshold' is. Your central icon of tree, woman and serpent, for example, assumes the reader has read *The Myth of the Goddess*.[6] A quotation from or reference to that book would not only clarify, but avoid the charge which is bound to be made by the ignorant that this whole concatenation of symbols is a farrago of your own febrile imagination. Nearly all your references to figures and types from mythology or folklore need a brief simple exposition, such as you give for kundalini.

What is your objection to giving the sources of your quotations from the Notebooks? You deny your readers the possibility of looking any of them up. And wouldn't it help you to get back to them if you needed to?

A few more specific points. p.18b I don't understand the last line.

---

4 Sagar, *Literature and the Crime Against Nature*, pp. 287–9.
5 In 1964 Hughes had reviewed, and been deeply influenced by Mircea Eliade's *Shamanism*. *Winter Pollen*, pp. 56–9.
6 By Anne Baring and Jules Cashford. See also 5 January 1990.

p.43 Sphinx, not sphynx.

44. I don't like 'consultants'. How about 'guides' or 'familiars'?

46. Isn't it the deity which is hidden from the Universe, and not the other way round?

At the bottom of that page the simile of ovum and sperm obscures rather than clarifies the meaning. This is a very difficult page. I can think of no folk-tales where the questor is invited to kill his animal guide at the threshold of the spirit world. Why? How about some examples? I would need a lot of persuading that the killing of the bird is a necessary act for which the mariner is rewarded. This is directly contrary to every account I know including my own, and your own unexceptionable account on p.78?

49. The second half of p. 220 of *The Wise Wound* has an idea you might find useful in relation to the mariner's shedding of his own blood.[7]

59.It is impossible to follow your description of 'the old four-line ballad verse' without an example.

78. 'Wordsworth contributed the albatross'. Any reader who is not familiar with the Wordsworth note on this might be in some doubt as to whether you are speaking literally or figuratively.[8]

88. 'Concretization and thereby debasement'. There is surely no harm in 'concretization' unless, as here, into inadequate images; indeed it is essential to poetry. But your underlining suggests that it is not the inadequacy of the concretization but the concretization itself which is debasing. It's an ugly word anyway. Can't you get rid of it?

89. What purpose is served by the word 'Unitarian'? As I understand it the Unitarians were and are more open-minded and tolerant than most of the Protestant sects. In my youth I knew a Unitarian minister in Bradford (father of Alan Bullock), who took his texts more often from Blake and Lawrence than from the Bible. My Encyclopedia describes the Unitarians as:

> A group of Christians who reject the doctrine of the Trinity and the divinity of Christ, believing instead in the single personality of God and regarding Christ as a religious teacher. They have no formal creeds but stress reason and conscience as the bases of religion and view human nature as essentially good: they therefore also reject orthodox Christian teaching on original sin and atonement.

---

7 By Penelope Shuttle and Peter Redgrove.
8 Wordsworth gave the following account of his contribution to 'The Ancient Mariner':
   Much of the greatest part of the story was Coleridge's invention but certain parts I suggested; for example, some crime was to be committed which should bring upon the old Navigator, as Coleridge afterwards delighted to call him, the spectral persecution as a consequence to that crime and his own wanderings. I had been reading in *Shelvocke's Voyages*, a day or two before, that while doubling Cape Horn they frequently saw albatrosses in that latitude, the largest sort of sea-fowl, some extending their wings twelve or thirteen feet. 'Suppose', said I, 'You represent him as having killed one of these birds on entering the South Sea, and that the tutelary spirits of these regions take upon themselves to avenge the crime!' The incident was thought fit for the purpose and adopted accordingly (Jared Curtis, ed., *The Fenwick Notes of William Wordsworth*, Humanities Ebooks, 2011).

We are half-way through The Iron Woman as the children's bedtime book (Bernard got me a proof copy). They are spell-bound, and Melissa, who is coming to the end of her teaching practice, wishes she could have used it with her eleven-year-olds. Ursula (who has just had her eighth birthday) has composed her first song. She had no help at all with words or music. A really dramatic piano score, like Britten's setting of 'Waly, Waly'. The words go:

> I'm astray on the wild and windy moor
> With my true love by my side.
> We'll be married on Wednesday morn
> And she will be my bride.

> We'll stay together . . . for ever
> For I love her with all my heart.
> We're alone on the wild and windy moor
> And we will never part.

She knows nothing yet of Wuthering Heights!
    All the best   Keith

10th June 93

Dear Keith
    Here's the last section of the Coleridge — clearer and a bit more to the point (to my point, I mean).[9]
        Love to all   Ted

12 June 93

Dear Keith — I don't think you should let my elaborations dint your feelings about your own. Largely, my notions are not sufficiently simplified, whereas yours are — you have a much clearer sense of your audience. So you are able to make deep openings very simply, clearly — without any feelings of difficulty. But as you say, mine needs, first of all, to be <u>translated</u>. Mainly, it needs translating from merely unnecessary complication (trying to say everything at once) to simple step by step. When I take trouble, it quickly begins to look straightforward — and after all none of these things is new.
    Yes, you are right — this time maybe I should give some clarifying notes, maybe even reference (a list of books about

---

9 'Postscript: The Snake in the Spine'.

shamanism for instance). (Also, reference to the tree & the Goddess literature. The tree, the serpent & the Goddess).

My hope always is, students will start finding these appendages (to the poems) more interesting than critical commentary — and will go to look them up.

Could you bear to list the places where you think I could do with a clarifying note of that kind? I would be really grateful. My sense of what is necessary, in that line, is defective.

My copy editor — a very clever girl, well read, (who is also a great fan of this essay) didn't know what Samadhi was/is.[10]

Yes maybe the ovum/sperm idea is a bit out of proportion. But all those stories to the other world & rebirth are analogues of sperm → dying into → egg → to be transformed therein by a female → to new birth/revelation etc.

'Guardian of the Threshold' — surely you've met those stories. The little fox, the little horse, the bird, the lion, etc etc — that instruct the adventurer how they must be killed before etc etc. All stories where Dragon must be killed to release maiden, or treasure, where Sphinx, or monster must be killed to release destiny, etc.

One of the most standard features, in some form or other.

Problem is — who is my reader? A student who has only just begun to study such poems (and knows nothing). Or the enthusiast — who knows everything about the poem except my slant? From experience, I know the second sort don't miss the opportunity to jeer at my efforts to contact the first sort.

No, I have to think of you and one or two others, or be gagged, really.

I didn't specify the Notebook quotes for the simple daft reason that I copied the quotes from British [actually London] Library Vols (£20 worth of postage) and didn't note every number — only the occasional ones — because I didn't at the time foresee how useful they might be as evidence in this Court. And also, I thought — whoever is curious ought to read the whole of the Notebooks anyway. What point can there be in merely checking the quote I use — to see if I'm getting it word perfect?

There is a wonderfully interesting passage (7th August, 1826)

10 Samadhi, in Hinduism, Buddhism, and Sikhism, and Yoga, is a high level of concentration which has been described as a non-dualistic state of consciousness in which the consciousness of the experiencing subject becomes one with the experienced object, and in which the mind becomes still. See also footnote on p. 303.

where — while considering an abstruse theological possibility — about his landlady's Mrs Gilman's piety — he [Coleridge] suddenly has a vision, looking through the branches & foliage of Elm trees at the setting sun. It is an exact replay of The Mariner's looking through the ship's masts — and brings him to the same kind of ecstatic realisation (condensed & without sea-snakes — unless the sea-snakes have secreted themselves in Mrs Gilman). Worth a chapter — but enough's enough.

The point is — reading the Notebooks with my argument in mind, you find corroboration on nearly every page. So — if I can tease my reader into doing that, my main witness becomes Coleridge himself.

But how can I get those numbers for my quotes (the note numbers —) without getting the Notebooks back, & going through them again.

Yes, I'll check those places where Unitarianism gets in the way. Still, even as a Unitarian he was awfully sharp in principles, deeply puritan in his idealism, (his anti-Catholicism is almost angry with purest prejudice). So his Unitarian latitude was also the half-liberal planetary system around a Christianity, solar centre, that incorporated Milton, pretty well whole & entire. According to his Notebooks. Speaking generally.

Yes, 'consultants' was a joke — a poor one.

The Universe here, obscured from the deity (i.e. as if lost)

But I've altered that (my editor thought as you do.)

O.K. I'll make you a list of stories where the (even helpful) animal has to be killed. At this point in my argument, I'm merely showing how it fits into a traditional dream/epic pattern — as the sacrificial animal (the animal which is also the God/Goddess). One Basis, surely, of the sacrificial idea — the earthly (animal or human) form of the deity is killed, to open access to the deity's unearthly reality. No sacrifice, no communion.

Yes, I'll look up the Wise Wound. Though here I'm simply/mainly identifying the continuity of the idea — from Sufferings of Cain.

I'll send you the Myth Metre Rhythm essay, when I get a copy — a great deal in that about Coleridge's metres etc. (This essay began as a Note — to that). So they'll go together in this prose book, (which I'm titling 'Winter Pollen')

Yes, I'll look at 'concretization'.

Ursula's song is beautiful isn't it? It's like the real thing.

Glad she/they like Iron woman. I'll write about the Lawrence.

Love to all   Ted

[12 June 1993]

Dear Keith — Your remarks set me fiddling with the final 2 pages. So here is where they now stand. (A few minor corrections, too, in earlier pages).

Love to all   Ted

17 June 1993

Yes, of course I know some stories with guardians of the threshold, but not every reader who knows some of these stories will recognize the dragon, Sphinx or whatever under that title. Also you mention stories I don't immediately recognize — little fox, little horse, bird, lion — where? What puzzled me particularly was your apparent conflation of the guardian of the threshold (which I'd always thought of as hostile, monstrous) with the shaman's animal familiar or the questing hero's benevolent animal guide.

Surely there are many readers between the two kinds you specify, the beginner and the expert. People who have long known and loved the poems and understood them at an adequate level for their own enjoyment or for teaching them to schoolkids or even undergraduates, but who have never been stimulated to go deeper than the received and obvious meanings . . .

Yes, you're right about the Notebooks. Not worth the bother and expense.

Here is the list you ask for of references which could profit from clarification, or simply an example or two, or a signpost to where clarification can be found. A bibliography or some bibliographical notes directing readers to Eliade, Campbell, Jung, Baring and Cashford or whatever would not only be useful in itself but would make it harder for your ignorant detractors to give the impression that you are on a private ego-trip into fantastic or at least totally uncharted territory;

'Kubla Khan' is short enough for you to reprint the whole poem at the head of your discussion of it.

7. The role of oak and snake in 'the cosmology of Norse myth' and 'the inner world common to many Shamanic traditions'.

9b. What is a Hamadryad?

12. 'Orphic song'.

15. 'Psyche's incognito visitant' (omit?).

18b. The last line is incomprehensible to me.

19. 'Flute of Marsyas'. 'Triple Mother'.

20. 'Orpheus-like or Bran-like'. 'tutelary spirit'.
25. 'like Orpheus'.
43. 'like the goblins of the sangsara on a Tibetan tanka'.
45. 'Keeper of the Threshold'.
46. 'the typical story of that kind' — examples.
63. First five lines.
82. Quetzalcoatl = Plumed Serpent.
83ff. The Snake in mythology.

Have you seriously considered getting a word-processor? It would save you hours of typing on work like this. You could make all the changes you wanted, big or small, without any retyping — move bits around. A terrific boon — though it does take a while to learn how to use one in the first instance, like driving a car.

All the best   Keith

27th [June] 93

Dear Keith,

Thank you for the note. I will look at all your suggestions. As you say, there are many readers between the two kinds — between the extremes. But your suggestions — of the points that need a note or clarification — suggest that you too are imagining readers on the margins of illiterate.

For Hamadryad — surely most dictionaries supply: 'Dryad — i.e. nymph — that lives in a tree, as Naiad is a nymph that lives in running water. A large poisonous snake of the Cobra family. Also, type of large Abyssinian baboon.' Yes, I suppose even The Baboon maidens. On the other hand, maybe it would be as well to supply just that fragment of the dictionary (under Naiad, the Oxford even supplies 'tutelary spirit of a stream' etc)

Orphic music — the sort that moves rocks and timbers. But maybe that's too remote. I'll delete that. Though Orphic Song also charmed the Underworld and liberated Orpheus' lost beloved etc — as Coleridge's 3 poems did. And Orpheus lost Euridice when he turned to make sure of her credentials, just as Coleridge lost the 'Abyssinian maid/Nightmare Life In Death/Heaven's Mother/ Geraldine when Wordsworth took him by the ear and twisted his head, saying: 'you think this is your lost beloved, but look more closely, my dear fellow, she is a heap of bones and maggots' But I will cut Orphic.

Psyche's incognito visitant — wouldn't anyone far enough into Romantic poetry to be making head or tail of my essay know, via Keats' Ode to Psyche, that this visitant was Eros — though Psyche's sisters had persuaded her it was a giant serpent. As told in The Golden Ass. Perhaps the note, as such, would add to the suggestiveness of my essay. Maybe I should assume total ignorance and insert the note.

When you say the last line on 18b is incomprehensible, I feel I really have failed to communicate. My only point is: if any traveller, post the publication of Kubla Khan, had written this diary passage, if Ruskin or Tennyson or somebody of that kind had written it, we would say — consciously or unconsciously they are plagiarising the 'savage place' in Coleridge's poem: his poem showed them how to feel about such a combination of effects. Now since it is Coleridge himself writing this passage (five or six years after Kubla Khan being written), it is more explicit about the <u>savage women</u>, right there in the water, and — my coup de grace — it introduces the 'lovely lizards' right where (at the peak of his ecstatic response to the whole scene) they or it ought to appear in the poem but are or is suppressed, i.e. the whole hidden presence of the alligator is allowed, in this diary note, to come into the open as 'lovely lizards'. As if the lizards were indeed an aspect of those 'savage women'. It's a great pity that he forgot to note — in the diary — that the women were <u>singing —</u> can you imagine that scene, in that place, with the women <u>not singing</u>. I should think it's extremely likely that they were — or just had been, or would later. What I'm implying is that exactly the same primal scene enthralled him here, in the diary, as produced the vision in the poems — but the diary as I say is more literal about the actual components, whereas the poem leaves them in suspension, suppressed or only obliquely suggested. I suppose what I am say[ing] is that this diary note validates what I have said so far about the poem.

By Flute of Marsyas I was making the allusion to the basic, primitive instrument of a kind of Pan, which Marsyas was. I thought he was stock enough common knowledge to readers, again, who have bothered to read this far into an investigation of Coleridge. Zbigniew Herbert can make an allusive poem about him without need for a note: perhaps readers are content to find his poem 'obscure'.

My meaning was that the gigantic musical instrument of the Alph, as I've descriptively assembled it — eruption from an explosive source, eruption from a cosmic reptile, through the love bellowings of an alligator, through the throat of a nightingale, through the Abyssinian maiden's dulcimer and tender seductive but dementing song — could by no great stretch of metaphor be called an elemental flute of the god Pan, alias Marsyas: Marsyas because just as in Coleridge this music is challenged, and defeated, by the music of the orthodoxy, so Marsyas entered a contest with the music of Apollo and was defeated, as you know. And then flayed by Apollo — as Coleridge was flayed by the official committee of the orthodoxy, chaired by Wordsworth. So in 'flute of Marsyas' I was trying to get a lot for my money — but evidently in an obsolete coinage.

'Triple Mother' is making a passing point about Loki's (very confused) parentage. I'll cut it.

Orpheus and Bran, as you know both had heads that sang and continued to give oracles after their death. Looking them up again in Graves I see what I had forgotten: he regards them as in some respects the same figure (both Crows). But if you think I need to supply a note, I will. I simply feel apprehensive about making that kind of nursery note considering what I have to say about some other things.

Tutelary spirit — maybe I'll include that in a Hamadryad note. But I think, what would I think if I saw such a note — explaining tutelary spirit — in an essay by Coleridge, or by any modern literary commentator? The whole piece would suddenly assume an awkward air — a classroom in Dartmoor prison maybe. Would Empson need to explain it, or any of my esteemed colleagues? Perhaps they would.

Like Orpheus, as above. I'll delete it.

Goblins of the Sangsara etc. I suppose the point is to make a comparison with a similar situation in a completely different religious cosmology which is yet at this point identical. A Tanka and Sangsara could hardly be explained in a brief, informative note, without the whole metaphor appearing merely ornamental. Later on, I fit Coleridge into that very cosmology, with his Kundalini serpent. And so if this were a book one might take off from that metaphor of the Tanka and expand into a chapter that would more fully prepare the context for my last chapter about his hidden affinity with Indian asceticism. You see my point: the metaphor is central to what I am eventually saying about Coleridge — but, as you note, too brief for anybody who does not know the context of those two terms — tanka and sangsara, though they are commonplaces of one of the world's three great religions. Maybe it's best I simply leave them as a lump of obscurity.

I didn't feel Quetzalcoatl needed more than I gave him ('mexican redeemer god etc etc') — but now I've added the Note about Neumann's books I shall leave it to the readers. Likewise the 'snake in mythology'.

I will make a brief note about Keeper of The Threshold. And I will make the first five lines on page 63 clearer.

I shall never do any more of this. I don't think any of your questions would have surfaced if we had both been living in the US thinking of US readers. There, we would be thinking of a readership with a rough easy half-familiarity with all this stuff. Here, we are thinking of the militant opposition to knowing anything about anything, So here you need to nurse your under-exposed reader along like some molycoddled, [sic] spoilt child who will squall and abuse you if you say anything he doesn't know. Maybe I exaggerate. But I feel it is incredibly debilitating — this conviction that the ordinary ignorance, which was always massive, has now taken control and is in power, in every corner of cultural life. It's the ultimate triumph of the old law: if he can read, hang him. But more subtly presented via Education Committees and TV Production Managers. Whatever we say, it's not so in the U.S.

Maybe the mistake is to think that this is anything to worry about.

Faber spontaneously produced this reprint of these three books. First and third slightly trimmed, slightly changed, two or three bits added. Middle one slightly changed here and there but not as much as I once planned. The first one needed its photos I think. But evidently we are doing a de luxe reprint: more and new photographs by Fay, all the verses about that locale that I can scrape together.[11] The other two are better without illustrations, but could not be worse in any other typeface. Faber is incurably blighted by their

11 Published in 1994 as *Elmet*.

Brand Image obsession — imposed on them by Pentagram (who don't therefore have to apply their minds to each production in turn, they just throw them one after another onto the conveyor belt to come out in the same sardine-style can — occasionally a different colour). But in future it will be a condition of my contract: typeface.

Yes, you're right about a wordprocessor. I daresay this last four years it would have saved me two full working years.[12] But I've finished with prose except narratives, which don't need much correction as a rule.

I wrote The Iron Woman up to the point where the girl helps her to clean herself at the river — or leads her to the river and watches her clean herself then turned to the Shakes Book. Then never went back to the Iron Woman for the two years. As soon as the Shakes book was done, I finished The Iron Woman. So the Shakes is a kind of Note to Page 25 of the story.

The week after I sent it off, I read in The New Scientist that Japanese Scientists have found a method of reducing the kind of plastic that is mostly used — the kinds of plastic mostly used — to a single simple substance which burns with a pure heat.

love to the family   Ted

1 Aug. 93

Dear Keith —

At Farrar, Straus & Giroux: WES ADAMS

FARRAR STRAUS & GIROUX INC

19 UNION SQ WEST

NEW YORK, N.Y. 10003

At Faber — Christopher Reid[13]

I managed to take account of almost all those suggestions you gave me, in the Coleridge piece. Thank you a lot for that. I combed out one or two other bits of spaghetti, I think.

I'll get Faber to send you a set of the proofs (it will be 400 pages, or thereabouts). WINTER POLLEN.

12 Ted believed that the manipulation of a pen, pencil or brush activated the right-hand (creative) hemisphere of the brain, but that using a keyboard was a left-hemisphere (mechanical) function. See my essay on 'Ted Hughes and the Divided Brain' in the Journal of the Ted Hughes Society, 1 (Summer 2011), www.thetedhughessociety.org.

13 I had asked Ted for the names of these commissioning editors with a view to sending them my proposal for Literature and the Crime Against Nature.

Just going to Canada for a few days, do one or two readings. Rather resent going — all the time wasted on that prose, just when I'd found a way through.[14] Priorities! But I need some cash.

Love to all the family   Ted

14 October 1993

Can you tell me if there are or are going to be US editions of any of the following: *Moortown Diary*; *Rain-Charm*; *Three Books*; *Dancer to God*; *Iron Woman*; *Winter Pollen*.

I'm no nearer finding a publisher for *Literature and the Crime Against Nature*, or finding out what is going to happen to me at the university next year. Melissa has an interview next week for a job she wants very much at a school in Accrington. Once she has a permanent job I shall be in a position to take early retirement if I just get sick of the whole academic fiasco. Manchester is advertising for a chair in Critical Theory. They are all disappearing up their own arses.

I finished my pond and waterfall, and, though I say it myself, it's very beautiful. Just as I envisaged it. We have it floodlit in the evenings. We bought two goldfish for the children, two silver rudd, and caught several tiny minnows. One of the goldfish died. I glimpsed the minnows occasionally, but the other three I've never seen since they went in. If they are dead, where are the bodies? There are lots of herons round here, but when they visit a pond they usually leave an unmistakable trail of wreckage as though a large dog has been cavorting there.

For Ted's reply see his letter of 2 December.

25th Oct 93

Dear Keith,

It will be nice to see you in York.[15] And it would be nice to have some time — but I've committed myself to relatives back in Mytholmroyd. Then back to the overload here. I expect York will be — who knows what cupboards will disgorge God knows what. Well, just lower the brow and push through. It's a charity event. Though I'm not the charity.

WINTER POLLEN is 460 pages. Trying to correct one or two things I fell through into pits full of alligators. As I knew I would. Which is why I always put it off. Chunks of life. I've just sent off

14 I presume that Ted meant that he had resumed work on *Birthday Letters*.
15 I attended a reading Ted gave with Tony Harrison at the Theatre Royal, York, on 31 October.

today a nightmare of corrected proof, rejigged pages etc. I'd hoped to send the proof of the Coleridge piece maybe somewhere for cash, but I've messed it about so much it's no longer suitable.

Did you see the little column of Ad for Reg's Mermaid's Purse in The Independent? He sold out the whole edition within the next 24 hours. Is that the book or the nature of the edition? Faber had about 2,000 Cats And Cuckoos for two years and never sold one. Eventually Reg and I took them back. He's selling his in fifties, to art galleries, National Trust Shops etc. Any ideas?

Love to the family   Ted

3 November 1993

Dear Ted

That was a splendid reading on Sunday. It was particularly exciting to hear so many new poems. How near publication are any of these? I enjoyed Tony Harrison too — you make a good pairing. Are you going to publish 'Old Oates'?

Introducing one of the poems about your father you said that he was in the First Fifth Lancashire Fusiliers which landed on Gallipoli on 6 May, and that only eleven men 'got off'. The Gallipoli landings began 25 April 1915. But according to army records, your father did not enter the Balkans operational area until 22 July as a member of the Ninth Lancashire Fusiliers (the First Fifth was not created until February 1918, when your father joined it). There were fresh landings at Sulva Bay, Gallipoli, on 6 August in which your father probably took part. The last British troops left Gallipoli 8 January 1916. The 9th left Gallipoli with only 4 officers out of 29, and with fewer than 100 men. So the figure of eleven (or seventeen as Olwyn recalled it to me in a letter twenty years ago) cannot refer to the whole regiment, but presumably to the landing party or battalion or company of which your father was a member. I take it you were just speaking from your memory of what your father had told you and family traditions? Do you have any records against which to check any of this?[16]

5th Nov. 93

Dear Keith —

Sorry you didn't come round to the bar afterwards — stayed there quite late, with Tony H & Barry Rutter.[17]

---

16   I had recently acted as external examiner for a PhD thesis by Colin Fraser on 'Reshaping the Past: The Personal Poetry of Ted Hughes', in which Fraser had researched the army records.

17   Barrie Rutter had played Silenus in Tony Harrison's The Trackers of Oxyrhynchus at the National Theatre

Tried to read too much — so lost control of the last ten minutes. Meant to end very differently.

Interesting what you say about Lancs Fus. I only recall my Dad's 'First of the Fifth' — he had a jingle about it which I've forgotten. His DCM. Watch has 1/5th, but he got that in Sept 1918.

I never actually asked him just where he landed, would you believe it. But if he joined up, as he did, in Bury & within a day or two of war being declared (in the queue, he was two away from Billy Holt),[18] I had assumed he joined the 1/5th then. — I understood it was in existence then. (See 'Hell's Foundations' — that book about Bury.) And I understood that only the first conscripts (first few days) went into the 1st. After that, it was 2nd & 3rd. Still, I'm not sure! Then he was in Egypt etc.

The survivors I remember not as 11 but as 3. I assumed, of the Battalion. I should have some old papers, about the details, regimental details, I mean.

What I'm really interested to learn is the Army record of his Grandfather — called Major, was also a Major, and served (circa 1870) on Gibraltar. 'Major Major of the Rock' was how Grandma etc identified him — that was his tag. He married a Spanish woman. I wonder who she was.[19] Where Olwyn's nose came in. Used to have a picture of her — small, thin, very dark. My brother's hair was blue-black.

But if I could locate him — interesting.

I hope the Nature book prospers.

Yes, I have a lot of verses, but I'm not sure I don't like them better unpublished — or at least uncollected.

Love to Melissa & family Ted

2 Dec 93

Dear Keith —

Can't answer about the U.S. editions. 'Moortown Diary' — I should say is unlikely, because of old Harper Edn, though that's

---

in 1990. In 1992 he had founded Northern Broadsides, a touring company (based in the historic Dean Clough Mill in Halifax, West Yorkshire), which soon built up a formidable reputation performing Shakespeare and classical texts with an innovative, popular and regional style, often in unconventional locations (The Tower of London, cattle markets, churches, indoor riding stables, Victorian mills).

18 See 16 July 1980.

19 George Major married June Ratcliffe.

out of print. Rain-charm — very unlikely. 3 books — don't know yet. Dancer to God: Farrar Straus bought Faber Sheets — published it year before last. 'Iron Woman' — at the moment is running foul of U.S. Political Correctness in a big way. 'Winter Pollen' — don't know yet, but I'd hope so, some time.

The general opposition to me personally in the U.S. (Feminism in College & University English Faculty Committees — & in Libraries & Bookshops) has really made me, quite spontaneously, begin to delete the U.S. from all my reckonings. The males who might support don't seem to raise their voices.[20] Maybe what I write is simply of no interest to them. The damage has been done. That's my impression. I can't go lecturing/reading, to raise my stakes — because I meet crazies. So.

How is it the students themselves don't get sick of Critical Theory — ? that's what beats me. Still — it's easy power, I suppose. A degree in Lit Crit theory — then straight into investigative journalism!

Mystery about fish bodies. It always puzzled me. Have you an eel? They will nip out small fish — especially minnows. Yes, and a heron. I watched a heron pick out 35 somethings in 5 minutes (timed) this last year — on the Thurso.

Did Melissa get the job?[21]

Love to all   Ted

'The Iron Man' is pretty good — reviewers just wanted to block Pete's comeback.[22]

---

20 A notable exception was Leonard Scigaj, who wrote to me in July 1991:
    Every one of Ted's Harper and Viking adult poetry volumes since Crow is out of print in the U.S., both hardcopy and paper. Last semester I taught Crow and River back to back to undergraduate seniors, and they loved both. But I had to use my credit card and a cable call to Faber & Faber to have thirty paperback copies of River sent across the ocean to do it.
21 Melissa, who had been doing supply teaching for some time, was applying for a post as a primary school teacher. She began full-time teaching in September 1994.
22 Pete Townshend's rock opera The Iron Man had opened at the Young Vic on 18 November, to largely hostile reviews. It had been available since 1989 on Virgin records, V2592. When the production closed, the huge Iron Man was dismantled, and reassembled in a barn at Moortown farm.

1994

Hughes read with Heaney at the Sheldonian in Oxford. In June he set aside his almost complete translation of Euripides' *Alcestis* in order to begin translating Aeschylus' *Oresteia* at the request of John Durnin of the Northcott Theatre, Exeter. In August he attended the International Poetry Festival in Struga, Macedonia, where he was invested as the Golden Wreath Laureate for that year. On 6 October, the first National Poetry Day, Hughes read with Simon Armitage at the National Theatre. By now Hughes was writing more poems about Sylvia Plath, eight of which he included in his *New Selected Poems* (1995).

5th Jan 94

Dear Keith — wrote this for a group who are interested in making a historical/Shakespearean pageant (an epic drama) out of Shakes, the background history, and my book. Does it give too much away (make a reader feel no further need to read the book) for a more general publication? Or do you think it would make a reader want to read the book?[1]

I've asked them to send you a reviewers copy of Winter Pollen.[2]

Happy New Year & love to you all — Ted

8 Jan 94

Dear Keith —

You're right about the 1/5. I've dug out his battered papers. He joined in <u>Rochdale</u>, 22nd Sept 1914 — the 2/6. So when he got to be in the 1/5, as on his DCM watch, I've no idea!

Have a good 1994

Love to all   Ted

20 Jan 94

Dear Keith —

Yes, your note jolted me into action, so I've written to Leonard.[3] Only slight complication is that the children own all the Plath

---

1 See Appendix X.

2 I reviewed it in *Resurgence*, May/June 1994. See Appendix XI.

3 The note, no longer extant, presumably referred to the use of an image by Baskin on the cover of my forthcoming book, *The Challenge of Ted Hughes* (1994).

Rights — and one is in Vancouver, or suspended between Vancouver & Fairbanks, while the other is in Wooroloo, Western Australia. But I don't see why there should be a problem.

Pity I've had to write off the U.S. Strange business!!

Have you been seeing these programmes about Britain's big cats. Carol watched one (leopard size, black) for two or three minutes.

They'll be sending you a 'Winter Pollen' next week, for what its worth.

Warn Ursula — there's bears in them thar woods.

Love to all   Ted

21 April 94

Dear Keith —

'The Achievement' came — looks quite a neat book.[4]

I was in Italy & met a writer (Italian) doing — giving — a long series of lectures on 'Nature' in English lit. I told him about your chapters and he's very keen to see them naturally. He translated 'The Iron Woman'. Sweet fellow. Writes verse, has a little vineyard. Any chance of him seeing them?

I'm plugging away at one thing & another. Fending off distractions, mainly. Everything O.K.?

Love to the family   Ted

A decision had been taken to replace the Extra-Mural Department at Manchester, a fully academic department, with a Centre for Continuing Education, a purely administrative department. This meant that all forty-odd academic staff of the department had to be relocated, most of us in the appropriate internal department.

3 July 1994

At last I know what is happening to me at the university. After no-one doing anything about my future for nine months, despite all my questions and promptings, I had to go to the Vice Chancellor. He said that the English department did not want me because my work 'did not fit what they saw as their changing profile' . . . I take it to mean that they are going to phase out the teaching of literature altogether and just do critical theory and media studies. I was introduced in refectory a few weeks ago to a young man doing a course

4 In fact, The Challenge of Ted Hughes.

in the English department, and when I asked the subject, he replied 'soap operas'. I accepted the V.C.'s offer of enhanced early retirement. I am well out of that.

9th July 94

Dear Keith,

Here is the Italian's address. Riccardo Duranti [. . .] Very nice chap — good translator, too, evidently.[5]

Perhaps your Academic crisis is part of the greater crisis — English studies gradually turning into something that has nothing to do with the original concern, enjoyment of books and literary works. The way a snake's skin gradually separates itself, till it lies there as an object on its own, a trophy of a different kind, for the snake-skin collector. While the snake escapes renewed, to live its own unpredictable life.

Perhaps a whole new branch of communal activity should be organised — The Enjoyment Of Literary Works as Lumps of Life. Or, as Doorways Into Life.

Perhaps — an extra mural business. Utterly separate from the Academy. A wing of the Arvon Foundation maybe.

While the University Departments dry out, go crusty, drop off —

What mystifies me is — how it is that young students, wanting only to write and live, year after year succumb to those tortures. Is it that — when they apply — they don't know exactly what lies ahead, but expect something quite different (something that will help them to write etc). Do they go in under this utter misconception of what Eng Lit is?

You remember my story: Varsity[6] at Cambridge asked the 400 new students of English what they wanted to do after University? All but about twenty wanted to be writers of some kind — that's why they were reading English. Of my whole year, only one — Anthony Hopkins who wrote and may still write TV plays[7] — ever

5 Riccardo Duranti himself wrote to me on 20 July (Ted having given him my address), asking for a copy of *Literature and the Crime Against Nature*. I have no record of any subsequent correspondence. His address has been omitted.
6 An independent student newspaper.
7 Hughes is confusing the actor Anthony Hopkins with John Hopkins (1931–98), who wrote the scripts for *Z Cars* in the sixties, and whose quartet of plays *Talking to a Stranger* (1966) was described by George Melly as 'television's first authentic masterpiece'. He continued to write screenplays and television adaptations for the rest of his life.

emerged into the literary world that I knew. Same year after year, presumably. Yet in those days the torments were mild — frosty breath of Leavis, fall-out through US students of US New Crit.

If only some newspaper would do that survey year after year: after about ten years there'd be some evidence. I get letters from the casualties in their second and third year — wails from no man's land. Brian Cox knows exactly what I mean and thinks the same.[8] Maybe Arvon should do it.

But there's no evidence to show to the unsuspecting young. And, like the old, postgraduates stay quiet about the damage, or justify it somehow. Couldn't you organise it, with the Guardian?

I believe it's a good idea to shorten the book.[9] Two books. My heart sinks when I see over three hundred pages. (Spite of my own doorstops.)

Planning a new Selected including much more of everything, with a few new things at the end — nearly a Collected.[10] Also, a Complete Animal etc Poems — with a section for younger readers. Though young readers read all of them, seem to. But those I aimed at younger readers have softer tips.

Good to hear about the fish.

Love to all — Ted

5 October 1994

I am planning to treat myself to a retirement present in the form of a large greenhouse, which I shall attempt to turn into a miniature tropical rain forest. There will be a pool with a cascade and tropical fish and water lilies. Behind it bamboos and in front ferns. Arching over it will be a dead tree trunk carrying bromeliads, air-plants and epiphytic orchids. All round the walls will be flowering climbers such as passion flowers and abutilon. Any remaining planting space will be for food plants for tropical butterflies. There will be a bench so that I can sit in there and think about working . . . Now I have all winter to prepare the site and gather information and advice.[11] This interests

---

8   In 1989 Brian Cox had chaired a committee on the teaching of English, but the Thatcher government had no interest in the Cox Report. He had retired in 1993 to concentrate on writing poems, but also served as chairman of North West Arts, and of the Arvon Foundation.

9   I was becoming desperate to find a publisher for Literature and the Crime Against Nature, which was the fruit of over twenty years' work, and was wondering whether I should divide it.

10   The 1995 New Selected Poems contained 276 poems. The eventual Collected Poems contains over 1,000.

11   It soon became evident that this scheme would be both impractical and ridiculously expensive, so I settled for an aviary.

me far more than doing any more mere research or critical writing. Even when a book is published these days, you feel you might just as well have posted the manuscript into deep space.

6 Oct 94

Dear Keith —

Your green-house world sounds like a "flight into paradise" — out of this dumped other world.

Yes, that piece in the Spectator belongs about 1975 (part of a session of afterwork on the Crow story — so, that vein, as you divine correctly.) Coming across it lately it struck me with a certain truth to nature. Never seen the point made elsewhere — though the phenomenon ruins a fair proportion of lives, or a fair proportion of most lives.[12]

Put about 20 newish pieces in a New Selected (much fuller) Poems — for next year. Some pieces about S.P. etc.[13]

Strange things being said about Lawrence via Frieda's biog.[14]

Love to the family   Ted

11th Nov. 94

Dear Keith —

Thought these might interest you.[15]

I hope all's going well.

Love to the family   Ted

12 'Playing with an Archetype', 24 September 1994. This was announced as a 'new poem', but it reminded me so strongly of 'The Lamentable History of the Human Calf' that I told Ted that it read more like something circa 1970. The theme of both poems is that marriage is a perpetual gamble for higher and higher stakes until the man has lost everything.
13 New Selected Poems contained eight poems which were subsequently to be published in Birthday Letters, five of them previously unpublished. They attracted very little attention.
14 Rosie Jackson, Frieda Lawrence (Pandora, 1994).
15 Ted enclosed two copies of an offprint of 'the Poet Laureate's National Poet' by Anthony Paul, from A. J. Hoensclaars, ed., Reclamations of Shakespeare (Rodopi, 1994).

1995

The Dream Fighter and Other Creation Tales was published. In February, Hughes read at the Bath Literature Festival. He interrupted his work on *The Oresteia* to translate Wedekind's *Spring Awakening* for the Royal Shakespeare Company, but returned to it in May, and completed it in October. Circumstances prevented the Northcott from staging it. In August Hughes visited British Columbia, where he was interviewed by Thomas Pero (published in *Wild Steelhead & Salmon*, Winter 1999). He translated more Ovid. Hughes now began to work towards a whole book of poems about Sylvia Plath, to be called, initially, *The Sorrows of the Deer*. He also embarked on the huge task of preparing an archive of his manuscripts for sale (eventually to Emory University, Atlanta). At the invitation of Tim Supple, Hughes translated Lorca's *Blood Wedding*. He was a founding trustee of the Westcountry Rivers Trust.

Early in 1995 Ted told me that he was planning to sell his massive collection of his own manuscripts. He asked me for suggestions about possible buyers, and also if I could help by providing descriptive catalogues of the contents of each box, to enable him to identify material he did not want to include in the sale, either because he might want to return to it, or for personal reasons. In February I spent a weekend at Court Green. The manuscripts were in about fifty large boxes the size of tea-chests (some of them I think were tea-chests). One of the first boxes we came to was Crow material, so I chose to begin with that. I worked on it for the whole weekend. I brought three other boxes home with me, chosen more or less at random. One contained River material, one A Primer of Birds, and the third Sylvia Plath manuscripts. I suggested returning to Court Green in mid-April.

20th March 95

Dear Keith —

Thank you for the various things. Your chapter will be useful to me.[1] Pointed up certain things in just the right way for me. Also the Kitto — which I hadn't seen. Strengthens my faith in Aeschylus' canniness. Main problem, in these plays, is to give the active details of imagery etc real dramatic life — projected, active, leverage on the listener. To give each image the role of a sort of actor. If you can't do that, then the passages seem simply too long. However.

---

1 Since Ted was working on his translation of *The Oresteia of Aeschylus* (1999) I sent him my chapter on it, 'The Oresteia and the Superannuation of the Gods', from *Literature and the Crime Against Nature*, and H. D. F. Kitto's *Greek Tragedy* (Methuen, 1961).

Yes, I think what you've done with the Crow stuff is ideal.
O.K. think of 11–18th April.
Yes, number the pages — good idea.
  Love to Melissa & all   Ted

21 May 1995

Dear Ted
    I thought you were intending to call on your way home from Scotland, to pick up some of your boxes. In the event, it's just as well you didn't, since I have never lifted up a single box. It has been just hand to mouth with classes (my last class as a member of staff is next Wednesday) and with preparations for my Italian study tour (*Lawrence and the Etruscans*). The tour operator who is supposed to be organizing it has done nothing, withheld information, given misinformation . . . So I am having to do everything myself. I may be able to make a start tomorrow. Next week we are camping in Scotland. After that I should be able to do a bit. But there have been some changes in my circumstances since I last saw you which are going to affect my availability.
    First, Melissa has got a full-time appointment. She has been doing supply work hitherto. This will increase my domestic and family responsibilities. Second, developments in relation to my ecocriticism book seem to be leading towards putting the two books back into one, but cutting it down considerably by eliminating quotations from and references to secondary sources, and by conflating both the Greek chapters and the Shakespeare chapters. This will mean a lot of additional work on something I have already been working on for twenty years. Third, Mansell have asked me to prepare a revised and extended edition of the TH Bibliography, taking it up to the end of this year. Again a lot of work. Fourth, I have been trying for decades to get some publisher to let me do a proper edition of Lawrence's paintings, and suddenly I have been offered a contract to do just that. Add to this the fact that I am already late in handing over to the Cambridge University Press a large new critical study of DHL (*A Deeper Reality*), which is nowhere near finished, and you see that my retirement is not going to be spent cultivating my garden – not for a few more years anyway. Nor am I going to have as much time to devote to your manuscripts as seemed likely when I took it on . . .
    What I want to suggest, therefore, is that I will do what I can, but that you should see if you can find someone else to do a sizeable chunk (perhaps the bulk if they are available) or I might hold you up intolerably. You may know several people, but it seems to me that the ideal person would be Ann Skea.[2]

2 See 7 June 1988. In 1994 Ann Skea had published *Ted Hughes: The Poetic Quest*, a study with many unique insights.

27th May 95

Dear Keith —

Sorry to hear that I'll be losing you. But maybe Anne Skea is a good suggestion.

Also, it must be good that you're full of projects.

Thanks for the Rylands Library connection. I don't know what I can do till I've got a better idea of just what the archive amounts to. I don't suppose anybody would buy it blind. And how could I value it in its present state.

Just translated Wedekind's 'Spring Awakening' for the RSC.[3] Strange play.

Faber are doing that Coleridge essay as the Intro to a selection of the poems — all the poems I mention in the piece.[4]

Love to all — Ted

29 May 1995

There are some revised carbons where the revision does not appear in the printed text either in *River* or *Three Books* or *New Selected Poems*, all of which use the unrevised text. So what is the status of this revision? For example, the ending of 'The River', which in all the printed texts is:

It is a god, and inviolable.
Immortal. And will wash itself of all deaths.

is revised as:

It is a god, and though murdered, and murdered,
Immortal. And will wash itself of all deaths.

Which is to be preferred? There are many other examples . . .

I've just heard from Ann Skea. She has no commitments beyond the end of July, and is planning to come over. So she could be available to work for you for virtually the whole of August, if you want her. Also, she has excellent computer skills, which might come in useful.

We are off to Scotland tomorrow, camping north of Oban. But the first morning we have booked to go on an otter watch at six on a nature reserve

---

3 The Royal Shakespeare Company.
4 Ted Hughes, ed., *A Choice of Coleridge's Verse* (Faber & Faber, 1996).

where they promise your money back if you don't see one. None of us has seen a wild otter, so that will be exciting.

4th June 95

Dear Keith —

Thanks for the letter & details.[5]

'To educate the children' — became 'On the Tarka Trail' (Three Books)

'Stripping Salmon' was in the 1st Ed. of River as 'The Morning Before Christmas'. 'Crathie' became 'Dee'. (?)

<u>Status of Revision</u>. Yes, sometimes I make a change in a copy — then simply lose track of the copy. More often, revert to the original. I would have to look at them all!!!!

I made a whole lot of corrections in a copy of Flowers & Insects — then lost the copy.

The end of river is printed as I want it.

Ann Skea is a very good suggestion. I'll ask her — could you let me have her present address. I've got it somewhere, but —

Hope you saw some otters.[6]

What you're discovering — in the way of possibly unused revisions — is the sort of thing I'm very curious about. Then again, there should be a lot more MS of the river poems, somewhere.

    Love to all   Ted

19th Oct 95

Dear Keith — I changed my mind about the archives. Ann eventually came down for 3 days to stay at our cottage — just holiday. It struck me reading through what you had done,[7] that though you itemised everything perfectly, I myself, reading your list, had no idea exactly what most of the items were. Since quite a lot of

5   I was now working on the River manuscripts, and had sent Ted a list of poems which were either unpublished or published under different titles.
6   We did not on that occasion, but have done so on subsequent visits to NW Scotland.
7   I had completed my listing of the three boxes, Crow, River and A Primer of Birds, but not of the Plath material.

the material is miscellaneous drafts of unfinished or unpublished things, and since in among — as I've discovered — are all kinds of other things, some of which I would not want anyone to see, it became clear that I simply had to do it myself. So I made a start, and got a good way — discovered all kinds of things, and definitely felt the benefits of re-familiarising myself with all that long ago preoccupation. So I'm pressing on — making simple notes & breaking each group down into numbered folders. Up to 89, so far. Discovered a few S.P. mss & a whole children's story I'd forgotten — besides masses of verse which has a kind of interest for me.

What I'm especially curious to see, as I get towards the end — still some way off — is exactly what is missing.

In your Bibliog. Section A., 2nd page, last item (Collected Animal Poems) you omit Vol II — What Is The Truth.

I should have a copy of Reckless Head for you — I'll dig it out.

I'll also look for the Motion Bradbury New Writing — I think I got a couple of copies.[8] Pretty sure I got only one copy of the Causley Tributes (mine was Little Whale Song)[9] and one of the Spender (an elegy from Cappriccios [sic] plus the Stones poem out of Mermaid's Purse — titled parts I & II.)[10]

Spring Awakening was pretty surprising — quite shockingly effective in parts.[11]

Also translated Oresteia (Faber will do it. And maybe the Northcott, if we can agree terms),[12] made a Coleridge Selection — my Snake In The Oak essay, plus all the poems which belong to or touch that mythos). Translating some more Ovid for a vol.[13]

8 Andrew Motion and Malcolm Bradbury, eds., New Writing 2 (Minerva, 1993).

9 Michael Hanke, ed., Poems for Charles Causley (Enitharmon Press, 1982).

10 Barry Humphries, arr., A Garland for Stephen Spender (Tragara Press, 1991).

11 First performed by the Royal Shakespeare Company at the Barbican on 2 August 1995.

12 The Oresteia was first performed not by the Northcott Theatre in Exeter, which had originally invited Hughes to make the translation, but by the National Theatre in 1999, directed by Katie Mitchell. For a full account see Roger Rees, eds., Ted Hughes and the Classics (Oxford University Press, 2009), pp. 20–21.

13 In 1993 Hughes had contributed translations of four stories from Ovid's Metamorphoses to Michael Hoffman and James Lasdun, eds., After Ovid (Faber & Faber, 1994), and had enjoyed doing them so much that in 1996 he produced twenty-one more as Tales from Ovid.

Yes, I have the ivory fox. Let you see it some day.[14]
Love to all   Ted

14 The most recent story in Hughes' collected stories, *Difficulties of a Bridegroom*, was 'The Deadfall',
    written in 1993. At the end of the story, Ted and his brother, as boys, are burying a dead fox, when Ted
    picks up from the loose soil a little ivory fox. This more-than-coincidence is of a piece with his earlier
    encounter with a mysterious old lady:
        What made me feel slightly giddy was the way I'd found it while we were actually burying that fox.
        I did not know what to make of any of it. I could not see any way past it. When I thought about it,
        I felt a ring tightening round my head. But there was the ivory fox in my pocket, so smooth and
        perfect. And after all these years, here it is, just as I found it. And still I do not know what to make
        of it. Or of that old lady either. If it was an old lady.
    I'd asked Ted if they had really found such an ivory fox.

1996

Hughes finished his translations from the *Metamorphoses*, twenty-five in all, which were published in 1997 as *Tales from Ovid*. He wrote many more poems for *Birthday Letters*. In October *Blood Wedding* was performed at the Young Vic. In December he translated 250 lines of *Sir Gawain and the Green Knight for The School Bag*, then attempted to complete the translation, but managed only another 566 lines. (About half of these were published in *Selected Translations*.)

14 Jan 96

Dear Keith and Melissa —

Thank you for the hospitality, last Friday. I enjoyed my visit, meeting the children in their latest phase. I'm sending Aaron the skull of the first badger I ever skinned — about 1967 (I've got a photo somewhere of me skinning it).[1] The occipital ridge has been gnawn [sic] slightly by rats. I found it as I searched in the roof for the box of skulls that Nicky used to have — which I can't find (I think he must have traded them long ago). The badger was never with them — so survived. Fangs have gone — I made ear-rings of them, as I remember.

The aviary impressed me mightily. Interesting future for it. A stately pleasure dome.[2]

I made the small mistake that night of glancing at an Anthology of modern criticism. A mistake, in that I stayed awake too long at it. I wonder what it will all look like in 200 years time. But here and there it was much more interesting than I'd expected — what's the Hungarian's name?[3]

I plodded on a little bit with the inventorising. Occasionally very surprised to find things totally strange to me. Not sure how much

---

1 See plate 5.
2 My new aviary had a heated bird-room, with an octagonal flight attached, thirty-two feet in circumference. Inside the flight was a pool with a cascade, a dwarf eucalyptus, a pink-berried mountain ash, and a bench. I had not yet acquired any birds when Ted saw it, but it was intended to house Australian finches, especially the endangered Gouldian finch. All were captive bred, and I bred them successfully myself for eight years, before deciding that even a 'stately pleasure dome' (the phrase is from 'Kubla Khan') was no more than a golden cage.
3 David Lodge, ed., *20th Century Literary Criticism* (Longman, 1972), contains an essay on 'The Ideology of Modernism' (1963) by the Marxist critic Georg Lukács (1885–1971).

can ever be salvaged or reprocessed. Everything changes. I regret not writing far more of certain things — the kind of thing that seemed too easy. They're the pieces that seem most useful to me now. But it's a big shock — reviewing your old track through the jungle. As if everything happened in a midnight tropical storm. I suppose I kept or published the odd moments that seemed to enjoy a momentary clear view. I'm not sure they were always the most interesting.

But I do feel a need to do something quite different. A bad sign? To be rid of all these old nests, to round up the animal pieces, (as I've long intended to do. I'd hoped 'What Is The Truth' was a last procession of the toys.)

I suppose school has swallowed everything & every body again. You were right about the journey — 5 ½ hours.

　　love to you all　　Ted

27 July 96

Dear Keith —

It was always my intention to sling into a big box any mag. etc that published anything of mine — and a spasmodic revival of this intention has saved some things. But my feeling is — many things have slipped through & gone. My chaos is finally dissolving me back into the basic original state, I think.

I've about gone through my archive — mystified by all kinds of gaps. And recently the MS of Adam & The Sacred 9 was sold somewhere — when did I sell that? I know I sold some things to you, & that you converted them at some stage, but I've forgotten what.[4]

When you say you could 'come down and go through the stuff myself' I have to smile. The 'stuff' is just a litter of odd things scattered among the huge paper chaos. Insofar as it's been up to me, that side of things has been utterly neglected. I have a low view of all this at the moment. Such a mountain of sorting out!

My efforts to get the mess I've made of everything under control is really my occupation these days — just handling the past.

I can't promise that I'll be able to do much more than begin to

---

4　I had bought the archive in April 1977, and sold it about 1983 to help to pay for our new house.

assemble any publications that might be useful to you that I come across.

I had a fox-skull for Aaron, & it's fallen down behind the glove compartment in the car!

Love to all — Ted

26 Aug. 96

Dear Keith —

Lovely picture of the adders.[5]

That signature is mine allright — not one of the original run, maybe one of my author's copies that I sold some time. Could be a transposed photograph of a signature?? Who'd bother. But yes, it's mine — familiar variant.[6]

Haven't recovered the skull yet. Have to send him another.[7]

I hope the birds are perking.

Love to all   Ted

Do you sniff an upturn in Lawrence's fortunes?

15th November 1996

Dear Arren —

I thought you'd like a rattlesnake tail, to scare your mother.

Keep happy   Ted

2nd Dec 96

Dear Keith —

Not sure where that passage came from — but it was part of a little Foreword. I thought I had a proof of the book — kept surfacing, but sank again. If it reappears, I'll let you know.

I wish to God I could stop writing these paragraphs for people. Another recently as foreword to 'The Lizard's Question' — an élite anthology of semi-sacred texts given to Prince Philip at his recent 75th Birthday Celebrations. Set up by Arts for Nature (run by the

---

5 I had photographed an adult and baby adder together at the Serpentarium in the New Forest.
6 Someone had asked me to verify what purported to be a signed book, and I was unsure.
7 Ted did send Arren the fox skull, together with the skull of a large unidentified bird.

Duchess of Abercorn — descendant of Pushkin). A rather weary piece, I'm afraid.

Just translated a few fittes of Gawain for our School Bag Anthol.[8] So it goes on.

Is the vivarium happy.[9] Nice to have a second childhood, isn't it.

Love to all   Ted

3rd Dec 96

Dear Arren —

How's the vivarium?

Not sure rattlers do shed their rattles.[10] But they do get served up in restaurants — maybe lose the rattle on the way.

Keep your Dad and Mum at it and your sister
Ted

28 Dec 96

Dear Keith —

Have I answered your enquiry about the bibliography?

If I haven't, it would be because I have no suggestions. I seem to have a less than complete notion of everything that goes on in my name. Even if I had tried quite hard, I doubt if I could have assembled a copy of every published thing as it appeared. I'm told something of mine was in The New Statesman a couple of weeks ago. First I'd heard.[11]

I hope you're all well — snakes & birds inc.

Got stuck into translating Gawain — not sure it's a good idea. Did about 250 lines in 2 days, for The School Bag, so thought I'd do the rest in 10. Mistake![12]

Have a good 1997
Love to all   Ted

---

8   The School Bag, edited by Hughes and Seamus Heaney (Faber, 1997), contained Hughes' translation of lines from Part IV of Sir Gawain and the Green Knight, the encounter with the Green Knight at the Green Chapel.

9   Arren now had a large vivarium with a corn snake.

10   They don't; rather, a segment is added with each shedding.

11   An excerpt from Ted's translation of Ovid's Metamorphoses had appeared in the New Statesman on 20 December.

12   Hughes went back to the beginning, and apparently abandoned his translation at line 566. Lines 163–231, 276–325, 392–492 and 516–566 are printed in Weissbort, Selected Translations, together with the lines from The School Bag.

1997

In April Hughes was diagnosed with cancer. He selected eighty-eight poems from the hundred or more he had written for *Birthday Letters*. He did not make the decision to publish them until November. After fruitless negotiations with the Almeida and Royal Court theatres, in April Hughes signed a contract with the National Theatre for *The Oresteia*. (Katie Mitchell's production opened in 1999.) In August Jonathan Kent of the Almeida invited Hughes to provide a version of Racine's *Phèdre* for Diana Rigg. *Tales from Ovid* won the Whitbread Book of the Year prize.

14 July 1997

Dear Keith —

How goes it.

I've been off-colour, as they say, but pulling out of it now.

Matthew Evans is Chairman of the Committee set up to review the situation of the Lending Libraries. He asked me to compose some verses as a sort of figurehead — so here's what he's got.[1]

I'm trying to put a mass of things together. Not quite sure what it will look like, finally. But I'd like to be rid of it — i.e. dump it on the public.

I hope the family's in good feather, and all the birds happy and under control.

Love to Melissa & yourself

Ted

Craig Raine is publishing an Anthol of New Writing (with some female whose name I forget).[2] He's using 3 new pieces (new, old i.e. unpub.) of mine. You asked me to let you know. Did you see Frieda's poems in this last London Mag?[3]

The Intro. to By Heart is the final version (the one in School Bag is not).

---

1 'Hear It Again'. See Appendix XII.
2 Carmen Callil and Craig Raine, eds., *New Writing 7* (Vintage, 1998).
3 'Three Old Ladies' and 'Nothing', both collected in Frieda Hughes, *Wooroloo* (HarperCollins, 1998; Bloodaxe, 1999).

Did you see my piece in the Guardian? Does it persuade you either way?[4]

15 July 1997

'Hear It Again'. I'm afraid I don't much care for these sort of occasional argumentative rhyming poems. ('Rain Charm' is the only Laureate poem I ever go back to.) Somehow the rhymes, which should clinch the meaning, seem to trivialize it. Also it seems very long to serve as 'a sort of figurehead'. I feel you could write much more powerfully on the same subject in prose . . .

I have read your piece on hunting with great interest. You seem to have David Bellamy on your side. You ask if it persuades me. Well, yes and no. You may well be right that if hunting were banned, and if no effective protection could then be enforced, the deer and foxes would suffer, perhaps literally, certainly numerically. I am all for pragmatic approaches to such issues. But your argument takes a great deal for granted and leaves a great deal (including the whole moral and spiritual dimension which characterizes your poems about animals) out of account. Even within the narrow terms of your own argument I have some reservations.

My own position is something like this. I do not want to live in a society and bring children up in a society in which it is regarded as normal, acceptable, perhaps even admirable to torture and kill animals — any animals — for fun. It is already illegal to do this to domestic and farm animals, and to selected species of wild animals — badgers and otters, for example. I can see no reason why it should not be illegal to cause unnecessary suffering to any animal. Such a law would be difficult to enforce, especially in the wilds of the West Country. But the fact that the law cannot protect citizens in day-time city streets is no reason to legalize mugging! You imply that human nature in relation to animals is a constant. But I believe great changes have taken place in my lifetime, and particularly in the last twenty or thirty years, People are much better educated about animals and their place in the scheme of things. A major contribution has been made by television programmes. Your own work has made a far from negligible contribution. A year or two ago I was watching a major golf championship in the States on television. Suddenly everyone froze as a large snake emerged from the rough onto the green. Thirty years ago the nearest golfer would have clobbered it to death without a qualm. On this occasion there seemed to be complete spontaneous agreement among the golfers, officials and spectators that the first priority was to ensure the safety of the snake. Play was suspended for a considerable time as they consulted about the best course of action — best for the snake. There is now far more sympathy for the hunt saboteur than for the huntsman. Far more people now care about animals than ever before. Millions care enough to

4 On 5 July the *Guardian* had published Ted's essay 'The Hart of the Mystery', which argued against the hunting ban (see Appendix XIII).

belong to countless organizations for their protection. For the first time in our history there are votes in the protection and welfare of animals and their habitats.

The alternative to hunting is not a free-for-all. Farmers must obviously have the right to use humane methods to protect their stock and crops. But given the will, it is surely not impossible to devise effective methods of keeping up the numbers of deer and foxes.

The field sports fraternity are all in a panic as they see their long era of power and privilege coming to an end.

15th August 97

Dear Keith —

I woke this morning thinking — I must write to Keith, must do something about that cataloguing he did, must send a skull or two to Aaron, must think of an equaliser for Ursula, etc. So I get up and here's your letter.

Yes, I know what you mean about the library piece. etc.

2 different Oxford editions give 2 different readings — I changed that line, in proof, to fit one of them.[5]

Two different attitudes to poems, aren't there. There's the making of stylistic artefacts — where the subject matter is simply usable material, and there's the truth-seeking exploration of the subject matter, where you're simply searching out the electrical life and the circuits. Shakes' sonnets are the first — wrought-doublets and costly codpieces. The big speeches in the plays the second. I suppose the ideal desirable thing is the first — using material which has been put through the process of the second internally and exhaustively. Is the best of Yeats like that? The best of Frost? The first is entertainment, creating beauty objects. The second religion/science.

The Hunt piece was making a real point. That protection does work in the West Country. Partly because we're an island. Poaching from outside is heavy — and very nasty — but not yet heavy enough to affect numbers (of deer, obviously).

But imagine what would happen to any stag or hind that wandered into Heptonstall crags — or onto Manor Farm opposite Mexborough.

5 As the second line of the Chaucer quotation which opens 'Hear It Again' Hughes has: 'Cometh al this newe corne yer by yere'. I had alerted him to the fact that in the Oxford *Works of Geoffrey Chaucer* it reads: 'Cometh al this newe corn from yer to yere'.

Wouldn't last two days. Never would have, in 200 years.

And where are the foxes in the wild Calder Valley? When I first went into Lumb Bank, one day I met 3 or 4 men halfway up the Lane with dogs. They were Savile's gamekeepers. A fox had been seen going into that valley, (week or two before) and they'd traced it to a pile of rocks in the wood down towards Hebden. They'd come miles to get it (they were way off Savile's land — though l think he owns the hill-face opposite L.B. and the green strip at the top of L.B. lane.) All the time my brother and I roamed those hillsides, we never saw a fox or heard of one — except that one in Crimsworth Dene.[6] When I went to Mexborough, the first time I walked on Manor Farm (across the river) I saw a dead fox — then saw others, all dead, later. I saw one living cub, caught it — and the farmer killed it. I got hold of another fox-cub in Holderness and my landlord — he kept chickens — killed it.

But I know these West Country farmers — and these West Country boyos too. One of the reasons I came to Devon, thinking of living on Exmoor, was the possibility of knocking over the occasional deer — subsistence.

On the other hand — yes, the Hunt! That horse culture! When a man/woman gets up on a horse in his/her hunting kit he/she becomes something quite awful, as a rule. It has something to do with the nervous fear of what your horse might do if you relax your despotic control of its every move. But also to do with (a) being mounted & therefore $2/3$ big powerful animal (b) being in a uniform (out of your normal self) with a rigid funny hat (the hat crucial to attitude — as cavalry and commanding officers have always known) and (c) suddenly being in the role of King William's barons. Decent folk become instantly dreadful. I've been in some scenes!

Also, I've known for some years what a hunted deer goes though physically. And a hunted fox. And a fish being caught, for that matter.

For years I've kept having an idea that I daren't quite formulate: why aren't wild animals simply given the legal status of fellow citizens. As you say — there is a big mass change. But West Country farmers — !!! Deprived of the Hunt by Blair & Prescott. That puts Blair in the role of William the Conq. God help the deer then! You know, when the Tories wouldn't give public libraries increased

---

6   Hughes is referring to the fox described in the story 'The Deadfall' in *Difficulties of a Bridegroom*.

index-linked funding, those mild, civilised, responsible citizens <u>began to sell off the books</u> — beginning with the rarest & oldest. For some years now some booksellers (one in Museum St) have operated almost wholly in library sell-offs. I expect you know about that. But the motive was only secondarily to raise cash — primarily it was good old human nature, bureaucratic spite. Oh, well, if they wont etc etc they mustn't expect us etc etc. That's how it went. That's well known, in the business.

There's been a catastrophic quiet destruction of the libraries throughout Britain that few people seem to know about it. (Hence my rhymes.)

Too bad about the Gouldians. Can't you isolate the males?[7]

I'm putting together a vast pile of pieces about S.P. & me — those few at the end of New Selected were picked from them, or some of those few. Very much the second kind of voice — rough. Not even that. Basically, my model was 'a letter'. Poetical effects incidental. Very self-exposing, I suppose, unguarded — my attempt to write about those things without aesthetic exploitation or concern for my artistic reputation. I no longer give much thought to that. Except to write clearly and expressively. Simply. No style. Plain.

It will bring the sky down on my head, if I publish it — about 90–100 pieces.[8] But so what. The sky's fallen anyway.

One notion was — to set down something for F[rieda] & N[icholas]. Written at odd times since the early seventies. Now I've had enough of it. The whole business has sat on top of me too long — done me no good at all.

Anyway, love to you all, Ted

p.s. Manchester is off. I just don't feel like that sort of jamboree at the moment.[9]

7 I was having some success breeding other species of Australian finch, but none yet with my Gouldians.
8 In the event it was very important to Hughes, for Cabbalistic reasons, that there should be exactly eighty-eight poems in *Birthday Letters*. See 'Poetry and Magic I: *Birthday Letters*' (http://ann.skea.com). Ted's claim that that the book had 'no plan' was not strictly true. Ann Skea demonstrates that it was extremely carefully planned on a Cabbalistic grid.
9 Ted had been due to give a reading in Manchester on 9 November.

2nd Oct 97

Dear Keith —

Interested to hear how the birds and serpents are going. Is it an advance on technicolour fish? Certainly on invertebrates. From the contemplative to the cerebro/vigilant mode — lunar to solar.

You see how wretchedly stripped to the bare chassis this fox-skull is. Before it got lost in the bowels of my car it was in good shape — as mortal remains go. Even had most of its teeth — the prettiest of all the fittings. But I'll look out for another.

What is the bird's skull? I never knew. Not a heron.

Are you still keeping track of where I publish things? If so — I'll try to keep you informed.

Those pieces about S.P. in the end of the New Collected are probably too obscure (not the pieces about Assia).[10] I've put together about 90 — full context makes them read more openly. Still thinking whether to pub. or not. Probably not, but it would be a burden gone.[11]

Love   Ted

10 Nov. 97

Dear Keith —

Going through my pile of mail I meet your Diana poem and can't remember if I replied.[12]

Well, like everybody else, like me, you were grabbed by the mob current undertow — against your inclinations?

I lay awake early the Thursday morning and made mine up — working backwards from the flower on the gun, which had struck me as the oddest image of the whole event. So there we are.

I thought best to keep clear of the hound complication and go for the pop deification — Diana as Mary as Christ.

Big revelation of (a) mass unconscious has been deculturalised & appropriated by secular pop (Elton John & applause for a memorial address) (as for a speech in a chat show) (b) mass feeling

---

10 Eight poems about Assia from *Capriccio*, and eight about Sylvia which were to be in *Birthday Letters*, had been included in *New Selected Poems* in 1995.

11 In fact the book had been with Faber since August.

12 Hughes' poem on the occasion of Princess Diana's funeral, '6 September 1997' (*Collected Poems*, p. 861), was published in the *Guardian* and elsewhere on that date. I had sent Ted my own poem on her death, of which I can now find no trace.

for symbols of royalty (without her royal connection, Diana was just another Sloane) gargling away there under the pavements. But I liked your verses.

Love to the whole zoo   Ted

17ᵗʰ Nov. 97

Dear Keith —

What do you make of this? Are my fortunes changing? Or what?[13]

Keep a secret till mid-January. I put together about 88 pieces about S.P. and me, our times together and various matters appertaining thereunto. In the end I couldn't go on sitting on it. Costs too heavy & in the currency I can least afford to pay. No revelations. Just a fuller memoire [sic]. Written between 72 and this last year. No plan. But it's taught me a lot — about myself, seeing it all set up together. I've asked F & F to send you a copy, when they're printed (No review proofs)

<u>Don't speak about it</u> — otherwise there'll be a whole Galippoly [sic] of entrenched weaponry mounted ready. Totally vulnerable as it is.

Love   Ted

13 Ted enclosed an appreciative article by Harriet Zinnes, 'And he shivered with the horror of Creation', *The Hollins Critic*, 1 October 1997.

1998

Birthday Letters was published in January to an overwhelmingly positive response. It won the Forward, T. S. Eliot, Whitbread, and South Bank prizes. Hughes and Daniel Weissbort finished editing Yehuda Amichai: Selected Poems, published by Faber in 2000. In May Hughes began 'blocking out' a stage version of Gilgamesh for Tim Supple. In June he finished Alcestis. The Paris Review published a major interview with Hughes in its Spring number. Phèdre opened at the Malvern Festival on 6 August. On 16 October the Queen presented Hughes with the Order of Merit. Hughes died in London on 28 October, aged sixty-eight.

[c. January 1998]

Dear Keith —

This is an out-of-the-way publication you might not know about.[1] Old verses — from Morrigu days.

Love to all   Ted

Alongside the whole poem Ted writes: 'Their idea to align it like this!' Next to the second stanza he writes '24½ lbs.', and against the final stanza: 'between 30 & 40 lbs.'.

4 March 98

Dear Keith —

Any news of Literature and the Crime Against Nature?[2]

I'm lying low — reading nothing in this amazing dust-cloud over my book, shutting my ears too, though I get to hear. Not sure what to make of it.[3]

Just put together about 250 of the best translations of Yehuda Amichai. With Daniel Weissbort.[4] Not sure if any publisher will take it on — so much of his has been published here, but usually

---

1 The note was written on a photocopy of 'Some Pike for Nicholas' from Waterlog, 7 (December 1997/January 1998).
2 By this time, having received seventy-six rejections, I had abandoned my attempts to find a publisher. It was not published until 2005.
3 Birthday Letters was published on 29 January, sold an unprecedented number of copies, and received widespread critical acclaim.
4 Published by Faber in 2000.

spoiled by a large proportion of unsuccessful translations. Recently a very big collection became his official presence in the U.S. — and killed every poem stone dead, pretty well. All done by one man and his wife.[5]

Love to all, and the creatures   Ted

5 March 98

Dear Keith —

I'm replying to a letter of yours in a heap from last January — I was away for a period and never caught up. Till now.

You ask about the Head Poems — the Mokomaki as I recall only contained 3 or 4. I don't know how many there are, but I like the best. 'Halfway Head' is in an Anthology coming out next Month — edited Carmen Cahill [sic] & Craig Raine.[6] With 2 other pieces — (all by different heads!)

I was thinking the other day I ought to push the Heads a bit further. I'll see how many there are — but I had the odd note for quite a few.

I see there's a translation of 'Widdop' from Elmet in Jordi Dolci's new book (in Spanish).[7]

Some things in an Italian magazine — which will surface again. (And I'll tell you).

Some things in the Turkish newspaper, Cumhuriyet — ten of 35 translated by one Coskun Yerli. (Another letter from last winter that I just answered). All from River. He tells me they'll make a book — but heard nothing since.

I'll try to find the Spanish How The Whale. In fact, if you like, I'll send you a pile of photocopied covers & title pages, from foreign editions. I keep them.

Heard rumours recently that SP's journals from 1959 to 1963 (end of 62) were 'seen', in the sixties. They must have existed, for sure, because I burned one covering the last couple of months — and at that point (early 63), that must have been a continuation of

5 Stephen Mitchell and Chana Bloch, eds., *The Selected Poetry of Yehuda Amichai* (HarperCollins, 1992).
6 Callil and Raine, eds., *New Writing 7*.
7 In 1997 Jordi Doce had published 'Two Extremes of a Continuum: On Translating Ted Hughes and Charles Tomlinson into Spanish', in *Forum for Modern Language Studies*, 33, 1. In 1999 Hiperion, Madrid, published his bilingual edition of *Crow*.

journals right up to it. Strange business — trail's gone cold at the moment.[8]

Love to all   Ted

15 April 98

Dear Keith —

You could get a copy of 'Caryatids' from Smith College Library — by Fax, I imagine. The Curator to speak to is Martin Antonetti — very nice man — and Smith phone is (413) 585 2906.[9]

I'm not sure that it was in Chequer — might have been Granta.

Point of the Cader Idris ref. Dan Huws, who wrote the 'dismemberment' of Caryatids — which pained Sylvia very sharply — eventually (after S.P. & I were married) became (with his German wife Helga) her friend, quite close. When she died he wrote the enclosed.[10] The connection with Cader Idris is: Tradition says, whoever climbs Cader Idris and spends a night on top, either goes mad or becomes a poet. I never asked Dan if he was thinking of Cader Idris when he wrote his 'O Mountain'. As far as I'm concerned, it has to be Cader Idris. 'The white noise' — is simply all that went into making his little lament, while S.P. made the climb, in his vision, in the snow (the great snow of that February).

---

8   The journals from 1950 to 1959 were at Smith College. Frieda and Nicholas, who held the copyright, had authorized Karen Kukil, curator of the Plath collection there, to edit them. The later journals could not be found. The earlier journals, together with 'fifteen journal fragments and notebooks, written between 1950 and 1962' were published by Faber in 2000.

9   The January 1956 issue of *Chequer* contained two poems by S.P., 'Epitaph in Three Parts' (*Collected Poems: Sylvia Plath*, 337) and '"Three Caryatids without a Portico" by Hugo Robus. A Study in Sculptural Dimensions' (*The Laughter of Foxes*, 49). In *Broadsheet*, a weekly Cambridge cyclostyled review, Ted's friend Daniel Huws commented on these: 'Of the quaint and eclectic artfulness of Sylvia Plath's two poems my better half tells me "Fraud, fraud", but I will not say so: who am I to know how beautiful she may be'.

10 'O Mountain', in Daniel Huws, *Noth* (Secker and Warburg, 1972).

   We know our crags, our climbs, our controlled terrors,
   As we know our own hearthsides. We manage nicely.

   The clouds of selfishness rift and terribly
   Turning our foothills small and grubby appears
   The mountain soaring against a blue heaven,
   Bulking beyond conceivable ascent.
   Yet while we slept was a breaking body climbing.

   Where the winds of the world pour unendingly
   Wildly whistling to no one, let the mind hover
   And its eye make out in the dazzle, O Mountain, O Man,
   The frail figure on the white virgin peak.

Dan was/is very aware of Cader Idris. He and Luke Myers (our American) went up Cader Idris and brought me a stone — shaped like a fox's head, snout & 2 big ears — off the top. I don't think they stayed up there for the night.

You could be right about the dates.[11] Probably I elected that date to prominence because she made a great point of my doing her Father's horoscope and made me aware of the anniversary (— though at the time it was to my mind not an important factor in the sequence of events) but over the years it imposed itself as mightily significant, in retrospect, because the next truly decisive day in our life was another Friday 13th.

The three lines were:

  Thumbed no stony horny pot
  But a certain meaning green
  Gulls mulled in the greenest light

which is the last verse of a piece titled I think Hermit at Outermost House. (Outermost House was a house on Cape Cod — made famous by a book with that title.)

What a great thing to see the children doing so well. Michael Morpurgo met Aaron [Arren]. Said Aaron's school is away the best & best run he's ever visited.

Love to all   Ted

11 May 98

Dear Keith —

Have you thought about the Harvill Press — for <u>Literature for Survival</u>. Christopher Maclehose (is that spelt right?)[12] is chief Editor and an enlightened type.

Phedre opens at the Malvern Festival in August, then goes to the Albery Theatre in September. Diana Rigg Phèdre, Toby Stevens Hippolytus. The Oresteia starts end of 1999 — at the Cottesloe. Kate Mitchell directing it.

Tim Supple is doing some of the Ovid at Stratford this

---

11 In '18 Rugby Street' Hughes wrote:
                    You were pausing
        A night in London on your escape to Paris.
        April 13th, your father's birthday. A Friday.
      I had pointed out to Ted that the date in question was actually Friday 23rd March. Plath returned to Ted at Rugby Street on Friday 13 April, *after* her trip to Paris.
12 Correctly MacLehose.

summer.[13] And we've been talking about some actable form of Gilgamesh, which I'd love to see.[14] (Did you see Tim Supple's marvellous Comedy of Errors?)

I've got most of a version of the Alcestis, with a more developed interlude about Heracles. Thought I'd show it to Barry Rutter.[15]

Greenfinches were dying like flies round our bird table earlier this year — some epidemic. Could your birds have caught something.

I hope you're all well — love   Ted

5th June 98

Dear Keith —

all going well?

Just a note to say a poem of mine just came out in a very strange Irish Magazine — Céidhe[16] — (just, just, just!) After-gasp of B.L. Surprising little poems from Teddy Lucie-Smith. Catholic Review from the far West — full of matters strange to one a little removed from those needy parishes.

I'm just blocking out Gilgamesh for Tim Supple (the Young Vic director) to then convert to stage action, for next year. Not sure how deeply I'll go into it (in way speech & narration), but it's an old ambition. In fact, it's a very shapely tale — 2 brothers, tragic equation & coda in fascinating (post Tiamat/Marduk) form.[17]

Love to all,   Ted
Also in New Writing 7 — 3 poems.

17 June 1998

I am following through the imagery of wardrobe in Birthday Letters, which surfaces in 'A Pink Wool Knitted Dress' and 'The Blue Flannel Suit' – the importance of this imagery underlined by

---

13   Tales from Ovid opened at the Swan Theatre, Stratford on 9 April 1999.
14   The Epic of Gilgamesh, one of the earliest surviving works of literature, originated as a series of Sumerian legends and poems.
15   The world premiere was by Rutter's Northern Broadsides at Dean Clough Mill, Halifax, on 14 September 2000.
16   Céide: a Review from the Margins, a journal founded in 1997 by three Catholic priests: Brendan Hoban, Enda McDonagh and Kevin Hegarty.
17   See 5 January 1990.

You had only to look
Into the nearest face of a metaphor
Picked out of your wardrobe.

The significance of Sylvia's dress is clear enough: it is your dress I am looking at. I'm almost sure that I have read somewhere that Aurelia[18] gave you a suit (was it for the wedding) which you couldn't bring yourself to wear – but now I can't find the reference anywhere. Is it correct? The words 'My wreckage / Was all of a sudden a new wardrobe, unworn' would seem to partially confirm it.

In 'Epiphany' – and perhaps elsewhere – are you consciously referring to Grimm's 'The Golden Bird'?

22 June 98

Dear Keith —

I assume from the note arriving today that I did answer your queries.

'Epiphany' — no, if The Golden Bird is there it was quite unconscious. Your pointing it out surprised me.

I seem to remember that Aurelia did produce a suit — after I got to the U.S. But which was it? I did buy a dark heavy flannel suit (hardly ever wore that — hated it). The only U.S. garment I quite liked was my black coat — heavy material. Also some where there a light grey suit (I'm wearing it in the Faber photograph) which I also disliked.[19] I have always detested suits — and blazers.

All these garments went to the bonfires that somebody lit in the 3 main bedrooms at Lumb Bank, in 1970 [actually 1971]. (Along with all my letters, up to that point).

Just for curiosity, enclose some notes I sent to questions from a German translator.[20]

I haven't got a Galway map, but I recall on my last visit making sure of the spelling — 1993 or 4 — of Aughresburg, and it is an e.[21] Strange Lough — contains very big trout, among many Loughs that have only tiny ones. Separated from the sea by a narrow rim of land.

---

18 Aurelia Plath, Sylvia's mother.
19 The famous photograph by Mark Gerson of Hughes with T. S. Eliot, W. H. Auden, Stephen Spender and Louis MacNeice taken at Faber & Faber on 23 June 1960 at a party in honour of Auden. See plate 3.
20 See Appendix XIV.
21 In *Flowers and Insects* we find 'A Violet at Lough Aughrisburg', but in *New Selected Poems* Hughes changed the spelling to 'Aughresberg'. The correct spelling is Aughrisbeg (Galway).

I've been intrigued, I must say, by the maze of interconnections between those BLs. Considering how I wrote them, months often years apart, never thinking of them as parts of a whole — just as opportunities to write in a simple, unguarded, intimate way — to release something! Nor can I recall how I came to shuffle them into that order — following chronology of subject matter was the only rule, I think.

So glad to be rid of it — whatever it is. I've translated Eurip's Alcestis (did most of it before the Oresteia) with a developed section — the drunken Hercules scene. Thought I'd show it to Barrie Rutter.

Love to all   Ted

Give us a call, 30ᵗʰ July or near.

2 July 98

Dear Keith —

Such a flurry of mail lately — I'm not sure I answered this one of yours, 13ᵗʰ June. Did I send that letter to Dan? I was intending to see him — but have not managed it.

I'm sure he no longer has any trace of the article he wrote.

When Pan asked me to write about an otter we were sitting more or less stripped in a 95° swelter. He asked S.P. to write about 'Lorelei'. (She knew an old German song about the Lorelei.) She ended up with Lorelei and Full Fathom Five. I remember she sat reading and occasionally writing, in one position, all day, and ended up with both.[22]

Love to all,   Ted

22 Both Hughes and Plath wrote poems called 'Ouija'. Hughes' note on that poem in Plath's *Collected Poems* reprints her 'Dialogue Over a Ouija Board'. The 'spirit' which spoke to them through the Ouija board said that it's name was Pan; not the Great God Pan, but a little spirit that lived at the bottom of an iceberg. I had asked Ted if he or Sylvia had written any poems other than 'An Otter' in response to suggestions from Pan?

In an unscripted radio discussion with A. Alvarez in 1960, Hughes gave a detailed account of writing 'An Otter' in response to a suggestion from Pan. There Hughes described this 'spirit' as 'presumably some combination of the unconscious mind of the two of you combined on this particular device to spell out messages – not a spirit at all I don't think, but just the ideas that don't quite come into consciousness – the ideas that you're just slightly repressing, that you're half aware of – these are the ideas that come out on this planchette board. In other words, they're ideas from your own mind, very much so'.

On the single occasion when Daniel Huws participated in such a session, he became very bored, and deliberately spelled out fake answers to the questions being asked of Pan. He had Pan say that its favourite poet was Shakespeare, and its favourite line 'never, never, never, never, never'. Someone asked what the next line was. Huws improvised: 'Why shall I ever be perplexed thus? / I'd hack my

15 July 1998

Dear Ted

Yes, you forwarded my letter to Daniel Huws. It seems he has kept all the *Broadsheets* and *Chequers* from those Cambridge days. He sent me photocopies of his piece on 'Caryatids', and also two things you published under pseudonyms: 'Song of the Sorry Lovers' (Peter Crews) in *Chequer* in 1954, and your review of *Chequer* in *Broadsheet* in 1955 (Jonathan Dyce).

I have now finished and enclose the first draft of the first chapter of the proposed new book.[23] I wonder what you will think of it. Don't feel you have to read it if you'd rather not . . .

I have always felt it was a mistake publishing those *Crow* poems without any indication of their larger context. And you have obviously tried to do that belatedly by publishing articles on aspects of *Crow*, and by giving a good deal of the background whenever you have done readings from *Crow*. I have transcripts of several of these. But the new audiobook version is by far the fullest. It seems to me tremendously useful, almost essential to avoid new readers repeating the misreadings which the book suffered not just from common readers, but from reviewers and professional critics. It is a pity that it should be available only to those who happen to buy the audiobook, and not available in print at all. How would you feel about publishing a transcript of it as an appendix to my book?[24]

I wonder why, in all the many versions I have heard from you of the ogress episode you only ever mention the same three of the seven questions. Do you not want to disclose what the other four questions are, and which poems are the answers to them? It has always seemed to me that there are far more than seven poems which could be Crow's answers to these questions. Why does he have to give only one answer to each? Would it not fit better with the idea of her weight increasing with a wrong answer and decreasing with a better one if he gave at least two answers to each, or more, learning each time from the mistakes of the previous one?

Did I tell you that Ursula got a distinction in grade 6 violin? She missed one by three marks in grade 6 piano. Both of them have had excellent reports. It will be difficult to decide what subjects Ursula will do for GCSE, since she seems equally good across the whole range. I suppose she will concentrate on the Arts. We went to the school play at Arren's school last night. He played Shakespeare, appropriately, since he is very familiar with most of the plays. I've been telling them the stories for ten years, and we have seen several productions.

We have brought forward by two days our trip to Cornwall, so we shall

---

arm off like a rotten branch / Had it betrayed me as my memory'. Ted was delighted. Huws wondered whether something similar had happened on other evenings with the Ouija board: 'Ted persisting until one of the company, out of boredom or desperation or whatever, began to speak' (Huws, *Memories of Ted Hughes*, pp. 43–4).

23 'From Prospero to Orpheus'.

24 In the event I used all this material in the appendix, 'The Story of Crow'.

now be passing down the A30 on the morning of Tuesday 28th. I'll ring you nearer the time to see if it will be convenient to call.

All the best. Love to Carol. Keith

18th June [actually 18–19 July] 98

Dear Keith —

Got your letter and chapter — which I've read. Your account of the cooperation between S.P. & me is pretty much as I see it — so far as it goes. Obviously, I could add a vast amount of detail. And even something more of her influence on me. But it is clear as you've done it, and supports what you say about my changing attitude to the whole event, and my failure, in the end, to turn it positive — which makes BL just the book you describe.

I have wondered — some justification I think — if an all-out attempt much much earlier to complete a full account, in the manner of those BL, of that part of my life, would not have liberated me to deal with it on deeper, more creative levels — i.e. where the very worst things can be made positive, where the whole point of the operation is to turn deadly negatives into triumphant positives, in the total picture. On the autobiographical level, that can be difficult, because — if things cannot be got off that level, and onto the creative level (i.e. a bit forgotten, maybe), then they simply stay as if they were a recurrent stuck dream that simply goes on delivering its inescapable blow. Two things kept me stuck on the autobiographical level. One — a moral reluctance to deal with the episode directly, as material for an artistic work. As I might — or as one might — find a close metaphor in some dramatic action & make a play of it or bury the main features of it in the plot of a novel. As even Tolstoy did — quite deliberately. That seemed to me reprehensible, not truly creative. When poets did it — as Snodgrass, then Lowell, then Sexton did — picking it up from each other — I despised it. In poetry, I believed, if the experience was to be dealt with creatively, it would have to emerge obliquely, through a symbol, inadvertently — as in Shakes. Venus & Adonis, or Ancient Mariner or Christabel, or Lamia, or Eve of St Agnes, or something of that sort. And in fact with me, in retrospect, I can see that it began to emerge in exactly this fashion in Crow — which I started in 1965, just after coming from Ireland, where I'd found a way out of a 3 year impasse, with Skylarks. But I was still too close to the experience, maybe, to deal with it quickly enough, and those years were devoured too by other preoccupations, mainly centred round the children & my mother, who died in 69, after Assia.

This revival, in A's death, of S's, and in my mother's death a big psychological melt-down with accidental complicating factors, knocked Crow off his perch. (I wrote the last of them a week before A's death — on my way to take her looking for a new home in Northumberland, returning from which, she died.) Then I escaped from it all into working with Peter Brook — total suspension of my own writing except for that little myth of sinister import and total inner stasis, Prometheus on his Crag, which I was tinkering with in Iran.

But I was pulled inescapably back onto the autobiographical level of S's death by the huge outcry that flushed me from my thicket in 1970–71–72 when Sylvia's poems & novel hit the first militant wave of Feminism as a divine revelation from their Patron Saint. And never gave me another moment to let it all sink away to the levels on which I might deal with it naturally & creatively. Nor to escape constantly more hectic involvement with it — on that autobiographical level.

This arrest, of what I might have made of Crow, and of that material in other truly creative works, held me till I more or less abandoned the effort — and from the piece about Baskin (took a year almost), the piece about Eliot (a few months), the new Introduction to Ecco Press' republication of the Selected Shakes, which turned into Shakespeare & the Goddess[25] (2 years, staying up till 3 & 4 a.m. destroying my immune system), I took refuge in prose. Oh, yes, & the Coleridge essay & revisions of the Winter Pollen pieces, maybe the best part of a year, though it was all done by early 1994. Still — 5 or 6 years nothing but prose — nothing but burning the foxes. (That fox was telling — prose is destroying you physically, literally: maybe not others, but you, yes.). Finally, I cracked. I got together all the BL letters, wrote some more — with mighty relief, and did what Carol could never have borne 3 years before (when I did put some into the New Selected) published them. A thing that I too had always thought unthinkable — so

---

25 Hughes wrote a new introduction and concluding essay for the 1991 second edition of *A Choice of Shakespeare's Verse*, published in the USA by the Ecco Press as *The Essential Shakespeare*.

raw, so vulnerable, so unprocessed, so naive, so self-exposing & unguarded, so without any of the niceties that any poetry workshop student could have helped me to. And so dead against my near-inborn conviction that you never talk about yourself in this way — in poetry. So at bottom, somewhere, I do now have the feeling of having committed some kind of obscure crime, publishing them. But there is no way I could have gone on letting all that business gag me, knowing, with Sylvia's reputation as my environment, I could never escape with her onto the other levels. There simply was no more time, and I was feeling pretty low, physically. Once I'd determined to do it, & put them together, & started repairing them wherever I could, & writing the few last ones, I suddenly had free energy I hadn't known since Crow. Which went into Ovid, then the Oresteia, Phèdre maybe — and parts of Alcestis, (which I haven't done anything with yet).

Hence the tone, etc, of B.L. God knows what sort of book it is, but at least none of it is faked, innocent as it is. And I must take some uplift from the consistency of the interconnections — though I wrote them over such a long time, rarely re-reading them, merely adding another now & again, never regarding them as a single structure — in fact the book has a structure, intricate, & accurate so far as I can judge. Solidly of a piece, somehow. So I can't care what people say. It has worked for me — better than I'd thought possible. Though I see now that any traumatic event — if writing is your method — has to be dealt with deliberately. An image has to be looked for — consciously — and then mined to the limit: but not in autobiographical terms. My high-minded principal [sic] was simply wrong — for my own psychological & physical health. It was stupid. The public interference, later, was just bad luck. Though it deflected me into Season Songs, Moortown, Gaudete, River, Elmet, Cave-birds etc — lots of little things I'm glad to have got down.

I'd written almost all the Wodwo poems before S.P. died. After I left her she kept typescripts of Out, Green Wolf, New Moon in January, Heptonstall, Full Moon & Frieda & a few little experimental improvisations & versions of Lorca that I'd made, on her desk. They were there when she died. I think she got certain things from them. Also a piece I never collected — The Road to Easington, to which her reply was The Bee Meeting, mocking the rhythms with a different meaning i.e. your escape is my funeral. That's how she read it, I think, eventually, though she was excited by it when I wrote it.

After her death — 2 or 3 weeks later, I wrote The Howling of Wolves, & finished Gnat-Psalm, I think. (Might have finished that earlier — or much later. Drafted it before she died.) After the Wolves, the Song of the Rat. Then nothing till I went to Ireland — and eventually got to Skylarks. About 3 years, of rubbishy efforts, radio plays, prose, in there.

About Otter: Yes, Pan asked me to write it, whereupon I dutifully wrote Part I. Felt I had got somewhere, but nowhere like far enough. Later on — days, couple of weeks — I was writing something else, (forget what) when I became aware of a written scroll hanging somewhere in the air just to my right. It was verses, not perfectly distinct but just legible — rather like the retinal distortions you can experience sometimes in a slight migraine. I copied the words down — and the whole poem came out as it is in Part II, exactly as it is, I think. Very odd experience, but so involuntary — so oddly pushed onto me — that I assumed that Pan was presenting his version of Otter as a mild hallucination. It recapitulates most of the themes of the first — but in visual close-up, with more subjectivity, more delicately, far better.

About the 2 levels, in that essay on the poems & the Bell Jar.[26] I believe that the lower level, the unalterable experience, can be changed — if the ritual is strong enough, or if the 'experience' is weak and malleable enough. With her, the experience was hellish strong, and her ritual — The Bell Jar — not strong enough. And the Ariel poems were not so much triumphant ritual — as double-tongued, triumph & doom. The most triumphant — Ariel itself, the poem — is a prophecy of suicide. If we had got back together mid-Ariel, or even any time before she died, maybe, the ritual could have been confirmed. New experience would have re-enforced it. She would probably have been able to hang on to all her new energy & enlarged personality. But accidents accelerated that last week to free fall 32ft per sec per sec.[27] we ran out of time — by days, I think. So I shall always believe. The horrors visited on us that last week, by well-meaning busybodies, brought her to that state where she was helpless at that most dangerous moment — when a neurosis

26 'Publishing Sylvia Plath' in Winter Pollen.
27 The accelerative power of Earth's gravity on a free-falling object.

overcome suddenly makes a last effort and stabs its victim in the back. Evidently a well-known regular occurrence, in similar cases. So I have to think.

But don't let this complicate your account, which is true on this point, in essentials.

And yes, it's true — because I accepted her temperament & its apparent needs as a given set of facts, to be tended, humoured, cared for, cured if possible in the long-term, and did not impose on her a whole new pattern of behaviour more actively extraverted & organised towards a disciplined engagement with the world, — I surrendered the chance to change her in other ways than by inward concentrated search for the essential voice of an essential self. If she had married a lawyer, a banker — as her mother wanted her to — well, God knows, maybe that would have been hopeless. God knows what way of life would have been better than the one we followed. Though in retrospect, it does read like the scenario written by her father that she had to perform — and which I unwittingly directed so vigourously [sic], with such fixed ideas, making such sacrifices, thinking we had all time ahead.

The landscape at Mex. was Manor Farm, old Denaby — the land you see immediately across the river (Don, not Dearne) from Mexborough Station. Now one big ploughed field. A copse hanging down the near face of the right hand hill was the setting for my story the Rain Horse. Across the river you can see the dips & hollows in the high earthen river bank. I know that farm, as it was in the late thirties early forties, better than any place on earth.[28] A year or two ago I went back to look at the farm building itself. Shock of my life. It would shock you too, if you saw it.

First to take an interest in my writing was our form mistress in my first class — a Miss Mcleod, who was also the Headmistress. Fine looking woman — I fell in love with her, somewhat. Next was Pauline Mayne — then about 23. She touched off my passion to write poetry. I used to write long lolloping Kiplingesque sagas, about all kinds of things. She pointed to a phrase — describing the hammer of a wildfowlers' gun breaking in the cold 'with frost-

---

28 There is a remarkable parallel between this recollection and a passage Lawrence wrote in a letter following his last visit to 'the country of my heart':

From the hills, if you look across at Underwood wood, you'll see a tiny red farm on the edge of the wood. That was Miriam's farm, where I got my first incentive to write . . . I know that view better than any in the world.

chilled snap'. 'That's poetry' she said. And I thought, well if that's poetry that's the way I think so I can give you no end of it. She became a close friend of my family's — still is I suppose. Then came John Fisher — demobbed. For a while it was Pauline and John together. I was in love with both, so they could teach me anything. John F had only to exclaim about the unearthly mightiness of Beethoven — whom I had never knowingly listened to — for me to become such a sotted addict of Beethoven that his music dominated my life till I left University & lost my gramaphone [sic] & radio. Even so, ever since, it has preoccupied me at some level. I still listen to it in preference to anything else. That's education, I suppose.

The Pike we caught was big — very big — but not 40 lb. Nicholas' 1st pike, in Ireland, was twice as big. (He's never caught one bigger — caught it on his mother's birthday, at Six-mile Bridge — home town of Edna O'Brien).

No, the night fishing did not involve trespassing. We just liked fishing on into the dark. I've always liked fishing at night. Although, it's true, poaching is more exciting than legal fishing — night or day.

I climbed to the top of Scout Rock first when I was about six — yes, that was late. But our side of the valley I'd been climbing as long as I could remember, certainly from 3 or 4. And the moors there were higher than Scout Rock — level with the moors behind & beyond Scout Rock. My mother's mother's family — Smiths — farmed above Scout Rock. I used to go up to that farm, occasionally, with her — but only along the top edge of Scout Rock, much later with my brother. There's a path, at the brink. Impressive outlook — more so than from the moorline opposite (above Height's Road — behind the Skip Inn and the Golf course). Impressive outlook into the valley, that is. Ewood — the home of my mother's father's family, the Farrars — is opposite, big house gone, but many of the outbuildings still there. Crowded now by housing developments.

Moorland had an effect on me — still has. The moment I get to heather, everything feels better. I shall live in Caithness yet. (Like the top of the Pennine Moors, but in fact a plain, with the most marvellous wild, neglected rivers going through it. The whole area a bit neglected — too flat & desolate for tourists, too poor for the old crofting population: a landscape of little ruins, alive with Northern birds.) But I felt it very early, very strong, the feeling for heather.

Orpheus was the first story that occurred to me after S.P.s death. I rejected it: I thought it would be too obvious an attempt to exploit my situation — I was too conscious of that obviousness. I saw my little note about it, the other day. The shock twist was that Pluto answered: No, of course you can't have her back. She's dead, you idiot. Too close to it, you see. I wrote the musical play in 1971, same time as the Max Nicholson essay, in a farmhouse in North Devon that I'd escaped to after A's & my mother's death, trying to sort out marriage dilemmas etc. Wrote it in the spirit of a bagatelle. Should have gone on and written lots more things in that vein — but life intervened, production lines were destroyed, I had to start afresh elsewhere, in time. (In fact, I got married and went off with Peter Brook.)

I'm babbling on. I'd intended to make this succinct — (less of my scrawl to test you.)

Crag Jack was my grandfather — Dad's father, Irish. A dyer, died age about 40 from pneumonia. He's the subject of my piece 'Familiar'.[29] Came down out of Crag Vale (leads up through the deep gorge opening South from Mytholmroyd). Family legend makes him a local sage — solved people's problems, wrote their letters, closest friends the local Catholic and Wesleyan Ministers, though he spent a lot of time in pubs. Said to be a great singer. No photo, left my Dad a 3 year old orphan (and his younger brother — and older sister). Mystery man. A geneologist [sic] up there — a Hughes — tried to trace his origins, but failed, though there are other Hughes' about. Probably came from Manchester or Liverpool. My Dad's mother's father was a regular soldier, surnamed Major, rank of Major, known in the family legend as Major Major of the Rock — permanently stationed at Gibraltar, where he married a Spaniard, small very dark woman, Arab-looking, high thin nose like Olwyn's. Often thought I'd like to learn more about them — should be possible through Army records on Gibraltar. Granny died age 92 or so in the mid-forties. My brother's nose is like a comic Julius Caesar — he had blue-black straight hair.

The 'magic landscape' behind the Old Denaby landscape was Tarka the Otter's N. Devon. In 38, when we moved to Mex. my

---

29 Hughes is referring to the 'Familiar' in *Elmet*, not that in *Capriccio*.

brother went off to Devon as a Gamekeeper's assistant — age 18, his last free year before the war. My life over old Denaby was a dream life — keeping going alone the life I'd lived with him. Made doubly so by Williamson's Tarka the Otter — which I found in the School library in 1941, and kept out, on & off, for 2 years — till I knew it by heart pretty well. By then, my brother was gone right away, into North Africa — where he stayed till the war ended, and after. So his paradisal life as a Gamekeeper (he still calls it the happiest year of his life) in Devon, made more actual by Williamson's book, became the inner life I simply went on living — but alone. I lived it in that double vision — the real manor farm over Old Denaby, & the imagined world of Tarka. He was like my surrogate father — old enough for that.

Later on, I teamed up with a boy in my sister's class[30] — whose father was the gardener on Crookhill Estate above Conisborough. The big house was a Sanatorium for miners with T.B. The 100 acre park & woodlands were ours. He shared my obsessions. I became a member of that family, pretty well, till I went into the RAF. He married my girl friend of the day — no rancour or problem — and went on to become Head of Parks in Hong Kong for 18 years. We spent all weekends, and all long summer evenings together, fishing, shooting. Bicycle crazed too: we rode all over South Yorks, Derbyshire & into Nottinghamshire, fishing.

The Devon dream must have stayed with me. When S.P. and I moved down here in 1961, we looked at quite a few houses. I wanted a place up on Exmoor — near deer, sea-bass & sea-trout. Idea was to be self-sufficient. But I ended up here. First morning of the 1962 trout season, I went out at dawn (to get back by 9 am — for Sylvia's writing stint) and was walking across the meadow towards the river when an otter jumped out of the ditch in front of me, and went bobbing along toward the river — into which it vanished. I suddenly realised what I'd done. The Taw is one of Tarka's two rivers. I never again saw an otter on the Taw — in thousands of hours night & day. Saw plenty on the Torridge — Tarka's birth-river — later on, when it became an otter sanctuary, for nursing the otters released from hand-rearing.

So my Mytholmroyd landscape, my Old Denaby landscape, & North Devon, all flowed into one — through my inner life with my

30 John Wholey.

brother — present the first 7 years, absent ever after. (When he left the RAF, he went to Australia).

His absence left me to my sister — who took his place as my mentor. She was the prodigy at School — and I see now she had marvellously precocious taste in poetry. When my teacher began to make remarks about my writing, my mother went out and bought a whole library — 2nd hand — of classic poets. All the Warwick Shakespeares, & everything after. Eventually Olwyn got me into the Shakespeare. They coached me, somehow — perpetual expectations. And Olwyn as you know is a formidable force. So all that started up alongside my shooting & fishing obsession. The later teachers — Pauline Mayne & John F.— became close friends of my mother's & Olwyn's, & of mine, of course. So, I was in that cooker from age of about eleven — and totally confident that I belonged in it, so by 16 I had no thought of becoming anything but a writer of some kind, certainly writing verse. When I sat my entrance exam to Pembroke, John F sent a notebook of my poems to the College Master — S.C. Roberts. When I got back, our latin master Neil, had composed a latin epigram on my ignominious failure. If it had been decided by my answer papers, he would have been right — but Roberts liked my poems. He persuaded them to take me on as a 'dark horse'. So I heard later.

That's pretty much how I got to Grammar School too. My mother had made a close friend of the headmaster at the Junior School — Schofield St. He bought his tobacco in the shop.[31] When I failed the preliminary for the 11 plus, she persuaded him to let me sit the actual exam. I wrote a long essay on how I wanted to be a gamekeeper, spent all my exam time on it. And got through, with 2 others. So I had some funny luck, in those days.

Babbling on again. It's too easy, writing about yourself. I hope it helps.

Yes, do give us a card or call when you're coming this way.

Interested in what you say about the audiobook commentary on Crow — yes, publish it as an appendix by all means.[32]

I only ever mention the 3 answers to the ogress because they are the only three I've published.[33] Each one was a big thing for me —

---

31 Hughes' parents had a newsagent's and tobacconist's shop in Mexborough.
32 *Ted Hughes: Crow* (Faber/Penguin Audiobooks, 1997).
33 Among the manuscripts Hughes sold to Emory, Neil Roberts found many other questions Hughes had thought of for the ogress. I discuss these in *Ted Hughes and Nature*, p. 108.

it's not easy to find that pitch. And not be repetitive — from piece to piece. Others are in chaotic draft. But I have all the questions — which I would never disclose, for fear of disrupting what might be getting itself ready.

Tiger-psalm was originally one — but took off on a different plane. It's that headlong huddle of first lines, crowding towards the right conclusion — with the authentic feeling of the plight identified by the question: somehow, absolutely everything in me has to be in on it — I've made too many attempts at them that just skid over the top. I should have tried again, maybe, when I was doing the Oresteia. I certainly had all the right material white-hot, that year, maybe still have.

You must be proud of Ursula & Arren — you've got that right, whatever you might think you've got less than right.

Having a foolish struggle to set brief prose intros to the U.S. editions of Phèdre & Oresteia. Farrar Straus want me to do something like the piece I did for the Ovid. To make a series — of 3 — for Schools! What can you say about the Oresteia in 3 or 4 pages? There's a review in today's Times by Fredrick Raphael, of a reissue of Burckhard's Rise & fall of Democracy in Greece, that I wouldn't mind stealing complete.[34] Better than burning the foxes.

This is too long.

Love to you all   Ted

Have you read Tom Paulin's marvellous book about Hazlitt?[35]

In early August I went to the world premiere of Ted's translation of Racine's Phèdre at the Malvern Festival knowing Euripides' Hippolytus, but not Racine's version of the story. My letter to Ted about the play is lost, but its substance was as follows. Racine acknowledged his debt to Euripides, but his version shows little understanding of what Euripides was about. There is no sense of the determining power of the two goddesses, Aphrodite and Artemis, and no sense that Hippolytus' coldness is anything more than adolescent priggishness. Racine misses the significance of Hippolytus to the extent that Hippolytus' indifference to women is explained by the fact that he just hadn't met the right woman yet, and Racine provides just such a woman for him in the form of a beautiful imprisoned princess, Aricia, who does not exist in any earlier tellings of the story. Racine's Hippolytus has no tragic flaw, and his gruesome death is gratuitous. I asked Ted why he had undertaken to translate such a poor play when he could have been translating the Hippolytus or The Bacchae.

34 Jacob Burckhardt (1818–97), The Greeks and Greek Civilisation (HarperCollins, 1998), reviewed by Frederic Raphael in the Sunday Times.
35 Tom Paulin, The Day-Star of Liberty: William Hazlitt's Radical Style (Faber & Faber, 1998). See Hughes' letter to Paulin in Reid, Letters, pp. 729–31.

14 Aug. 98

Dear Keith —

Your letter is a bit melancholy. That was awful, I can imagine, getting your trailer tent smashed up — by your sister-in-law! I always avoid travelling in convoy — when I'm behind, I do daft things I'd never normally do, trying to keep up or at least not overtake. And when I'm in front, I'm always worrying about my train of vehicles — not getting them into difficulties at roundabouts and lights & yes lay-bys. I always make a destination where we can meet up, then all get there solo. Will insurance fix it? Can't fix the history.[36]

Well, I see one or two reasons for Christopher Reid rejecting the book — did he see all the book or the outline?[37] If I wrote the kind of book, I would never show 'outlines'. There's a Jewish Proverb: (one of Leonard's favourites) 'Never show fools (i.e. anybody) half-work'. They always find fault, see the negative problems, — take it, basically (unconsciously) as a finished work, anticipate woodenly.

But maybe you showed him the whole thing.

Now if you'd discussed it with him as a possibility — a chapter about this, another about that, he would have said 'We'd very much like to see it'. Because 'hearing' anticipates positively. For some reason. Usually. No?

I heard from Nick Gammage[38] that Leonard's latest cooperation with me is being touted in the trade as 'poems kept out of B.L. for X reasons'. etc.[39] Quite a few I did keep out because I thought enough is enough. I asked Leonard and he complained his distributor 'took it into his head' etc. Usual story — the commercial dumpster. They didn't fit, or didn't belong.

I'm sending you a Xerox of it, to burden your file. I doubt if you'd want to bankrupt your lineage trying to buy one. (Please don't lend it and let it be duplicated — not sure I should have let him have 2 or 3 of them.)

---

36 In fact the insurance paid for a much better trailer-tent, which Melissa and I are still using.

37 I had sent Christopher Reid, as reader for Faber, what I had so far written (most of it) of The Laughter of Foxes. He had found the book lacking in critical objectivity, and 'disconcertingly ventriloquial', which I thought as insulting to Ted as to me.

38 Nick Gammage was editing The Epic Poise: A Celebration of Ted Hughes (1999), which was originally intended as a celebration of Hughes' seventieth birthday in 2000, but became a memorial volume.

39 Howls and Whispers. Ten special copies and a hundred ordinary, all signed by Hughes and Baskin. The price of the ordinary copies was $4,500.

These Lt editions deals always have twisty consequences — not sure they're worth it.

Did I tell you about Richard Gilbertson — trying to sell his diary observations, about me & mine in the sixties.[40] He sent a sample to Faber — which they rejected. Somebody won't.

Dear old Gilbertson. There's an underside to that story — he will hardly be able to mention that.

Cheer up Keith. Your kids are turning out little Aces, your finches are breeding. You had a great time in Cornwall.

My phone is [enclosed]

You didn't give an address so I couldn't contact you to call anyway. You could have had cream tea and I could have given you some Laureate sherry, and shown Arren my skulls, and given him a skin or two.

  Love to all   Ted

You were watching the wrong play. Racine's play is 5 universes away from the Euripides. Authentic suppression of the Female by Puritan intellectualism (Pascal as you know also Jansenist). Crucial moment in French Culture — never recovered. I read it as a (subconscious) analysis & total dramatisation of his (Racine's) rejection of the Theatre (Phèdre) and his reversion to the Jansenist brainwashing of his youth (against which his whole Theatre adventure had been a defiant resistance and escape). Hence Aricia etc. Yes, I was asked to do it. Production has quite a way to go, but it should be OK by Sept & London.

7 October 1998

Dear Ted

Sorry to hear from Ann Skea that you were prevented by a bad cough from doing your reading at the National.

As you know, I'm doing a piece for Nick Gammage's book. I've now finished the second draft, which Nick is perfectly happy with. But because of its unusually (for me) personal nature, I don't want to go any further without your approval. Please let me know if you are unhappy about any part of it and I will either change it or drop it. If you are unhappy about the whole thing, I can

---

40 Richard Gilbertson was a Cornish bookseller and publisher who had published Hughes' *Animal Poems* in 1967, *Five Autumn Songs for Children's Voices* in 1968, and *The Martyrdom of Bishop Farrar* in 1970. In 1986–7 he had published a series of nine articles in *The Bookdealer* describing the large collection of presentation copies he had received from Ted in the late sixties.

easily do something quite different for Nick (though I understand from him that my contribution is of a piece with most of the other fifty).

You remember that you said I could publish your commentary on *Crow* from the Faber audiobook in *The Laughter of Foxes*. It sounds as if it is being read rather than improvised. Does that mean that it exists in some written form? If so, could you let me have a copy? Otherwise I'll simply transcribe it from the tape, and send you the transcript in case you want to change anything.

My Bolton WEA class began yesterday. It is the first time in over forty years that I am letting the students choose the entire syllabus. I arrived at the first meeting not knowing what any of the texts would be, except that they would all be chosen from *By Heart*.[41] . . . I ask the students who have chosen a poem to launch the discussion by saying why they chose it. The old lady who went first on 'Piano'[42] suggested that in old people nostalgia is a substitute for falling in love in the young; but nostalgia in a young man of twenty-five is an 'affliction'. Better than many critics!

I now have three baby Lavender finches nearly ready for fledging. I spend half my time collecting insects for them.

Get well soon.   Keith

10 Oct 98

Dear Keith —

Thank you for the piece.[43] Letter first.

No, what you say seems fine to me. I don't see that you break any taboos.

As for the Crow audiobook commentary, best if you transcribe it & let me rejig it. I wrote it out, because I know, in improvising something already gone over many times, you can get into a waffle & waste a lot of time.

I like the old lady's remark about nostalgia.

Now the piece:

(1) In your first year, (my third) I had switched to anthropology. I don't recall that I ever went to an English lecture again (I went very rarely even in my 2nd year).[44] And I went to very few Anthropology

---

41 *By Heart: 101 Poems to Remember*, edited with an introduction by Ted Hughes (Faber & Faber, 1997).
42 By D. H. Lawrence.
43 The first draft of my contribution to *The Epic Poise*.
44 In my piece I had recalled seeing at lectures a conspicuous figure in a burgundy corduroy jacket (at a time when we all wore blazers or sports coats and duffle-jackets), so large that he always sat where he could sprawl into the aisle, and usually not disguising his boredom. I thought it was probably Ted. My first year, 1952–3, was in fact Ted's *second*, so we did overlap for a year as students of English.

Lectures — a few of Glyn Daniels. Mainly, from my year 2 onwards, I spent my days at the University Library. My year 3, I became embroiled with a girl,[45] eventually lived with her somewhere in Cambridge, living partly in London, partly in Cambridge, tangled with various girls. Wrote The Jaguar, The Thought Fox, The Casualty, Wind, Vampire etc. Met Sylvia early 1956 — lived here and there in Cambridge, & occasionally in London till we married, and from Autumn term 1956 lived in Eltisley Av.

I wore corduroy jackets from about 1951. As I recall, I never wore a burgundy coloured one . . . I wore a grey one, which I eventually died [sic] black — about 1953. Maybe I did have a burgundy one at some point — which I also died [sic] black. But I don't remember it. I remember the grey, the 2 different jackets, and that both were died black eventually. I gave one of them, I think, to Joe Lyde.[46]

I got the corduroy cheap from my Uncle's.[47]

I wore the last black one up to marrying Sylvia & going off to Spain. Returning Sept 1956, to lodge at Eltisley Av. I then started wearing a thick Brown & Black Harris Tweed. I lay low, because I felt, I suppose, that I was in enemy country. First two years, I didn't feel much social self-confidence.

Maybe the person you saw was Mark Boxer. He was very tall, wore as I recall a Burgundy Corduroy jacket, and never hid his boredom — sketching caricatures & laughing out loud.[48] I was a quiet type, an outsider.

Burgundy would have seemed a little bit too affectedly Oscar

45 'It must have been that summer that Ted met Shirley. She was an undergraduate at Newnham. She never joined the male company at the Anchor but would come and lean over the railings of the bridge. Ted would see her and be off. She was a tall, attractive, shy girl, with a farouche air. She is commemorated in Ted's poem "Fallgrief's Girlfriends"' (Daniel Huws, Memories of Ted Hughes: 1952–1963 (Richard Hollis/Five Leaves, 2010)).

46 Joe Lyde, an Irish jazz trumpeter and pianist, was a contemporary of Hughes at Cambridge. Daniel Huws writes: 'After Cambridge, Joe got a scholarship to Tulane University, for the sake of being able to play with bands in New Orleans. He returned to London and died young, of drink, the first of our contemporaries to die. Ted found him amusing in his uninhibited recounting of his escapades, and in his abrasiveness. Many, including Sylvia Plath, could not abide him.' Memories of Ted Hughes, p. 14.

47 Ted's maternal uncle, Walter Farrar, was a prosperous mill-owner in Mytholmroyd.

48 Mark Boxer was a Kingsman, and editor of the student magazine Granta, in which he published a poem about God 'washing his dirty socks'. The Vice-Chancellor demanded he be sent down, the first student since Shelley to be sent down for blasphemy. E. M. Forster spoke in his defence. King's succeeded in reducing the sentence to a week's rustication during May Week, which would mean that he missed the May Ball that ended it. The authorities forgot, however, that May Balls go on into the early hours and, on the stroke of midnight during the Ball, Boxer made a triumphant return. He later had a prominent career as an editor and cartoonist, and married the newsreader Anna Ford.

Wildish for me, I think. But I can't be sure. I changed a lot, end of my 2nd year.

It's true I often took an end seat.

Horrible Religious Error was written on the train to Manchester. I joined up with A., and we went North — after the reading — to find a new place to live, alternative to Court Green. Found a good place on the North Tyne. Saturday she went back to London, I went back to Devon — last time I saw or spoke to her. Last Crow piece I wrote. (She killed herself & Shura the Sunday afternoon).

P5 — penult. para:
The George is in Hatherleigh.
Never sold 'all the stock' — at one go. After 1976 sold it in bits and pieces. Possibly we were selling a few animals. (Never sold stock in Okehampton).

P 10/11: The Elk — my elk is dead, killed by a single shot.[49]
Later, my brother (in the story) brings in the ape-like creature that could not be killed — until after many shots, carefully placed. A sort of Bigfoot man/animal.
The elk is the last animal I kill.
After that follows the brother's Yeti/Bigfoot, the old woman of the animals, the flayed head, corpses & pelts all gone, the pursuit, of me, by the head, the return to the native village, the head now a flying goblin of screams & huge talons, my battle in the dark forest with the screaming head that seems to metamorphose, as I get the upper hand and kill it, into an unconscious beautiful Indian girl unknown to the local tribe. My taking her off, making her my wife — though she remains dumb & will communicate nothing of what she knows.
So the sequence goes: brother; brother gradually goes mad with the abundant slaughter of trophies; goes wholly mad, with

49 See 3 August 1978, and Appendix V.

slaughter of the Bigfoot; brother disappears but seems to have been killed & devoured by the little old woman — who comes up out of the river & goes back into it; only his flayed skull remains, on the empty graveyard of all they have killed (their carcasses, trophy skins & antlers having vanished); my brother's skull transforms to a flying head as it pursues me; I fight it in pitch dark; it seems to change to the beautiful unconscious unwounded girl. I marry her — and hunt no more, & she remains dumb.

Seems to me, that the brother, going insane as penalty for his treatment of the animals, eventually becomes that girl, my Cordelia. Funny business.

As your Elk would have become your wife — mother of your children. Perhaps.

Barrie Cooke is one of my 3 closest friends in Ireland. We used to go round looking at the Elk Skeletons — or just antlers — in old Irish houses & museums. He's a great feeling for such things.[50]

<u>Shakespeare</u>: Still can't see your problem fitting Venus & Adonis to Measure for Measure — up to end of Act II <u>Sc II</u>, and Rape of Lucrece to what follows (from half way though that speech.) That's the play in which we see how the Equation is put together to make the dynamo of the plot.

<u>I'm sending you a visual riddle.</u>[51] One pattern — as you see — can exist 'invisibly' within another, and not be arbitrary: it can exist there as 3 dimensional and one & only: i.e. ingenuity can't find any

---

50 In my piece for Nick Gammage, after comparing my story with 'The Head' I had added:
   In 1986 I bought Aidan Dunne's monograph on the Irish painter Barrie Cooke, because it contained Hughes' poem 'The Great Irish Pike', illustrated by Cooke. Here I found a magnificent painting by Cooke called *Megacerous Hibernicus* (1983). It is a painting of my beast, its face a mask of blood. Dunne writes of it: '*Megacerous Hibernicus* is a cloudy, epic vision of an elk, its body in profile, its head, and the great spread of its antlers angled towards us. Hazy, emergent, it stands against and blends into a moist, dark blanket of space, like a murky soup of time, suffused with a misty light . . . It is a ghostly presence, hazy and evanescent, but the pale shafts of skeletal bone, the red sinewy trails of pigment, flowering antlers webbed with veins, and its heroic, questing attitude, surveying us through the centuries, indicates a resurrected, sentient state.'
   I like to think that Cooke's purer vision represents a later stage of the resurrection of the same elk, the same violated but unkillable holy life in our common consciousness.
51 These Magic Eye images, or random dot autostereograms, were appearing weekly in one of the national newspapers at that time. It was quite revelatory when the hidden image, after long staring, would suddenly take shape in three dimensions behind the completely different apparent image.

more, & it has as strong a reality, or stronger, than the superficial more obvious one, (once you see it) (and before you lose it again).

Also, the 2nd pattern is not easy to find — you might not be able to find it at all.

And there are other differences too, naturally.

This riddle merely demonstrates that a powerful pattern — a powerful 'other image, on another level', can exist, and yet be very difficult to locate and define, within it.

But Imagine that in each case, the invisible pattern is the Equation, evolving from play to play, while the key minutiae details, by which the existence of each depends on the other, are from play to play extremely varied. Does that make it easier? Or harder? Bring the picture close to your nose, let your eye-focus drift (without going into a total blur), then move the picture slowly away from your eyes. After a while, the hidden image will separate itself. Lovely concentrated sensation, as it comes clear.

I'd like 2 years to rewrite the Shakespeare simply & more briefly.

Hamlet & Measure for Measure are not the most lucid chapters — Hamlet was very early, M for M I tried too hard.

After a certain point, as my perception clarified itself, the book wrote itself.

———————————

Not sure about the penultimate para on p.17. Won't you simply raise righteous anger & opposition? Pointlessly.[52]

Main problem of the book: it is too long; it deals with every play, & leaves nothing to the reader; it needs the reader to know Shakespeare better than all but a very few do; style too complicated; I added too much arcane material.

It's strange, you know, but I have the impression that we know each other better, and have met far more often, than you imply — in this piece. Maybe it's your computer — formalising what ought to be more casual & intimate. We'll get the low-down on computers, pretty soon.

Love to all.   Ted

---

52 I imagine this paragraph expressed in no uncertain terms my contempt for the philistinism of the reviewers, particularly those from the Oxford Shakespeare establishment. I deleted it.

11 October 1998

Dear Ted

I'm doing some work on *Remains of Elmet*, trying to make sense of the order, among other things. Ann managed to make some sense of it in her book,[53] but she was using the first trade edition, where the order was Fay's, not yours. I can make more sense of the order in the Rainbow Press edition than I can of your order in *Three Books*, more or less retained in *Elmet*. The new order looks like the old order merely shuffled, though presumably, knowing you, it is highly purposive. The only purpose I can half-detect would be to deliberately undermine the tendency of the first order to move towards more upbeat poems in the last ten. By removing two of the most positive poems — 'High Sea-Light' and 'In April' — altogether, and by moving two more 'There come days . . .' and 'The Trance of Light' to near the beginning, you relinquish that brighter ending. Is that deliberate?

[pm 14 Oct. 1998]

Dear Keith — Elmet —

Yes, Elmet's 3 orderings: only the first one works. That was Fay's — with maybe a nudge or two here and there from me.

As I think I told you at the time, I began the writing with autobiographical pieces (the Canal Poems, Mount Zion etc). then that diabolical fear of subjectivity argued me into writing impersonal 'mood pieces', to accompany the photos without conflict of visual imagery and specific descriptions. Still, I managed to do it without disrupting the general wholeness of the inspiration.

Later on when the idea of an edition without pictures came up, I made another mistake — and tried to introduce more of an autobiographical content. Here and there converting 'mood pieces' (Hardcastle Crags) to autobiographical meditations (Leaf Mould). Not sure what to make of the results. But I think the genuine inspiration for the whole scheme had gone — had faded quite a bit. A mongrel effect.

When the Limited Edition, with photos, came up, I gradually realised the moment had passed. I finished some more 'autobiographical pieces' 'Climbing into Heptonstall' etc. but utterly different in spirit. Fay's photographic vision of the region had also changed — and her style of photography. In the end I

---

53 Skea, *Ted Hughes: The Poetic Quest*. In the original edition the poems were accompanied by Fay Godwin's photographs.

simply piled together everything related to Calder Valley — and more or less left it again to Fay. Unsatisfactory, though I like her pictures.

Because of this coming and going, I never got the text, let alone the order of it, that I wanted. I feel I let Fay down, somewhat, except that first time round.

The correct or reasonably working order is still to be found.

Best would have been to build the whole sequence around my father & mother, and let Fay's pictures provide backdrop, merely. I would then have a book that I wanted, and that others could relate to.

Best   Ted

14–15 October 1998.

Dear Ted

Your comments on my piece will be extremely helpful . . .

What a pity that the person I remembered so clearly from Mill Lane lecture rooms wasn't you. It could well have been, as you say, Mark Boxer. It made a good story, but I will drop it. I've corrected all the other factual errors, of course.

I know I could have said a lot more about 'The Beast', and in fact had already written about it at some length, but I wanted that material for The Laughter of Foxes, not this supposedly little piece. The only reason I didn't send you the new material about the brothers and the slaughter of the animals was that I didn't want to overwhelm you with several things of mine all at once. But I enclose the pages now . . .

Much of our correspondence on your Shakespeare book, looking back over it, seems to be concerned with unresolved disagreements about particularly, Isabella. In the very last paragraph of the book you say:

> From the point of view of woman, everything is different, in the sense that the 'tragic error' belongs exclusively to the psychology of the man (except where woman imitates man).

But Isabella seems to me the perfect example of woman imitating man. She wants all intercourse between the sexes, even speech, to be banned. She abhors extramarital lovemaking more than any other vice. She regards the law by which her brother is condemned as just. She is more ruthlessly legalistic than Angelo: 'I had rather my brother die by the law, than my son should be unlawfully born'. She despises anyone who values life and love more than honour. She speaks one of the most inhuman lines in Shakespeare: 'More than our brother is our chastity'. She has disbranched herself from her material sap as effectively as Goneril. She is pure Adonis in her total rejection of the claims of love. She is a female Angelo, which is part of her attraction for him . . . So I can't see Isabella as corresponding in any way to Venus. And Mariana is as perfect an embodiment of Venus as one can find – offering total unconditional love, and being spurned by a narcissistic puritan – yet you don't mention her, don't seem to have any place for her in your application of the equation.

Yes, I love those hidden pictures. I can usually do them quite quickly. But I haven't yet been able to do the two you sent . . .

This piece was never intended to be a complete account of our relationship. It never occurred to me to try to make it that. Just certain carefully selected highlights. I wanted the piece to have a certain coherence, theme, the relationship between you as poet and me as critic (which of course is only part of our total relationship). What is important to us might not be of much general interest. Also, I am invading your privacy enough already. We have corresponded a great deal over nearly thirty years. Your sense of our relationship probably derives mainly from that. We haven't met all that often. Must be over three years since the last time, when I took you to your reading in Bath. You don't seem to come north as much as you used to. Anyway, I have added a few extra touches to counteract what you took to be the implication that we knew each other less well than we do.

I don't think the computer is to blame. I know your theory of the pen being linked to the right side of the brain etc. And you may be right as far as the first drafts of poems go. But for prose a word-processor doesn't have any of the disadvantages of a typewriter. With a typewriter you are always conscious of all the trouble it will cause if you get anything wrong and have to type it all out again. With a word processor you can bung anything down, in the knowledge that any changes can be easily and quickly made. You can delete, move, insert, with two clicks of the mouse. If you had done the Shakespeare book on a word-processor you could have saved hundreds of hours, and possibly your health.

Just got your second letter. O.K. I won't attempt to read anything into the order of poems in *Remains*. By the way, although I have had it since it was published and skimmed and dipped before, I had never read Ann Skea's book properly, cover to cover, and with time to go back to most of the poems, until this last week or two. You must have been delighted with it. It seems to me by far the best criticism written about your work so far. It's all good, but the chapters on *Remains* seem particularly fine. What a pity it didn't get published by Faber or someone who would have got it noticed. I wouldn't know about it myself if Ann were not a friend of mine . . .

My Lavenders have fledged now. I must go and catch some more insects. It's a still evening for once, and the midges are out in numbers.

Love to Carol.   Keith.

Appendices

Appendices

Appendix I

From a transcript of Hughes' dating of all the poems in *The Hawk in the Rain* in a copy at Worcester Polytechnic Institute, Massachusetts.

'The Hawk In The Rain' London 1956 Rugby St.

'The Jaguar' Cambridge 1954, 4th verse, the Beacon; 5th verse Cambridge 1956

'Macaw and Little Miss' British Railways 19th June 1956

'The Thought-Fox' London 1955, Rugby St.

'The Horses' Cambridge, 1956 November Eltisley Av.

'Famous Poet' Cambridge 1956 Eltisley Av.

'Song' Patrington 16th June 1949 3 a.m.

'Parlour-Piece' Cambridge 1956

'Secretary' London 1955 Rugby St.

'Soliloquy of a Misanthrope' London, Rugby St. 1955

'The Dove Breeder' Cambridge Station, 1956

'Billet-Doux' London Rugby St. 1955

'A Modest Proposal' Cambridge, Eltisley Av. Sept. 1956

'Incompatibilities' Benidorm, Spain July 1956

'September' Spain, July 1956

'Fallgrief's Girl-Friends' London, Parson's Green, 1955

'Two Phases' The Beacon 1955

'The Decay of Vanity' London Rugby St. 1955

'Fair Choice' The Beacon, 1956

'The Conversion of The Reverend Skinner' Todmorden 1954

'Complaint' The Beacon 1956 May

'Phaetons' The Beacon 1956 May

'Egg-Head' The Beacon 1956 Sept.

'The Man Seeking Experience Enquires His Way of A Drop of Water' The Beacon 1956 Sept.

'Meeting' Spain Aug. 56

'Wind' The Beacon 1955–6

'October Dawn' Cambridge, Eltisley Av. Oct. 56

'Roarers In A Ring' Paris 1956 June

'Vampire' Cambridge 1956

'Childbirth' The Beacon 1955

'The Hag' Parson's Green, London 1954

'Law in The Country Of The Cats' Parson's Green, London 1954

'Invitation To The Dance' Todmorden 1956

'The Casualty' Cambridge 1956 Oct.

'Bayonet Charge' British Railway June 14th 1956

'Griefs For Dead Soldiers' London, Rugby St. 1956

'Six Young Men' The Beacon Sept. 1956

'Two Wise Generals' Cambridge, April 1956

'The Ancient Heroes and The Bomber Pilot' Cambridge, Eltisley Av. 1956

'The Martyrdom of Bishop Farrar' Spain, Aug. 1956

Appendix II

This appendix combines a list of the poems included in the photocopy typescript of *Cave-Birds* enclosed with Hughes' letter of 20 March 1975 with the commentary sent in May. The titles Hughes gave to Baskin's drawings on the typescript are in brackets.

(A Hercules-in-the-Underworld Bird) THE SUMMONER.
The hero's cockerel innocence, it turns out, becomes his guilt. His own self, finally, the innate nature of his flesh and blood, brings him to court.

I WAS JUST WALKING ALONG.
The defendant, in the decent piety of his innocence, is surprised. What has he failed to take account of?

THE ADVOCATE.
He is given some indication of the nature of the charge. What is he guilty of exactly? Being alive? Or of some error in the use of his life?

AFTER THE FIRST FRIGHT.
He is confronted in court with his victim. It is his own demon whom he now sees for the first time. The hero realises he is out of his depth. He protests as an honourable Platonist, thereby re-enacting his crime in front of his judges. He still cannot understand his guilt. He cannot understand the sequence of cause and effect.

(A Titled Vulturess) THE INTERROGATOR.
The crime, which seems to be a form of murder, brings into question the death penalty. The interrogator for crimes involving death collects the evidence from the accused.

SHE SEEMED SO CONSIDERATE.
Convinced now of his guilt, the defendant wishes only to understand it. But he is mystified. The interrogator seems to be offering him an ambiguous atonement.

(An Oven-ready Piranha Bird) THE JUDGE.
The visible representative of natural law does not partake of its splendour.

YOUR MOTHER'S BONES WANTED TO SPEAK, THEY COULD NOT.
It seems to the defendant that the court is confusing his victim with some other personage for whom he felt only love and concern.

(A Hermaphroditic Ephesian Owl) THE PLAINTIFF.
His crime implicates him in wider and wider responsibilities. His victim takes on a form which is progressively more multiple and serious, progressively more personal and inescapable.

IN THESE FADING MOMENTS I WANTED TO SAY.
He comprehends some contradictions of his guilty innocence and his innocent guilt.

(A Raven of Ravens) THE EXECUTIONER.
He is sentenced to death. The raven of ravens takes possession of him.

(A tumbled Socratic Cock) THE ACCUSED.
The physical life of the cockerel is offered up to the creator, the sun-being who, in the aspect of judgement, is a raven.

FIRST, THE DOUBTFUL CHARTS OF SKIN.
Sentenced, and swallowed by the raven, the hero finds himself on a journey, which leads him, not to death, but to the start of a new adventure.

(A Death-Stone Crow of Carrion) THE KNIGHT.
He is no longer anything like a cockerel. Possession by raven has transformed him into something more like a crow for his new trials in the underworld. As a knight, he dedicates himself to whatever shall be required of him.

SOMETHING WAS HAPPENING.
While the hero undergoes his vigil, the helper begins to work for him, calling on the eagles.

(A Double Osprey) THE GATEKEEPER.
The eagles have agreed to weigh him in their balance.

(A Flayed Crow) THE HALL OF JUDGEMENT.
The eagles allow him a new chance in their world.

(A Maze Pelican) THE BAPTIST.
But first he has to be washed in the waters of the source.

ONLY A LITTLE SLEEP, A LITTLE SLUMBER.
Reduced to total dependence on the help of the eagles, the hero begins to feel first stirrings of humanity again.

(A Sunrise of Owl) A LOYAL MOTHER.
He is offered an easy option by the eagle owl.

AS I CAME, I SAW A WOOD.
Much as he would like to take this beautiful option, he cannot.

(A Monkey-Eating Eagle) INCOMPARABLE MARRIAGE.
The monkey-eating eagle claims to be his daughter in the heaven of eagles. Whether he likes it or not, he now has to marry her and become the child in her womb.

(A Stud Cockerel Hunted Into a Desert) THE CULPRIT.
His marriage, the opposite of a physical marriage, is celebrated by driving out of him a cockerel, as a scapegoat, a sacrifice to the eagles.

AFTER THERE WAS NOTHING THERE WAS A WOMAN.
At moments it seems as if he were increasingly human, but somehow as if unborn, as if he were in the womb of some female, who is herself of dubious reality.

(A Scarecrow Swift) THE GUIDE.
It seems as if his real journey through the heaven of eagles were only just beginning.

HIS LEGS RAN ABOUT.
The version of the earthly woman revives more strongly and he is no longer entirely unborn, though not completely born either, with consequent confusions.

(A Crow of Prisms) WALKING BARE.
At the same time he seems to be journeying into the sun.

BRIDE AND GROOM LAY HIDDEN FOR THREE DAYS.
Somehow the earthly woman has become his bride. They have just found each other, hardly created yet, on an earth not easily separable from the heaven of the eagles.

(An Owl Flower) THE GOOD ANGEL.
The sun-being, in its aspect of benevolence, is an owl, which also is
a flower. The judgement of the eagles, evidently, is that he should be reborn.

(A Ghostly Falcon) THE RISEN.
He is reborn as a falcon.

FINALE.

Appendix III

The contents of a projected collection, *Caprichos*, which was never published, and bears no relation to *Capriccio* (1990).

1. 'No came from the earth'
2. 'He wanted to be here'
3. 'I walk'
4. 'The prisoners'
5. 'When it comes down to it'
6. 'If mouth could open its cliff'
7. 'The oracle'
8. 'When dawn lifts the eyelid'
9. 'A man stepping from every tedious thing'
10. 'Face was necessary'
11. 'He cast off the weight of space'
12. 'A deathly sleep'
13. 'He was frightened'
14. 'Dead, she became space-earth'
15. 'The earth locked out the light'
16. 'Nevertheless rejoice'

2 (as 'Halfway Head') and 5 (as 'Reckless Head') are in *Mokomaki*.

3, 6, 7, 10, 14 and 15 are six of the 'Seven dungeon songs' in *Moortown*.

8 and 16 were published in the Australian periodical *Aspect* in 1978.

11, with small changes, became 'For Leonard and Lisa' in *A Primer of Birds*.

1, 4, 9, 12 and 13 are unpublished.

Appendix IV

Four poems by Keith Sagar
praised by Hughes.

THE NIGHTINGALE MAN

There was this garden
Right there just off the sidewalk
Among the shops and office blocks.
It was shabby, trodden and littered.
There were a few little pools
With concrete paths.
In the far corner was a big bush
With many small birds in it.
One of them was singing
Very loud and metallic
Or perhaps it was a phonograph.

And a man stood on the sidewalk
Almost swamped by the rush-hour
   crowds.
He shouted to the passers-by
That these were nightingales
And for a dollar he would call one
To come and sit on your head and sing.

Someone gave him a dollar
And he whistled
And a nightingale came
And sat on his grizzled head.
He had a hard time making it go
To the other man.
Then it sang.
There was quite a crowd watching.

A little girl with tightly bound hair
With plastic flowers in it
Walked stiffly between the pools
Like a little oriental lady.
I don't know if she was part of the act.
One of the nightingales came
Uncalled
And sat on her head.
But it did not sing.

I'll tell you where it was.
Just a couple of blocks from
That big brothel where the women sit
In those huge first-floor windows,
Twenty or thirty of them
(Beauties most of them)
Waiting to be picked out.

BICOLOUR BLENNY

What sticks up from that coral-head?
A blob of mud with alert tilting eyes?
Look closer.
A sooty cricket with Martian antennae?
No.
Just a mud-coloured blenny
Propped on his primitive fin-feet
On perpetual look-out.

Here comes a shrimp,
Perfected and preserved
For just this moment –

The blenny launches upwards –
An inch of sooty chest –
Then suddenly he is on fire –
A jet of flame leaps upwards from the tail
And fires the long dark body.

Slaked with shrimp, the fire subsides
Into its coral-head grate.
The flaming skirt is folded neatly
Into its niche;
While the lugubrious square head
Pretends once more
To know nothing about it
To be nothing but mud and greed.

ANTEATER

A is for Anteater
Who watched his aunt eat her
Breakfast in wonder and pain,
For the ants that she ate
Reappeared on her plate,
Having eaten their way out again.

WOMBAT

The Wombat walloped the wallaby
From Battersea
To the London Zoo
And there he battered the kangaroo;
For the wombat
Loves combat.

Appendix V

'The Beast' by Keith Sagar

It was late May and a late spring. The sun was bright but not burning. There were flowers everywhere. The air was rich with scents, and the cypresses rustled softly to themselves. We were among the first to arrive that morning. A group of screaming schoolchildren was soon left behind: and we soon lost each other in the maze of tombs.

The area of the necropolis would have looked tiny on any map; but because of the crowdedness of the tombs and their apparently random arrangement, in reality it seemed vast. It had nothing whatever of the gloom, the clammy morbidity of an English graveyard. Here the word resurrection seemed more than the empty token it has become in Christianity. Somewhere, in some form, the Etruscans who had been buried here are dancing again and smiling still, in this world or another.

I strayed further and further from the trodden paths, glimpsing my friend in the distance less and less frequently. Birdsongs were now the only sounds. Most of the tombs were circular, about fifty feet in diameter, and domed. The tumuli were all wildly overgrown, and ablaze with broom. Handsome green lizards sunned themselves on the walls, posed to be photographed, then, at the crucial moment, scuttled off towards the dark entrances, and stood for a second at the thresholds, brighteyed against the blackness. Steps led down to the entrances, most of which were blocked with rubble. Some of the tombs were flooded, and the stairs disappeared into a phosphorescent green scum. A few were open, and cobwebs guarded their darkness and silence.

Time slowed as the sun climbed. I walked through waist-high flowers round the circumference of a high tomb, and suddenly came upon an opening at my feet the size of a house, a sunken court. An intact staircase led down to it from a far corner. I had seen nothing like it before. I could see no way to the stair but by leaping a five-foot gap with an unsure footing and a fall of some twenty feet. I jumped it safely and descended the stair. There was a doorway in the middle of each wall. All were blocked. But one not completely. I crawled through. When my eyes adjusted to the darkness I could see nothing but rubble-strewn empty chambers, and was about to turn back when I caught a glimmer of light ahead – another exit. With great difficulty I scrambled through.

With every step the temperature fell and the air became more dank. I became aware of a greenish eerie light. I emerged at the head of a steep valley with strange primitive trees and giant mosses and ferns. The sides of the valley were close and sheer and the sky looked far up. It was cold, and there were neither birds nor flowers. Nothing moved in the unnatural stillness. I moved slowly forward, intruding on the last fastness of an earlier world-age, long before the Etruscans, long before civilizations existed or joy was known.

Beneath the ancient trees like standing fossils, something took shape, something brown and beastlike. It did not move. I approached in fear. It was some great elk-like beast with massive antlers. But what was wrong with it? Its stillness was not the stillness of a cocked lizard, nor yet the stillness of death. With a pang of horror I saw that it had no eyes, just black holes where its eyes had been. It must be dead, long dead. But it was not dead. It made a sound, a sound I heard with my spine, the sound of aeons of accumulated agony and resignation. The beast could neither live nor die. It stood in an attitude of utter wretchedness. And I saw that what I had taken to be antlers were not all antlers. Among the antlers were shafts of wood driven into the skull and wedged there. The beast had long ago lost the will or the strength to try to dislodge them. Fear gave way to compassion. Very gently I touched one of the smaller shafts. The beast did not move. I grasped the shaft and gently pulled. Slowly it came away, leaving a bottomless hole like the eye-sockets. Slowly I pulled out another and another, inching them out as gently as I could, though the beast made neither sound nor movement. An hour or so it took to remove all the shafts. I stood back and wondered what the point of my intervention was. The beast had stood thus for centuries. Surely it could feel nothing. Then I remembered that sound. Had the beast actually made it, or had I imagined it?

Now I looked at the cavernous face of the beast, and the beast looked at me. With its empty eye-sockets I knew that it looked at me. And I knew that, though I saw no tears, it wept. And I knew that its weeping was a remission of its agony.

Appendix VI

Hughes' introduction to *The Reef and Other Poems* by Keith Sagar.

There is a kind of poetry which I find, say, in Stephen Crane's writings as I find it (in much greater intensity) in Tolstoy's. Behind that tensely objective prose, so sharply focussed on material activity, one feels another vision, of a different order of things.

It's not quite a simultaneous vision of some spiritual truth of things, behind and different from the material truth, though it is that too. Whatever it is, it's a vision of a world of strange forms, and strange doings, within the observed one, and it leaks through to us when it does with a shock.

Tolstoy wrote no poems, but Stephen Crane did, and they reveal his struggle to isolate that deeper poetic intuition of his in a pure form. They are written in the same language as the prose, and yet quite a few of them are undoubtedly poetry. Moreover, they give a poetic pleasure of a rare kind.

On the surface, Crane's poems look like an attempt to be simpler than simple — a moral strenuousness to be 'as true as truth's simplicity, And simpler than the infancy of truth', in disregard of aesthetic concerns. They are anti-poems, of a sort. Writers who try this road usually end up in spite of their moral seriousness only with poorer and poorer truisms, and emptier and emptier simplifications, and most of Stephen Crane's attempts end up just there. But when he succeeds, they are very different.

There are two kinds of simplicity, after all. The common type belongs to simplifications made this side of the experience of the complexity of the subject; and is achieved by retreating from it. The rare type belongs to the observations made on the other side of the subject, when the experience of having gone through the complexity has changed the observer, and brought him to a direct grasp of the inner sources of the subject, which are always simple. The first common type has the simplicity of excluding all but a few salient effects. This other rare type has the simplicity of an inclusion of everything in a clear solution. We recognise the difference, because we recognise in this latter kind that the observer has paid in full for what he records, and that has earned him a superior stake in reality, which is not common. Good folk rhymes have this kind of simplicity — experience itself seems to have produced them. (It's certain that very few poets have ever been able to add to them.)

Maybe this helps to explain why this kind of poetic simplicity is more often something latent in prose than pure in poetry. To succeed in any degree in producing it, a writer needs a strong imaginative grasp, and exhaustive accurately-imagined experience, of common reality at many levels as well as tenacity, and a good compass. Maybe he also needs a touch of that martial/ascetic brand of temperament — usually alien and even hostile to aesthetic sensibility — to provide the reckless drive towards essentials, and the readiness to abandon the verbal charms of conventional poetry.

In Archaic and Primitive Arts, and in Modern Art, this drive usually finds something slightly grotesque and sinister (and shows its connection incidentally to the art of children and 'folk'.) But at its best it is not marginal (Picasso, Kafka).

In Crane, when it works, it produces little visionary parables, as it did (with infinitely greater illumination) in Blake — visionary yet rough, hand-made, utilitarian, hacked out against the grain rather than modelled with cultural refinements.

Tolstoy shows himself of the same family when he describes one character, in a mystified way, as 'a blue triangle'.

What saves such as this from being just one more poetic invention of a rather facile kind is the anti-aesthetic context in which it appears, the exacting ethical tone of the whole work. It is a notorious fact that the slightest 'improving' touch from a skilled poet — of the sort whose language is willy nilly saturated with the latest technical refinements and cultural mannerisms — kills a folk-rhyme or a Blake Song stone dead. That sort of simplicity — so deep and impersonal and somehow all-inclusive — cannot be faked. It is natural to the spiritualised morality of the statement, and to a sense of words derived from that, and true to it. It's the old, absolute requirement: to be possessed by the priorities, and to be sensitive to the right words for the priorities, of a subject from outside our ego's usual daily performance.

No doubt this is an odd place for such a lengthy description of a certain kind of poetry. But it seems to me worth the trouble here, in a foreword to poems by Keith Sagar, because though I'm surprised to find it, I feel something of this kind of poetry in his work. In my opinion, that's its value. These words will have been justified amply, if they can suggest to one reader that he look at the poems in this light.

Keith Sagar's verse is manifestly plain. When I first met these pieces, I could not put my finger on just what it is in them that rings so true, and that kept bringing me back to look at them again, and that gave me such a definite pleasure when I did. I could recognise in them, everywhere, his special brand of humour (serious) and the way it blends into the fascinated attention — a very special quality in itself that he brings to whatever interests him. I could also sense and enjoy his very original and private relationship to the natural world. I felt there was a real person in these poems, to whom things happened in a real way, and interestingly. I like his attitude of affectionate, unsentimental, workmanlike practicality towards small things — very like his use of language in the poems. And I appreciated his quiet skill — the deft and solid simplicity of his patterns. Again and again, with the baldest economy, he seemed to me to get it just right.

But what surprised me most of all, I think, was the way these parables, and cool sinister anecdotes, the microscopically-exact fish in their intent lives, even his brief pensées, have touched that place in my imagination where some folk-rhymes, some archaic and some modern pieces of art, certain tribal sacred objects, certain slightly occult experiences, even the poems of Edwin Muir, among other things, live together on the other side of personality and fashion and many a grander cultural monument. Poems that move towards that world seem to me very much worth creating and having.

Appendix VII

Letter from Henry Moore to Keith Sagar.

26th March 1980

Dear Keith Sagar,

I am sorry it is only now I am answering your letter of 30th January about your very interesting idea of a poster poem of Ted Hughes.

I admire Ted Hughes' poetry very much indeed – for me he is the best of living English poets . . . (I have the 'Elmet Poems' book, illustrated by the beautiful photographs of Fay Godwin).

However, I am so very much behind with all my work commitments, that I know I cannot find the time to do anything for you by the date of the Conference and exhibition you are organising for his 50th birthday.

Will you please tell him this, but also say what immense pleasure I get out of his Elmet Poems, (and I agree with you that there is a strong Yorkshire connection between us).

With best wishes,

Henry Moore

Appendix VIII

'A Reply to my Critics', *Books and Issues*, nos. 3–4 (1981). A reply to criticisms of Hughes' poetry which had been published in the previous two editions of *Books and Issues*.

I haven't seen Aidan Coen's article about my verse, but reading Mr. Brinton's letter, where he volunteers some opinions of his own, it occurred to me – not for the first time – that I should perhaps have taken more trouble to bridge the culture gap that seems to render my poem *Crow* nearly inaccessible to some readers.

Maybe I assumed too confidently that readers would share my weakness for the particular literary tradition in which the poem is set – or in which I tried to set it. I realise now that a reader who is unfamiliar with the Trickster Tales of early and primitive literatures, or who can't concede that those folk productions have any place in the canon of serious literary forms, is going to try to relate my poem to something more familiar; what usually comes up is Black Comedy of the modish, modern Continental sort. I think this is misleading, and I will try to say why.

Black Comedy (as I understand it) and Trickster Literature have superficial apparent resemblances, to be sure. But they are fundamentally so opposite that those seeming resemblances are in fact absolute opposites, as negative and positive are opposites.

Black Comedy is the end of a cultural process, Trickster Literature is the beginning. Black Comedy draws its effect from the animal despair and suicidal nihilism that afflicts a society or an individual when the supportive metaphysical benefits disintegrate. Trickster Literature draws its effects from the unkillable, biological optimism that supports a society or individual whose world is not yet fully created, and whose metaphysical beliefs are only just struggling out of the dream stage.

In Black Comedy, the despair and nihilism are fundamental, and the attempts to live are provisional, clownish, pathetic, meaningless, 'absurd'. In Trickster Literature the optimism and creative joy are fundamental, and the attempts to live, and to enlarge and intensify life, fill up at every point with triumphant meaning.

In Black Comedy, great metaphysical beliefs lie in ruins, and the bare forked animal has nothing but a repertoire of futilities. In Trickster Literature metaphysical beliefs are only just being nursed into life, out of the womb and the soil, and the bare forked animal has a repertoire of all untried possibilities.

It is easy to confuse the two with each other, because historically they sometimes co-exist, and psychologically they often do so – or at least they do so up to the point where the negative mood finally crushes out all possibility of hope, as very often demonstrated in our day, so that the biological processes of reproduction and renewal cease. Black Comedy expresses the disintegration and misery of that, which is a reality, and has its place in our attempts to diagnose what is happening to us. But Trickster Literature expresses the vital factor compressed beneath the affliction at such times – the renewing sacred spirit, searching its depths for new resources and directives, exploring towards new emergence and growth. And this is how the worst moment comes closest to the best opportunity. 'When the load of bricks is doubled, Moses comes' etc.

But an alert sensitivity can distinguish between the two easily enough. In Black Comedy, the lost hopeful world of Trickster is mirrored coldly, with a negative accent. In Trickster Literature, the suffering world of Black Comedy, shut off behind thin glass, is mirrored hotly, with a positive accent. It is the difference between two laughters: one, bitter and destructive; the other zestful and creative, attending what seems to be the same calamity.

In the individual life, Black Comedy corresponds to the materialist disillusionment of inescapable age and illness, as if it were founded on the breakdown of the cells. Trickster Literature corresponds to the infantile, irresponsible naivety of sexual love, as if it were founded on the immortal enterprise of the sperm.

At bottom, this is what Trickster is: the optimism of the sperm, still struggling joyfully along after 150 million years.

Cultures blossom round his head and fall to bits under his feet. Indifferent to all the discouragements of time, learning a little, but not much, from every rebuff, in the evolutionary way, turning everything to his advantage, or trying to, being nothing really but a total commitment to salvaging life against all the odds, perpetuating life, renewing the opportunities for all the energies of life, at any cost. Plenty of other qualities, some of them dubious enough, spin round that nucleus, but the trajectory is constant. The sperm looking for the egg – to combine with every human thing that is not itself, and to create a new self, with multiplied genetic potential, in a renewed world.

In the literature, the playful-savage burlesque of Trickster's inadequacies and setbacks, which is a distinguishing feature of the style, is an integral part of the deep humane realism. And it is this folk-note of playfulness, really of affection and fellow-feeling, which does not date, no matter how peculiar and extreme the adventures.

All the annihilations and transformations that befall Trickster are reminiscent of what used to happen to some gods. This agon is like the perpetual replay archive of all that ever happened to living organisms, as if all life could pool its experience in such beings, and it defines the plane Trickster lives on, the dimension of psychic life through which he fares forward, destruction-prone but indestructible, and more than happy, like the spirit of the natural world, a green endlessly resurrected god in a wolf-mask, only intermittently conscious perhaps, blundering through every possible mistake and every possible sticky end, experimenting with every impulse, like a gambling machine of mutations, but inaccessible to despair. And rescuing through everything the great possibility.

The morality of the sperm is undeniably selfish, from all points of view but its own and the future's ('A standing cock knows no conscience' – Scots proverb) and innate in it is a certain hardness of ego, over-purposeful, nickel-nosed, defensively plated, all attention rigidly outward and forward: the ego of the sign for Mars. But the paradox is, this spirit has at the same time no definable ego at all – only an obscure bundle of inheritance, a sackful of impulses jostling to explore their scope. And from beginning to end, the dynamo of this little mob of selves is a single need to search – for marriage with its creator, a marriage that will be a self-immolation in new, greater and other life.

This spirit of the sperm, as Trickster, may be generalised, simultaneously base and divine, but it is not at all abstract. His recurrent adventure is like a master plan, one of the deepest imprints in our nature, if not the deepest, and one of our most useful ideas. We use it all the time, quite spontaneously, like a tool, at every stage of our psychological recovery or growth. It supplies a path to the God-seeker, whose spiritual ecstasy hasn't altogether lost the sexual *samadhi*[1] of the sperm. A little lower, like the

---

1 A Sanskrit word, meaning, in Hinduism and Buddhism, a state of such intense concentration that the distinction between self and not-self disappears (see also 12 June 1993). In 'Strangers', a poem written at about the same time as this essay, Hughes wrote:

The sea-trout, upstaring, in trance,
Absorb everything and forget it
Into a blank of bliss.
And this is the real samadhi – wordless, levitated.

'Sexual *samadhi*' may thus have something in common with the Elizabethan concept of coition as a 'little death'.

hand of his Fate, it guides the Hero through his Hero-Tale, embroils him, mortal as he is, in tragedy, but sustains him with tragic joy. Beneath the Hero Tale, like the satyr behind the tragedy, is the Trickster Saga, a series of tragicomedies. It is a series, and never properly tragic, because Trickster, daemon of phallic energy, bearing the spirit of the sperm, is repetitive and indestructible. No matter what fatal mistakes he makes, and what tragic flaws he indulges, he refuses to let death detain him, but always circumvents it, and never despairs. Too full of ideas for sexual *samadhi*, too unresolved for spiritual ecstasy, too deathless for tragic joy, he rattles along in biological glee.

Each of these figures casts the shadows of the others. The Trickster, the Hero, and the Saint on the Path, meet in the Holy Fool. None of them operates within a closed society, but on the epic stage, in the draughty wholeness of Creation. And each of them, true to that little sperm, serpent at the centre of the whole Russian Doll complex, works to redeem us, to heal us, and even, in a sense to resurrect us, in our bad times.

This particular view of the Trickster Tale was my guiding metaphor when I set out to make what I could of *Crow*. The form proposed itself, by way of the unique possibilities of the style and tone, as a means of domesticating many things that interested me, and that were interested in me, and that I could find no other way of coming to terms with at the time. And I was conscious, too, that the overall theme offered a good outcome for me personally.[2]

I don't know if this account will modify readings of such pieces as 'Truth Kills Everybody'. That poem seems to attract particularly sharp dislike.

'Truth Kills Everybody' records one of Crow's face-to-face encounters with the object of his search: the spirit link with his creator. It is an inner link, naturally, and the meeting is internal.

The hostility and energy of the confrontation are the measure of a gap – the difference in electrical potential between the limited, benighted-with-expectations-and-preconceptions ego of Crow at this point, and the thing he seeks to unite himself with. Much is projected. The mood is the appropriate one of the Old Adam *in extremis* – where shocking things are done and undergone in a sort of dreadful, reckless glee, with wild laughter.

Since Crow's understanding is so inadequate, and his procedure so mistaken, the thing defends itself with successive cuttlefish ink-clouds of illusion – composite symbols, each one recombining the various changing factors of the fight, in a progression.

Crow can either give up, and escape back into his limited self-conceit, or he can press on till he breaks through to what he wants. But since what he wants — to lose himself in that spirit-link with his creator – means the end of his ego-shell, then that break-through will destroy him as the Crow he was. But he does break through, and he is duly exploded. That is the chief positive step that Crow ever takes, but even this he takes wrongly.

Taking it too suddenly, unprepared and ignorantly, by force, he can't control the self-transformation. The spirit-light emerges as shattering flame. So his momentary gain

---

2 *The Life and Songs of the Crow* was to have been an 'epic folk-tale' in prose, studded with hundreds of poems. The tale drew not only on trickster mythology, but on the whole body of myth, folklore and literature with which Hughes was familiar. Like all quest narratives, it was to end with the protagonist emerging from the darkness of his crimes and sufferings into a raw wisdom, the healing of the split within him, and the recovery of his own deepest humanity, all expressed in images of ego-death, rebirth. and marriage.

He had written about the first two-thirds of the story when the second great tragedy in his life, the deaths of his partner Assia and their daughter Shura (to whom *Crow* was dedicated), caused him to abort the project, since he no longer felt that he could validate in his own experience the happy ending which the story demanded. He published in *Crow* only a selection of the already-written poems, ending at the point where Crow's regeneration was about to begin. He later came to see that widespread misinterpretation of *Crow* was inevitable, given the absence of the larger context. See 'The Story of Crow' in Sagar, *The Laughter of Foxes*.

destroys him, and is itself lost. He reappears elsewhere as the same old Crow, or rather as not quite the same. A Crow of more fragments, more precariously glued together, more vulnerable.

In this context, the annihilation has nothing to do with the annihilations in Nazi Germany, or even in a fox-hunt. The images were all taken from memorable dreams, which in this poem I tried to set in an interpretative context. It's possible, I suppose, that I interpreted wrongly, but remembering the physical effect the assembling of this poem had on me, I believe not. That's neither here nor there, I know, in what a reader finds on the page, but it persuades me that any sense of ease in the contemplation of annihilation, in this poem, is not mine.

Crow is like most of us – he directs involuntary blinkered aggression against what he most wants to unite with in himself, and what most wants to unite with him. But at least he doesn't displace his distorted attack sideways, and project it against some outer substitute. In this case he has the wit to recognise the cause of his fear and fascination, and to hang onto it. So he gets somewhere, for a while.

The Annihilation in this poem is part of 'the fury of a spiritual existence', in Blake's sense. It is like all the other misfortunes Crow undergoes, the deaths he dies, throughout his adventures. They are the sort that pass, maybe, without the flicker of an eyelid, but which nevertheless decide, I think, our minute by minute ability to live.

Naturally, what isn't there in the verse will have to stay invisible, (just as what isn't there in the reader will never be found in any verse) no matter how the intended drift is explained. But a more graphic idea of the context – of the traditional convention I set out to exploit, as far as I could, and of the essential line and level of the narrative, which might make some misreadings less likely – ought to have been part of those published fragments.

'Close reading' is evidently not enough to save us from misreading, or to break through the projection of fixed ideas, conditioned reflexes, preconceptions, etc. which often seem to be the only lenses we have – witness Mr Brinton's[3] misquotation of 'Truth Kills Everybody'. In one main sense, that poem is about just the sort of misreading it seems to provoke: the cuttlefish ink-clouds, behind which the real nature of the thing escapes, are Rorschach blots, of a kind.

3 Ian Brinton subsequently became Head of English at Dulwich College, and Editor of The Use of English.

Appendix IX

John Carey, then Merton Professor at Oxford, reviewed *Shakespeare and the Goddess of Complete Being* in the *Sunday Times* on 5 April 1992, under the heading 'Shaman Scandal'.

Carey began his review with the statement that 'the ideas for this book came to Ted Hughes in a dream'. Hughes had described the dream in question as merely a 'contributory incident' in the proofs of the book, and dropped it altogether from the published text.[1] The ideas in fact came from a lifetime of as deep a familiarity with Shakespeare as anyone has ever had, from a remarkable knowledge of world mythology, from a long relationship with the Swedish theatre director Donya Feuer, and from his 1971 introduction to *A Choice of Shakespeare's Verse*, with its crucial interpretations of *Venus and Adonis* and *The Rape of Lucrece*. Carey's failure to mention any of these is indicative of his determination, from the start, to be as reductive as possible.

After a brief, garbled, tongue-in-cheek summary of the book, ignoring all Hughes' disclaimers about his readings having only a shadowy life behind the more conventional and accessible meanings of the plays, he concludes that the book is 'tedious mumbo-jumbo', 'a preposterous pick 'n' mix myth-pack', 'an act of grotesque, donkey-eared vandalism'.

It must be said that the majority of reviewers shared his contempt. Hughes' reply, published in the same paper on 19 April under the heading 'Battling over the Bard', is reproduced here.

Recently, on The Late Show, I watched a self-confessed feminist, laughingly paralysed by her fixed ideas about life in general and about me in particular. In my book, Shakespeare and The Goddess of Complete Being, I have translated the Complete Works into the holiest book of all feminism's Holy Books, and Lisa Jardine did not know how to open it.[2]

Two Sundays ago, John Carey did no better in the Sunday Times, in what he told readers about that book. Bigotries bushed over his spectacles, he brayed about "vandalism" and lashed out with his hooves.

He demonstrated as a glitzy public entertainment his astonishing (at least, in an Oxford Prof of English it's surely astonishing) inability to see that Shakespeare is not one writer but two. Not simply and exclusively one of the greatest realists (like Tolstoy), but also, at the same time, the greatest of our mythic poets (like Keats). Which is exactly what Tolstoy didn't like about him. Tolstoy hated in Shakespeare what Carey cannot see. He hated the musical dominance of the mythic substructure. He called its effects (because he couldn't see the thing itself, either) "depraved" and "unnatural". They were the cause of what he regarded as hopelessly false characterisation, ludicrously unreal situations and plots – the cause, in general, of the pervasive "great evil" that he found throughout Shakespeare. Notoriously, Tolstoy connected the "depravity of imagination", in art as a whole, with the "evil" of music.

He wrote The Kreutzer Sonata, like an illustration in a sermon, to demonstrate just this. In The Kreutzer Sonata he "proves" how this "evil" of art is epitomised in its

---

1 See 9 July 1992.
2 Lisa Jardine (b.1944), the daughter of Jacob Bronowski, published *Reading Shakespeare Historically* (Routledge) in 1996. She is now Professor of Renaissance Studies, and Director of the Centre for Editing Lives and Letters, at Queen Mary, University of London.

demonic source, the "evil" of music, and how this music is inseparable from, as if it emerged from, sexuality, but in particular from female sexuality – from her ruthless (he called it a "devil") need to reproduce life. In this way, he transposed his hatred of the "mythic music" in Shakespeare, through his terror of "the dreadful thing" in music, through his hatred of female sexuality, to his hatred of birth itself. In other words, for Tolstoy at that point, life itself had become the "evil thing".

We prefer to reverse this Calvinist madness and re-name the source of life, calling it good instead of evil, whereupon female sexuality became a blessing, not a curse. So, following Tolstoy's argument in reverse, we convert music to a blessing, likewise, as it emerges from this source. Music rises from the origins of consciousness into visible imagery as the vital patterns of myth, which becomes thereby the original blessed language of life imposing a dance figure on its meanings. The mythic poet speaks not in the language of the realist's negotiation with outer circumstances, but directly the language of the sources of life. Which is why we value Eliot, Yeats, Keats, Coleridge's early poems, Blake, Milton and Shakespeare in a category separate from all the others. But for Carey, in Shakespeare, this language does not exist. The only play of Shakespeare's that Tolstoy could half tolerate was Othello. To express his hatred of female sexuality and music, Tolstoy stole (unconsciously) the situation of Othello for The Kreutzer Sonata. But whereas Shakespeare's Othello (the one Shakespeare hero who positively dislikes music) threw away "a pearl richer than all his tribe", and knew too late that he had made a hideous mistake, Tolstoy, not satisfied that his destruction of female sexuality, in his tremendous story, was final enough, went on to write a fanatic moral tirade, virtually in defence of the murder. This utter renunciation of what Tolstoy called the "evil" thing finds its pallid, remote but unmistakeable [sic] echo in Carey's three-fold denial of the mythic poet in Shakespeare.

My book simply traces the organised shape and working of the mythic complex in this other Shakespeare's head, and shows how it expresses itself through the work of the great realist. This complex, which is the mythic substructure of Shakespeare's imagination, is in turn inevitably, in the thick of the religious crisis of that time the mythic structure of Reformation Christianity and of the matrix of pre-Christian religions from which it issued, as they were mediated through his temperament. This religious inheritance shaped every Western society, and the minds of their populations, and still largely determines our own. Only Carey, or his like, could pick all this up (easy, it's nothing to him) and crush it together into his tabloid, popsicle phrase, "a preposterous pick 'n' mix myth-pack". Or dismiss its presence in the plays as "an occult ingredient". It's irrelevant to him. It was body and soul for Eliot, Yeats, Keats, Coleridge, Blake, Milton — in an obvious way — as for Shakespeare. But Carey stares at it like Caspar Hauser at a box of alphabet letters,[2] or like a bouncy, pink-necked young subaltern of the Raj squinting at a Hindu temple. It's all "mumbo jumbo" he says. You have to wonder what he tells his students. And how he marks their papers.

He tells Sunday Times readers that none of Shakespeare's plays fits my theme because none of the tragic heroes happens to be cold-blooded — which according to him I have made an absolute first requirement. They're all hot-blooded, he says (seeming to laugh). But Carey misreads everything, skipping along, snatching for soundbites. Readers can judge for themselves. What has to happen to Hamlet's hot blood before he can banish Ophelia to that nunnery (and to her death) and frighten his mother so that she thinks he's going to kill her (as indirectly he does bring about her death)? What happens to Othello's hot-blooded love, for him to be able to kill in cold blood the Desdemona he worships? He has to plunge, as he says, into the "icy current and compulsive course" of the frozen state of will that can reject and not feel. How does the royal champion Macbeth steel himself (or freeze his heart) to kill King Duncan? How does hot-blooded Lear flash-freeze his adoration of Cordelia, so he can banish

2   Caspar Hauser was a German youth who claimed to have grown up in total isolation in a dungeon.

her? How does Timon bring his great hot love for Athens and his friends to the reversal of temperature at which he can curse them to "destruction" (and all mankind with them).

Shakespeare goes to some lengths to describe what has to happen to Coriolanus's hot-blooded devotion to Rome in the name of his mother and wife before he can become inhuman enough to roast them all to ashes, as he intends. How does Antony's burning passion for Cleopatra turn to the cold steel that tries to kill her? How does Posthumous freeze his heart against all women and send a hit-man to kill his adored wife? How does Leontes anaesthetise what turns out to have been his great love for his wife Hermione to the numb point where he can strive to condemn her to death, while he throws her baby into the wilderness? Each of these plays, it seems to me, turns on this moment, where the hot blood becomes . . . whatever it takes to murder the one on whose love your life depends. My book merely analyses what lies under that moment. Carey says it does not exist. Which plays has he been reading all these years?

Carey regards this change, from the passionate lover to the insane murderer, which always happens at a particular, sudden moment, as some daft invention of mine – a "gory antic", as he describes it, out of my Crow. He would know, if he knew what he ought to know, that my Crow is Bran of the Tower Ravens, Bran who was Apollo (a Crow god) plus his son, the Crow demi-god Asclepius the Healer (whose mother was the white Crow goddess Coronis), was the god-king, a Crow god, of early Britain, where he was also the Llud who was Llyr who was Lear. More mumbo jumbo to make him smile.

That rictus of derision on Carey's face distorts his mind's eye too. He goes through my book, sticking his tongue out at everything, with the mental freedom of one of those blinded donkeys that spend their days plodding in a small circle, turning a millstone, and then, when they're let out into the open landscape, go on plodding around in the same small circle.

Appendix X

Introductory and concluding paragraphs in 'A Brief Guide' to *Shakespeare and the Goddess of Complete Being* sent by Hughes to Michael Kustow. Born in 1939, Kustow joined the Royal Shakespeare Company in 1962, and worked with Peter Brook, whose biography he subsequently wrote. In 1973 he became an Associate Director of the National Theatre, where he staged a Platform Performance of *Gaudete* in 1977. From 1982 he was the first Commissioning Editor of Arts for Channel 4 television for seven years. Since then he has worked as an independent writer and director.

5 Jan 94

Dear Michael,

Here is a brief crib, to open up my book and guide your eye to the essentials of my argument. Once those have been grasped, everything else is simply filling in the details — corroborating those essentials. If I could have relied on readers to grasp the essentials, and fill in the details out of their own knowledge, as you see my book could have been a hundred pages — or maybe only these ten. In the book, I went doggedly though each play — persuaded that ninety nine readers out of a hundred who might feel interested in the idea would be uncertain in their memory of the plot detail of most of the plays, and the hundredth, an expert, would resist my specialised approach with other preconceptions. The argument is not really very complicated. If you know the mechanics of the myths, and their role in the religions, it's extremely simple, since they provide all the engineering of the basic Equation, that has not changed in five thousand years. That background, knowledge, though, seems to be in short supply. It is the kind of knowledge that has been anathematized in our English tradition since the 17th Century. So prejudice against is heaped over ignorance of, for many readers. But maybe that is changing slowly.

An important part of my argument in the book is that Shakespeare's dramas give form and expression to a balancing act between mutually hostile religious currents of immense force.

This balancing act rode what was in fact a moment of crisis (from Henry VIII's rejection of Katherine to the Civil War) in the conflict between two religious myths — a conflict in which one of the myths finally overpowered the other (and attempted to exterminate the other).

A necessary background to the character and behaviour of these myths is the history of their conflict — which goes back to the religious revolution in early Sumeria where the Jehovah-like God Marduk overthrew the Great Goddess Tiamat and made the Universe out of her remains. This revolution recurred in Old Testament Israel where Jehovah overthrew the Great Goddess Anath/ Ashteroth/Astarte etc etc. Secreted in the Bible, it recurred again at the Reformation where the God of militant Protestantism/ Calvanism [sic] overthrew the Great Whore of Babylon alias the Papal Empire in Northern Europe. It was naturalised into English political and domestic life when Henry VIII rejected the saintly Katherine, his Catholic Queen, and opened England to the Protestant takeover, which duly followed — culminating eventually in the Civil War.

At each point, the basic situation — rejection and attempted annihilation of the Goddess and all her representatives by a Puritan Male Deity — is that of the opening of Shakespeare's TRAGIC EQUATION. His dramas explore the psychological consequences of that initiating act.

Once naturalised into English life, by Henry VIII's decision, the conflict worked out in religious/political/social consequences that put England through what I describe as an internal 'somersault' — where what began as a Catholic nation, part of the Papal Empire, ended up as a Puritan nation, religiously self-determined and independent. I sketch this aspect of the conflict, as it affected the life and psychology of individual citizens — their dream-life and neuroses. Each of the two myths involved has a particular story. Historically, and psychologically, one of the myths (that of the Male God) grew out of the other (the myth of the Goddess and her divine child). But as religions they are seperate [sic], and so their myths have been seperated, and each regards the other as its enemy. In the Reformation, as in Modern Northern Ireland.

Shakespeare naturalised these two myths in his two long narrative poems: VENUS AND ADONIS and LUCRECE. His great coup was to fit these two stories together, as a dramatic plot. In this way he unearthed The Tragic Equation. That is to say, when he demonstrates how the tragic action of the myth of the Puritan God emerges inevitably out of the situation of the Goddess and her Divine Child (who becomes her divine consort), he has restored the two myths, the two stories, to the single psychological continuum of cause and effect which created them in the first place as the most inclusive image of mankind's innately tragic psychological life.

***

A thorough chart of the events, personalities and decrees of the day would suggest a seething matrix of one big event struggling to happen — out of which Shakespeare's figures and situations rise like dreams of explanation and prophesy, i.e. like the apparitions out of the witch's cauldron.

Maybe the great unspoken protagonist is the proleptic Ghost of Cromwell, attended by Milton's subconscious mind — as Lear with his Fool. He staggers through the plays, trying on the masks of the various heroes, while voices out of the future strike at him like lightning and pelt him like roaring gusts of wind and rain etc, and Charles I scampers in and out naked, already lost, looking for the womb that will bear him, like a soul in the Bardo. Well, what we need is a team of apprentice Shakespeares, and it could be a good show.

The background of the myths seems confusing only to readers who don't recognise the powerlines running through it. In the one lineage, already mentioned, the current comes through the Sumerian God Marduk, to the militant Jehovah/Christ of Lutheran Protestantism, who rode into battle finally as the War-God of Cromwell. In the other lineage, the current comes through Tiamat, the Great Goddess destroyed by Marduk. From her, it descends in four streams, (four that are relevant to my argument about what is relevant to Shakespeare's use of the Equation). One of these was the mythos of Isis, which pervaded the whole Mediterranean world — and so spread to the British Isles, saturating the foundations of the Celtic (Irish and Arthurian) tradition. Another was the mythos of Venus and Adonis, which derived directly from the Astarte/Baal variants of the Middle East, and also spread throughout the Mediterranean. Another was the mythos of Attis and Cybele, the most extreme variant of the Venus and Adonis Branch, which also spread — as a religion favoured within the Roman Empire — throughout what would become the Christian world. It became especially significant for Christianity in that its main cult centre was Tarsus, where Saul grew up. St Paul's attitudes, habits of feeling, and in general the temperamental imprint that he set on Pauline Christianity, sprang directly from his early immersion in the fanaticism of the Attis Cult. The fourth stream came through the Eleusinian Mysteries, in a form of the Great Goddess cult that pervaded the classical world (and met its own Reformation, in a sense, in fifth Century BC Athens, where the resulting conflict helped shape Athenian tragedy), and emerged into Gnosticism as early Christianity's most serious rival, producing the myth of Sophia which gives Shakespeare the basic structure and function of his transcendental coda. Christianity digested all these Goddess influences, and braided them into its own single current — not impossible since they were all variants of a single religious idea: the myth of the Great Goddess and her Divine Child either male or female. Where the child is male he grows up to be sacrificed as her consort.

Eventually, at the Reformation, Christianity restored the situation of the Goddess and her divine child/consort (stage 1 of the Tragic Equation) to the Full Tragic Equation, as first laid down in the myth of Marduk and Tiamat, by allowing the consort to mature into a Marduk/Jehovah — who destroyed the Great Goddess.

All the myths referred to, in other words, are members of this single family — tragic family — and only need to be learned for their actions and significance (in modern life too) to be understood. And for their dynamic presence in Shakespeare's operations to be appreciated.

Appendix XI

'Pollen for a Waste Land'. A review of *Winter Pollen* in *Resurgence* no. 164 (1994) by Keith Sagar.

In the last ten years literary criticism has virtually disappeared from publishers' lists, where it has been replaced by critical theory. The theorists, having demonstrated to their own satisfaction that there is no such thing as imagination or meaning or Nature, have withdrawn from the real world (there being no such thing) into their self-chosen Purgatory where they walk in a ring, eyes fixed on the feet of the one in front. In the midst of this Waste Land, this winter world, Ted Hughes' new book comes like a miraculous blessing of pollen.

The greatest poets have always been the greatest critics, for the simple reason that imagination requires imagination to respond to it. The poet struggles to awaken the atrophied or undeveloped imagination of the reader. But when the reader is as fully awake as the poet, the sparks begin to fly. Most poets have lacked the time or inclination to produce more than a smattering of informal insights. Those who have produced substantial criticism – Coleridge, Eliot, Lawrence – operate on a plane far beyond academic criticism. Few people, even among those alive to Hughes' stature as a poet, have bothered to seek out his scattered, inaccessible criticism.

We owe a great debt to Bill Scammell, first for persuading Hughes to allow the occasional prose to be collected, then for selecting so impeccably: also to Faber for producing such a large and handsome book at, these days, a not unreasonable price. With the publication of this book, hot on the heels of his *Shakespeare and the Goddess of Complete Being* (which John Moat described in *Resurgence* as the first proper hearing given to Shakespeare), Ted Hughes establishes himself as the next in this sequence. *Winter Pollen* is the most important collection of literary essays since Eliot's *Selected Essays* and Lawrence's *Phoenix* in the thirties.

The book begins with some early autobiographical pieces, testifying to the importance of the spirit of place – the West Yorkshire moors and industrial valleys – in forming Hughes' imagination, providing him with a stock of stark images which were easy to match with those his father fed to him from his experiences of the horrors of the Dardanelles, images of a constant struggle between vitality and death. The fox soon became his totem. Reading English at Cambridge it was a charred fox which told him in a dream that he was killing his inner demons. In his third year he changed to Archaeology and Anthropology, an area of study which not only became fruitful for his poetry, but earned him a living through the sixties, when he reviewed books in these fields in the weeklies almost every month.

Perhaps the most significant of these was his review of Mircea Eliade's *Shamanism* in 1964. The function of the shaman is to visit the spirit world on behalf of the tribe: 'The results, when the shaman returns to the living, are some display of healing power, or a clairvoyant piece of information. The cathartic effect on the audience, and the refreshing of their religious feeling, must be profound.' Hughes saw that all he admired most in poetry, and had been striving for in his own, was shamanic, that shamans were engaged in the same Heroic Quest: 'The shamans seem to undergo, at will and at phenomenal intensity, and with practical results, one of the main regenerating dramas of the human psyche; the fundamental poetic event.' The nature of that event, whereby, insofar as he can psychically correct himself, the poet heals and fertilizes others, is the subject of most of the essays.

The greater the poet he is discussing, the deeper his engagement, the more exciting his insights. The process culminates in his recent essay on Eliot (the first poet to explore our desacralized landscape, to stand 'at the centre of revelation in this age'), his new long essay on Coleridge (here published for the first time), and his phenomenal book on Shakespeare (here represented by one chapter and by the 1971 essay from which it evolved).

When imagination is allied to high intelligence, and plays upon such a body of learning, the result is wisdom. Scammell speaks of Hughes' willingness to take on 'the very largest social, aesthetic and metaphysical issues . . . Each of the pieces is rewarding in its own right, quite often dense with intellectual excitement as Hughes grapples with the elusive stuff – verbal, social, physical, psychic – that goes to make up creation; and each, as well as throwing light on his own poems and habits of thought, marks a point in the larger trajectory of his own poetic "myth", or schema, by means of which he position himself in the modern chaos.'

That schema has become steadily more ecological. There are pieces here which will appeal directly to *Resurgence* readers: Hughes' lengthy 1970 review, for example, of Max Nicholson's *The Environmental Revolution*, which reads like a vivid high-speed scan of all the future preoccupations of *Resurgence*: 'the salvaging of all nature from the pressures and oversights of our runaway population, and from the monstrous anti-Nature that we have created, the now nearly autonomous Technosphere . . . the mindless greed of big industry, and the shameless dealing of the government departments who promote and protect it . . . the industrial poisoning of the water systems . . . the opportunism of some farmers, who act as if history were finished, and their soil would not be needed after another thirty years . . . the cynicism of the chemical industries', the confident ignorance of economists, and much more; but against this 'the re-emergence of Nature as the Great Goddess of mankind', the scientific confirmation of the old myths and poetic vision of nature as a single organism, the re-assembling of the scattered dry bones of insulated specialisms.

The basic Western myth is the quest for the lost life: 'when the modern mediumistic artist looks into his crystal, he sees always the same. He sees the last nightmare of mental disintegration and spiritual emptiness . . . But he may see something else. He may see a vision of the real Eden, "excellent as at the first day", the draughty radiant Paradise of the animals, which is the actual Earth, in the actual Universe . . Eden when it is poisoned to the point of death, its efforts to be itself are new in every second. This is what will survive, if anything can . . . But while the mice in the field are listening to the Universe, and moving in the body of nature, where every living cell is sacred to every other, and all are interdependent, the Developer is peering at the field through a visor, and behind him stands the whole army of madmen's ideas, and shareholders, impatient to cash-in the world.' The proper business of both art and science is to discover, and of education to teach 'a proper knowledge of the sacred wholeness of Nature, and a proper alignment of our behaviour within her laws.'

A major obstacle to such knowledge and alignment has been the anthropocentric assumption by Western culture of the God-given right to judge nature by human moral standards, and to condemn her as 'red in tooth and claw'. Our sentimental nature poets, turning a blind eye to predation, have inadvertently encouraged this. Hughes sets himself from the beginning to look nature in the face, not to extenuate anything, but to try to see her in her own terms, not ours. He was appalled by the 'world made of blood' he forced himself to contemplate, a world brimming with woe, 'a cortege of mourning and lament'. In the worst years, he sought ways, under the influence of Buddhism, to detach himself from the world and the body, but found that such detachment was a greater violation than the suffering of incarnation. Gradually, his vision of nature cleared, allowing him to see violence in nature as 'within the law' – 'The tiger blesses with a fang.'

It is not the violence of the natural world which should appal us, rather the violence which has been done to our '"divine" faculty of spontaneous allegiance to the creator's law' in the name of 'our customary social and humanitarian values'. These values serve to 'protect the familiar human condition, that is alienated from its spiritual being as it is from its animal integrity and from a lucid acceptance of the true nature of the activities by which it survives', activities such as those conducted on our behalf in the abattoirs and factory farms, not to mention 'our extraordinary readiness to exploit, oppress, torture and kill our own kind, refining on the way all the varieties of the lie and all the pleasures of watching others suffer, and violating in the process every law and sacred trust'.

At the end of this essay, 'Poetry and Violence', Hughes declares his allegiance to the movement which in the last few decades has brought almost to a mass market such formerly esoteric material as sacred texts, mythologies, collections of folklore: 'countless changes have slowly but surely returned the Paleolithic world, the Pagan or natural world, to "sacred" status.' He hails the 'massive resurgence of something as archaic and yet as up to date – as timeless, and as global – as the "sacred" biology of woman . . . And the universal movement in which all these different currents make one tide is the movement to save the Earth by a reformed good sense and sensitivity – to correct the régime of our "customary social and humanitarian values", as it advertises itself, and rescue not only humankind from it, but all other living things: to rescue "life" itself.'

But in drawing attention to Hughes' contribution to ecological thinking and polemic, I risk giving a distorted sense of the book as a whole, and of the importance of Hughes as a writer of prose or verse. His essential subject is the poetic imagination, which unifies inner and outer realities, and seeks to heal the split of Western dualistic consciousness. The poet seeks metaphors for his own nature, and in the great poet those metaphors turn out to be universal. We are all criminals against nature, including our own nature, being judged by great literature. Unlike the prose ecologist, the poet is not handing down truths from a position of privileged intelligence, but is himself a representative criminal on trial at the bar of his own imagination, submitting to its correction. His poetry might be at one stage the cross-examination, the display of the evidence against himself, at another the confession, at another the judgment and punishment, and finally, in the greatest poets, the renewal, the return to the world, shaman-like, with healing gifts.

Marvellous as these essays are, one must go to the poems both for the seeds and the fruits of the essays. It was in the poems of the seventies that Hughes struggled painfully towards a biocentric vision, to accept and be accepted by the goddess. The prayer-like epilogue poems in *Gaudete* were the fruit of that struggle:

> The grim badger with armorial mask
> Biting spade-steel, teeth and jaw-strake shattered
> Draws that final shuddering battle-cry
> Out of its backbone.
>
> Me too,
> Let me be one of your warriors.
>
> Let your home
> Be my home. Your people
> My people.

Through this long and painful process Hughes earned the right and the ability (more than any other poet known to me) to fertilize and sensitize the imagination of the reader and for that reader to resacralize the world. There is no richer gift than such poetry. Hughes tends to work in large mythic sequences which cannot be represented in anthologies or even in his own *Selected Poems*. The book I would therefore recommend (apart from his splendid books for younger readers) is the recently published *Three Books* (Faber), which contains *Cave Birds*, *Remains of Elmet* and *River*. These are holy books in the sense Lawrence intended when he wrote 'a book is a holy thing and must be made so again.' The last poem in that book, as in the *Selected Poems*, is called 'That Morning', and records an experience in Alaska, an experience of what Blake would have called 'fourfold vision':

Solemn to stand there in the pollen light
Waist-deep in wild salmon swaying massed
As from the hand of God. There the body

Separated, golden and imperishable,
From its doubting thought – a spirit-beacon
Lit by the power of the salmon

That came on, came on, and kept on coming
As if we flew slowly, their formation
Lifting us toward some dazzle of blessing

One wrong thought might darken. As if the fallen
World and salmon were over. As if these
Were the imperishable fish

That had let the world pass away –

There, in a mauve light of drifted lupins,
They hung in the cupped hands of mountains

Made of tingling atoms. It had happened.
Then for a sign that we were where we were
Two gold bears came down and swam like men

Beside us. And dived like children.
And stood in deep water as on a throne
Eating pierced salmon off their talons.

So we found the end of our journey.

So we stood, alive in the river of light
Among the creatures of light, creatures of light.

Appendix XII

'Hear it Again'. Composed at the request of Matthew Evans, Chairman of the Library and Information Commission, July 1997.

HEAR IT AGAIN

'For out of olde feldes, as men seyth,
Cometh al this newe corne yer by yere,
And out of olde bokes, in good feyth,
Cometh al this newe science that men lere.'
Chaucer: *The Parlement of Foules*

Fourteen centuries have learned,
From charred remains, that what took place
When Alexandria's library burned
Brain-damaged the human race.

Whatever escaped
Was hidden by bookish monks in their damp cells
Hunted by Alfred dug for by Charlemagne
Got through the Dark Ages little enough but enough
For Dante and Chaucer sitting up all night
looking for light.

A Serbian Prof's insanity,[1]
Commanding guns, to split the heart,
His and his people's, tore apart
The Sarajevo library.[2]

Tyrants know where to aim
As Hitler poured his petrol and tossed matches
Stalin collected the bards —
In other words the mobile and only libraries —
of all those enslaved peoples from the Black to
the Bering Sea
And made a bonfire
Of the mainsprings of national identities to melt
the folk into one puddle
And the three seconds of the present moment
By massacring those wordy fellows whose memories were
bigger than armies.

---

1 In the copy he sent to me Hughes inserted here the following note: '— An ex Eng. Lit Prof and famous critic (Serbian). The other half of Karidzik for a while. Since shot himself.' Radovan Karadžić is a former Bosnian Serb politician. He is currently detained in the United Nations Detention Unit of Scheveningen in The Hague, accused of war crimes.
2 In a second note Hughes wrote: 'the great treasure-house of Jugoslavia – and the Serbs in particular'.

Where any nation starts awake
Books are the memory. And it's plain
Decay of libraries is like
Alzheimer's in the nation's brain.

>And in my own day in my own land
>I have heard the fiery whisper: 'We are here
>To destroy the Book
>To destroy the rooted stock of the Book and
>The Book's perennial vintage, destroy it
>Not with a hammer or a sickle
>And not exactly according to Mao who also
>Drained the skull of adult and adolescent
>To build a shining new society
>With the empties . . .'

For this one's dreams and that one's acts
For all who've failed or aged beyond
The reach of teachers, here are found
The inspiration and the facts.

>As we all know and have heard all our lives
>Just as we've heard that here.

Even the most misfitting child
Who's chanced upon the library's worth,
Sits with the genius of the Earth
And turns the key to the whole world.

>Hear it again.

Ted Hughes, July 1997

Appendix XIII

'The Hart of the Mystery', *Guardian*, 5 July 1997

With the countryside lobby's marches set to reach London next week, Ted Hughes argues that it is the pact between farmers and animals created by hunting that preserves thriving numbers of red deer and foxes in areas such as Exmoor.

In the present debate about hunting with hounds, one big question is in danger of getting lost. If hunting is to be banned, what then happens to the deer and the foxes?

Dick Lloyd, the historian of Exmoor's red deer, has produced a graph which shows how the ups and downs of the West Country deer population have matched the ups and downs of the staghunt for the last 350 years. The political aspects of this process are no small part of it. Since they took shape with William the Conqueror, and stepped into the open during the Civil War, it is not hard to see how they have come to bedevil the modern issue. But simpler mechanisms are enough to be going on with.

In early times, the red deer were preserved, nominally for the king, by inheritors of the baronial rights, who organised their own hunt under royal licence. In those days, the threat to the deer came from the other side – from the indigenous farmers and enterprising young countrymen, those inheritors of English Saxon attitudes towards what had imposed itself, brutally, as a foreign army of occupation. Such men saw the deer as chattels of the enemy. Through successive reigns, these opposing positions became entrenched in the tradition of country life. Hence the legends.

Up to the Civil War, the arrangement worked well from the deer's point of view. Then the Civil War broke it up, and the hunt's protection evaporated. The West Country red deer population immediately collapsed. By 1660 it was almost extinct. One doesn't have to suppose that social vengeance prompted the massacre. Human nature was quite enough – as with animal populations everywhere. What endangers profit will be exterminated. What can be cashed in on some market will be feverishly cashed in – i.e. exterminated. This tendency may be out of control in our modern world, but it was always there. The rare thing, the unnatural and usually impossible thing, is to hit on a system of control *that works*.

After the Civil War, and before the Exmoor herd disappeared completely, a north Devon family, who inherited some of the baronial outlook if not all the rights, formed the North Devon Staghounds and reintroduced organised hunting. With deer imported from Germany, the herd quickly recovered. When the population reached something around 250 it levelled off, and for the next 125 years never fell much below 200. This now seems like quite a small number for such a large area of wild country. But the hunt's system of control obviously had its problems. What had nearly annihilated the herd after the Civil War was still in the offing and waiting for its moment – which came.

When the North Devon Staghounds fizzled out in 1825, their small powers of protection went, and the deer population collapsed just as surely as before. By 1850, it had fallen to about 50 – most of them said to be maimed and peppered with gunshot wounds.

No doubt partly in response to this crisis, the Devon and Somerset Staghounds then came into being. Farmers had participated in the hunt before. But either by policy or natural development or both, farmers now make up the main body of the new hunt. In this period, staghunting became the sport and concern of the ordinary farmer. As a result farmers, and with them the country people in general, began to change their minds about the deer. And it was here that the mysterious thing occurred – something that could never have been contrived by legislation or in any way enforced. Everybody began to protect the deer. The exceptions were too few to make a difference. The staghunt had been appropriated somehow by the whole West Country farming way of life. As a result, all north Devon and Somerset became virtually a free-range deer park. And the deer did more than recover. By the end of the 19th century, when a second hunt, the Tiverton Staghounds, was formed based on the first, the herd numbered close on 1,500. In 1905, 300 could be exported to Germany – as a surplus.

Then came the First World War, and the deer population dipped again, this time under a deliberate policy of the two hunts, to protect crops and supply food. In 1917, a third hunt, the Quantocks Staghounds, joined in the war effort. In the Second World War, the emergency was even more acute, and the herd continued to shrink. But after the war, when things eased off, with three hunts fully operational the deer population soared again, as it has continued to do ever since, right up to the 1995 census of 2,500 animals – far more than ever before in recorded history.

This must be one of English conservation's most impressive success stories. And yet it depends on a single fragile psychological factor – what I have called that 'mysterious thing'. The hunt itself is helpless to protect the deer. The secret lies in that strange agreement among the farmers and country people of the sprawling region, a decision arrived at God knows how, to refrain from killing the deer.

The effects of this unspoken contract are so real that West Country farmers far from the hunt's heartland now find themselves going to some trouble to protect odd groups of resident red deer. I know one farmer 30 miles from the hunt's usual limits who was recently tolerating over 20, on less than 300 acres. Few such farmers would suppose they were preserving deer for the hunt. Many of them will have little direct interest in it. But staghunting touches deep tribal springs. This attitude to the red deer has a pride and sovereignty all its own. And this is one way in which these men can confirm their solidarity with the inner life of the region: they refrain from killing the deer.

Even so, the agreement is precarious. This protection is granted to the herd on a condition. The moment the hunt is banned, everything changes. The deer instantly lose all symbolic meaning, as the totems of a special way of life. Ejected from their sacred niche in the community, they suddenly belong to everybody and nobody. They have become vagrants, deprived of all status. Or rather, they have a new status – one that is dangerous to them. They now belong to a government that has just proved itself unsympathetic, even hostile, towards the West Country farmer's way of life. And this government having taken the deer from the farmer, has straight away dumped them back on his fields as expensive squatters. To be fed and cared for by him.

Meanwhile, those enterprising young locals look at the deer with new eyes. What they now see are huge, unclaimed packages of saleable meat and exciting fun just wandering about. If the ban comes, the survival of the red deer will depend on what these farmers and locals take it into their heads to do. What will they do?

Will they revert to basic human form and do what they did after 1642 and again after 1825, on those earlier occasions when the hunt withdrew its claim from the herd? It seems at least quite likely that they will. Not all at once. Gradually they will get there. And the law that cannot protect citizens in day-time city streets will not be able to do much for those big, naïve animals, so readily convertible to cash, in sparsely populated north Devon and Somerset criss-crossed by so many convenient access and escape routes. If the law cannot afford to help the deer, who can? The shortage of legal weapons will stimulate ingenuity. The poaching gangs will feel that bit more competitive.

For most people, the latest piece of science about the suffering of the hunted red deer has already settled the question of whether or not to ban staghunting. But that tender concern for what red deer can suffer should go further. Do we really want the Exmoor herd? Or can we live happily without it, as we never give a thought to the bears, the wolves and the beavers? The debate has concentrated on the effects the ban will have on country people – the act so symbolic, the shock seismic, with all manner of unpredictable consequences for our fissile society. But we should keep in mind what will happen to the red deer themselves when people wake up from the spell of the hunt.

This uncertain future is not confined to the deer. Foxes should be pricking their ears. If Exmoor's deer are too readily convertible to cash, foxes interfere with income. For the moment, they enjoy the same indulgence as the red deer: the spell of the hunt. But what happened in north Devon in Jack Russell's time can be reversed.

Jack Russell, who popularised the terrier that bears his name, was a fanatic fox-hunter through the mid-19th century. He would hunt six days a week. When he tried to start up a hunt at Iddesleigh, in north Devon, he found the country around all but empty of foxes. Whenever a fox was spotted, it was marked down, then with a great ringing of church bells the whole parish would turn out to find and kill it. In a land of sheep, chickens, ducks and geese, that was considered the right and proper fate of all foxes. At first, Jack Russell had to compete with the mob for these rare beasts. But he was an unusual man, and the extraordinary force of his character eventually began to persuade local farmers that his method was better. One or two of them constructed artificial dens, foxes were imported, and he got a small hunt going. That did the trick.

At this point, exactly as with the Exmoor Staghunt the mysterious thing happened. The spell of the hunt took hold, and the country folk began to protect foxes. One record tells how 'before two years were over, so far from persecuting the fox many a moor farmer would rather have lost the best sheep in his flock than see the gallant animal killed in any fashion except by hounds'. Against heavy odds, this attitude has persisted. One result is that many foxes have been killed by hounds. But another result (more important, I imagine, from the fox's point of view) is that foxes now swarm in abundance where formerly there were none – or only those odd visitors instantly killed. Not long ago the first meet of the local hunt was held at Jack Russell's village, Iddesleigh. They began at a small wood close by. A friend of mine who watched it told me: 'The whole wood exploded with foxes. Twenty foxes! Hounds were running everywhere.'

The sheep-farmers shoot and snare foxes occasionally, but in general that easy tolerance prevails, intact enough for the foxes to flourish – like the red deer – perhaps as never before. And yet for foxes, too, the contract is flimsy. Any good excuse to kill them finds men ready. For a while in the 1970s, when a fox pelt could fetch £25, I knew of fox-trappers who were setting lines of 300 snares. So here again, if the spell of the hunt were to be lifted, it seems likely that country people would revert to their common sense, and their market economy, where the only virtue of a fox is to be dead.

Before we ban these hunts, perhaps we should make sure we have a new method of control (of the people) and preservation (of the animals) half as effective and simple as this strange system that our history has produced for us. That is, if we really do want the animals.

Appendix XIV

Extracts from a letter dated 16 June 1998 from Hughes to Andrea Paluch and Robert Habeck, who translated *Birthday Letters* into German.

Dear Andrea and Robert,

I hope you're finding something of interest in my BIRTHDAY LETTERS. You will have located the general style of those pieces, I trust. I wrote them without any thought of publication, over twenty years, writing just one or two now and again. My aim was to find a language so simple, so psychologically <u>naïve</u> and naked, that my sense of communication with her, directly, so to speak, could feel free and unself-conscious. And insofar as I did find that intimate wavelength, the pieces carry the life that makes me want to keep them. Here and there, the more obviously 'poetic' effects may be a little denser, and the manner more elliptical, but if that other quality — the intimate immediacy of the voice — were not uppermost, I would not have included those particular letters. I did exclude quite a few that guarded themselves (most poems are highly defensive one way or another) too effectively. My whole point was to get certain things off my chest — but in that intimate way, directly to her. It was a kind of necessity. And it would have been far better for me if I had done the whole thing, finished and off my back, twenty five years ago. In fact, I decided to publish these only six months before they came out.

I do not know if that concentrated immediacy and intimacy is easy to find and maintain in German. It is not easy to find and maintain in English. But the simplicity and plainness perhaps gives a translator little option — no opportunity for developing images, or introducing rhetorical skill: all I tried to do was strip myself child-naked and wade in.

p58. 'flitting towards their honey'. The most famous English poet of the First World War (died of a mosquito bite on the Gallipoli campaign) was a famously beautiful youth, a graduate of Cambridge University, called Rupert Brooke. His sonnet 'If I should die, think only this of me . . .' was far and away the best known 'war-poem' and probably, among the mass of the people, still is, though as a poet he has on the whole worn badly, and was gradually eclipsed by the much more slowly emerging work of such as Wilfred Owen (whose most famous poem, STRANGE MEETING, lies behind the piece of mine in Birthday Letters titled A PICTURE OF OTTO, p 193). Even so, up into the thirties and forties, Rupert Brooke symbolised the glorious happy innocent etc priviledged [sic] Cambridge student world of that First World War generation. Still does, to a degree. As such, he became a legend in the University, and his life came to typify the ultimate idyll of Cambridge University student life.

The most romantic thing a student can do, at Cambridge, is take out a punt (a river-boat) on the river Cam, and go with a group of friends upriver, winding through willowy meadows, the mile or two to the village of Grantchester, (which is incidentally the setting of one of Chaucer's lewdest, funniest and most famous Canterbury Tales.) Once you get to Grantchester, if it is a suitably sunny day, you can have (you could have, even in my day, but not any longer, the house now belongs to a notorious politician, novelist etc — Jeffrey Archer) tea on the lawn of the Old Vicarage. In Brooke's day, the church clock was permanently stuck at ten to three. (In my day, too, it was still stuck at ten to three — but immobilised, by then, as a memorial to Rupert Brooke.) This punt trip to Grantchester was a journey deep into the Cambridge mythos of Rupert Brooke's vanished world. What linked him particularly to Grantchester was a poem he wrote (in the Café des Westens, in Berlin) in 1912, a floridly Edwardian overflow of nostalgia for — the Old Vicarage garden, at Grantchester. (And there was also — another memorial touch — always honey for tea.) In my day, every student in Cambridge quickly became aware of the closing couplet of this poem

>Oh yet
>Stands the Church clock at ten to three?
>And is there honey still for tea?

So that poem (and its lost world) is what I touch in those lines.

'Flitting' — you don't ask about this word, but in English it precisely conveys the swift, brief, barely glimpsed flight of a tiny bird from one bush to the next. Or of a ghost, substanceless and again barely seen, moving lightly across a hall or corridor or past a window. Or — again in a very precise usage — it is used of families who (perhaps to escape paying their rent) load up all their belongings at night and vanish from the house they have lived in. (From this, especially in the North of England, it is used more generally of any change of house.) I suppose I lean on the bird, the ghost, and a little, perhaps, on the loaded vehicle and its passengers disappearing (into their questionable futures, into the past, into some equivalent, it may be, of the First World War).

p128: you quote 'winding wounds' — but the actual words are 'Wind-wounds' where the wind is the March or April wind blowing, and the model for this compound usage might be 'Flesh-wounds' — making the daffodils concentrated, jaggedly-raw, pulsing and spasming holes or rents in the living body of the wind (wounds which will soon heal away and vanish). And somewhat as if the daffodils were each the bladed, exploded object that made and was still lodged in the wound, twisting in it — as the wind twisted.

p138: 'It' refers syntactically and in truth to the 'door': — In the English the succession of 'open it', 'through it' leaves little room for the third it to refer to anything else. Though the door is also the 'elm', as you see. And I seem to remember, in some deleted bit of the first paragraph, I made much clearer what I was strongly aware of, that the Elm Tree is (all over Europe) the tree at the door of the underworld, a death tree, and the curious coincidence is there, for the knowledgeable reader as for me, that S.P.'s very first ARIEL poem, the poem in which her new voice arrived with a bang, is titled ELM, and is about a gigantic Elm (actually three elms close together) that overshadowed our yard. In other words, that was the poem in which the mythos of her father emerged fully into her work, bringing its own great problem with it. In fact, I suppose that is what my piece is about.[1]

p150: the image in the previous couplet, 'Your page a dark swarm' brings together SP bending over the bees (bending over the beehive with its roof off), SP bending over her page (where the letters as she composed writhed and twisted, superimposed on each other, displacing each other), her page, as a seething mass and depth and compound ball of living ideas — carrying, somewhere in the heart of it, in the heart of the words, of the phrases, of the poetic whole struggling to form itself, the vital nuclei of her poetic operation — her 'self' and her 'Daddy' — and finally, her poem (in process of composition there on her page as she bends over it) as a swarm of bees clinging under a blossoming bough. You know that in late Spring (about the time of year of my piece) thriving bee-colonies throw off a 'swarm'. Most of the population of the hive goes off. While outriders go looking for a new place to build the new hive or nest, the mass of the bees congregate in a thick ball, around the Queen, all clinging to each other and to some bough. Then they are said to be 'swarming.' If you're an expert, you can hold a box or sack under them, shake the bough, and the whole lot will drop off into it. You can then take them to a new, empty hive. Otherwise they would eventually go right away, to some hole in a tree or under somebody's roof, and you would lose them.

So, as you see, I keep all these aspects in soft focus. The lit blossom is also SP's face. The bough is also her 'slender neck'. The bees are also her Ariel poetry. I maintain the figure by juxtaposition rather than syntactic coercion.

p163. In English, Genie, Guardian Angel and Demon Slave are sexually undetermined, though the tendency might be to imagine them Male. But they could, more specifically identified, be acceptable as Female. I take advantage of that vagary of gender, to claim the whole creature, whichever and whatever it is, as 'Like a Fish-mother' — i.e. as a being that has in some way produced you from her womb, and now wants to protect you by eating you (as some fish do, and even as under certain conditions some animals do). So it is 'She'.

Select Bibliography

Books by Ted Hughes

A full description of all Hughes' books, contributions to books and periodicals, translations of his work, broadcasts, and recordings, books and articles about him, up to the end of 1995, can be found in *Ted Hughes: A Bibliography*, by K. Sagar and S. Tabor, Mansell, 1998.

Unless otherwise stated, all UK titles are published by Faber & Faber, London; US publication details are in square brackets.

The Hawk in the Rain, 1957 [Harper & Brothers, 1957]
Lupercal, 1960 [Harper & Brothers, 1960]
Meet My Folks! 1961 [Bobbs-Merrill, 1973]
How the Whale Became, 1963 [Atheneum, 1964]
Recklings, Turret Press, 1966
Wodwo, 1967 [Harper & Row, 1967]
Poetry in the Making, 1967 [*Poetry Is*, Doubleday, 1970]
The Iron Man, 1968 [*The Iron Giant*, Harper & Row, 1968]
ed. *A Choice of Shakespeare's Verse*, 1971 [*With Fairest Flowers While Summer Lasts*, Doubleday, 1971]. Hughes' introduction is reprinted in *Winter Pollen* as 'The Great Theme: Notes on Shakespeare'
Seneca's Oedipus, 1969 [Doubleday, 1972]
Crow, 1970 [Harper & Row, 1971]
Poems: Ruth Fainlight, Ted Hughes, Alan Sillitoe, Rainbow Press, 1971
Selected Poems: 1957–1967, 1972 [Harper & Row, 1973]
Prometheus on his Crag, Rainbow Press, 1973
Cave Birds, Scolar Press, 1975; trade edn Faber & Faber, 1978 [Viking, 1979]
Season Songs, Rainbow Press, 1974 as *Spring, Summer, Autumn, Winter*; trade edn Faber & Faber, 1976 [Viking, 1975]
Moon-Whales and Other Moon Poems [Viking, 1976]
Gaudete, 1977 [Harper & Row, 1977]
ed. *Johnny Panic and the Bible of Dreams and Other Prose Writings*, by Sylvia Plath, 1977 [Harper & Row, 1979]
Moon-Bells, Chatto & Windus, 1978
Orts, Rainbow Press, 1978
Moortown Elegies, Rainbow Press, 1978; Faber & Faber, 1989, as *Moortown Diary*
Adam and the Sacred Nine, Rainbow Press, 1979
Remains of Elmet, Rainbow Press, 1979; Faber & Faber, 1979 [Harper & Row, 1979]; repr. Faber & Faber, 1994, as *Elmet*
Henry Williamson, Rainbow Press, 1979
Moortown, 1979 [Harper & Row, 1980]
Under the North Star, 1981 [Viking, 1981]
A Primer of Birds, Gehenna Press, 1981
ed. *Collected Poems by Sylvia Plath*, 1981 [Harper & Row, 1981]
Selected Poems 1957–1981, 1982 [*New Selected Poems*, Harper & Row, 1982]
The Great Irish Pike, Appledore Press, 1982

ed. with Seamus Heaney, *The Rattle Bag*, 1982
ed. with Frances McCullough, *The Journals of Sylvia Plath* [Dial Press, 1982]
River, 1983 [Harper & Row, 1984]
What is the Truth? 1984 [Harper & Row, 1984]
Mokomaki, Eremite Press, 1985
ed. *Sylvia Plath's Selected Poems*, 1985
Flowers and Insects, 1986 [Alfred A. Knopf, 1986]
The Cat and the Cuckoo, Sunstone Press, 1987
T. S. Eliot: A Tribute, 1987
Tales of the Early World, 1988 [Farrar, Straus and Giroux, 1991]
Wolfwatching, 1989 [Farrar, Straus and Giroux, 1991]
Capriccio [Gehenna Press 1990]
Shakespeare and the Goddess of Complete Being, 1992 [Farrar, Straus and Giroux, 1992]
Rain-Charm for the Duchy and Other Laureate Poems, 1992
A Dancer to God: Tributes to T. S. Eliot, 1992 [Farrar, Straus and Giroux, 1993]
The Mermaid's Purse, Sunstone Press, 1993
Three Books: Remains of Elmet, Cave Birds, River, 1993
The Iron Woman, 1993 [Dial Books, 1995]
Elmet, 1994
Winter Pollen, ed. William Scammell, 1994 [Picador, 1995]
New Selected Poems, 1995
The Dreamfighter and Other Creation Tales, 1995
Difficulties of a Bridegroom: Collected Short Stories, 1995 [Picador, 1995]
Wedekind's Spring Awakening, 1995
Collected Animal Poems, 1995
ed. *A Choice of Coleridge's Verse*, 1996
Lorca's Blood Wedding, 1996
ed. with Seamus Heaney, *The School Bag*, 1997
ed. *By Heart: 101 Poems to Remember*, 1997
Tales from Ovid, 1997 [Farrar, Straus and Giroux, 1999]
Birthday Letters, 1998 [Farrar, Straus and Giroux, 1998]
Racine's Phèdre, 1998 [Farrar, Straus and Giroux, 1999]
Howls and Whispers [Gehenna Press, 1998]
The Oresteia of Aeschylus, 1999 [Farrar, Straus and Giroux, 1999]
The Alcestis of Euripides, 1999 [Farrar, Straus and Giroux, 1999]
Collected Plays for Children, 2001
Collected Poems, ed. Paul Keegan, 2003 [Farrar, Straus and Giroux, 2003]
Collected Poems for Children, 2005
Selected Translations, ed. Daniel Weissbort, 2006 [Farrar, Straus and Giroux, 2008]
Letters of Ted Hughes, ed. Christopher Reid, 2007 [Farrar, Straus and Giroux, 2008]

Critical and Biographical Studies Cited

Bishop, Nicholas, *Re-making Poetry: Ted Hughes and a New Critical Psychology*, Harvester Wheatsheaf, 1991
Dyson, A. E., *Three Contemporary Poets: Thom Gunn, Ted Hughes and R. S. Thomas*, Macmillan, 1990
Faas, Ekbert, *Ted Hughes: The Unaccommodated Universe*, Black Sparrow Press, 1980
Feinstein, Elaine, *Ted Hughes: The Life of a Poet*, Weidenfeld & Nicolson, 2001
Gammage, Nick, ed., *The Epic Poise: A Celebration of Ted Hughes*, Faber & Faber, 1999
Gifford, Terry and Roberts, Neil, *Ted Hughes: A Critical Study*, Faber & Faber, 1981
Huws, Daniel, *Memories of Ted Hughes: 1952–1963*, Richard Hollis/Five Leaves, 2010
Rees, Roger, ed., *Ted Hughes and the Classics*, Oxford University Press, 2009
Robinson, Craig, *Ted Hughes as Shepherd of Being*, Macmillan, 1989

Sagar, Keith, *The Art of Ted Hughes*, Cambridge University Press, 1975; extended edn 1978; digitally reissued 2008

————, *Literature and the Crime Against Nature*, Chaucer Press, 2005

————, *The Laughter of Foxes: A Study of Ted Hughes*, Liverpool University Press, 2000; rev. edn 2006

————, *Ted Hughes and Nature: 'Terror and Exultation'*, Fastprint Publishing, 2009

Sagar, Keith, ed., *The Achievement of Ted Hughes*, Manchester University Press, 1983

————, *The Challenge of Ted Hughes*, Macmillan, 1994

Scigaj, Leonard M., *The Poetry of Ted Hughes: Form and Imagination*, University of Iowa Press, 1986

————, *Ted Hughes*, Twayne, 1991

Scigaj, Leonard M., ed., *Critical Essays on Ted Hughes*, G. K. Hall, 1992

Skea, Ann, *Ted Hughes: The Poetic Quest*, University of New England Press, 1994

West, Thomas, *Ted Hughes*, Methuen, 1995

Index of Works by Ted Hughes

General Index

Abse, Dannie 81
Adams, Norman 92
Adelaide Festival 52–3
Aeschylus
  The Oresteia 239, 244, 248, 254, 264, 267, 271, 278
Africa 25, 119, 127-8, 131, 276
Aftermann, Alan 53
Alaska 84, 93, 130, 138, 141, 143–4, 150, 159–60, 165, 168, 172, 317
Alchemy 4, 6, 27, 101, 103, 131, 209
Alexandra, Duchess of Abercorn 252–3
Almeida Theatre 254
Alvarez, A. 105, 171, 267
Amichai, Yehuda 21, 54, 137, 261–2
Amis, Kingsley 141
Anath 27, 311
Anderson, Jane V. 117, 161
Antonetti, Martin 263
Aphrodite 27, 191, 278
Apollo 232, 310
Archer, Jeffrey 323
Arden, John
  Sergeant Musgrave's Dance 35
Arnold, Matthew 76
Arts for Nature 252
Arvon Foundation 43, 84, 100, 120, 125, 127, 132, 134, 172, 241–2
Asclepius 310
Ashteroth 311
Aspect 296
Association of Verbal Arts 129, 132
Astarte 311–12
Astrology 4, 41, 152, 216, 219
Atlantic Salmon Trust 143, 148
Attar, Farid ud-Din
  The Conference of the Birds 21
Attis 312
Auden, W. H. 4, 11, 79–80, 82, 266

Baal 312
Baldwin, James 127
Baldwin, Michael 81
Bananas 14, 66
Bangladesh 170, 178
Banks, John 83
Bardo Thödol 33, 35
Baring, Anne, and Jules Cashford
  The Myth of the Goddess 179, 224, 229
Baskin, Leonard 30, 36, 41, 43–50, 57, 61, 70, 72, 78, 86, 91, 101, 118, 121, 128, 145, 239,

270, 279, 293
  Cave Birds 61, 160–76, 293
Baskin, Lucretia 91
Bate, Gillian 11, 214, 227
Baudelaire, Charles 88
Beckett, Samuel 2, 168
Beer, Patricia 82
Beethoven, Ludwig van 274
Belfast Review 7
Bellamy, David 255
Bergonzi, Bernard 159
Bermelin, Robert 117–18, 125–6, 135
Bernard, Kenneth 100
Betjeman, John 16
Bishop, Nicholas 167–8
Blackford, Richard 70, 84–7
Blair, Tony 257
Blake, William 74, 92, 164, 215–16, 225, 302, 307, 309, 317
Books and Issues 304
Bown, Jane 95
Boxer, Mark 282, 287
Braasch, Holger 115
Bradford Grammar School 13
Bradshaw, Graham 214
Bran 27, 36, 155, 310
Branch, Tony 72
Brinton, Ian 304, 307
British Broadcasting Corporation 66, 114–15, 183
British Columbia 161, 165, 244
British Council 3
Britten, Benjamin 226
Brodsky, Joseph 71, 171, 173
Brontë, Emily 100
  Wuthering Heights 100, 226
Brook, Peter 10, 21, 41, 115, 218, 270, 275, 311
Brooke, Rupert 323–4
Brownjohn, Alan 120, 221
Bruno, Giordano 195, 215–16
Bullock, Alan 225
Burckhardt, Jacob
  The Greeks and Greek Civilization 278
Burgess, Anthony 185
Burgess, Susan 53
Burnet, John
  Early Greek Philosophy 129
Butler, Jan 71

Cabbala 4, 12, 215